Congratulations F
winning The
Award for Acad
Excellence, 2017

Best regards
Ronald D Lee
KHSO1
September 2017

MW01200218

KH601

"And Ye Shall Know the Truth and the Truth Shall Make You Free"

Richard G. Irwin

My Life in the Central Intelligence Agency

Jacksonville, Florida ♦ Herndon, Virginia
www.Fortis-Publishing.com

KH601

"And Ye Shall Know the Truth and the Truth Shall Make You Free"

By Richard G. Irwin
My Life in the Central Intelligence Agency

ISBN 978-0-9777884-8-4 (hardcover)

Library of Congress Control Number: 2010926936

Published by Fortis Publishing
Jacksonville, Florida—Herndon, Virginia
www.Fortis-Publishing.com

Manufactured in the United States of America

Dedication

This book is dedicated, to my mother and father, Edith and James Irwin; two of the warmest, kindest, loving, parents that ever lived. May they Rest in Peace.

In addition, I would like to dedicate this book to my wife Karen and my children Kelly, Matthew, and Kathleen. While I cannot bring back all of the birthdays that I missed, holidays, soccer games, or dance recitals, I hope that after reading this book, you will have a better understanding of where I was and why I was not home. Karen, you especially have always been there for me through thick and thin, good times and bad.

Karen gave up a lucrative career as a Conference Planner with EDS to accompany me to Honduras during the 1980s (one month after the U.S. Embassy Annex in Tegucigalpa was set on fire during a demonstration), with a 15 month old and a three month old baby, six months after purchasing a brand new house. Prior to our departure, she had to sell our townhouse, purchase a new house, pack, and unpack. All of this while pregnant and working full-time while I was TDY to Swan Island off the coast of Honduras for several months. This from a woman who never even had been outside of the United States except for our honeymoon to Acapulco.

Lastly, I would like to dedicate this book to my deceased sister Ruth Ann, my sisters Regina and Chris, and my brother Jim.

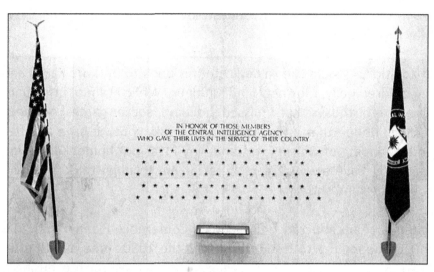

Contents

Contents (continued)

Acknowledgments

I would like to thank Nancy Shipley who provided the first editing prior to KH601 going to Adducent Inc. for further editing & book design; without her assistance, I would never have been able to get this book finished.

Next, I would like to thank my neighbor Brian Foster, a computer wiz, for all the time that he spent keeping my computer up and running during the three years it took me to write this book.

Thanks as well to Dennis Lowery and Jim Zumwalt from Fortis Publishing for helping me get this book published.

Lastly, I would like to thank Bill Kilgore and his family for their kind hospitality each Fall for letting me relax and unwind from the pressures of work during hunting season at their farm Kildary Acres in Airville, Pennsylvania.

Prologue

Sitting on the stairs of the Lincoln Memorial during the afternoon of 31 December 2004, I wanted some time to be by myself prior to driving home to celebrate New Years Eve with my family.

Earlier in the day, I officially retired from the Central Intelligence Agency (CIA) after 28 years of service. Little did I know that this journey would take me to 87 countries around the world; afford me the opportunity to become fluent in Spanish, Italian and French; work under eight Director's of the Central Intelligence Agency (DCI's); go to the White House to serve a President; and end at a newly created domestic agency known as the Department of Homeland Security (DHS) as part of the largest U.S. government reorganization in the past 50 years.

As a CIA covert operations officer, I had the opportunity to serve at the "right time and the right place" on several historic occasions, and was fortunate to have been involved in some of the most successful operations in the annals of the Agency. Stories normally told only inside the hallowed halls of the CIA. Along the way, I battled communism with the Contras in Central America; witnessed the rise of global terrorism, al-Qaeda, and the events that led up to 9/11; and laid my life on the line in Afghanistan.

As I closed my eyes and reminisced, it seemed like only yesterday that the phone rang at my girlfriend's house one morning in August 1977. Karen reached across the bed and said, "It's for you – some guy who says he is from Washington." The man introduced himself as being from the CIA and asked me if I was still interested in a position with the Central Intelligence Agency although a year had passed since my initial application. When I replied "yes", the man told me to report to CIA Headquarters in Langley, Virginia on September 11 – a date, not only affiliated with a new beginning in my life, but also one, which, 24 years later would forever be immortalized in history with the attacks on the World Trade Center and the Pentagon.

Chapter 1

"We're looking for you; special men and women who still have a spirit of adventure. There are not many of you. One in a thousand maybe."

I was born on 6 February 1955 to James and Edith Irwin during one of the blizzards of the century, and was raised on a small farm in Breinigsville, a rural community outside of Allentown, Pennsylvania. The name Irwin is believed to have derived from the ancient Celto-Scythick word Erin-Viene, or Erin-Wiene, meaning "a true or brave Westland man." My great-grandfather, Bernard John Dowling Irwin's heroic actions in Arizona in 1861 earned him the Congressional Medal of Honor (the first on record). On my mother's side, Sir Joseph Lister III was credited with inventing the first antiseptic.

* * *

While growing up, I always wanted to be a Pennsylvania State Policemen, mostly because of a 6'4" State Trooper who often attended mass in uniform at St. Joseph's Catholic Church in Fogelsville, where I had served as an alter boy. Bernie Buhosky was an enormous man with a deep, resounding voice. As a child, he would frequently tell me tales of what it was like being a State Trooper.

In the fall of 1976, during my junior year at York College of Pennsylvania while studying Police Science, I filled out an application to be a Trooper with the Pennsylvania State Police. I had heard that they were expecting approximately 10,000 applications for 150 positions in a class that would commence in the fall of 1977. The starting salary was $10,213 per year. At that time, the Pennsylvania State Police had few women and even fewer minorities. I remember taking the examination and, to my surprise, did very well scoring a 98% out of a 100. After my interview however, I received a letter informing me that I had not been accepted into the ranks of Pennsylvania's finest. I later learned that the applicant review board had accepted applicants who had scored considerably lower on the exam to fill their hiring quota. The only consolation was that a good friend of mine, Paul Evanko, would not only become a Trooper but eventually would go on to be the Commissioner of the Pennsylvania State Police.

Initially crushed, I took the advice of one of my college professors and decided to apply to several Federal agencies (the CIA, the FBI, and the U.S. Secret Service). My interest in the CIA was piqued after seeing a recruitment advertisement in the Philadelphia Inquirer one weekend:

"We're looking for you; special men and women who still have a spirit of adventure. There are not many of you. One in a thousand maybe. You are a bright, self-reliant, self-motivated person we need to help us gather information and put together a meaningful picture of what is happening in the world. One of an elite corps of men and women. You can rely on your wits, your initiative, and your skills. And in return enjoy recognition, positions of responsibility, life in foreign places, plus knowing that you belong to a small very special group of people doing a vital, meaningful job in the face of challenges and possible hardship. You will gain valuable experience because the opportunity we offer would give you the chance to develop your ability to take charge, make decisions, use your imagination, be creative, and work with others. Among the qualifications: a college education, U.S. citizenship, and foreign language aptitude. If all this sounds too good to be true, you owe yourself a closer look. Send your resume in confidence."

The ad then provided an address in Washington DC and ended with:

"No obligation and we'll keep your inquiry confidential. Central Intelligence Agency--It is time for us to know more about each other. An equal-opportunity affirmative-action employer."

During the wedding of a high school friend, I casually mentioned to the daughter of my high school principal, Nancy Hershey that I was interested in applying to the CIA. Much to my surprise, Nancy told me that her uncle was employed there. I was so excited that I immediately contacted her father, Donald, who, in turn, put me in touch with his brother-in-law, Douglas Climenson. A week later, after writing Douglas Climenson, I received a reply from a CIA personnel representative along with information on the CIA, an application and how to apply. The date was 30 August 1976.

Several months after submitting the application, I received a letter on 22 December 1976 telling me to report to 1820 North Fort Meyer Drive in Rosslyn, Virginia. After checking into the Marriott Hotel in Rosslyn, I reported to the building at 9:00 a.m. the following morning and was interviewed by a middle age personnel officer who, after allowing me the opportunity to provide a quick overview of myself and why I wanted to join the CIA, did not seem overly impressed with my credentials. I did not understand why, though, after all, I was a 21-year-old junior in college with a 3.00 GPA whose only job experience was as a construction worker, a security guard, a bouncer, and a bartender. Following the initial introductions, the personnel officer provided a long-winded, carefully rehearsed, recruitment speech, which he probably had given a thousand times.

"Richard, the mission of the CIA is to collect, evaluate, and disseminate foreign intelligence to assist the President and senior U.S. Government policy makers in making decisions relating to National Security. The CIA does not make policy. Rather it is an independent source of foreign intelligence information for those who do. The CIA is authorized to engage in covert actions at the President's direction in accordance with applicable law and carefully selects well-qualified people in all fields of study. Scientists, engineers, economists, linguists, mathematicians, secretaries, accountants and computer specialists are but a few of the professionals who are continually in demand."

The personnel officer continued by comparing the Agency's work to that of an academic institution, claiming that academic institutions required research, careful evaluation, and writing of reports. The major difference, in his opinion, however, was that reports generated by the CIA ended up on the desk of the nation's policymakers. The personnel officer added that, *"The selection for Agency employment was highly competitive and employee requirements included a Bachelor's degree from an accredited college or university, a GPA of 3.00 or better, excellent oral and written communication skills, strong interpersonal skills, and high levels of trustworthiness, integrity and loyalty to the U.S."* Coming to what would be the end of the interview; the personnel officer leaned forward in his chair, looked me in the eye, and told me that due to my age and lack of experience it would probably be very difficult for me to enter onboard with the Agency as a full-time staff employee. Much to my surprise, however, he then asked me if I would be interested in working as a contract security guard and wanted to know if I would be willing to relocate to the Washington DC area following my college graduation. After a year of employment as a contract guard, I could apply for a staff position.

When I replied that I was interested, and would do just about anything to get my foot in the door with the Agency he continued by saying that all applicants had to undergo and complete successful occupational testing to include an aptitude test, writing test, personality inventory, two personal interviews, a thorough medical and psychological examination, a polygraph interview, and an extensive background investigation before entering on duty. When I told him that the background investigation, polygraph and medical examination would not be a problem, he encouraged me to maintain my GPA and finish my degree and that processing generally took between nine to twelve months.

Shortly after the interview I received a letter on 5 May 1977 saying that the CIA had completed a review of my application and that they would be processing me for a security guard position, on a contract basis; a GS-5 at $9,303.00 per year. The letter added that the final appointment was dependent on a number of factors such as character and reference investigations, and processing procedures.

On 27 May 1977, a letter arrived requesting that I return to Washington DC. This time I was given a battery of psychological and sociological aptitude tests with questions such as: "Would I rather be an airline pilot, or an airline flight attendant", a two-day physical, and a polygraph examination, which lasted the better part of four hours. During the polygraph pre-interview, I was informed that a person taking a polygraph did not pass or fail. Rather they favorably complete testing, do not favorable complete testing, or the results are found to be "inconclusive" or "deemed deceptive". With the latter, I was told that the person was considered to be lying or fabricating. I considered myself lucky. I passed the polygraph the first time even though I had admitted to experimenting with marijuana during my freshman and sophomore years of college. In addition to asking numerous counterintelligence questions, such as: "Have you ever been part of a subversive group, been involved in any subversive activities, or a plot to overthrow the Government of the United States," I was asked several lifestyle questions about my finances, drinking, drug usage, and character. In addition to probing into my honesty, integrity, trustworthiness, and loyalty, I was also asked if I had ever been involved in any homosexual activity since my 18th birthday. Today the homosexual question is no longer asked after an applicant was denied admission to the CIA in the mid-1980s after admitting to homosexual activity, sued the CIA, and won in a case commonly referred to as the "John Doe" case. Up until then, the Director of Central Intelligence (DCI) had the final say as to who would be employed in the CIA and who would not, using National Security as his argument for rejection.

Following the polygraph, I was told that I had to submit to a background investigation where a government investigator would interview my friends, peers, neighbors, high school teachers, college professors, employers, and co-workers. I was informed that the investigator would ask many of the same questions as the polygraph operator and would be looking to see if the person they interviewed would recommend me for a position of trust and responsibility with the U.S. Government.

Although a year had passed since my initial application, when I finally received the phone call informing me to report to CIA Headquarters in Langley, Virginia in late August 1977, I was 22 years old and did not have a clue of what I was getting into. The only thing I knew about the Agency was what the recruiter had told me, what I had read in books and newspapers, or heard on television and in the movies. I later found out that, despite receiving over 100,000 applications, the CIA had only hired 54 people that year (1977) and I was lucky to have been one of them. I never met Douglas Climenson in the 28 years that I was employed by the CIA, but I owe him a great deal of gratitude for helping me get an interview, which led me to being accepted into the Agency.

Arriving promptly at 8:00 a.m. on 11 September 1977, a day and month, which would later be synonymous with several ruthless terrorist attacks on the United States, I gave my full name and Social Security Number to the Security Guard at the main entrance of the CIA Headquarters.

According to the CIA's Factbook on Intelligence, the original Headquarters building was designed in the mid 1950's by the New York firm of Harrison and Abramovitz, designers of the United Nations Building. Located about eight miles from downtown Washington, DC, the grounds were envisioned by the Director of Central Intelligence, Allen W. Dulles, as projecting the atmosphere of a college campus. As the population of the Agency increased, it was determined that another building needed to be constructed. The New Headquarters Building was designed in the early 1980's by the Detroit architectural and engineering firm of Smith, Hinchman & Grylls. The new building is joined to the west façade of the original building and includes two six-story office towers connected by a four-story core area. The building is steel/glass as compared to the pre-cast concrete construction of the original building. *The cornerstone of the original building was laid on 3 November 1959, and construction was completed in November 1963. Construction of the new building began in May 1984. The cornerstone was laid by then Vice-President of the United States, George Herbert Bush, on 1 November 1985. Occupancy of the new building began in June 1988 and was completed in November 1989. The original building consists of 1,400,000 square feet and the new building contains 1,100,000 square feet of space. The buildings and grounds comprise 258 acres.*

After parking my car, I followed a steady stream of employees into the main lobby. To this day, I still get chills up and down my spine when entering the main foyer of the CIA. The first thing I remember seeing was the enormous Agency seal on the floor. The design of the seal was approved and set forth on 17 February 1950 in President Truman's Executive Order 10111. In the Executive Order, the seal is described in the heraldic terms as follows:

SHIELD: Argent, a compass rose of sixteen point's gules.

CREST: On a wreath argent and gules an American bald eagle's head erased proper.

Below the shield, in red letters on gold scroll is the inscription "United States of America"; and in white letters encircling the shield and crest at the top the inscription "Central Intelligence Agency"–all on a circular blue background with a narrow gold edge. The interpretation of the CIA seals is: *The American eagle is the national bird and is a symbol of strength and alertness. The radiating spokes of the compass rose depict the coverage of intelligence data from all areas of the world to a central point. The shield is the standard symbol of defense. Intelligence provided to our policymakers is used to help defend our country.*

To my right were numerous stars etched on the Wall of Honor silently, but permanently, immortalizing those CIA officers who lost their lives in the service of their country. Below the wall, a glass-encased Book of Honor displayed the names of those whose names can, in death, now be revealed. This simple, but starkly elegant, memorial was sculpted in July 1974. To my left, what caught my eye most was a biblical verse etched on the wall, which characterizes the intelligence mission in a free society. It reads:

"AND YE SHALL KNOW THE TRUTH, AND THE TRUTH SHALL MAKE YOU FREE."

JOHN VIII-XXXII

To the right of this simple inscription was a life-like bronze statue of Major General William J. Donovan, the Director of the Office of Strategic Services (OSS) and forerunner of the Central Intelligence Agency. Adjacent to the statue, an open book displayed the names of the OSS officers who lost their lives in the line of duty.

After gazing in awe at the lobby of the CIA for several minutes, I was met by a man who introduced himself as a security officer from the Office of Security. I was then ushered into a private room where the security officer proceeded to lecture me on the CIA's "Code of Conduct" and zero tolerance "Drug Policy". Following the lecture, I signed a consent form acknowledging the fact that, although I had experimented with marijuana, I would no longer condone to such activity as an Agency employee. If I violated this agreement, I would be terminated immediately.

I was then escorted to the badge office where I received my Agency Badge KH601, as Employee Number 0687991, and a four-digit code, which I had to memorize to use the new security access control system, which allowed employees access into the main headquarters building. After receiving my new Agency badge, I met with a personnel officer and signed what seemed to be a thousand forms to include a life insurance policy form, a health insurance policy form, a beneficiary statement, and a notification of next of kin form. With the exception of my immediate family and several close friends, no one knew that I had applied and was accepted into the CIA. Thank God, in that I was told from that day forward that I would be undercover and would not be able to reveal my Agency affiliation until the day I retired. The personnel officer then handed me a piece of paper with the name, address, phone number, and a point of contact for my new cover employer.

All I can remember was fear that I would never be able to spit out this long-winded cover story if pressured to do so. Although I was expecting to work at the CIA Headquarters compound, I was surprised when told by the personnel officer that I would be working at a covert Agency facility in Northern Virginia. I was then provided a map with directions to the site and was told to destroy the map upon arrival. With some trepidation, I drove directly to the site where I gave my name to the security guard at the main gate who told me to proceed to the visitor parking lot in front of the main building.

During the initial check-in with my security supervisor, I received a uniform, a schedule and was told that I would have to work rotating shifts since the facility operated 24 hours a day, every day of the year. The facility, which I quickly learned, was the U.S. Government's premier satellite reconnaissance facility. Much of the work performed at this location was eventually compromised when William Kampiles (who worked as a watch officer at the CIA operations center in Langley from March to November 1977) took a copy of the technical manual for the KH-11 reconnaissance satellite system after resigning from the CIA, and sold it to Soviet intelligence for $3,000. Kampiles was later caught, tried, convicted of espionage, and sentenced to 40 years in prison.

In that the facility was less than two years old, the majority of the security guards working there had been employed by the Agency in Vietnam and transferred to the site in 1975 shortly after the war ended. Much to my surprise, however, I was not provided a weapon– only a whistle; so much for security at one of the Agency's most secretive sites! By the end of my first day, I was so excited by the day's events that I had forgotten to make a reservation at a local hotel. I had not even thought about where I was going to live so after a co-worker named Patsy B. suggested that I look in the Washington Post for rooms to rent, I picked up the Post and eventually ended up renting a room in a house in Woodbridge, Virginia. If it were not for the hospitality and cooking of my good friends Ray and Mary Esparza, I probably would have starved that first year.

My roommates at the time believed my cover story that I was a security guard at a local government facility and never tried probing further. After several months of rotating shifts, I was permanently assigned to the day shift, which I readily accepted, although I still worked almost every holiday. I got along well with those I worked with but my supervisor, a good old boy from the south, repeatedly reminded me that he was not impressed with my college degree. I later found out that he used to deliver bread and milk to the site before signing on as a guard.

During the first month of my employment, the new DCI, Stansfield Turner, visited the site where I was working. Turner had been appointed by President Jimmy Carter and one of his first moves, shortly after being sworn in as DCI, was making good on one of President Carter's campaign promises to clean out the "cowboy" elements of the Agency. In what has commonly been referred to as the "Halloween Massacre", Turner handed out pink-slips, firing 800 case officers from the Agency's Clandestine Service, known as the Directorate of Operations (DO) on 31 October 1977; a move that to this day does not bode well with the majority of Agency employees. Turner tried to justify his decision by claiming that the Vietnam War was over and that the DO was overstaffed. One rumor at the time was that Turner was "hell bent" on firing the chief of one of our overseas offices as part of this cleansing effort and had narrowed his choice to a chief of one of our smaller offices. The chief, when informed of Turner's decision, in an electronic message known as a "cable", politely replied, in what has been described as the shortest cable in CIA history, with two words--"F--- You".

Two months after beginning my employment, I decided to visit Washington DC on my day off with some friends who had come to visit from out of town. The day was 15 November 1977 and Shah Mohammed Riza Pahlevi of Iran had been invited to the White House as a guest of President Jimmy Carter. Although the government had received information that Iranian dissidents were planning to hold large demonstrations to protest the visit, with some information indicating the possibility of violence, my friends and I decided to visit Washington DC anyway. Interestingly, when informed of this information, President Carter made it clear that he did not want a large police presence around the White House and, therefore, the order was given to the U.S. Park Police, the law enforcement entity responsible for maintaining security around the ellipse, to remain out of sight on buses in full-riot gear while approximately 50 U.S. Park Police officers patrolled the grounds on horseback. As the anti-Shah demonstrators began marching down Pennsylvania Avenue towards the White House, many were carrying signs and banners advocating the overthrow of the Shah.

Unbeknownst to the police officers, however, the protesters had cleverly concealed 2x4 pieces of lumber and ladders behind the banners and signs. When the demonstrators tried to breach the perimeter iron fence surrounding the White House using the ladders during a ceremony that President Carter was hosting for the Shah on the South Lawn of the White House, the U.S. Park Police quickly moved in on horseback. Unveiling the 2x4's, the demonstrators quickly swung at the horses, bringing both the animals and riders to the ground. As my friends and I watched in horror and disbelief, we observed some protestors drive large nails into the underbellies of several of the horses, while others embedded large fishing hooks, attached to fishing lines, into the horses to pull them and their riders to the ground. Within minutes, several mounted policemen and policewomen were pummeled amid screams and tear gas as swarms of police officers rushed to their aid from the buses surrounding the ellipse.

I do not know how many brave men and women were injured that day, but I am sure that many of the police officers were permanently disabled. As tear gas began exploding in the air, workers from a nearby construction site began running to the scene to join in the fray, many of whom began beating the demonstrators. Attack dogs and water canons were unleashed in an attempt to suppress the unruly crowd. The next day, the front page of every local newspaper carried a photograph of a teary-eyed President Carter and the Shah due to the amount of tear gas that had floated over the South Lawn of the White House complex. Other photographs showed dogs attacking the demonstrators and construction workers beating the hell out of several of them. Interestingly, there were no photographs of the demonstrators pummeling the horses or the heroic mounted police officers in the field that day.

* * *

One year to the day after serving as a security guard, I accepted a staff position with the Agency as an intelligence assistant in the Directorate of Science and Technology (DS&T) as a GS-7. My job consisted of retrieving and filing target folders and building target packages for photographic interpreters who spent hours analyzing and interpreting rolls of satellite imagery pertaining to the Soviet Union, the Middle East and other "hot spots" around the world.

Receiving my First Promotion to GS-7 in 1978 from Mike Poole

Ten months later, I was promoted to a GS-8, and became a research assistant, editing reports, which the photo interpreters produced. In that everyone worked rotating shifts and long hours, I really got to know my co-workers and supervisors very well. On our days off, we frequently played golf together and even had our own softball team known as the "Flyers".

One night in February 1979, while working the midnight shift, we received imagery of the U.S. Embassy being overrun in Tehran; the pictures were immediately blown up and made into briefing boards for the President. This was the first time that the U.S. Embassy in Iran was overthrown. On the second more famous occasion in November 1979, American hostages were held for 444 days. The buildup to the fall of the U.S. Embassy in February 1979 began on 16 January 1979 when the Shah and his family secretly boarded a plane and were flown out of Tehran to Egypt. On 1 February, exiled religious leader Ayatollah Ruhollah Khomeini returned to Iran from France, where he had been living in exile for 15 years, to lead a revolution against Shah elected Prime Minister Bahktiar. Nine days later, on 10 February 1979, the revolt commenced when Iranian Air Force cadets staged a pro Khomeini demonstration at the Doshan Tappen Air Force base at Farahabad and the Iranian Army was called to restore order. The next morning thousand of Iranian's rushed to the Air Force base, stormed the gates, and seized automatic weapons and grenades. For the next few days, hundreds of Iranians took to the streets, walking or driving in front of the U.S. Embassy waving automatic weapons and yelling anti-American slogans such as "Yankee go home".

On 14 February 1979, when pro-Khomeini supporters forced their way over the walls and into the U.S. Embassy, those working at the complex were fortunate at that time to have a security officer named Bill A. assigned in Tehran, along with his wife, Caren. As the students stormed the embassy, the 20-member U.S. Marine security detachment tried to repel the attack by using tear gas. Unfortunately, the Marines had to request permission to deploy the gas *five times* before U.S. Ambassador William Sullivan granted approval. As shots rang out throughout the embassy complex and as armed attackers made their way to the post communications center (PCC) on the top floor of the chancery that was serving as the embassy safe haven, Ambassador Sullivan ordered the Marines to drop their weapons in an office adjacent to the Ambassador's suite and give up without a fight. Although this decision probably saved a lot of lives, according to Bill, at least some of the Marines got to send a few of their attackers to their graves that day as they were coming over the walls prior to Ambassador Sullivan's order. As everyone was escorted to an outside area near the motor pool where they were frisked and lined up against a wall in front of a hoard of photographers and angry armed gunmen, a Khomeini spokesperson eventually arrived and ordered the students to leave the area. Buses were called and the students departed with arms raised high in defiance.

Following the overthrow of the embassy, the State Department asked that all Americans leave Iran. For the next several days, Bill assisted in the evacuation of numerous Americans living in Tehran, spending countless hours helping families gather their personal belongings, close up their houses, and take care of their pets prior to boarding chartered Pan Am 747's. Several days later, Bill and Caren got their chance to leave Tehran on the last Pan Am flight out along with 28 other Americans who Bill helped smuggle out of the country thanks to a friend of his. As the 330 passengers boarded the 747, the pilot came on the intercom and said that there would be a delay as armed Iranian Revolutionary Guards boarded the aircraft. As the guards walked up and down the aisle bearing a photograph of a beardless man, one of Bill's colleagues sitting next to him remarked, "What are we going to do?" to which Bill replied, "There is no way that I am leaving this plane. They are going to have to shoot me first." Then, for the next two hours, each time when the Iranian Revolutionary Guards pressed a gun to Bill's bearded face and asked him if he was the person in the photograph, he softly replied "no".

When the Iranian Revolutionary Guards were satisfied, the pilot got on the intercom and said that he had received permission to depart. As the plane lifted off, all 330 passengers began applauding, the bar was opened, and the passengers proceeded to drink everything onboard. A second round of applause ensued when the pilot announced that they had just departed Iranian airspace and, when the plane finally arrived at Frankfurt, Germany, Bill was greeted by a fellow officer named Billy H. Although Bill and Caren were fortunate to depart, they left all of their personal belongings behind except for their dog, Smokey. Regrettably, with everything that he had done to save lives during the fall of the American Embassy in Tehran, Bill was not recognized for his efforts. To this day, Bill will tell you that many of his Iranian colleagues were tortured and killed after their names were found in files that were not destroyed that day when the U.S. Embassy was turned over to the Iranians.

When order was restored at the U.S. Embassy by the Iranian coalition government, Khomeini aide, Dr. Ibrahim Yazdi offered to provide the embassy with approximately 150-200 Iranian soldiers and security police for compound security under a former SAVAK member named Mashallah Kahsani, who had been serving as the security chief for the embassy security force. Nine months later, on 4 November 1979, this same individual, Mashallah Kahsani led the charge against the U.S. Embassy where this time, 13 U.S. Marines and 39 other Americans would be held for 14 months prior to being released. Sixty-six individuals were originally taken hostage on that day, 14 were released leaving 52 American citizens to remain imprisoned.

After the U.S. Embassy was overthrown for the second time, President Carter authorized a Top-Secret mission named "Operation Eagle Claw," to free the hostages wherein U.S. helicopters were to carry Delta Force commandos from a carrier in the Persian Gulf to a point outside of Tehran where they would spend the night and begin the rescue the next morning. However, the complicated mission, which involved refueling the helicopters at a spot in the Iranian desert labeled "Desert One", was aborted on 25 April 1980 after three of the eight helicopters suffered mechanical failure and one of the helicopters collided with a refueling plane killing eight U.S. servicemen.

When militant students stormed the U.S. Embassy in Tehran this second time in November 1979, the site where I was working was again one of the key sources of information for the U.S. Government. One of my co-workers, a fellow security guard at the site, had a brother named Joe who was assigned as a U.S. Army military policeman on the Defense Attaché's staff at the embassy in Tehran when the embassy fell into the hands of the Iranians. The guard's brother, we were later told, had collaborated with the Iranian hostage takers. As many may recall, for the 444 days that the hostages were being held, there was always a discrepancy as to the number of hostages taken. This was due to the fact that many, including Tom A., Bill D., and Mel K. were held in solitary confinement for most of the time—over one and a half years. A State Department political officer named Mike M., who was suspected of being a CIA officer by his captors, also spent much of his time in isolation. When the hostages returned home, President Reagan held a huge ceremony on the South Lawn of the White House for 51 of the 52 hostages. The only one not invited was the U.S. Army Staff Sergeant mentioned above.

Although I did not know Tom A. or Bill D. personally, I did know Mel K. and enjoyed hearing him recall many of his stories from this period after he was released. Each day his captors would tell Mel that many of his fellow hostages had been set free in an effort to get him to talk and added that he, too, would be released if he told them what they wanted to hear, but he never did. Mel claimed that he viewed his incarceration as a game of "cat and mouse" providing only bits and pieces of useless information. He was always scheming to escape and one of my favorite stories was of the day he was bitten by a large German shepherd while trying to escape. Over the course of several weeks, Mel had complained to his guards that he was not feeling well and told them he was having trouble sleeping. A doctor was summoned, who gave him some stomach medication and sleeping pills. One evening, Mel tied his bed sheets together and slipped out of the window of his cell some 20 feet from the ground. Before climbing down with the use of his makeshift rope, he had placed the sleeping pills in several pieces of soap meat and thrown them out the window. A German shepherd, tied up below his window, consumed the meat and fell into a deep slumber. Unfortunately for Mel, however, the medication was not strong enough, and the dog awoke barking and ravenously tore into his ass as he tried to escape with his pants falling down to his knees requiring him to get several stitches. Mel was beaten and tortured following this attempted escape and spent several days tied to a chair blindfolded with his hands tied behind his back.

This was not the first time that he had been tortured and beaten. Mel claimed that like many of his fellow hostages, his captors would frequently put their weapon in his mouth and squeeze the trigger only to hear the click of an empty weapon—a sick ritual accompanied by their laughter. After his release, the first thing Mel asked for was to be polygraphed, to demonstrate that he never provided any information to his captors although he was tortured and beaten daily. Sure enough, to his credit, the polygraph supported Mel's claim that he never gave his captors any pertinent information.

I later ran into Mel in Central America in 1989. Mel and several other U.S. Government officials were there providing training. One day Mel and several of his co-workers commandeered a blue bus similar to those that shuttled government employees around Washington DC to the various satellite offices. The buses were referred to as "blue birds" due to their distinct dark blue color and the locations of the buildings typically stenciled on the front above the windshield as an indication of where the bus was headed. After allowing the passengers to exit the bus, Mel and his colleagues decided to gather around for a photograph armed with a variety of weapons. They sent the photograph back to Washington DC but, unfortunately, several senior officials did not find the photograph humorous and, subsequently, Mel and his colleagues were reprimanded for the stunt. The last time I asked about Mel, I heard through a mutual friend that he was killed by a drunk driver in a car crash in California in 2002; a real tragedy as he was a good man and a true hero.

* * *

After serving at the aforementioned site, my goal was to become a security officer in the Office of Security within the Directorate of Administration (DA) or an operations officer in the Directorate of Operations (DO) now known as the National Clandestine Service (NCS).

During the 1970s and early 1980s, most of the CIA's Office of Security leadership were former FBI agents, many of whom continued to maintain the FBI mindset. One day, while talking to the

Deputy Director of Security at the time, Edwal J., I mentioned that I was torn between joining the Office of Security or the Agency's Clandestine Service. His reply was quite simple, "the DA is the white world, Richard; and the DO is the black world." Back in 1980, and as it is today, the Office of Security was responsible for providing a comprehensive, worldwide security program that protects Agency personnel, programs, information, facilities, and activities. Through a system of formal classroom training courses, on-the-job training, and rotational assignments, most of which are in the Washington, DC area, security careerists become exposed to a wide variety of security disciplines. Security careerists are expected to work in fast-paced environments, be highly organized, analytic, enjoy working with others, be willing to work in a variety of different positions -- domestically and overseas -- and must be willing to move every two to three years. Although the Office of Security claims that the interests of an individual are taken into consideration when job assignments are made, security careerists have to be willing to accept positions and develop skills to meet the mission needs of the CIA.

Most security officers begin their career as investigators prior to becoming clearance adjudicators, area security officers, or overseas security officers. Some go on to become counterintelligence analysts, polygraph examiners, financial investigators, or computer forensic investigators. Security officers are also deployed as liaison officers at other Intelligence Community partners, to non-security offices within the Agency, or assigned to other U.S. Government agencies to respond to all questions and issues relating to security, resource and program management, budget and finance, and policy and plans. As analysts, security officers are placed in positions where they are expected to collect and analyze security or counterintelligence related information.

In addition to the Office of Security, I began exploring the possibility of working in the Directorate of Operations (DO). The CIA's clandestine service can best be described as the front-line source of clandestine information on critical international developments from terrorism and weapons of mass destruction to military and political issues. The mission of the DO requires clandestine service officers to live and work overseas, making a true commitment to the Agency. The Agency likes to brag, "This is more than just a job — it's a way of life that challenges the deepest resources of personal intelligence, self-reliance and responsibility." Eventually, I was interviewed by the DO's Latin America and Africa

Divisions, hoping to be accepted into the Agency's Clandestine Service Trainee (CST) program or the Professional Trainee (PT) program.

The CST is an intensive training program that the DO uses to groom and prepare officers for the foreign intelligence-collection challenges facing the world. The PT program is an entry-level employment program for recent college graduates where applicants accepted are assigned to Washington, DC for several months, during which time they work in two disciplines – as a staff operations officer and as a collection management officer. At the end of the program, PT's are assessed and evaluated for movement into the CST program, the traditional pipeline to serving overseas as an operations officer or collection management officer; and in Washington, DC as a staff operations officer. Operation officers are assigned one of the toughest jobs in the U.S. Government – collecting foreign intelligence. To do this, an operations officer establishes and maintains networks and personal relationships with foreign "assets" in the field. Operations officers work with collection management officers to determine what kind of assets to seek and what information is needed. In addition to establishing and maintaining networks and personal relationships with foreign "assets" in the field, operations officers must live "under cover" – a necessary challenge that is part of their clandestine role.

The collection management officer serves as the connection between the operations officer in the field and the foreign policy community. These officers are responsible for guiding intelligence collection and directing its dissemination. Managing the collection effort requires determining what U.S. policy makers and intelligence analysts need to know, and then communicating those requirements to the operations officer. To be effective, they must understand operational tradecraft and international issues. Collection management officers serve overseas and in the Washington, DC headquarters, while staff operations officers contribute to the clandestine service mission primarily from the Washington, DC headquarters, providing fast-paced research and case management in support of their colleagues overseas. This includes monitoring counterintelligence issues and providing support needed to deal with our foreign contacts in the field. Staff operations officers must be knowledgeable on both operational tradecraft and international issues in order to enhance their interaction with field-based officers.

Operations officers and collection management officers spend a significant portion of their time abroad, on tours of two to four years. Typically, operations officers will serve 60%-70% of their careers overseas, while collection management officers will serve 30%-40% of their careers overseas. Staff operations officers, although based in the Washington, DC area, travel overseas on a temporary basis. There are some fundamental qualities common to most successful Agency operations officers, collection management officers, and staff operations officers, including a strong record of academic and professional achievement; excellent writing skills; problem-solving abilities; and highly developed interpersonal skills. Overseas experience and languages are important factors.

Directorate of Operations officers must be perennial students in the sense that they are required to seek answers, learn other languages, and study other cultures to enhance their abilities to deal effectively with foreign cultures and societies. By the very nature of this clandestine business, DO officers are placed "under cover" and expect limited external recognition for themselves and their families. Instead, the Agency has its own internal promotions, awards and medals, and makes every effort to recognize their accomplishments. In addition, DO officers are paid well in terms of regular, taxable income, and they receive non-taxable overseas allowances that generally permit them to focus on their work and enjoy a decent standard of living. The majority of DO officers live comfortably by the American standard of living, make significant contributions that affect our National Security, and experience a high level of job satisfaction and camaraderie throughout their career.

* * *

During the spring of 1980, while playing rugby for a local Northern Virginia rugby team (NOVA), I fractured my right shoulder and had to have extensive surgery to repair it. The surgeon, who happened to be the same surgeon for the Washington Redskins football team and the Washington Capitols ice hockey team, Dr. Pat Palumbo, cut off my collarbone and clavicle, tied my ligaments in knots, and put a metal plate in my shoulder with six-inch pins and screws. I was in the hospital for several days. When released, a friend picked me up and drove me to my girlfriend's house in York, Pennsylvania to recover.

While recuperating from the surgery, I received a phone call from the Office of Security informing me that I was going to be interviewed as a candidate. The next day, I departed Pennsylvania at

4:30 a.m. and drove to Langley in a 1976 stick shift Mustang. Fortunately, I was not pulled over by a police officer that morning because if I had been, they would have seen a young man dressed in a three-piece suit with a tightly wrapped bandage around his upper body trying to shift gears by placing his left hand through the steering wheel.

As I arrived at Langley for the 9:00 a.m. interview, I realized that I was running late. I parked the car and raced to the interview room only to hear voices from inside the room say, "I guess that we can proceed with the next interview in that it appears that this candidate is not coming". Upon entering the room, the three interviewers, two men and a woman, were aghast to see a sweating young man with a bandage wrapped around his entire upper torso, talking at 100 miles per hour trying to explain why he was late. For the next 20 minutes, I then proceeded to tell everyone about the injury and the lengths to which I had gone to get to the interview that day.

Several months later, after being selected on 28 April 1980, I was told by one of the interviewers that the impression I had made on the panel that day was the reason I had been selected.

My Special Agent class consisted of a number of agents that were both men and women. The Director of Security at the time was William (Bill) K., who served as a father figure for many of the new agents. Our advisor was a seasoned veteran of the Office of Security named Andy B., who went on to be the head of our Chicago Field Office for many years. The class coordinator was Maureen B., who eventually went on to become one of the most senior females in the Office of Security.

The first day I walked into the second portion of the class, I was met by an impressive figure standing over 6'5" tall and weighing close to 260 pounds. His name was Bill A. and he dubbed me the "Boston Flash", a reference to the field office where I would be going after graduating from the training. I liked Bill right from the start and, ironically, ending up working for him on four different occasions spanning 12 years during my career. To further cement our relationship, Bill was a fellow rugby player. After completing the class, the first advice he gave me was to look up an individual who played for the Boston Rugby Club, which I did shortly after my arrival in Boston.

Chapter 2

"Adventures in a Domestic Field Office"

Following graduation, I packed up my things and drove to Boston, Massachusetts on 23 June 1980. After checking into a downtown hotel, I decided to walk to the harbor and could not have been luckier because, sailing vessels known as "Tall Ships" were in town that day. For the next several hours, one after another passed in front of me, including the 295-foot U.S. Coast Guard ship known as the Barque Eagle.

The following day, I walked to the Boston Field Office (BFO) at 10 High Street where our office was located on the seventh floor of a ten-story building. My first impression upon entering the foyer was the décor. In addition to large photographs of the President, and the Secretary of Defense, there were pictures of soldiers on the walls with captions underneath them such as "I am a soldier, if captured I will only provide my name, rank, and serial number." Apparently, the office interior decoration had not changed since the 1950's. While gazing at the décor, I was met by a host of older agents. At 25, I was the first young agent assigned to BFO in some time.

In those days, the Office of Security had field offices in Boston, New York, Washington, Miami, Chicago, Los Angeles, and San Francisco. The Special Agent in Charge (SAC) in Boston was a tall Irishman by the name of Paul B. Paul had gained fame in the Office of Security working on the West Coast in California on several compartmented programs involving satellite reconnaissance with companies that had contracts with the Agency. The Assistant Special Agent in Charge (ASAC) was another Irishman named Dick O. Like many who had become SAC's or ASAC's in the Boston Field Office, both Paul and Dick had previously served as agents in Boston when they were younger. Some of the agents who had served with them at the time remained there, choosing to stay in that type of work rather than return to Headquarters in Washington DC, along with the head clerk at the time, Gloria R.

I liked Paul and Dick, both of whom I consider to be two of the finest supervisors I have ever worked for during my career. Paul further impressed me when he closed the office at noon on my first day and said that we were going to have lunch at a local German bar,

"Jackie Wurts", where we proceeded to eat bratwurst sandwiches and drink pitchers of dark German beer for the better part of two to three hours. Later, after returning to the office, one of the first things I had to concentrate on was finding an apartment. Paul suggested that I focus my search on the north shore above Boston, because most of my work would be north of the city.

Departing the office that afternoon, I began a slow drive up Route 1 and settled in Marblehead, a small, historic town on the ocean, 12 miles north of Boston, well known for sailing, excellent restaurants, and high priced real estate. Walking into the first real estate company I came to, I was soon shown a small three-room apartment in an old estate house on One Green Street, near a historic century-old cemetery and a pond known as "Red's Pond" several blocks from the ocean. The apartment had hardwood floors, French doors leading out to a small balcony, and a fireplace in both the living room and bedroom. I signed the contract that afternoon for $450 per month–incredible in comparison to today's rents. That evening, I rode my bike to the ocean to overlook the water at the Boston Yacht Club and a man approached me who introduced himself as Dick Levine. After sizing me up, Dick asked me if I had ever crewed on a sailboat before. Although I replied I had not and that I had no sailing experience, Dick asked me if I was interested in learning how to crew. This led to me sailing almost ever day after work aboard a 32-foot "Etchel" class similar to the Olympic class sailboat known as the "Soiling". The name of our boat was the "Dixie" which, now rests at the bottom of the Marblehead harbor after a collision with another sailboat.

The next day, I was provided a new 1980 Chrysler "K' car, a set of U.S. Government credentials and a set of CIA credentials signed by DCI William (Bill) Casey in the event that we had to assist in protecting the DCI, DDCI, carry classified information, or support anything of a National Security interest in the New England area. After several weeks in the Boston Field Office, I began to fall into a routine where each evening I would map out a strategy of where I would go the following day to interview people. After compiling information, as agents we had to dictate a report into a machine known as a Dictaphone, which recorded the information. The report was then transcribed by a secretary and handed back to the agent for review several days later. In Boston, we were fortunate to have an excellent secretary by the name of Eva D. who could type more than 100 words per minute. Eventually we were provided with a small pocket cassette recorder, which made recording much easier.

The competition to complete cases in BFO was strong and even more so among the various field offices. Completing 15-18 cases per month in Boston was the norm and, averaging 20 cases per month, as I had been doing for three years, was the exception to the rule. With numbers like that, it was no great surprise that BFO ranked number one most of the time among the other field offices.

After several months at BFO, I finally visited Harvard University. Walking from the field office to the subway station, I boarded the Red Line to Harvard Square. Having never taken a subway before in my life, this turned out to be quite an interesting experience. As was the custom in those days, I was dressed in a three-piece suit and wearing a tan trench coat as fall was approaching. Shortly after sitting down, a man holding a bottle in a paper bag sat down on one side of me, while an overweight, disheveled woman, who appeared to be "homeless", sat on my other side. By the odors emitting from both of them, it was apparent that neither of them had bathed for quite some time. The stench became even more obtrusive in that the train's heater, located under our seats, was forcing out hot air. When the women got up to depart, I noticed her seat was wet. Apparently, she had urinated in her pants as she sat. As the urine began to drip down into the heating system under our seats, the man next to me holding the bottle in the paper bag began vomiting. The smell of the urine and vomit was too much for me to handle. Although I was two subway stops from Harvard Square, I decided to get off at the next stop and walk the remainder of the way; so much for taking public transportation in Boston.

After my first year at the Boston Field Office, SAC Paul B. announced that he was going to retire and a fellow Special Agent by the name of Jed K. and I were put in charge of Paul's retirement ceremony. Wanting to do something special for Paul, Jed and I decided to arrange a dinner at one of his favorite restaurants in Boston's South End, the "No Name Restaurant", followed by a basketball game at the Boston Garden with Paul's beloved Celtics. The "No Name Restaurant" sat at the end of the pier where the British poured tea into the Boston Harbor to avoid paying taxes on 16 December 1773. Although famous for its seafood, the restaurant really did not have a name.

Having grown up in the Boston area, Paul was a huge Boston Celtics fan. The only problem was that the Celtics were in the midst of the Eastern Conference Finals with their fierce rivals, the Philadelphia 76ers. Boston, at the time, had Larry Bird, Cedric

Maxwell, Robert Parish, Chris Ford, Tiny Archibald, Kevin McHale, M.L. Carr, Gerald Henderson, and Rick Robey. The 76ers, on the other hand, had Julius Irving, Darryl Dawkins, Maurice Cheeks, Steve Mix, Andrew Toney, and Caldwell Jones. Tickets were impossible to come by but not for two determined BFO agents such as Jed and myself. Our first stop was the Celtics main ticket office at the Boston Garden where Jed and I approached the ticket clerk and asked to purchase 35 tickets for the game between the Celtics and 76ers on Friday evening. After the ticket clerk replied "no way" and finally stopped laughing, we asked if there was anyone whom we could talk to in the Celtics organization who could help us purchase the 35 tickets. The clerk suggested that we speak to a person in the Celtics front office and gave us the name of an individual. Contacting them and not being shy, Jed and I proceeded to flash our U.S. Government credentials and began to tell the story that we were arranging the retirement party for a one-star General who was returning to the Boston area after serving for many years at the Pentagon in Washington, DC.

We continued that the General was a huge Celtics fan and as a farewell, he wanted to see them play the 76ers. When we stated that we were looking for 35 tickets for Friday evening, the Celtics representative replied that, although it was impossible to get all 35 seats together, he would try to get several seats of two and three tickets in several different sections throughout the arena. When we told him that we preferred to keep everyone seated together, his reply was, "Sorry, this is the best that I can do". Not to be deterred, Jed and I asked if there was anyone else, we could talk to in the Celtics organization. Given the name of one of the Vice Presidents, we arranged to meet him.

We presented our U.S. Government credentials and informed the VP that we had a two-star General coming up from Washington, DC who was retiring in the Boston area, and continued that the General was a huge Celtics fan, wanted to see a game for his retirement, and then asked if we could purchase 35 tickets for Friday night's game. When the VP replied that he could give us three sets of 10 tickets in various sections, and one set of five tickets in another, we thanked him profusely, and asked if there was anyone else in the Celtics organization that we could talk to while, we were there. Chuckling, the VP replied that the only other individual who could authorize this type of ticket purchase was a Senior Vice President who worked directly for the infamous General Manager of the Celtics, Red Auerbach—so we asked if he could arrange a meeting.

Several minutes later, Jed, and I were standing in front of the Senior VP to General Manager Red Auerbach.

With our U.S. Government credentials extended, we proceeded to tell the Senior VP the story of a three-star General who was retiring in the Boston area from Washington, DC after serving in the military for more than 35 years. We continued that the General was from the Boston area, was a huge Celtics fan, and we were hoping to show our appreciation by getting him tickets to see the Celtics/76ers game on Friday evening. Much to everyone's surprise, except, of course, Jed and I, that Friday evening, Paul and 35 members of his entourage, including the Director of Security, Bill K., were sitting behind the Boston Celtics bench watching the Celtics beat the 76ers that night. What Jed and I had not bargained for however, was Paul's picture being flashed on the huge television screen above the playing floor during the game recognizing him for more than 35 years of military service as a General in the U.S. Army. Although Paul gave Jed and me a dirty look at the time, he later thanked us profusely by taking the two of us afterwards to Boston's infamous North End for pizza, beers, and Italian cannolis. Paul never asked us how we got the tickets and we never told him.

When Paul B. retired, he was replaced by Jack P. as the Special Agent in Charge (SAC) – another former BFO special agent who had served in Boston during the 1960's. Jack had gained fame in the Office of Security working on the Hughes Glomar Explorer Project. Sun Shipbuilding and Dry-Dock Company built the Hughes Glomar Explorer in 1973 for an intricate CIA undertaking to raise a Soviet nuclear submarine that had sunk in the Pacific, resting on the ocean floor nearly 17,000 feet below the surface. The Soviet Golf-II Class ballistic missile submarine sank on 11 April 1968, approximately 750 miles northwest of Hawaii. Naval intelligence at Pearl Harbor had tracked the submarine and learned of its fate through underwater listening devices. After months of futile searching by Soviet vessels, it became apparent that only the U.S. knew the location of the sunken submarine. Global Marine supervised construction of the Glomar Explorer, at a cost in excess of $200 million dollars, and operated it from 1973 to 1975 under contract to the U.S. government. The Glomar Explorer went to sea on 20 June 1974, found the sub, and began to bring a portion of it to the surface. The Soviets watched the "deep-sea mining" operation with interest, but did not attempt to thwart it. Unfortunately, an accident during the lifting operation caused the fragile hulk to break apart, resulting in the loss of a critical portion of the submarine.

As a young Special Agent, Jack had also walked down Pennsylvania Avenue side by side with First Lady Jacqueline Kennedy and French President Charles de Gaulle during President Kennedy's funeral procession on 25 November 1963. In that the assassination took place during the Cold War, it was at first unclear whether the shooting was part of a larger attack upon the U.S. When President de Gaulle was told that the U.S. Secret Service was concerned about his safety, Jack overheard President de Gaulle comment, "If Mrs. Kennedy is walking down Pennsylvania Avenue, then I will be by her side."

* * *

An avid golfer, former SAC Paul and I would meet from time to time to play golf. As is the case today, the government car was only to be used for "official business". An agent was cautioned about using the car for anything but "official business", which included stopping by a store for a loaf of bread or milk, even if the store was on the way home. Usually, if an agent had to make an "unofficial stop", their excuse was always that they had to make a phone call (in those primitive days before cellular phones).

To have golf clubs in the trunk of your government car was the ultimate sin – grounds for disciplinary action or even dismissal. So when Paul called me one day after he had retired to meet him after work to play golf, I threw my clubs in the trunk although I knew I was breaking the rules and would be reprimanded if I got caught. To cover myself, I purposely arranged to have an interview in the area near the golf course that day. However, much to my surprise, before arriving at the golf course, Jack summoned me to the office. Several minutes after my arrival, Jack asked if he could borrow my car and, unbeknownst to me, was on his way to pick up the Director of Security, Bill K., who was flying into Boston from Washington, DC. As fate would have it, when Jack opened the trunk and saw my golf clubs, not only was he embarrassed, I was screwed. Upon returning to the office and questioning me, I told Jack that I was wrong and, therefore, would accept the consequences for my actions. I never let Jack know that I was planning to play golf with his predecessor, Paul, however, and unless Jack reads this book, he never will know it. This incident quickly got back to Headquarters in Washington, DC and to the various field offices around the country. I was later told that it was used during class as an example of what not to do as a Special Agent. Several years after this incident, Paul shrank to less than 150 pounds and eventually died of cancer. I still carry his prayer card with me today–he made that much of an impression on me.

* * *

On a cold, snowy 13 January 1982 morning, my beeper went off and I was summoned to the office by Jack, who calmly closed the door after I entered. Jack, who was always concerned about his weight, was usually at his desk eating carrots and celery, or on the floor doing pushups or sit-ups in his suit. As was the case when anyone was summoned to the SAC's office, I thought that I was in trouble and had done something wrong.

Much to my surprise, however, Jack began by saying that he had an important assignment for me, one that I could not discuss with anyone else in the office. Rumors of five Libyan terrorists entering the United States through Canada to assassinate President Ronald Reagan had been circulating in Washington DC for several months beginning on 4 December 1981 when the *New York Times* reported that a five man Libyan "hit team" had entered the United States. In response, the Immigration and Naturalization Service had sent a seven-page memo stamped "Extremely Sensitive" to all of its major border crossings and airport offices. Two days later on 6 December 1981, Libyan President Mohmmar Qaddafi appeared in a live interview on ABC televisions' *This Week with David Brinkley*. Speaking from his private office in Tripoli, Qaddafi heatedly denied that he had sent any "hit team" to the United States or any assassination squads. Although composite sketches of the five alleged "hit men" had been posted on television, the U.S. Government wanted photographs of these individuals distributed immediately.

Jack announced that I would be traveling to Fort Kent, Maine, the most northern town on Route 1 along the U.S./Canadian border, and would be met by several officials from the U.S. Customs and Immigration Service; a U.S. Secret Service agent; and an FBI agent who would be arriving from Washington. The next morning, I awoke to a driving snowstorm, dressed in my favorite three-piece suit, put on my Herman Survivor boots, a heavy winter Gore-Tex parka and headed to Logan International Airport where I boarded a small 20 passenger Bar Harbor Airlines Corsair shuttle. The afternoon before, an Air Florida 737 jet (Flight 90) crashed into the Potomac River in Washington, DC after taking off from Reagan National Airport, killing 74 passengers. The plane had crushed several cars and killed five people on the 14th Street Bridge before violently splashing into the icy Potomac River and sinking. Subsequent rescue efforts yielded only five survivors from the airplane. Crash investigators concluded that the crew's failure to use the engine anti-ice mechanism caused large amounts of ice and snow to gather in the engines without being melted. To say that I was a little tense about my flight was an understatement. I was scheduled to fly from Boston to Bangor, Maine and then from Bangor to Presque Isle, Maine.

Upon arriving in Bangor some 45 minutes later, the pilot came on the intercom and announced that he would not be able to continue north to Presque, Isle; the weather had worsened and everyone had to depart the aircraft. After the other passengers were off, I worked my way up to the front of the aircraft and stuck my head in the cabin. We normally carried U.S. Government credentials, but on this occasion, I was allowed to take my CIA credentials, which had been signed by the DCI, Bill Casey. Presenting them to the stunned pilot and co-pilot I announced that I was a Special Agent with the CIA's Office of Security, on a special mission involving National Security.

I further informed them that I needed to get to Loring Air Force Base, home of the B-52 strategic air command (a cover story, which I had quickly devised to cover the fact that I was heading to Fort Kent). Surprisingly, the pilot radioed the tower and asked permission to continue to Presque Isle. Although the pilot identified me as a Special Agent, he never revealed my Agency affiliation. Upon receiving permission to depart, the pilot offered me a seat in the cockpit with him and the co-pilot. For the next quarter hour, I watched in awe as maintenance men used brooms to sweep the snow off the wings of our aircraft as a small Cessna single engine taxied ahead of us to help clear the runway. After taking off, I remember the pilot jokingly say that it would be a short flight – less than fifteen minutes. Even to this day, I still cannot understand how the pilot flew the plane in that the snow was coming down so hard the windshield wipers could barely keep up. Thank God for instruments. Finally, after what seemed like an eternity, we landed and proceeded to skid along, oblivious to the fact that we were actually on a marked runway. After my heart started beating again, I asked the pilot and co-pilot if I could buy them breakfast and a coffee to which they readily agreed. It was 10:00 a.m. My instructions were to be in Fort Kent by 4:00 p.m. so I thought I had plenty of time. My next daunting task, however, after consuming a large breakfast of scrambled eggs, sausage, toast and home fries, was to find a rental vehicle to drive the 86 miles from Presque Isle to Fort Kent along Route 1.

Unfortunately, due to the weather everything, with the exception of the restaurant, was closed at the airport including all of the car rental companies. After unsuccessfully calling every car rental company in the phone book, I decided to call Jack. When ASAC Dick O. answered the phone, I explained my dilemma. His response is one that I will always remember, "Richard, all I can ask is that you try". With that hanging over my head, I proceeded to ask everyone I could find in the airport if they knew of anyone who would rent me a vehicle. Finally, I was given the name of someone whom I promptly called and, thirty minutes later, a Chrysler K car with front wheel drive arrived and I was off to Fort Kent via Route 1.

Since the snow was still coming down hard with huge drifts beginning to form, I can still recall saying to myself, "How am I ever going to be able to continue?" As fate would have it, though, a large snowplow pulled out in front of me and began to clear the way. As I settled back to listen to music, little did I know that the snowplow driver's job was to plow the entire 86 miles from Presque Isle to Fort Kent. Driving along at less than 20 miles per hour, it was difficult to imagine snow piled as high as the telephone lines on the side of the road and drifts covering the back of barns and houses in flat fields known for growing potatoes. Four hours later, I arrived in Fort Kent and looked at my watch. It was 10 minutes to four o'clock. I cannot tell you how proud I was when I pulled up to the border crossing, presented my credentials, and asked to speak to the Officer in Charge. I was told that the U.S. Secret Service agent and the FBI agent, both of whom I was supposed to meet, had called and stated that they would not be arriving until the next day.

For the next seven days, travelers from 36 different countries entered this small border crossing at Fort Kent, Maine, but no one fitting the description or profile of the five individuals whom I had risked my life carrying their photos and bio information that day in early January 1982.

* * *

On another occasion, while visiting Maine, I pulled into the town of Bath known for its shipyards and ironwork. It was early evening and the temperature was dropping rapidly. With the snow lightly falling, I checked into a small motel and asked the owner if I could have a quiet room for the evening. In his down home east Maine accent, he softly replied, "You do not have to worry about noise, young man. You are the only guest I have for the evening".

After dinner, I headed to my room to get some much-needed rest. Later that night, as I was preparing for bed, I heard a vehicle pull up in front of my room, which, ironically, was the furthest room from the main reception building. As the vehicle parked, I looked outside and noticed a large white van with "Tidy Deity Diaper Service" stenciled on the side. Shortly thereafter, a man, a woman, and a small dog exited. Much to my dismay, the man put a key into my door and it opened. When I told him the room was occupied, the man immediately apologized and departed with the woman and the small dog in bay. The man then entered the room adjacent to mine and for the next four hours proceeded to make love to the women in a fashion and exuberance, which I can honestly, say, I have never heard before. To say that the woman was a "moaner and groaner" was an understatement. To make matters worse, as they made love, their damn bed frame kept banging up against my wall and the small dog never stopped yapping. Finally, after what seemed to be an eternity, everything in the other room got quiet and I finally fell asleep. The next morning, I looked out the window and noticed that the van was gone. As I was checking out, I casually mentioned this bizarre incident to the owner who almost choked on his coffee while apologizing and said that he had not rented any rooms nor had he given any keys out to anyone that evening.

Yet during another visit to Maine, when checking with my office one morning, Jack told me that he had just received a call from the wife of a former CIA security officer informing him that her husband had passed away during the night. Not knowing whom to contact for assistance, the widow called Jack for advice. Jack told the woman that he had a Special Agent in the area that would be visiting her shortly to lend a hand. Upon calling the woman, to my surprise, she sounded relatively calm recalling the story of how her husband had passed away during the night and was still in their bed. After getting directions to her residence, I told her that I would be there in 25 to 30 minutes.

The majority of Maine is very rural; so her directions were something like this: "Head north on "such and such" road from the center of town until you get to the first major intersection some 20 miles from town. Turn left at the big red barn on the corner and pass the next five dirt roads on the right side of the road. At the sixth dirt road, turn right and proceed ½ mile down the lane to our house."

Sounded simple to me. Thirty minutes later, I had found the intersection with the big red barn, turned left and was counting the dirt roads on my right. At the sixth dirt road, I turned right and drove 500 or 600 yards. Upon reaching the top of a small rise, I was astonished to see that the road ahead of me disappeared into a pond. As I tried to brake, my vehicle slid down the hill and into the pond, breaking the ice along the way. Luckily, only the front tires were submerged in the water. Looking behind me at the small incline, all I could think of was how am I going to get out of this mess. On top of that, I was running late to meet with a woman who had just lost her husband. Although I was in suit, when I was in Maine, I always wore Herman Survivor boots and a heavy winter Gore-Tex jacket so, I opened the driver's side door, put one foot on the gas peddle and the other foot on the ground with my back to the doorframe. Ten minutes later, sweating and muddy, my car was out of the pond thanks to front wheel drive. The second part of this nightmare began when I tried to get up the small icy incline in reverse as my tires spun furiously. After what seemed like an eternity, I finally reached the top of the hill while all along thinking of what it would have been like if the car had flipped over on its roof and slid back into the pond with me inside, dying without a trace.

When I finally arrived at the house, a woman met me with an "aghast look" upon her face. Apparently my appearance so unnerved the woman that she spent the next 30 minutes making me tea and getting me out of my wet, muddy clothing and into some new clothes, courtesy of her deceased husband. Upon returning to Boston, I submitted my expense account voucher to be reimbursed for my suit to be dry cleaned and unbelievably was told by the chief clerk, Gloria, that I would not be reimbursed since I had waited to get the suit dry cleaned in Boston rather than finding a 24 hour dry cleaning garment place in Maine. Apparently, Gloria had never taken a trip to upstate Maine in the wintertime.

* * *

At times, in addition to conducting interviews, as Special Agents we were asked to provide support to the DCI. On one occasion, I was told that the DCI would be meeting the head of one of the Intelligence Services off the Coast of Martha's Vineyard and was tasked with providing support during the meeting.

After driving an hour and a half from Boston, I boarded one of the ferries at Woods Hole and an hour later was at a hotel in Edgartown. Shortly after checking in, I was met by two advance agents from the DCI security staff who provided a briefing on what was going to transpire during the next few days. I was told that DCI Casey would be arriving in a small jet the following evening and afterwards would be transported to a yacht, which the Agency had rented, complete with chef, to entertain the director of this intelligence service. While several agents were assigned to the airport for the arrival and others assigned as drivers in the motorcade, I was told that I would be assigned to the yacht. All I can remember was that the meeting was delayed for one day due to the weather and several members of the crew and I were forced to eat a sumptuous meal consisting of lamb, stuffed grape leaves, rice and humus. Life for a 26-year-old agent was very good.

On another occasion, DCI Casey was asked to speak at Brown University as part of a lecture series that included several former DCI's. I was asked to provide support for this visit along with fellow Boston agent, Jed K. Upon arriving at the auditorium that evening our motorcade was greeted by a hostile crowd, many of whom were carrying signs claiming that the CIA was involved in genocide. To make matters worse, Casey, who was in his mid-70s at the time, had just broken his leg while playing golf several days earlier and was in a walking cast. As we led him into the auditorium, several protesters tried in vain to approach him but were hustled away by the local police. Shortly after he began his opening remarks, a host of students began to make "cat calls" while others stood up and began to publicly berate Casey. I could see that he was getting extremely agitated by this behavior and, shortly thereafter, he turned and walked off the stage. This incensed the crowd even more. As we quickly led him to the awaiting motorcade, a large number of protesters broke through the police lines and began pounding on the DCI's armored limousine and the escort vehicles, as we pulled away. Casey was so unnerved by the incident that he asked to be taken to the airport to return to Washington, DC rather than attend a reception at the hotel that the President of Brown University was hosting on his behalf. I can still remember, as the Director boarded the plane to depart that evening, he stopped and returned to personally thank us for our service—one of the few times that Casey ever spoke to us during these assignments.

* * *

In addition to providing support to the DCI, we were often called upon to assist with visits by Vice President George Bush who maintained a residence in Kennebunkport, Maine; Secretary of State

George Shultz who had an old farmhouse in Cummington, Massachusetts; and Secretary of Defense, Caspar Weinberger who had a residence in Bar Harbor, Maine.

In those days, a CIA communicator and a Director of Intelligence (DI) analyst, escorted by a Navy courier, hand carried the CIA presidential briefing known as the PDB to the President, Vice President and Cabinet members, such as the Secretary of State and Secretary of Defense, when they traveled outside of Washington, DC. After the highly classified PDB was left on the top of the roof of a vehicle driven by one of the Navy couriers and later turned into the FBI, DCI Casey decided to take away the courier privileges from the Navy and place it in the hands of Special Agents from the CIA's Office of Security. Shortly after Casey made this decision, I was summoned to the office by Jack P. one afternoon and was told that I would be escorting a CIA communicator and a DI Analyst with the PDB from our office in Boston to Secretary of Defense Weinberger who was at his residence in Bar Harbor, Maine. It was a six-hour drive from Boston to Bar Harbor, so we decided to give ourselves plenty of time and, departed at midnight to be there by 8:00 a.m. I was glad that we had because it snowed the entire trip. Upon arriving in Bar Harbor at 7:00 a.m., we decided to get breakfast and then head to Secretary Weinberger's residence. Arriving at precisely 8:00 a.m., we were met by one of Weinberger's aides who informed us that the Secretary was swimming in his indoor heated pool. Rather than invite us in out of the cold, however, we were told to return in an hour.

Since there is nothing—and I mean nothing—open in Bar Harbor in the wintertime, we decided to wait in our vehicle with the heater blasting. Finally, at 9:00 a.m., we knocked on the door again and were told by the aide to hand over the PDB to him. Although we politely informed the aide that the PDB was not to leave our sight, the aide reiterated that we were to hand over the PDB for Secretary Weinberger to read. Knowing that this was a battle that the communicator, the DI analyst, nor I was going to win; we reluctantly handed him the PDB and were told to wait in our vehicle until Secretary Weinberger finished reading it. Freezing our tails off, we returned to our vehicle and an hour and a half later, the aide handed the PDB back to us.

As we drove back to Boston, I called ASAC Dick O. and informed him of the reception that the three of us had just received. Dick's reply was "nobody treats one of my agents like that" and immediately got on the phone to Headquarters. I knew that somebody at DOD was going to have "hell to pay" for treating us that way and was proud to hear that Dick indeed asked Headquarters to "get on the horn" to DOD. Interestingly, the next time we had to support Secretary Weinberger, the aide that had been so rude to us in Bar Harbor was no longer at his side, and our reception was much better. On the other hand, when called upon to take the PDB to Vice President George H. Bush or Secretary of State George Shultz, we were always invited in and provided hot chocolate, or fresh muffins and cookies by Mrs. Bush and Mrs. Shultz.

Chapter 3

"Clearance Division and the Polygraph; Some Interesting Stories"

During the summer of 1983, after serving three years in the Boston Field Office, SAC Jack P. called me into his office and asked if I would be interested in joining the DCI security staff. Although I knew that this meant constant travel and long hours, I immediately agreed. Two days later however, during another conversation, Jack asked if I would be interested in working with Bill A. in a new security officer position in the paramilitary arm of the DO known as the International Activities Division (IAD). I was so excited about the opportunity of working for Bill again that I told Jack to withdraw my name as a candidate for the DCI security staff only to be informed several days later that George L., the nephew of the Chief of the Clearance Division, Willis R. had gotten the position in IAD. My new assignment was to fill George's former position in CD-5, a section of Clearance Division. CD-5 is responsible for clearing contractors that have staff-like access within the Agency. This meant that a contractor had to undergo the same security processing as that of a CIA staff employee, which included a full background investigation and polygraph.

I arrived in CD-5 on 20 September 1983, which, at the time, was located in the Old Headquarters Building (OHB); co-located with CD-4 responsible for clearing contractors for Special Compartmented Information known as (SCI). No one liked working in Clearance Division, but in the Office of Security, it was critical to understand the process for hiring and clearing personnel.

The Chief of CD-5 at the time was Bruce A., a native Hawaiian. Bruce was great to work for and someone I will always remember. He had served in the San Francisco Field Office and was well respected among his peers. There were only five or six of us in CD-5 at the time, so out section was close knit and eventually went on to break every record for closing cases in the Clearance Division at that time. Under Bruce's tutelage, we worked hard and played hard. He often rewarded us by taking the entire staff to the Vienna Inn for a lunch of cold beers and chilidogs. One day after having lunch, we mailed a chilidog to one of our coworkers named Debbie F. who was living overseas. It was moldy and full of mildew when it arrived, but Debbie cried and thanked us in a letter saying, "It was the thought that counted."

* * *

Unfortunately, one year into my tour, Bruce was diagnosed with cancer and passed away. His replacement was a former polygraph operator by the name of John G. who frequently entertained us with stories of some of his more interesting cases as a polygrapher.

One story that I will never forget involved an applicant who told John during testing that he had, had sex with a chicken. Although CIA policy called for polygraph operators to inform an individual that everything they say will be held in the strictest of confidence, when someone admits to something like this, the polygraph operator would normally stop the test, excuse themselves from the room and then proceed to tell everyone within earshot that they had someone who claimed that they had sex with a chicken. The entire office would then run to the two-way mirror to see who it was.

Another story was about a young woman in her early twenties who, as a contractor, was being considered for Agency staff-like access. In those days, in addition to asking questions pertaining to your sexual preference, the polygraph operator was permitted to ask questions about deviant sexual behavior. This woman was deemed to be telling the truth on all of the questions with the exception of the deviant sexual behavior question. The polygraph operator began to interrogate her in an attempt to resolve the issue. After repeated attempts to identify what was troubling her, the young woman finally admitted going to New York City one weekend and ended up visiting a private nightclub named "Plato's Retreat." Shortly after entering the bar, the young woman realized that everyone in the nightclub was naked. Soon after being coaxed by her boyfriend to remove her clothes, the young woman found herself in a compromising situation—another couple began kissing and caressing her and, much to her surprise, the other woman began to perform cunnilingus on her.

The polygraph eventually supported the young woman's claim that this was a one-time incident and her claim that she would never permit herself to get involved in such an act again, especially in light of the fact that she had broken off the relationship with her boyfriend. Still, the young woman was required to sign an Agency "Code of Conduct" statement. The "Code of Conduct" addresses the issue, states that the Agency does not condone this type of behavior, and mentions that further instances of this type of behavior could result in suspension or dismissal.

The next story involved another contractor. This man, an Admiral in the United States Navy, was judged to be telling the truth, except for the deviant sexual behavior question. Similarly as with the young woman mentioned above, the polygraph operator began to interrogate the Admiral in an attempt to resolve the issue. After repeated attempts, the man would not admit to anything or divulge what was troubling him.

On the third day of testing, a senior polygraph operator was called in to question the Admiral. After intense questioning, the man finally divulged that he recently had a serious argument with his wife and afterwards slammed the door and went out on the front steps of his house to "cool down". As he was sitting there, a small dog walked by and "just to get back at his wife", he took the dog into the garage and performed fellatio on it. This individual did not receive his clearance or access.

One story concerned a woman who was in her late fifties that was being considered for access. Her husband had just passed away and she claimed that she had to go back to work after being a homemaker for more that 30 years to support her family and, in particular, two children who were in college. During the polygraph test, the woman seemed truthful except on the criminal behavior question so the operator began to question her specifically on that topic. Despite their efforts, the woman would not say what was troubling her regarding that question.

The woman returned the second day, but the results were the same with the woman still being called "deceptive" on the criminal issue. Finally, after returning from lunch on the second day, the decision was made to have one of the senior polygraph operator's talk to her. After intense questioning the woman finally broke down, started to cry, and began by saying that she had never told anyone what she was about to disclose, not even her priest. The woman continued that while growing up as a young girl in occupied Poland during World War II, she and her older sister where walking home from school one day when a German soldier raped her sister. As the soldier was raping her sister, the woman claimed that she picked up a rock and began hitting the soldier in the head, several times, until he stopped breathing. Her sister then crawled from underneath the soldier and they both pushed his body into a ditch and left the scene. When asked if she believed that she had killed the soldier, the woman softly replied "yes." She added that she was 14 years old at the time and had been carrying around the memory and guilt for more than forty years. Further testing supported her admissions and, as you can imagine, the woman received her clearance.

My favorite story was about a man who sailed through the polygraph without any problems. At the end of the test when asked if there was anything else that he would like to divulge, the man replied, "yes." He then calmly stated that he had been reincarnated. When the polygraph operator asked him to elaborate on what he meant by reincarnated, the man claimed that he had been born in the south in Gulfport, Mississippi in 1846 under the name Jeremiah Jackson, enlisted in the Confederate Army when he was 16 years old, and was killed at the Battle of Shiloh on 6 April 1862. The man continued that he was then reborn in 1954 in Manassas, Virginia under the name of "William Jefferson"; (name changed to protect his privacy). The following day, the man returned and provided the polygraph operator a copy of a birth certificate in the name of Jeremiah Jackson who was born in Gulfport, Mississippi in 1846 and a death certificate showing that Jeremiah Jackson was killed at the Battle of Shiloh on 6 April 1862. He then produced a second birth certificate in the name of "William Jefferson" showing that he was born in Manassas, Virginia in 1954. The case eventually went to the Industrial Review Panel and, although everyone agreed that it was a bit odd, when no one on the panel, including the Agency psychologist, stated that they could dispute the man's claim, the man received his clearance and access.

The last story I can share involved a man who was having difficulty with the deviant sexual behavior question. When questioned, he calmly advised that he frequently performed auto-fellatio on himself. The man, who was very tall and thin, recounted that he could perform this act by sitting on the floor facing a wall with his legs in the air and afterwards would pull his legs towards him and put his penis into his mouth. At the Review Panel, the Agency psychologist noted that he had only heard of three other instances where a man could perform auto-fellatio, and in each instance, the individuals all had deep psychological problems and all three had been involved in other forms of deviant behavior. The decision was made that this individual not receive his clearance and access.

* * *

Each day, during the hour commute to the Gloucester Building, I would listen to a crazy radio-show host known as "The Greaseman" arriving to an overflowing inbox in a 10' x 10' office, which I shared with two colleagues Michael J., and Art F.

Our jobs consisted of opening new files on contractors being considered for staff-like access and scheduling their polygraph test. The process is known as the "whole person" concept to ensure that the Agency is looking at the entire person and not just a portion. To ensure that we were clearing the contractors in a timely fashion, we had to develop a "tickle-card system" (a method for reminders of open tasks and action items) to stay on top of each case and would put a "buck slip" on the file requesting that it be returned in 10 or 15 days so that the case never slipped through the cracks.

It was a never-ending process of trying to keep our heads above water. When all of the information was received from the various offices and the polygraph completed, as the case agent, we had to decide whether to approve or disapprove the candidate. If no derogatory information was identified in either the background investigation or the polygraph, we would fill out a sheet recommending approval and send it to the Chief of CD-5 and his superiors. If all three of them concurred with the recommendation to grant the individual access or the clearance, it was then granted. If negative information was found on the candidate, we had to write up a short report.

In those days before the personal computer, we had to write out each report in long hand or dictate it into a Dictaphone or pocket cassette recorder. The report was then passed to a secretary to type and returned several days later for our review making the entire process extremely slow. One day, Wang computers were installed on our desks, which sped up the process incredibly, since we could type our own reports, edit them, and send them on to the Chief of CD-5 for approval.

* * *

The morning of 24 October 1983, as I passed the office of the Chief of CD-4, Art O., I saw that his door was partially closed. As I entered to say good morning, I saw tears slowly streaming down Art's face as he raised his head from his desk. The day before, a five-ton Mercedes truck (roughly the size of a large dump truck) laden with the equivalent of over 12,000 pounds of TNT crashed through the perimeter of the compound of the U.S. contingent of the Multinational Force at Beirut International Airport, Beirut, Lebanon, penetrated the Battalion Landing Team Headquarters building and detonated. The force of the explosion destroyed the building resulting in the deaths of 241 U.S. military personnel including 220 Marines. Little did I know that Art O. was not only a

Marine, but had been one the most decorated Marines in the Korean conflict.

A month later, we received word that we would be moving to a new facility known as the Stafford Building in Tyson's Corner. The Deputy Chief of the branch at the time was an officer named Eric B. who had a large farm near Ashburn, Virginia, where I frequently used to hunt deer. After returning to Washington, DC from Los Angeles in 1975, Eric purchased a 38-acre farm from two elderly individuals who were getting divorced while in their late 60's. (At that time, Eric paid less than $150,000 for the property and 10 years later received a settlement of several million dollars to sell the farm to a housing developer.)

The Chief of the Branch was a seasoned veteran named Dick H. whose son, Tom, was also employed as a security officer. Tom was notorious for allowing a KGB defector to walk away from him during a protective assignment and re-defect to the Soviet Union.

The KGB officer was named Vitaly Yurchenko who, in 1985 after 25 years of service with the KGB, defected to the United States during an assignment to Rome. During subsequent interrogation by the Agency, Yurchenko accused two American agents of working for the KGB – Ronald Pelton and Edward Lee Howard. While Pelton was eventually convicted, Howard fled the U.S. before he could be questioned. On 31 October 1985, Yurchenko asked his Office of Security escort, Tom, if they could visit Georgetown to observe the Halloween festivities. Yurchenko appeared to have enjoyed himself immensely that evening in that several days later, on 2 November, he suggested to Tom that they again go to Georgetown for dinner. Tom agreed and the two men drove to the fancy Georgetown restaurant "Au Pied de Cochon". As the two men were having a drink, Yurchenko asked Tom if he could excuse himself to make a phone call and then disappeared. When it became obvious to Tom that Yurchenko was not going to return, Tom called his office for guidance.

Unfortunately, this was the first that anyone was made aware of this outing and by the time additional CIA and FBI officers arrived on the scene and began searching for Yurchenko, he had already reached the Soviet Embassy after crawling out of the bathroom window at the restaurant. A few days later Yurchenko boarded a Soviet aircraft and returned to Moscow. The following day, he appeared in a press conference arranged by the Soviets claiming that he had not voluntarily defected but rather had been drugged and kidnapped by the CIA. The entire episode brought suspicion about his defection story. Some suspected that he was acting as a "double agent" seeking to fool the CIA with wrong leads and misinformation to protect one of the USSR's most important CIA traitors, Aldrich Ames. That morning, a local newspaper captured the moment with a cartoon depicting an empty bar at closing time with chairs carefully stacked on top of tables. The only patron was a man in a trench coat and top hat sitting alone. The caption under the cartoon read: "Suddenly, intuitively, the awful realization hit CIA agent Bumworthy that his dinner companion, the Russian defector, would not be coming back!"

* * *

Prior to my departure from Clearance Division, I created a questionnaire that ultimately ended up saving the U.S. Government thousands of dollars. For my efforts, I received a cash award of $200 for coming up with the idea. Interestingly, a colleague of mine received a similar award of $1,000 for suggesting that the Agency place non-skid rubber mats on the internal stairways in the Headquarters building. Oh, well!

Chapter 4

"Learning the Ropes; My First Overseas Trips"

After a year and a half of serving in CD-5, I received word on 22 February 1985 that I was to be reunited with Bill A. who had just been promoted to the Deputy of the Overseas Security Support Branch (OSSB) under the chief of the branch, Ray H.

The mission of OSSB was to conduct comprehensive, physical security surveys to identify vulnerabilities at our DO offices and bases. Additionally, OSSB officers were taught to develop and implement a variety of contingency plans. In that the thoroughness of the security survey depended upon the level of expertise of the survey officer, I authored a manual keyed to the survey report outline, which served as a checklist covering all the areas of concern. This was eventually used by all of the OSSB survey officers as a guide for conducting the surveys and proved invaluable to the newly assigned security officers who had little or no experience.

In preparing the manual, I reviewed and analyzed all of the existing policies and restrictions to assure Agency compliance and am proud to say that this manual assisted the Office of Security in developing thorough and effective overseas security programs that focused on protecting personnel and classified information. OSSB security surveys included a threat and vulnerability assessment, information on the emergency destruction equipment used to destroy classified information, and the security containers used to store classified information.

During a survey, photographs were taken of all of this equipment as well as the compound, entrances and exits, and the entire Agency office. Before their departure, OSSB officers frequently wrote emergency plans and, in some instances, emergency evacuation plans while ensuring that these plans were integrated into any existing plans on hand. The second phase of the OSSB survey consisted of conducting residential security surveys for all of the Agency personnel to ensure that they had adequate security and appropriate emergency egress. Most medium to high threat posts at the time had alarm systems and, in some cases, static guards or roving patrols. In the higher threat posts, such as San Salvador, or Tegucigalpa, additional security measures were put into place as a deterrent to both criminals and terrorists.

The first few months of 1985 was spent in training. My boss, Bill wanted to create security generalists who, in addition to conducting surveys, could be called upon for additional support to the DO such as providing personal protection. In four months, I attended the following training: locks and safes; personal protection; firearms; high speed defensive driving; clandestine operations familiarization; crisis management; explosive awareness and recognition; post blast investigation; travel awareness; information security and fire fighting to serve as a first responder.

The Farm 1985

In those days, the DO had a course commonly referred to as "crash and bang." Although this course was reserved for DO officers who were being transferred overseas to "high threat posts," I was fortunate to attend it because I routinely was conducting security surveys at "high threat posts."

During this course, conducted at our training facility known as the "Farm", we got to shoot everyday and qualify on the three basic weapons of choice for the Agency—the pistol, the revolver, and shotgun. Around a specially designed track, we were taught to drive at high speeds and learned evasive maneuvers such as spinning the car around in a move known as a "forward 180 degree turn" or a "reverse 180 degree turn." We also learned how to use the vehicle as a weapon and crash it if necessary to escape a potential terrorist attack.

One phase of this training, while driving on roads that had been blocked off, we would encounter vehicles facing each other in the middle of the road wherein we were instructed to stop our vehicle, examine the situation, and then either depart in reverse or proceed through the center of the roadblock by ramming the vehicles. I cannot tell you what a rush it was to crash the vehicles—especially at nighttime.

I remember one of the instructors at the "Farm" who had been there forever by the name of "Red" (though in his late sixties, his hair was still red). On one occasion, he parked a small Chevrolet between a Cadillac and a large Chrysler Town and Country with the bumpers touching. When Red asked the class how long it would take the Chevrolet to escape if the occupants were attacked, the majority of the students replied in three to five minutes. He then calmly got into the driver's seat of the Chevy, started the engine, and proceeded to ram the car head first into the Cadillac in front of him. Putting the car in reverse, he slammed it into the Town and Country behind him. Now, with several inches in front and back, Red revved the engine and took the whole side of the Chevy off as he hit the rear of the Cadillac—blasting away from the area in a record of seven seconds from start to finish—an incredible feat that I will never forget. As Red returned to face the students, he said simply "if your life is in jeopardy, don't be afraid to damage your vehicle in order to escape."

In addition, we were put in situations to see if we could spot potentially dangerous situations ahead of time or "indicators of a potential attack" in what we referred to as "attack recognition". This meant driving at slow speeds around some of the rural roads that had been blocked off for the training. During this portion of the training, the instructors would set up scenarios to see how we responded.

One of my favorites involved coming to a stop sign as evening was approaching and seeing two vehicles parked along side the road with several individuals inside. From their appearance, it did not take us long to realize that neither the vehicles, nor the occupants of the vehicles, seemed to belong there. Then, without notice, a small explosive device detonated in front of our vehicle blinding us for a second or two. Our car would then purposely stall because a remote control "kill switch" had been installed in the vehicle without our knowledge, and then we would be attacked by a variety of small arms fire.

The object of this training scenario was to exit the vehicle from the passenger side door and then retreat along the side of it, to the rear of the vehicle, using the vehicle as cover until you escaped. Like most students, however, I exited the vehicle on the passenger side and proceeded to return fire with my weapon (equipped with paint balls); not a very smart move when you are heavily outnumbered.

Because the DO "crash and bang course" was difficult to get into for Director of Administration (DA) security officers, we were forced to develop our own course. The task for developing such a course was placed in the hands of OSSB officer, Mike H. Since the DO had first rights to all of the firearm ranges and driving tracks at the "Farm", for the driving portion of the training, Mike contacted a local racetrack, which specialized in Formula 1 racing. The owner, Bill S., had hired a former USAF Special Investigator named Jerry S. to head the defensive driver training and Jerry, in turn, hired several former Delta and Seal Team Operators to assist him. As part of the training, Jerry put together an "attack recognition" slideshow using photographs taken at the site of real incidents to demonstrate to the audience what a person might see before an attack took place. To this day, I consider this briefing to be the best I have ever seen. Following the slideshow, Jerry would then set up similar scenarios and ambushes on the track for the students to view first hand. During our first few visits to the racetrack, we used their instructors such as Cal F., a former Air Force OSI agent, and Lee C., a former Delta operator, and their vehicles.

Eventually, when we became more proficient, the Office of Security purchased several vehicles and we were allowed to lease the track and use our own instructors (who had been trained under the auspices of the racetrack instructors). Phase one of this training involved driving around the track in excess of 100 miles per hour, which pushed our driving skills and vehicle to the limit. The second phase of this training involved driving at normal speeds around the track and being ambushed by a variety of explosive devices and blank ammunition. In order to escape or evade these types of scenarios, we were taught the aforementioned "forward 180 degree turn", "reverse 180 degree turn" and a variety of right and left angle turns.

On one occasion, I remember seeing a vehicle turned over on its side and thinking that one of my fellow students may have been injured. As I pulled over and exited my vehicle to rush to the body on the ground, the individual, who I assumed was a student, calmly rolled over, produced a gun, and shot me with a paint ball. Another time, as I was following an ambulance around the track, the rear doors suddenly opened up and I was looking down the barrel of a 50-caliber machinegun that began pelting my car with paintballs.

These scenarios were even more nerve racking at nighttime when we would see the muzzle of a shotgun or pistol being discharged or a small explosion being detonated as we drove by. To say that our pucker factor was up during these scenarios was an understatement. Later, in addition to the local racetrack, we also used several other driving schools located throughout the United States.

Counterterrorism Driver Training

For the shooting portion of our training, Bill A. chose his good friend Bill C. to train us. Like Bill A., Bill C. was a mountain of a man who stood 6'5" and weighed close to 280 pounds. Bill C. had just returned from an extended TDY to Tegucigalpa, Honduras where he had been training Honduran para-military units. Firearms' training was held at one of our Agency facilities west of Washington, DC where we were taught combat shooting; drawing our weapon from our holster, and getting two shots off in less than two seconds.

When several of us became proficient marksmen, we continued our training at several private shooting schools. Since the OSSB did not have any weapons at the time, we received permission from the Director of Security to purchase a variety of pistols, sub-machine guns, shotguns, and an assortment of holsters, eye protection, and web gear. In order to transport our officers, equipment, and gear, I wrote up a purchase order to buy a new Suburban and had it signed by the Deputy Director of Security, at the time Dick L. However, after it was purchased, Dick claimed that he could not recall authorizing it.

* * *

My first trip overseas for OSSB was with a fellow officer named Jim C. in May of 1985. I will never forget this trip because I had the opportunity to visit the Galapagos Islands, and hunt for grouse and fish for trout in the mountains surrounding Quito.

My second trip was to Managua, Nicaragua in June 1985, a capital trying to rebuild from years of war and an earthquake that destroyed about 80 percent of the buildings and killed over 10,000 city inhabitants in late December 1972. Although millions of dollars in aid for earthquake victims and rebuilding projects flowed into Managua from abroad for years following the 1972 earthquake, when I arrived in 1985 the city still looked ravaged.

The purpose of my visit was to conduct a comprehensive security survey of our Agency office. Shortly after my arrival, I convinced the chief of our office, Steve M., to move the entire office into a Sensitive Compartmented Information Facility (SCIF), that we painted and carpeted one weekend, because at the time, there was a bill in the U.S. Senate requesting $38 million to support the Fuerza Democratica Nicaraguense (FDN)/Nicaraguan Resistance efforts to overthrow the Sandinista government headed by Nicaraguan President Daniel Ortega.

Managua, Nicaragua

Interestingly, every Thursday a large demonstration was held in front of the U.S. Embassy main gate by U.S. citizen groups calling themselves "Witnesses for Peace" and "Concerned American Citizens Living in Nicaragua." From the looks of them, most of the protestors appeared to be "remnants" from the 1960's "peace movement" that were in Managua protesting the U.S. efforts to overthrow the Sandinista government.

One weekend several friends and I jumped into two four-wheel drive vehicles with an interpreter and drove to the small town of Masaya, which was adjacent to a huge active volcano located about one hour southeast of Managua. Entering the village, the first thing we all noticed was an enormous thirty-foot sign constructed at the entrance to a Sandinista military installation overlooking the town which read, "Frente Sandinista de Liberacion Nacional (FSLN)".

Sandinista Fortress at top
(note 30' high letters "FSLN" on fortress wall)

In English, this translates to the National Sandinista Liberation Front. We had been traveling all day and were hungry and thirsty, so our first thought was to find a place to get a beer and something to eat. As we exited our vehicles, our interpreter began to get nervous and suggested that we leave Masaya immediately since the town was considered a Sandinista stronghold. I still remember the look on everyone's face as we entered a bar and it became so quiet you could have heard a pin drop. All of the patrons immediately stopped what they were doing and turned to look at us—five Americans dressed in blue jeans and khaki shirts accompanied by a Nicaraguan. Suddenly, the biggest Nicaraguan whom I had ever seen, dressed in a Sandinista uniform with the rank of Colonel, approached us and loudly asked in Spanish what we were doing in Masaya.

By his appearance and the stench of his breath, it was obvious that he had been at the bar for quite sometime. When we responded through our interpreter that we were American relief workers, the man pulled up his shirt and proudly displayed six bullet holes, which he claimed he had received while fighting the American-backed Contras. Not wanting to be outdone, I pulled up my shirt and showed him the scars I received from injuring my shoulder playing rugby, informing him through our interpreter that I received the scars from a Sandinista landmine. Knowing that I was probably lying, the Sandinista Colonel slowly smiled and asked us to join him for a drink.

Several hours later, after consuming large quantities of beer, the Colonel invited the six of us to his house for dinner, which, to our surprise, was located in the aforementioned Sandinista fortress overlooking Masaya. Upon arriving at the fort, we were escorted into a large room, which had been prepared with more food, beer, and alcohol. The drinking and eating continued until the early morning hours. Late in the evening as we departed, the Sandinista Colonel wrote down his name and phone number, handed the paper to me and then floored me by telling me in perfect English, *"Richard, here is my name and phone number. The next time you are in Nicaragua, call me and we will get together. Then I will find out the real reason why you are in my country."* As the shock of realizing, he knew English wore off; we bid our host farewell and drove back to Managua. The following morning when I told the story to the chief of our office, Steve M., he almost had a heart attack. *"Richard, what the hell were you doing drinking and eating with Colonel so and so and let's hope that the Ambassador does not find out."*

The following day, 6 June 1985, a $38 million dollar aid package was passed by the Senate. When the U.S. Government realized that the Nicaraguan Government was not going to close its embassy in Managua, I departed Nicaragua and flew to Tegucigalpa, Honduras. I later found out that the reason that Daniel Ortega did not close the U.S. Embassy in Managua was because this would have forced the U.S. Government to close the Nicaraguan Embassy in Washington, DC where many of President Ortega's close friends and family were living comfortably. (A year later, a supplemental bill for $100 million in U.S. aid for the Contras, was passed by Congress on 25 June 1986.)

U.S embassy in Honduras

Arriving at the airport in Tegucigalpa, I was met by the support chief named "Dusty" F. in an armored Chevrolet Blazer. Dusty eventually would go on to become the Executive Director of the Agency under DCI Porter Goss in 2005, but would later be forced to resign after the CIA Inspector General opened an investigation into Dusty's connections with two defense contractors accused of bribing a member of Congress, Randall "Duke" Cunningham, and Pentagon officials.

After getting into the Blazer, the first thing I noticed was a submachine gun lying on the floor by my feet. Dusty then handed me a pistol. When we arrived at our office, a friend of mine from our technical services office named Steve P. greeted me. I had met Steve earlier in the year during a training course and remember him telling me that he had applied to the Agency after graduating from American University but was not accepted because he did not have any experience. After being turned down by the Agency, Mick D. from our technical services office suggested Steve join the U.S. Marine Corp to get some experience. If he did so, Mick told Steve that he would consider hiring him. Four years later, Steve returned to Mick and held him to his promise claiming that he had done what Mick had instructed him to do—joined the U.S. Marine Corp and had obtained some experience. Apparently, Mick was so impressed that he kept his word and hired Steve.

As we were talking at the entrance to our office, Steve's hand-held radio began announcing that an individual was holding a woman hostage with a hand grenade at a small shopping center frequented by Americans one block from the Embassy. Steve immediately grabbed me and we raced to the scene. As we pulled up to the small shopping center in our car, we observed a man in his early twenties holding a young woman around the neck with one hand and an old German hand grenade known as a "potato masher" in the other hand. Much to my surprise, Steve exited the vehicle and starting filming the scene with a camcorder. As the police began trying to convince the young man to let the woman go, the grenade suddenly exploded killing the man and woman instantly right before our eyes. Quite an exciting morning considering the fact that I had only been in Honduras for a little over an hour and had not even had breakfast yet.

Later that evening, Dusty picked me up at my hotel and told me that we were going to the residence of the chief of our office, which sat on top of the mountain overlooking Tegucigalpa. Vince S. was having a dinner that evening for a Congressional Delegation known as a CODEL. As a security officer, my first thought was that the reason I had been invited was that Vince wanted me to provide armed security for the event. Much to my surprise, however, I was greeted warmly by Vince who asked me to join him and the CODEL staff on the terrace, which had a spectacular view of the city. When I asked Vince why he wanted a junior security officer to join such a distinguished crowd, Vince replied, "Richard, you just spent several weeks in Nicaragua and probably have more first hand knowledge and ground truth about what is happening there than anyone else in this room".

From Honduras, I proceeded to El Salvador where I had the opportunity to play softball with several U.S. Marines one week prior to the 19 June 1985 "Zona Rosa Massacre". That evening, four Marines had been sitting at an outdoor café known as "Chili's" eating American cheeseburgers and French fries in an area of San Salvador known as the "Zona Rosa" when a group of armed men opened fire at 9:00 p.m. The assailants were members of the Partido

Revolucionario de Trabajadores Centroamericanos (PRTC) which translates to the Revolutionary Party of Central American Workers; one of the organizations belonging to the Frente Farabundo Marti para la Liberacion Nacional (FMLN)—the National Liberation Farabundo Marti Front. The Marines, who were serving as security watch-standers at the U.S. Embassy in San Salvador at the time, were in civilian clothing and were unarmed. All four Marines, nine civilians, and one of the assailants died in the shoot-out. The "Mardoqueo Cruz" urban commando of the PRTC claimed responsibility for the killings and the FMLN defended the attack in a communiqué. Three of the attackers were eventually tried and convicted while a fourth attacker was amnestied.

Chili's restaurant in San Salvador

During my visit to El Salvador, I also had the opportunity to visit the town of San Miguel early one morning aboard a helicopter, along with Frank A., one of our logistic officer's, several hours after FLMN guerrillas attacked the military brigade there. Upon arriving, we were met by Dale B. another one of our officers assigned to the military compound who had survived the attack.

According to Dale, shortly before daybreak, several hundred guerrillas had crawled through the high grass to the fence line surrounding the military compound and threw homemade satchel charges filled with explosives onto the roofs of the Salvadoran barracks prior to breaching the fences with additional explosives and attacking the compound. The explosions killed many of the young soldiers who were sleeping inside the barracks. Some guerillas even found their way to the helicopter landing area and destroyed several of the Salvadoran military helicopters with explosive charges before being killed by Salvadoran soldiers.

Although the battle reportedly lasted less than one hour, I was surprised to see the number of casualties on both sides and was saddened by how young both the soldiers and guerillas were. My first thought was that most of them were young boys who should be chasing girls rather than dying in such a way. I had always envisioned a guerilla as a hardened, seasoned, veteran; something along the lines of a "Che Guevara". Although many of the young boys, forced into becoming guerillas at the age of 12, 13 or 14 years old were now seasoned veterans, they definitely were not adults nor what I had expected a guerilla to look like.

As I walked around the perimeter of the compound surveying the area, I noticed the remains of several guerillas that had been blown up by their own explosive devices. I later learned that many had not tested their time fuses. Believing that they had three minutes to throw their charges, unfortunately (for them), most had less time than that. Some had been shot before throwing their charges. When I asked about the sentries in the guard booths along the fence line, I was told that most of them had been killed while sleeping and later learned that the majority of them had been on duty for up to 12 hours. I also learned that most of the lighting surrounding the compound was not working or the light bulbs had burnt out and not replaced. Before our departure, I told the Salvadoran officer in charge that he might want to consider immediately implementing several security measures prior to the next FLMN attack.

San Miguel, El Salvador following FLMN attack. Note damage to the roof of the barracks.

Although I did not personally witness any abuse, as we departed that day I can still remember hearing the screams coming from the interrogation of the prisoners by the Salvadoran soldiers.

On TDY to Salvador 1985

Upon returning to San Salvador, I remember meeting with the Regional Security Officer (RSO) at the U.S. Embassy who informed me of an incident that had occurred the night before involving two visiting U.S. Government employees. According to the RSO, the U.S. Government employees had been driving home after the midnight embassy imposed curfew following a visit to a local whorehouse by the name of "Gloria's". As they stopped at a traffic light, an individual with a large stereo "boom box" on his shoulder casually walked in front of their car while crossing the street. As the light turned green, the driver beeped his horn, which in turn, led to the individual taking his stereo and throwing it through the front windshield of the U.S. Government employee's vehicle. Following this act, the driver reportedly exited his vehicle, drew his 9mm pistol, and shot several warning shots into the air in an attempt to get the individual to stop as he fled the scene. Unfortunately, for the U.S. Government employee, after hearing the shots, several local security guards exited the compounds that they were protecting and witnessed the U.S. Government employee shooting into the air.

The following morning, the individual who had thrown his stereo through the windshield was found dead in some bushes several blocks from the scene. Apparently, he had messed with someone else that evening that proceeded to shoot him with several rounds from a 5.56 rifle. When the RSO received information from the Salvadoran National Police of an American who had discharged his weapon in the air the night before, including a description of the two individuals, their vehicle, and the license plate number, the U.S. Government employees were called in for questioning and subsequently sent back to the U.S. for their actions.

After hearing the story I told the RSO that I had heard of a similar incident in Honduras involving a visiting U.S. Government employee who came to the RSO's office at the U.S. Embassy in Tegucigalpa one afternoon claiming that he had been the victim of a terrorist incident. When questioned further, the U.S. Government employee advised that earlier in the day he had been run off the road by several vehicles on the outskirts of Tegucigalpa and that the occupants had pointed weapons at him from their vehicles. After the incident, he claimed that he had chased the vehicles (all Toyota Land Cruisers with darkened windows) to a walled compound and watched as they entered. After departing his vehicle and walking up to the front door of the compound in an attempt to find out who lived there, the U.S. Government employee was met by a menacing individual who pointed a weapon at him and told him to leave. When the RSO asked the individual, what he was trying to prove by following the vehicles to the compound and demanding to find out who lived there, he stated that he wanted to get "even with them" for forcing him off the road. To make a long story short, investigation revealed that he had been forced off the road by a motorcade transporting the Head of the Honduran military and he was lucky that the General's security protective detail had not opened fire on him as he was chasing the motorcade to the compound. This individual was also sent back to the U.S. for his actions.

* * *

As I returned to Washington, DC, one day in late June 1985, a State Department Security officer by the name of Al B. came to visit Bill A. in OSSB. Al had been the Regional Security officer (RSO) in Beirut, Lebanon on 20 September 1984 when a truck bomb exploded outside the U.S. Embassy annex in Aukar, northeast of Beirut, killing 24 people. After hearing shooting from the guards who were trying to stop the explosive-laden truck as it raced past the security measures at the annex entrance that morning, Al ran to the front windows of the embassy to see what was happening as the truck bomb detonated. Lying in a pool of blood and torn to shreds by flying glass, Al claims that he was semiconscious when the first responders arrived and began triage. Seeing him in this state, the first responders covered Al with a sheet and proceeded to the next victim believing that he was dead. It was only after being put into a body bag did the first responders realize that Al was still breathing and began to administer first aid. Al spent the next 12 months in a hospital recovering from his wounds and his entire face had to be reconstructed due to the number of cuts he had received from the flying glass and debris.

After recovering, Al went on to head the State Department's Mobile Training Teams and Anti-Terrorism Assistance Programs. Al had come to see Bill that day to discuss the U.S. Government's decision to create an interagency rapid response team to respond to terrorist incidents. This new team became known as the Emergency Reaction Team (ERT), and later the Incident Response Team (IRT). Today this team is referred to as the Foreign Emergency Support Team (FEST). The ERT was created to provide the U.S. Government and host nations with rapid, coordinated, effective assistance following a terrorist incident and the ability to respond to such situations when U.S. assistance had been requested by the Chief of Mission (the President's top representative in the host nation), the host government, or directed by the President of the United States. The ERT was designed to provide a wide range of specialized skill not normally available on-scene. In establishing this response team, the Department of State was designated the lead agency for international terrorist incidents that took place outside of U.S. territory, other than incidents on U.S. flag vessels in international waters. The State Department would have the authority to act through U.S. Ambassadors as the on-scene coordinators for the U.S. Government. Once military force had been directed, however, the National Command Authority would exercise control of U.S. military forces. The Office of the Coordinator for Counterterrorism, within the State Department, was chosen to coordinate the ERT.

The ERT, like the FEST today, brought several unique capabilities not normally available at an affected U.S. Mission: crisis and consequence management assistance; capability to work 24 hours per day; additional communications; and selected expertise to augment U.S. Embassy staff. The ERT included a senior Foreign Service Officer as the Team Leader (with the rank of Ambassador), a deputy team leader, and an operations officer from the Department of State, Office of the Coordinator for Counterterrorism, as well as a combination of specialists from other departments and agencies.

In June 1985, the ERT became the IRT and Ambassador Robert B. Oakley, the State Department's Ambassador at Large for Counterterrorism, was chosen to head this effort. Ambassador L. Paul Bremer III eventually succeeded Oakley in heading the IRT. At the time, the IRT included five State Department officials; three FBI agents to include a hostage negotiator; three NSA officers; five Joint Special Operations Command (JSOC) officers; and 18 - 20 other officers from the Intelligence Community. Since its inception in 1985, the IRT/FEST has provided rapid assistance to Americans abroad and countries around the world that have suffered terrorist attacks.

One of the highlights of the IRT/FEST occurred on 20 December 1989 when the team was called on to support Operation Just Cause, the U.S. invasion of Panama. The invasion force consisted of a massive wave of conventional, airborne, and special operations forces including the U.S. Army's elite counterterrorist Delta Force, formally known as Special Forces Operational Detachment – Delta (SFOD-D), working in tandem with the 160th Special Operations Aviation Group, and supported by an AC-130 gunship from the 1st Special Operations Wing. One vital aspect of Operation Just Cause revolved around the rescue of an American citizen living in Panama named Kurt M. who was caught by members of General Manuel Noriega's Panamanian Defense Forces (PDF) using radio scanning and transmitting equipment procured in Miami to broadcast anti-Noriega messages. Kurt had been taken to the secret police headquarters building in downtown Panama where he was interrogated for three days, deprived of sleep, and forced to watch, as other prisoners were tortured in front of him. Kurt was then moved to a series of locations, ostensibly to eliminate any efforts by the United States to locate him, and eventually ended up at the notorious Carcel Modelo (Model Prison), a facility constructed in 1925 to house approximately 250 inmates. By 1987, the prison contained over 1,000 inmates creating brutal and claustrophobic living conditions. During his confinement, Kurt was kept in an 8' x 12' cell for nine months.

Initial planning for the operation began at Fort Bragg, North Carolina. Delta Force finalized mission-specific preparation for the rescue at a remote training facility in Florida. To enhance the ability of the assault team to penetrate the heavily guarded prison, a full-scale, three-story mock up was built. Its specific features were updated by reports from those military personnel who were permitted to visit Kurt in his cell. In this way, it was possible to rehearse the mission in total secrecy. In rescuing Kurt, Delta Force, supported by the air support teams, became the first American counterterrorist team ever to rescue an American hostage from enemy hands.

On 20 December 1989, General Manuel Noriega was overthrown and captured during the United States invasion of Panama. Following his capture, he was taken to the United States, convicted under federal charges of cocaine trafficking, racketeering, and money laundering, and remains incarcerated in a federal prison in Miami, Florida. Noriega was the de facto military dictator of Panama from 1983 to 1989 despite never being the official President of Panama. Although he was initially a strong ally of the United States while assisting Americans to arm and train anti-communists in Central America in the 1980s, in the late 1980s relations turned extremely tense between Noriega and the United States government when Colombian drug lords began using Panama as a drug smuggling and money laundering center.

In August 1998, two FEST teams deployed to Nairobi, Kenya and Dar Esalam, Tanzania in response to the al-Qaida bombings of the U.S. Embassies. The FEST played a key role is coordinating the U.S. government support to these embassies while providing the Chiefs of Mission with the best expertise available to mitigate the consequences of the two deadly terrorist attacks.

Later, on 12 October 2001, the FEST deployed in support of the American Embassy Sanaa to Aden Yemen to coordinate the response to the USS Cole bombing. The FEST set up in a local hotel and provided valuable support to the Ambassador as well as enhanced secure communications and reporting to Washington, DC.

Anyone assigned to the IRT had to be available to deploy in less than four hours. This included the time it took to load 15,000 pounds of equipment and gear into a dedicated truck, transport it to a dedicated aircraft, load the equipment and gear onto the aircraft, wait for all of the IRT members to show up, and then depart. The departure time was compounded by the fact that the JSOC officers had to fly from Fort Bragg, North Carolina in a dedicated aircraft to rendezvous with the IRT in Washington, DC. To be ready to deploy at a moment's notice, team members were authorized money to purchase an assortment of specialized clothing and gear, which they kept in the trunks of their personal vehicles. To transport the IRT, the U.S. Government purchased an aircraft and housed it at one of the local airports. The first 20 rows of the aircraft had been removed to store 15,000 pounds of equipment and gear. The next 20 rows had been reconfigured into a communications room and several small conference rooms, while the remaining seats in the aircraft had been redesigned to accommodate the IRT members.

Several months after establishing an Agency proprietary at one of the local airports, the Agency had to dismantle it and move the entire operation to an airport on a U.S. military base near Washington, DC after a Washington Post reporter began tracing the origins of the Agency Boeing 707 and published a story in the Washington Post. In tracing the aircraft, the reporter had discovered that the 707, under another proprietary, had been involved in transporting "oil drilling equipment" to Iran and that, the "oil drilling" equipment was actually anti-aircraft and anti-tank missiles being shipped to Iran as part of a secret covert plan involving arms sales to Iran, in return for release of the American hostages. Because U.S. officials believed that the Iranian-backed Hezbollah was behind the kidnappings of the U.S. hostages in Beirut, President Reagan was advised that a bargain could be struck with Iran—who would receive anti-aircraft and anti-tank missiles in return for release of the hostages. The premise for this plan was because Iran was desperately running out of military supplies in its war with Iraq, and Congress had banned the sale of American arms to countries like Iran that sponsored terrorism.

In August 1985, the first consignment of arms to Iran was sent -- 100 anti-tank missiles provided by Israel; another 408 were sent the following month. Because of the deal, American hostage Benjamin Weir was released from captivity after being imprisoned for 495 days. Only two other hostages were later released because of the arms-for-hostages deal. In July 1986, Father Martin Jenco, a Catholic priest, was released and the Administrator of the American University of Beirut's Medical School, David Jacobson, in November 1986. The arms for hostages deal eventually became public after a U.S. cargo plane was shot down over southern Nicaragua on 5 October 1986. Two of the crewmembers died in the crash, the third, pilot, Eugene Hasenfus, parachuted to safety and was captured by the Sandinista Army. This incident lead to one of the biggest scandals in American political history (known as the "Iran Contra Affair").

Chapter 5

"Combating International Terrorism Early On & the Creation of the Counterterrorism Center"

In the mid-1980s, a series of high-profile terrorist attacks galvanized U.S. policymakers to take the offensive against international terrorism:

- The 18 April 1983 bombing by Hezbollah operatives where a suicide bomber in a pickup truck loaded with explosives rammed into the U.S. Embassy in Beirut, Lebanon killing sixty-three people including 17 Americans, many of whom were employees of the CIA, including the chief of our office, Kenneth Haas and Middle East chief analyst Robert Ames.

- The 23 October 1983 bombing in Lebanon where a suicide bomber detonated a truck full of explosives at the U.S. Marine barracks located at Beirut International Airport killing 241 U.S. Marines and wounding more than 100 others.

- The 12 December 1983 bombing of the U.S. Embassy in Kuwait and a residential area for employees of the American corporation Raytheon killing six people and injuring 80.

- The 16 March 1984 kidnapping of the chief of our Beirut office, William Buckley, who died in captivity 15 months later.

- The 20 September 1984 Hezbollah bombing of the U.S. Embassy annex in Aukar, northeast of Beirut, where a truck bomb exploded outside the U.S. Embassy annex killing 24 people, two of whom were U.S. military personnel.

- The 3 December 1984 hijacking of Kuwait Airways Flight 221 on its way from Kuwait to Pakistan where two American officials from the U.S. Agency for International Development were killed by the hijackers when their demands to release 17 prisoners were not met.

- The 14 June 1985 Hezbollah hijacking of TWA Flight 847 enroute from Athens to Rome and forced to land in Beirut, Lebanon where the hijackers held the plane for 17 days and later shot and killed Robert Dean Stethem, a U.S. Navy diver, when their demands to release the Kuwait 17, as well as 700 fellow Shiite Muslim prisoners held in Israeli prisons, were not met.

- The 7 October 1985 Palestine Liberation Front Achille Lauro Italian cruise ship hijacking off the coast of Egypt where Leon Klinghoffer, a 69-year-old disabled American tourist, was killed when their demands to release Palestinian prisoners in Egypt, Italy, and elsewhere were not met.

- The 17 December 1985 airport bombings in Rome and Vienna killing 20 people, five of whom were Americans, by Palestinian terrorist Abu Nidal.

In response to these incidents, a task force chaired by Vice President George H. Bush was formed in early 1986 to address the problem of international terrorism. The task force concluded that U.S. Government agencies collected information on terrorism, but did not aggressively operate to disrupt terrorist activities.

As a result of these findings, the Director of Central Intelligence at the time, William (Bill) Casey, created the DCI Counterterrorist Center (CTC) on 12 February 1986 and directed it to preempt, disrupt, and defeat terrorists. CTC's mission, much as it is today, was to assist the Director of Central Intelligence in coordinating the counterterrorist efforts of the Intelligence Community by implementing a comprehensive counterterrorist operations program to collect intelligence on, and minimize the capabilities of, international terrorist groups and state sponsors. This enabled exploiting all-source intelligence to produce in-depth analyses of the groups and states responsible for international terrorism and the coordination of the Intelligence Community's counterterrorist activities. CTC's chief serves as Special Assistant to the Director of Central Intelligence for all counterterrorist matters. CTC's charter allows it to draw on all CIA resources and the talent of other U.S. Government agencies. CTC is guided by the definition of terrorism contained in Title 22 of the U.S. Code, Section 2656f(d):

"The term "terrorism" means premeditated, politically motivated violence perpetrated against noncombatant targets by sub-national groups or clandestine agents, usually intended to influence an audience. The term "international terrorism" refers to terrorism involving the territory or the citizens of more than one country. The term "terrorist group" means any group that practices, or has significant subgroups that practice, international terrorism."

The ultimate goal of the DCI Counterterrorist Center is to preempt, disrupt, and defeat terrorist activities at the earliest possible stage. CTC endeavors to exploit vulnerabilities within terrorist groups;

weaken terrorist groups' infrastructures so that they will be unable to carry out plans; work closely with friendly foreign security and intelligence services around the world through information-sharing on terrorists groups and training in preventing terrorist attacks; and pursue major terrorists overseas and help the FBI render them to justice.

DCI Casey placed the task of creating CTC in the hands of Duane "Dewey" Clarridge. Dewey was a seasoned veteran who had joined the Agency in 1955 and rose through the ranks of the DO. Before becoming the first Chief of CTC, Dewey had been the chief of our office in Istanbul, Turkey, and the Chief of the Latin America Division. During his three year tenure in the Latin America Division from 1981-1984, he directed several of the CIA's more notorious operations including the 1984 mining of Nicaraguan harbors – an act for which the United States was condemned in the 1986 World Court at the Hague. He was also instrumental in organizing and recruiting Contra forces to overthrow Nicaragua's leftist Sandinista government, which eventually grew to 20,000 members by the end of the conflict. In 1984, he became Chief of the European Division where he ran a successful counterterrorist operation prior to becoming the first Chief of CTC operating out of Langley.

Dewey's ideas were simple. In that terrorism is a transnational problem, the U.S. Government had to try to penetrate terrorist groups to find out who they were, to see what they were up to, and to find out who was supporting them financially, and logistically. With this information in hand, he was confident that the U.S. Government could then abort their operations. Dewey wanted to centralize the efforts against terrorism in one place and create a center that got around all the geographic and bureaucratic bullshit. In order to accomplish this task, he created a center with analysts from the DI working side by side with DO operations officers. He knew that to carry out the mission it was important to have President Reagan, Vice President Bush, and DCI Casey in his corner, all of whom told him, *"tell us what you want to do and we will support you."*

Dewey was charismatic and flamboyant. Having served as the Chief of the Latin America Division, he drove a convertible with a personalized license plate that said "CONTRA", wore expensive suits, and smoked the finest cigars. When establishing CTC, he was given unprecedented carte blanche by DCI Casey to choose anyone from any Directorate in the Agency to work in the center. One of the first moves he made was to choose Fred T. as his deputy, bringing him back to Headquarters from an overseas post where Fred served as the Chief of our office there. Fred served two years as Dewey's Deputy and then four years as the Chief of CTC after Dewey resigned.

When creating a center such as CTC, the first personnel always chosen are the support staff. One day in early February 1986, I was notified that the Director of Security at the time, Jim L. and the Deputy Director of Security, Wayne P. wanted to speak to me. During this meeting, I was told that the Agency was creating the Counterterrorist Center and that the next day I was to report as the First Director of Security. I recall after leaving their office that this was the first time in my career that I had been told the reason I had been chosen was that I was the best candidate for the job. Since I had traveled to over 50 countries while with the OSSB, I was confident that the experience I had acquired combating terrorism during these trips would assist me greatly in my new assignment.

Arriving in CTC, I was greeted by the new Chief of Support, Dave B. and Dewey's special assistant, Linda F., who I later worked with at the White House in 2002. Both congratulated me and welcomed me as the 12th member assigned to CTC. I was then introduced to Dewey, an individual whom to this day, I consider one of finest managers I have ever worked for. Dewey was one of the few senior officials in the Agency willing to take chances and he surrounded himself with the best and brightest that he could find.

Many senior Agency officials were opposed to the creation of CTC and were hoping it would fail. Most were jealous of Dewey and many were upset that they had to cough up bodies to support CTC. I can still remember that anytime there was an impending operation or mission, Dewey would bring together a small group of us into his office and go around the table one by one. He would ask his Chief of Operations, to outline the mission. Then he would proceed to the CTC lawyer and ask if we were operating within the constraints of the law. If the lawyer responded that he was not sure, Dewey would slam his fist down on the table and bellow, *"then damn it; find a way that we can conduct the operation without breaking the law!"* After going around the table, he would always finish by pointing to me and saying *"Richard, you better go along and ensure that we are prepared to back stop this in the event that anything hits the press."* His last words to all of us was always *"Good luck and don't screw up."*

Eventually CTC grew in the two years that I was assigned there (1986 to 1988) but was still quite small in comparison to the large number of personnel assigned to it today.

* * *

Although I mentioned several high-profile terrorist acts between 1983 and early 1986, the incident that truly forced U.S. policymakers and DCI Casey to take the offensive against international terrorism was the 16 March 1984 kidnapping of the Chief of our office in Beirut, William Buckley, who later died in captivity 15 months later. Casey had asked him to serve as the Chief in Beirut on the heels of the Beirut Embassy bombings. Buckley, a bachelor, with little or no family with the exception of a sister, was captured while departing his residence and reportedly had been carrying classified information in his briefcase.

One day Casey received photographs of Buckley tied to a chair with a newspaper depicting the date in his hands. Buckley was thin and his jaw appeared to have been broken. Rumor has it that Casey cried when shown the photos and vowed to do everything in his power to get Buckley released.

Shortly thereafter, a group of Special Activities Division paramilitary officers was dispatched to Beirut to find him. After identifying and capturing several of the individuals believed to be responsible for Buckley's kidnapping, one of them accidentally died during interrogation at the hands of one of our officers nicknamed "Crunch" who was later dismissed for his actions.

Buckley was the fourth person kidnapped by militant Islamic extremists in Lebanon. The first American hostage, American University of Beirut President David Dodge, had been kidnapped in July 1982. Eventually, 30 Westerners would be kidnapped during the 10 year-long Lebanese hostage-taking crisis (1982-1992). Americans kidnapped included journalist Terry Anderson, American University of Beirut librarian Peter Kilburn, and Benjamin Weir, a Presbyterian minister. While some of the prisoners lived through captivity, Anderson spent the longest time as a hostage–2,454 days— almost 7 years. Some, including Buckley, died in captivity or were killed by their kidnappers.

The second incident that forced U.S. policymakers and DCI Casey to take the offensive against international terrorism occurred on 15 April 1986 when an American soldier was killed after a bomb detonated at La Belle, a discotheque in West Berlin known to be popular with off-duty U.S. servicemen. A Turkish woman was also killed, and nearly 200 others were wounded. After U.S. intelligence intercepted Libyan government communications implicating Libya in the La Belle disco attack, President Reagan ordered retaliatory air strikes on Tripoli and Benghazi.

The operation on 15 April 1986, dubbed Operation El Dorado Canyon, involved 200 aircraft and over 60 tons of bombs. One of the residences of Libyan leader Muammar el-Qadaffi was hit in the attack, which, according to Libyan estimates, killed 37 people and injured 93 others. Two days after the U.S. retaliatory attack, the bodies of three American University of Beirut employees, American Peter Kilburn and British citizens John Douglas and Philip Padfield, were discovered near Beirut shot to death. The Arab Revolutionary Cells, a pro-Libyan group of Palestinians affiliated with terrorist Abu Nidal, claimed to have executed the three men in retaliation for "Operation El Dorado Canyon."

Shortly after establishing CTC, DCI Casey had this grandiose idea to hire former police officers due to their investigative skills and "street smarts", which he thought would be great assets when identifying and tracking terrorists. Therefore, with the assistance of Casey, all of the major police departments in the United States to include New York City, Los Angeles, Washington, DC, Chicago, San Francisco, and Miami were asked to recommend police, men and women who were approaching retirement age, to this program. Our goal was to hire several hundred police officers. Unfortunately, of the hundreds that were interviewed and eventually polygraphed, only a few were hired despite having to answer just three questions on the polygraph exam – the most important of which was "have you ever committed a crime or been involved in criminal activity." To add to the embarrassment, one of the police officers resigned two days after being briefed into the program, leaving less than a handful who earned the dubious distinction of being referred to as "Casey's Cops."

The second grandiose idea that Casey had, involved bringing senior U.S. corporate officials into CIA Headquarters. After providing an overview of what the CIA was doing to combat terrorism, Casey's goal was to get the corporations involved to see what they could bring to the table to combat terrorism. In that most large corporations had offices and personnel overseas, Casey wanted to stress that terrorists could strike anyone, anywhere, and at any time. Instead of bringing all the corporate executives in at one time, Casey decided to invite them in small groups of five to six. The executives were encouraged to bring along their Director of Security, a senior scientist, or a senior engineer. The objective was to put their personnel in touch later with CTC personnel to see if together they could come up with a better way to combat terrorism.

Before kicking off this idea, however, Casey collapsed at CIA Headquarters on 18 December 1986 and was rushed to a local hospital where he underwent surgery for a malignant brain tumor. During his stay in the hospital, several reporters claimed to have interviewed Casey while he was on his deathbed although Casey was incapacitated for most of the time and guarded by a security officer 24 hours per day. One reporter, dressed as a male nurse, did try to force his way into Casey's room but was intercepted by an Agency Security officer.

Casey later died on 6 May 1987 because of the brain tumor and his deputy, Bob Gates, resumed what Casey had started. Former United Nations Ambassador Jeanne Kirkpatrick provided a "fire and brimstone" eulogy at Casey's funeral where members of Casey's security detail served as his pallbearers. A memorial service was held in the auditorium at CIA headquarters for Casey on 2 June 1987 and William H. Webster, the newly appointed DCI who had formerly served as the Director of the FBI, made the opening remarks.

* * *

During my time in CTC, one of our case officers recruited an individual who provided information about the Hezbollah network operating in Europe. One claim was that Hezbollah had a large cache of weapons and explosives in the Fontainebleau Forrest in Paris, France.

The U.S. Government's relationship with France at the time was somewhat strained, so Dewey was eager to offer our assistance to the French in an attempt to locate the hidden cache.

In discussing this opportunity, one of our senior scientists recalled that one of the corporations, during the meetings at Headquarters with senior corporate executives, claimed that they had technology to find underground caches using a technique known as "microwave heliography." When approached, this corporation advised that they were willing to assemble a team to go to France and search for the underground cache using the microwave heliography equipment attached to an All Terrain Vehicle (ATV). Shortly after our initial discussions, the senior scientist called me at home from Dulles International Airport one morning at 7:00 a.m. claiming that he was getting ready to board a flight to San Diego to meet with the corporation team. The scientist went on to say that he had in his possession several blocks of C-4 explosives that were going to be used as training aids. Although the scientist swore that the chemical composition for the explosives had been removed, he added that the blocks still looked and smelled like C-4. The scientist was calling me wondering if he would have any problem going through security at the airport that morning, as he got ready to board his flight. After my heart started beating again, I told the scientist not to move until he heard from me. I immediately called my good friend, Keith M., who was the Director of Operations at Dulles at the time. When I informed him of the situation, I am sure that he thought both of us were crazy. To his credit, however, Keith immediately called Walt K., an FAA explosives expert who I knew from the Armor and Protective Systems Working Group. After explaining the situation, Walt made me swear on a stack of bibles that the explosive composition had indeed been removed from the C-4. The scientist was then met by several FAA security personnel and escorted through security to the plane. He was even bumped up to first class and upon arriving in Dallas, was escorted via a golf cart to his connecting flight where he was again placed in first class. To this day, I still do not think that this senior scientist realized the consequences of bringing the blocks of C-4 onto the plane that day because, in his mind, they were inert.

Within days after receiving this microwave heliography equipment, I flew to San Diego to brief the team and establish what is commonly referred to as a "bigoted program" at the corporation – a highly sensitive program where the "need to know" principle is necessary. Personnel read into such a program are placed on a special access list and are required to sign a release form advising them that they would be prosecuted by the law if they divulged any information pertaining to the program.

Our next daunting task was to get visas because the French required one to visit due to a number of bombings in Paris at the time. Because our team did not have sufficient time to obtain the visas, we arranged to be met by French intelligence and security officials at the airport in Paris. When we arrived at Dulles International Airport to depart, however, the United Airline agent would not let us board without visas. Not wanting to miss the flight,

I called the Director of Security for United Airlines, who I had just met in the aforementioned conference, and explained the need for our team to board the flight to London and then on to Paris. The Director of Security recalled that I had worked for Dewey, but still wanted a phone number to confirm who I said I was so I gave him the number of Bev S., Dewey's executive assistant whom he called to confirm my story.

Arriving in Paris with our team, we were met by several of our officers and members of the French police and intelligence services. After preliminary introductions, we were immediately taken to the Fontainebleau Forrest to set up and test our equipment. Two weeks of searching did not uncover anything. Then one day, during a routine search, our team found three rocks piled on top of each other in a densely wooded area. Expanding our search, we then found an arrow faintly engraved on a tree. Using our new "microwave heliography" equipment, we found two large underground caches containing 55-gallon plastic drums filled with weapons, explosives, money, and information, which eventually resulted in the arrest of some 75 Hezbollah operatives living in France. When we called CTC and reported our find, Dewey and the rest of CTC were ecstatic as well as the new DCI, Judge William Webster.

* * *

In August 1986, I was sent to a country in southern Africa due to a spate of bombings against the police force headquarters in this country, which also happened to be in the same building as the U.S. Embassy. As a rugby player, and thanks to Cofer Black, who was the chief of our office at the time, I got to meet the founder of modern day rugby, Dr. Danie Craven, and had him autograph some books and videos, which I brought back for Bill A. Before retuning home, however, I was asked to visit the small black African State of Lesotho because the U.S. Government had decided to establish an Embassy in Maseru.

As I was departing Maseru, I received an urgent message to fly to the Seychelles. There had been a coup attempt against the René regime by Minister of Defense Ogilvy Berlouis, who reportedly was being groomed to be the country's new pro-Western president. Berlouis led a group of 30 mercenaries and some 350 partisans in a plot known as Operation Distant Lash. Fortunately, the security forces quickly uncovered the conspiracy before the plotters could act and subsequently arrested Berlouis. Because of the plot, several

Seychelles People's Liberation Army (SPLA) members were forced to resign. As for me, upon my arrival in the Seychelles, I ended up scuba diving for five days with the chief of our office and his wife as I waited for the next flight to Europe to return to the U.S. Interestingly, this was not the first coup attempt in the Seychelles.

On 25 November 1981, Seychellois security forces put down a coup attempt sponsored by South Africa and remnants of Ian Smith's former Rhodesian regime when a group of forty-five European mercenaries, led by Colonel "Mad" Mike Hoare, arrived at Mahé International Airport on a commercial flight from Swaziland to overthrow long-time socialist President of Seychelles France-Albert René's regime. Colonel Hoare and the other mercenaries posed as members of the "Ancient Order of Frothblowers" (a charitable beer-drinking fraternity that had, in fact, died out after the Second World War), visiting the islands as tourists. Shortly after leaving their plane, an airport security guard spotted a Kalashnikov assault rifle in their luggage and this launched a gun battle in which hostages were taken. The Seychellois authorities quickly thwarted the coup attempt known as "Operation Anvil." Most of the mercenaries escaped after hijacking an Air India plane, which was sitting on the runway and forced the captain to fly them to Durban, South Africa. As soon as the aircraft arrived, however, the South African police arrested all the mercenaries. Three million dollars was paid to President René and his government by South Africa for the return of the remaining mercenaries detained in the Seychelles. Several of the mercenaries, including Colonel Hoare, served time in jail for their involvement in "Operation Anvil." Eventually, on 7 May 1985, Colonel Hoare gained his freedom because of a general presidential pardon.

* * *

One afternoon as I was sitting at my desk, we received a cable in CTC from a Middle Eastern country stating that one of their sources claimed that they knew where the American hostages were being held because the source's brother-in-law was one of the people assigned to guarding the hostages.

At the conclusion of the cable, the chief of our office in this country requested that a polygraph operator be immediately dispatched to Beirut to test the source. I immediately called our polygraph division and talked to the chief who informed me that the only one that he had in the area was their chief polygrapher located in a country in the Far East. Bernie F. was an Afro-American and at the time, because there were very few blacks in this Middle Eastern country, Bernie was asked if he would agree to being outfitted with a mask and gloves by our technical services office. He agreed, and after being fitted with the mask and gloves was transported to Larnaca and then flown in an Agency helicopter to the Middle Eastern country where he administered the polygraph and found the source to be telling the truth. With the results in hand, CTC wanted to implement a plan that they had devised to rescue the hostages using several foreign assets already in place so as not to show any U.S. Government involvement. That evening, I was told to drive to the airport with a technical services officer named Mike M. along with ten bags filled with money, gold bars, and an assortment of weapons, equipment and gear. Before our arrival, I again called my good friend Keith M. at Dulles International Airport. After telling him what we had, I asked him for assistance in getting Mike on the Delta flight to Frankfurt. To Keith's credit, the next thing I knew, Mike was on the Frankfurt flight where he then boarded a second flight to Larnaca and from there was shuttled into the Middle Eastern country aboard a helicopter. After arriving in country, Mike had to wait an additional three days before receiving authorization from CTC to pass the money, equipment and gear to the assets. CTC, in turn, was waiting for authorization from the National Security Council (NSC) at the White House to proceed. Unfortunately, when it was finally granted, the rescue team assaulted the suspect residence only to learn that the hostages had been moved the night before.

Following this incident, a senior CTC official named Howard F. was given the "green light" in September 1986 to set up a team to assist in locating the American hostages using individuals handpicked by a Major General. The 12 member team consisted of characters similar to those depicted in the famous film "The Dirty Dozen" – an explosives expert, a weapons experts, a motor cross champion, a computer wiz, a communications expert, and a financial expert skilled in transferring funds – just to name a few. When this team arrived in the United States, I met them and the General at Dulles International Airport outside of Washington, DC and escorted them through U.S. Customs and Immigration. At dinner that evening, I learned that the General had recently survived an assassination attempt and was lucky to be alive.

While driving through the "green zone" from East to West Beirut, his vehicle was stopped at one of the many checkpoints. When an argument ensued between the General's bodyguards and the checkpoint guards, he decided to exit his armored vehicle to talk with the guards. While approaching them, one pointed their AK-47 rifle at him. As the General began to explain who he was, the guard opened fire, shooting him through his hand and hitting him in the head and chest five times. As the bodyguards began returning fire, killing the checkpoint guards, they grabbed the wounded General and dragged him back to his vehicle. He believes that the reason he was not killed that day was his close proximity to the AK-47 when he was shot. In his opinion, the bullet hit him flat and did not have sufficient distance to begin spinning.

* * *

Several weeks earlier I had flown to Texas where I was met at the airport by one of our officers named T.J; a "kicker" known for his expertise in preparing parachutes which would be attached to cargo that was pushed out of the rear door of an aircraft. T.J. picked me up in an enormous blue Cadillac with a set of polished bullhorns on the hood. As we departed, he informed me that I would be driving to southern Texas where I would be meeting the foreman of a ranch owned by an oilman named Bill B., who had offered the Agency the use of his ranch. Mr. B. was a friend of Vice President George H. Bush and had married into a prominent Texas family. While cutting timber on their property, Mr. B's family struck oil and eventually became millionaires.

In order to look the part of a cowboy, I put on my oldest pair of blue jeans, a white cowboy shirt, a blue jean jacket, and a cowboy hat. I then rented a pickup truck and headed south to the ranch. Once I entered the main gate on the ranch, I still had to drive 20 or so miles to get to the ranch headquarters where I was met by Lloyd S., a huge man that stood 6'2" and well over 250 pounds. The first thing I noticed was that he had hands the size of baseball gloves. Although I assumed that T.J. had notified Lloyd that I was coming, Lloyd thought that I was a new ranch hand and instructed me to put my gear in the bunkroom. Not wanting to "break cover" until I had the opportunity to meet with Mr. B., I was escorted to the bunkroom and reminded that breakfast was at 6:00 a.m. sharp. The following morning I was treated to an enormous breakfast of eggs, bacon, ham, sausage, home fries, toast, and black coffee as thick as syrup. Following breakfast, I was told to saddle up a horse and ended up herding cattle into a pen with Lloyd for the next few hours. The cattle were then loaded onto the back of trailers to be shipped to Dallas. By mid-day, I was exhausted, and by evening, I was almost dead. When I asked Lloyd when Mr. B. would be arriving, I was told he was delayed for a day. Again, not wanting to "break cover," the next morning I was back at work herding cattle. Finally, late in the afternoon, I overheard Lloyd say that Mr. B. would be arriving that afternoon around 3:00 p.m. aboard his twin-engine aircraft and appeared somewhat surprised when I asked if I could drive with him to the runway to meet Mr. B. After he landed, I introduced myself to Mr. B., showed him my CIA credentials, and told him that I was with the Agency. I thought Lloyd was going to have a heart attack right there.

During the next several days, I was provided a tour of the ranch, which was roughly the size of Fairfax County, Virginia. Elk, whitetail deer, mule deer, antelope, and mountain goats populated the ranch. Once, when I asked Mr. B. how big his ranch was, he said, *"Richard, see that mountain range up there?" "Well, I own from that mountain range to that mountain range down there."* Mr. B. owned two other ranches, one of which we referred to as "snake pit" due to the number of rattlesnakes that inhabited the ranch. I can still recall when Lloyd decided to have a rattlesnake round up where the rattlesnakes are picked up using a long pole with a loop on the end and placed in a burlap bag before being skinned and cooked. I did not want any part of this ritual, so Lloyd told me to sit on some rocks out of the way. When Lloyd and the rest of the crew began to pour gasoline down the holes in between the rocks, I was soon surrounded by, what appeared to be, hundreds of rattlesnakes. While everyone laughed and laughed, I can assure you that I had to change my underwear before sitting down to a feast of fried rattlesnake and cold beer.

Following my discussions with Mr. B., I flew back to Washington DC, only to return to Texas several days later accompanied by a new CTC logistics officer named Frank W. and a recently hired administrative assistant named Mark S. After leaving the two of them in Texas, I returned to Washington, DC to bring the team back to the site aboard a "black flight". The trip is called a "black flight' because all of the windows are blacke ¹ and, therefore, the team does not have any idea where t¹ their flight or upon landing within the United St taken to ensure that the students remain in location of the facility and the identity of the

For the next several months, the tea Agency instructors in a variety of clandesti case officer training (spotting, assessing, developing and recruiting); tradecraft training (meeting someone securely); dead-drops; surveillance detection routes (SDRs); surveillance and counter-surveillance; secret writing; clandestine photography and video recording; debriefing and elicitation; report writing; basic analysis; and covert communications. Additionally, the team received firearms and evasive driving training and were subject to physical fitness training on a daily basis. One afternoon while training with the team, one of our officers called on the radio and said that he would be delivering a package to us. Minutes later, as one of our planes flew overhead, we looked up to see a small parachute opening and, seconds later, two cases of cold Budweiser beer landed at our feet.

To sharpen their skills, the team was flown to several U.S. cities to practice their new tradecraft, surveillance, and clandestine photography techniques. Their last practical exercise was conducted in a large European capital where the team was required to move around the city discreetly during a period of increased threat. On each of these occasions, I would accompany the team to ensure their safety and security. Because I was frequently questioned about who my traveling companions were during these trips – 12 bearded, ferocious looking men, I would calmly reply that they were members of their National Wrestling Team. Thank God, the men were of different sizes and weight since no one ever questioned me further after I gave them this response.

* * *

On Christmas morning in 1986 shortly after returning to Washington, DC to witness the birth of my daughter, Kelly, I received a call from an irate Lloyd S. telling me to get Frank W. off the ranch as soon as possible or he was going to kill him after spotting Frank's vehicle in front of his daughter Ginger's trailer that morning. I immediately called Frank and told him to pack his things and get on the next plane back to Washington, DC. Although Frank tried to explain, I told him that his actions were jeopardizing everything.

On 2 January 1987, seven days after my daughter, Kelly, was born, a fellow CTC officer named Paul D. and I drove the team to ...es International Airport where we boarded an Agency aircraft ...flight" to travel to one of our facilities to conduct explosive ...blast investigation training. Great pains were taken to ...e students remained in isolation to protect the location of this facility during their two-month stay with Paul and me. When I returned home, I was amazed at how much my new infant daughter, Kelly, had grown. Unfortunately, before deploying the team back into the Middle Eastern country, DCI Casey passed away in May 1987 and the seventh floor began to get "cold feet" about using such a team. Shortly thereafter, word came down that the team was to be disbanded and rumor has it that each team member was given one million dollars as severance pay and sent on their way. Looking back, I was shocked that no one bothered to conduct an "after action assessment" in that all of the team members were departing with a wealth of knowledge after being trained for nine months in clandestine operations.

* * *

A year after the training, I returned to present Mr. B. with one of the Olympic flags that flew over the stadium in Seoul, Korea during the 1988 summer Olympic Games, which I had received from a friend of mine, Rick P., who was working with the South Koreans during the games. Mr. B. was genuinely moved by this gift since he had four flagpoles in front of the main living area on the ranch and only three were flying flags. The first flagpole flew the stars and stripes; the second the State flag of Texas; and the third his corporation flag. The Olympic flag was hoisted up the fourth flagpole immediately after I presented it to him and I thought I saw the elderly Mr. B. shed a tear.

As the training in Texas was underway, the seventh floor granted CTC approval to train a second team of U.S. personnel known as the "U.S. Team" to follow suspect terrorists in an attempt to find out who was supporting them financially and logistically. A variety of men and women were selected for this new team – individuals with law enforcement, military, and corporate business backgrounds. All of them, particularly the women, spoke several languages including Arabic and Farsi. To facilitate their training, I found a large residence in the mountains and set it up as a classroom, sleeping and eating quarters. Colonel Tim G., who was the commander of the U.S. Marine Battalion in Beirut when the U.S. Marine Corps barracks was bombed in 1983, was hired to supervise and train this team. After an extensive training program similar to that provided to the first team, one of the first assignments in 1987 was to follow a member of the Amal Militia in Lebanon. In 1985, along with four other heavily armed terrorists, they had seized a Royal Jordanian airliner in Beirut and threatened to kill their hostages, including two U.S. citizens, unless their political demands were met. After two unsuccessful attempts to fly to Tunis, the hijackers returned the plane to Beirut, where they released the hostages, blew up the plane, and then fled from the airport.

Under the comprehensive Crime Control Act of 1984, which created a new section in the U.S. Criminal Code for hostage taking, and the Omnibus Diplomatic Security and Antiterrorism Act of 1986, which established a new extraterritorial statute pertaining to terrorist acts conducted abroad against U.S. citizens and interests, upon approval by the host country, it was determined that the FBI had the legal authority to deploy FBI personnel to conduct extraterritorial investigations in the host country where the criminal act had been committed. This enabled the United States to prosecute terrorists for crimes committed against U.S. citizens. With the new act in hand, capturing the Amal Militia member and putting him on trial was supposed to make the U.S. Government's intentions clear throughout the terrorist community – that the U.S. meant business. It further was intended to send notice to terrorists that "they could run, but they could not hide".

Shortly after receiving the task to locate the Amal Militia member, the "U.S. Team" enlisted the help of a former friend of his living in Cyprus to engage him in a telephone conversation in an attempt to lure the Amal Militia member to a yacht off the coast of Cyprus using a potential "drug deal" as bait. With "U.S. Team" members manning the tape recorder, the Amal Militia member admitted his role in the 1985 Royal Jordanian airlines hijacking. At the request of a "U.S. Team" member, the Amal Militia member accompanied the man as they boarded a yacht in the Mediterranean for what the Amal Militia member thought was the "drug purchase." Little did the Amal Militia member know that the yacht had been rented by the FBI, and that the enormous man of Greek heritage that embraced the Amal Militia member as he boarded the yacht was an undercover agent. As they tried to handcuff the Amal Militia member, the agent and he fell to the deck and the he severely sprained both his arms. He was then whisked away and placed aboard a jet to Washington, DC. Although the Amal Militia member initially suspected the Israeli's were responsible for his capture, on the eve of his trial he lamented, "I never imagined that I would be arrested by the American government!"

The elaborate operation involved the Pentagon, the FBI, and the Navy. Alongside the FBI on the yacht, several very attractive female CTC officers even went so far as to join their female FBI counterparts and sunbathe topless as part of the scenario. The Amal Militia member was the first international terrorist to be apprehended overseas and brought back to the United States to stand trial and his capture represented the first use of this new anti-terrorism statute. He was eventually convicted of conspiracy, aircraft piracy and hostage taking in the 1985 hijacking of Royal Jordanian Airlines Flight 402 in Beirut and sentenced to 30 years in a U.S. prison in March 1989 in the District of Columbia. Afterwards, terrorists began to take notice that the U.S. Government was serious.

After capturing the Amal Militia member, Dewey Clarridge was presented with a $25,000 cash award; one of only four awards presented to senior Agency managers that year. In Dewey's case, it was the second year in a row that he received this coveted award. He previously earned it as the Chief of the DO's Latin America Division. Of the four senior officials that received the award, one official did not do anything for members of his division; one brought donuts; and the third bought pizza for everyone in his division. Dewey, the class act that he is, gave $5,000 to his executive assistant, Bev, and told her to throw the best party the Agency had ever seen – and it was. The entire sixth floor corridor of the Old Headquarters building was lined with tables covered with the finest food and drink. Coolers were filled to the brim with beer, champagne, and wine. Huge prawns, caviar, smoked turkey, ham, and the finest desserts lined the tables. There even was a belly dancer that Dewey knew from his time in NE Division. If smoking were allowed in the Agency hallway, Dewey would have had the finest cigars. Leaving the Headquarters building that night via one of the exits in the basement I bumped into a young lady who seemed to be lost and somewhat inebriated (she must have had a hell of a time at the party since she had one leg in her panty hose and was dragging the other leg of her panty hose behind her).

Although Dewey claimed that he had no involvement in the illegal diversion of funds to the Contras or the subsequent cover-up, he was indicted in November 1991 on seven counts of perjury and false statements. When notified of the indictment, DCI Webster called Dewey into his office and told him that he was being demoted and relieved as the Chief of the Counterterrorism Center. Returning to his office, Dewey had Bev schedule a month long trip to several European and Middle East posts where he met with the leaders of several Intelligence Services. Upon his return, Dewey resigned and a farewell party was given to him in CTC, which rivaled the aforementioned party. Later, on Christmas Eve 1992, in the waning hours of his presidency, George H. Bush pardoned Dewey before his trial could finish. In addition to Dewey, President Bush also pardoned five of Dewey's cohorts in the Iran-Contra Affair including former Defense Secretary Caspar Weinberger, Elliot Abrahms, a former Assistant Secretary of State for Inter-American Affairs, former National Security Advisor Robert McFarlane and former CIA employees Alan Fiers and Clair George.

* * *

One afternoon before departing CTC, I received a call on my secure telephone from a man who claimed that he was with the Defense Intelligence Agency (DIA). After going secure, the man informed me that DIA, as the Federal Agency responsible for Prisoners of War (POW) and Missing in Action (MIA) soldiers, had a Laotian source who claimed that he knew where the remains of four deceased U.S. servicemen were located near Tchepone, Savannakhet Province in Laos. Knowing that an Air America flight had been shot down by hostile ground fire over Savannakhet Province in 1963, the DIA officer asked me if I could provide him with information on an individual named Eugene D., an Air America "kicker" believed to have survived the crash.

After receiving permission to review Eugene's file, I headed to the basement in the original Headquarters building and filled out a form requesting the file. When I opened it, the first thing that I saw was a huge notice on the inside cover that said, "This file will remain active until the year 2010." While reviewing I got goose bumps on my arms when I saw Eugene's original Air America application along with a photograph that he had submitted as part of his application. I learned that on 5 September 1963, an Air America C46 aircraft was hit by ground fire and crashed about two kilometers from Tchepone, Savannakhet Province, Laos. Eugene, Chui To Tik, and two Thai Nationals parachuted to safety, but were immediately captured by the Pathet Lao. Two crewmembers, Joseph C. and Charles H., were killed in the crash. Later, the Pathet Lao photographed Eugene and four other prisoners and published a leaflet naming the five as their prisoners.

Several times during their captivity, the entire crew was moved to different locations within Savannakhet and Khammouane Provinces. In early July 1966, Eugene and six other prisoners made an escape. However, only two of the seven, Dieter D. and one of the Thai Nationals who was part of Eugene's crew, reached safety. One report stated that Eugene was killed in the escape attempt, but the Thai National reported that he was last seen attempting to reach high ground. Additional information from an American escapee and a Thai captured with Eugene recounted his capture and prison chronology through 3 July 1966 – the last time they knew him to be alive with them in Khammouane Province.

Accounts of the prison escape included information that four of the seven prison guards were killed during the escape attempt. One Thai who escaped and was recaptured was not killed afterwards. Interestingly, there was one report that Eugene may have been alive as late as January 1968, but there was nothing in the file to corroborate this information. Lastly, I remember seeing a photograph of him obtained by Air America in May 1969 showing him in captivity circa 1965. In reviewing the file, it was evident that Eugene's family had not stopped looking for answers in that there were numerous letters in the file from family members and information that in 1972, Eugene's brother, Jerome, traveled to Laos in search of his missing brother.

I wish that this story had a happy conclusion, but it does not. The remains of the four POW/MIAs were returned to the United States, but DNA evidence revealed that Eugene's remains was not among them. Several years later while I was stationed in Honduras, I mentioned this story to a pilot friend of mine who was working for us on contract by the name of Lee G. When I mentioned Eugene's name, Lee became very emotional and told me that he had been employed by Air America and had known Eugene very well; a small world. Although the Pathet Lao openly admitted holding American prisoners of war, they insisted that the U.S. negotiate directly with them to ensure their release but, unfortunately, the U.S. never negotiated or recognized the Pathet Lao and consequently, not one of the nearly 600 Americans lost in Laos was ever released.

* * *

During the 1950s, a deteriorating political situation in Laos had allowed North Vietnam Army (NVA) troops and Pathet Lao guerrillas to seize the Laotian panhandle from the Royal Lao Army. Prevented by Geneva Accords from having a large military presence in Laos, the U.S. established a "Program Evaluation Office" (PEO) in 1958 as a CIA cover for anti-communist covert actions. One activity, begun in 1958, used Meo tribesmen for a small pilot guerrilla program, which soon became the largest clandestine army in CIA history. In the first year, using U.S. Special Forces White Star teams as PEO "civilians," a few CIA officers, and 90 elite Thai Border guards, an army of 9,000 Meo was trained for behind-lines guerrilla activity. Within 10 years, the Meo army grew to over 40,000 guerrillas, becoming the most effective fighting force in Laos. The CIA's covert airline, known as "Air America" supported the Meo as well as numerous other CIA-backed clandestine guerrilla armies. With the escalating war, a large U.S. military presence guaranteed that "Air America" could operate in relative obscurity.

With little fanfare throughout the war, "Air America" fought in the frontlines of unconventional war. "Air America" pilots reportedly flew "black missions" over North Vietnam, and the Laotian panhandle in every type of aircraft from 727 jets to small Cessna's and Porters transporting everything from combat troops (alive, wounded, or dead) to baby chickens, dropping rice to refugees, and specially trained Nung trail watchers into denied areas. As U.S. forces pulled out, "Air America" picked up the slack, straining to maintain the status quo. The communists drove the Meo from their homelands in the early 1970's, and as the Meo retreated, Air America was in the position of hauling (and feeding) tens of thousands of refugees. However, there were problems as the Agency fell under Congressional scrutiny of its worldwide paramilitary activities and public pressure to divest itself of Air America. South Vietnam's rapid collapse in 1975 signified the end of the clandestine war that began in Vietnam thirty years earlier.

* * *

Since I never miss deer hunting season, one day in late November 1987, I requested permission from Bill to go to Pennsylvania, knowing that I would be four hours from Washington, DC and, therefore, may or may not make it in time to deploy if called. When Bill asked me where I was going to hunt, I told him at a friend's cabin, in Potter County in northern Pennsylvania near the town of Sinnemahoning.

Reluctantly, Bill said that I could go and since we did not have cell phones in those days, he asked that I periodically check in with him. Prior to departing, I told Bill that I was hoping to have my buck within the first few hours of opening day and would then head back to Washington, DC. As luck would have it, at 7:00 a.m. on opening day of deer season, a big eight-point buck walked in front of my tree stand and I shot it. After gutting and dressing it, I tied the deer to the roof of my Jeep and headed home. As I stopped at a small bar in Sinnemahoning to get some breakfast, much to my surprise, I noticed a small index card on the cash register with my name on it and a message to call Bill A. The word "Urgent" was clearly scrawled on the card. Although my first reaction was that someone was playing a prank on me, I told the bartender whom I was and asked him about the message. He responded that a man by the name of Bill A. had just called asking for me, said it was urgent, and left a message to call him if I showed up. When I called Bill, he told me that we were deploying and to immediately head to the U.S. military base where the Boeing 707 was staged. When I asked him how he had found me, Bill replied, "Simple, you mentioned that you were hunting near the town of Sinnemahoning. I then called information and asked if there were any bars/restaurants in Sinnemahoning. When the operator informed me that there were only two bars/restaurants, I called and left messages at both locations with the bartenders knowing full well that you would stop at one of them prior to returning to Washington." I then jumped in my Jeep and drove as fast as I could to the U.S. military base where I was met by my deputy, Rob B., planeside minutes before takeoff.

As I was boarding the plane, I calmly handed Rob the keys to my Jeep with instructions to take my deer to a butcher and to tell my wife, Karen that I would not be home for dinner that evening. Unfortunately, as we were settling into our seats in the rear of the 707 aircraft, the pilot came on the public address system to inform us that the mission had been aborted. Earlier in the day on 29 November 1987, Korean Air Lines Flight 858 crashed into the Indian Ocean. Subsequent investigations revealed that North Korean agents planted a bomb aboard the plane. According to reports from South Korea, two North Koreans – a 70 year-old man, and a 26-year-old woman posing as father and daughter and carrying false Japanese passports – boarded a regular KAL flight from Baghdad to Seoul, placed explosives in an overhead luggage compartment, and disembarked at its first stop at Abu Dhabi. Nine hours later, the bomb exploded and the plane went down into the Andaman Sea off Burma. The man and woman went on to Bahrain where they were stopped and held for questioning, but prior to being interrogated, both ate poison ampoules hidden in the filter tips of cigarettes they were smoking. Although the man died, the woman survived and was extradited to South Korea, where she confessed on 23 December 1987.

* * *

Looking back at my time in CTC, I consider it one of the best assignments that I had during my career in the Agency because I got to participate in operations and do things not normally undertaken by a security officer. One such U.S. Government program involved "unmanned aerial vehicle's (UAV's) and "remote piloted vehicle's" (RPV's) using a Long-EZ aircraft. What made the Long-EZ aircraft unique was the fact that it was designed for fuel-efficient, long-range flights and could fly for over ten hours and up to 1,600 miles on 52 gallons of fuel. Equipped with a rear-seat fuel tank, the Long-EZ had flown for 4,800 miles. Burt Rutan had previously designed and flew in the "Voyager" aircraft with pilot Jeana Yeager non-stop and without refueling around the world for nine days, three minutes and 44 seconds between 14 and 23 December 1986. Sadly, singer and songwriter John Denver had died in a Long-EZ when it crashed on 12 October 1997.

Lastly, during my tenure as the first Director of Security in CTC, I had the opportunity to set up and administer two covert training sites, several proprietary's, safe houses and "bigoted programs." My time in CTC also provided me with a thorough understanding of using cover, backstopping, alias documents and accommodation addresses.

Chapter 6

"Supporting the Contra Program in Central America; Send Lawyers, Guns, and Money"

In December 1987, following extensive rehabilitation on my right knee to repair a torn meniscus and cruciate ligament which I had received while playing rugby for the Western Suburbs Rugby Football Club, I received a cable from the chief of our office in Tegucigalpa, Terry W. He asked that I return to Honduras to help oversee the "phase down" of the Nicaraguan Resistance FDN (Contra) supply program.

Swan Island

After the $100 million USD aid package to support the Contras was passed by Congress in June 1986, Swan Island was selected to serve as the principal storage and supply base to support the Contras in addition to other bases we had located throughout Honduras. During discussions with Terry, deputy chief of our office, Steve M., and our support chief, Jack K., I was asked to TDY to a small town, Aguacate, along the Honduran/Nicaraguan border – my second trip there. A year earlier, in October 1986, when assigned to CTC, I had been asked to TDY there to conduct a comprehensive survey of the site and, afterwards, implement security measures. The officer in charge at the time was a Special Activities Division paramilitary officer named George "Mick" M. His deputy was a Latin American Division officer named Tom F.

Upon my arrival, Mick and Tom greeted me warmly and let me share their quarters with them, which included getting to know their pet – a small scorpion that lived in their shower. As Paramilitary Officers, their primary responsibilities were to provide guidance, training, equipment, material, and financial support to the Contras. In addition to the training being conducted at this location (logistical resupply, cargo handling, parachute packaging), certain Contras were selected and flown to an undisclosed location outside of Honduras where they received additional paramilitary and offensive operations training accompanied by an Agency security officer.

I still remember the look on everyone's faces when the first flight landed and a security officer departed the plane dressed in a black trench coat and hat with a cigar in his mouth although the temperature was close to 100 degrees.

On another occasion, when the flight was delayed due to an aircraft mechanical problem, a young security officer had to stay overnight. In that this was his first support trip outside the country, Mick, Tom, and I decided to take him to one of the local bars, which also served as a whorehouse. Having never been to a whorehouse, and not knowing Spanish, the young man was very uncomfortable around the young women until one finally coaxed him into a back room. When he finally emerged 30 minutes later, he was grinning from ear to ear. However, when an article appeared in the local newspaper the next day mentioning that the area had one of the highest rates of AIDS, I thought the young security officer was going to have a heart attack. Although we kept trying to convince him not to worry in an effort to keep him from going into cardiac arrest, he departed that day as white as a ghost.

It was during this visit that I had the opportunity to meet an unemployed construction worker from Wisconsin by the name of Eugene Hasenfus. He was working as a cargo handler for a company named Southern Air Transport. Later Hasenfus would be aboard a Fairchild C-123 cargo plane on 5 October 1986 that was shot down over Nicaragua while delivering supplies to the Nicaraguan Contras. Although the two pilots died in the crash, Hasenfus was able to parachute to safety, having disobeyed orders by wearing one on the mission. He was subsequently captured by Nicaraguan government forces, tried, sentenced to 25 years in prison, but was later pardoned and released by Nicaraguan President Daniel Ortega in December 1986. Hasenfus' capture and detention helped uncover and publicize the Iran-Contra Affair because a black book of phone numbers in the wreckage tied the plane to an operation run out of Ilopango airbase in El Salvador, supported by anti-Castro exile Felix Rodriguez.

During this trip, in addition to visiting this small border town, I also had the chance to visit a second training site after receiving word from our officer in charge that he could not get his two drawer safe open. When informed of this problem I immediately drafted a cable to Art F., the same Art F. whom I had shared an office with while assigned to Clearance Division. Much to my surprise, I received a reply back from Art that no one could respond for a week so I decided to jump on a helicopter and fly to this site with a sack of tools and a bucket of chicken known as "Pollo Campero". After trying every possible combination in an attempt to open the safe, I eventually ripped off the safe's front door with a sledgehammer and chisel, removed the items, and then hauled the safe to a location where it was then blown up with explosives. Knowing that this might be the case, I provided the officer with a new safe that I had brought with me from our warehouse in Tegucigalpa. After returning to Tegucigalpa, I wrote up what I had done only to receive a blasting cable back from Art F. scolding me for my actions saying that I should have documented and photographed all of my actions – yeah, like I just happened to have a camera and video recorder with me at the time.

* * *

Because Congress had mandated that all activity pertaining to supplying the Contra's was to cease on 29 February 1988, several weeks after visiting those two training sites, I was asked by Terry and Jack to fly to Swan Island to ensure the safety and security of the inhabitants on the island. Swan Island lies 139 miles off the Honduran coast in the Caribbean and is approximately 3.5 kilometers long and 1.5 kilometers wide. Remote and densely forested it has a colorful history of involvement in U.S. covert operations. In addition to being used as the forward supply and storage base for the Agency's program to supply the Nicaraguan Contras from 1986-1988, the island had previously been used by the U.S. Government as a training site during the early 1960s. The only inhabitant on the island was a Honduran named Spencer Bennett who kept several head of cattle there. Spencer and I became good friends and I was saddened to hear that one New Year's Eve, while celebrating with his wife and some friends at a bar in Guanaja, Spencer was accidentally shot and killed when a man produced a pistol to shoot it in the air and the bullet struck Spencer in the side of his head.

Upon arriving at Swan Island aboard our Twin Otter aircraft, I was greeted by the officer in charge named John W. who asked me who I was and my purpose for being there. When I told him that I was a security officer sent by the support chief, Jack K., and the chief of our office, Terry W., to assist him with the phase-down of the program, using a few "choice" four-letter words John politely told me that he did not need any security officer and told me to get back on the plane to return to Tegucigalpa. When I reiterated that Jack and Terry had sent me, he rushed to his office to call Terry. My first thought was that he obviously had not been informed that I would be coming. Several minutes later, John returned and apologized. We eventually became good friends and I can honestly say that we made quite a team during my tenure on the island. Every time there was a problem, I ran interference for John claiming that I was from Washington, DC. Our friendship was enhanced by the fact that we both enjoyed snorkeling and diving, which we did together every day.

At the time of my arrival, there were 68 Americans assigned to Swan Island, 100 members of the Honduran Navy to support Honduran sovereignty, and 180 FDN Contras with full logistic support, communications, and administrative facilities. Our office was located in a small hurricane resistance shelter on the southeastern side of the island, which housed our classified information and communications equipment. Because we were concerned about the potential of an attack from the Sandinistas before the 29 February deadline, I worked with John to prepare emergency evacuation and destruction plans. All Americans were issued a "bug out" kit and we designated an area of the island where personnel would report in case of an emergency, In addition, we made sure that all of our emergency equipment was in good condition and in close proximity. During my time on the island, we began to reduce our files and all non-essential classified materials were destroyed on sight or shipped back to Tegucigalpa aboard our Twin Otter aircraft.

On the day of my arrival, I was introduced to the officers in charge (OIC) of both the FDN and Honduran Navy and eventually became an intermediary between these two constantly bickering factions. Although tensions were running extremely high in respect to moving the lethal and non-lethal material off the island, we were able to move approximately 340,000 pounds of material by air and another 360,000 pounds by sea during the next few weeks. On one occasion, the FDN OIC came to me complaining that the Hondurans were breaking into his warehouse and stealing quartermaster supplies (boots, socks, shirts, uniforms, etc). When he asked me if I could assist him in securing the warehouse, I immediately strengthened the doors, added some additional locking hardware, and perimeter lighting. Several days later when the FDN OIC informed me that his warehouse again had been broken into, I found an area where several rivets of the thin, tin wall had been removed and decided to place broken glass, nails, tacks and concertina wire along the inside so that anyone entering would be cut to shreds. The following night the warehouse was broken into yet again. When the FDN OIC complained to the Honduran OIC the following day, he added that a large quantity of blood was found at the scene, due to our new security measures. The Honduran OIC replied that he was confident that none of his soldiers were thieves and suggested that the FDN OIC look at his own men. This lead to the FDN OIC summoning all of his soldiers and lined them up in formation. He then walked up and down the line with a pistol in his hand swearing aloud that he would shoot anyone of his soldiers with injuries on their hands or legs. When he did not find anyone with these types of injuries, the FDN OIC asked the Honduran OIC to line his men up in formation to submit to a similar inspection. Sure enough, five soldiers stood in line with bandaged hands and legs with wounds, which they could not account for.

On another occasion, we received a message from Washington, DC stating that we were to begin removing the "Redeye" missiles off the island using our Twin Otter aircraft to move them to a Honduran military base in the town of Siuqutepac north of the Pamerola USAF base later renamed Soto Cano AFB. That afternoon, when we went to the container to open it, we were confronted by several armed Honduran Navy guards who, with weapons drawn, claimed that they had not received any information from their superiors relating to the transfer of the missiles from the island. For the next few minutes, we faced nervous young Honduran soldiers with weapons pointing at our faces until the Honduran Navy captain arrived. When informed of our mission, the young captain advised that he also had not been told of the transfer and, therefore, needed to receive permission from his commanding officer in Tegucigalpa. Eventually, several hours later, we were given the "green light" to transfer the "Redeyes" under the close supervision of a Honduran, Nicaraguan, and American Tri-commission.

Each day at 8:00 a.m. while serving on the island, all of the Americans would convene in the small office within the hurricane shelter for a morning briefing conducted by John. After reviewing cable traffic, we would then assist the Contras in loading various aircraft (DC6's, C-123's and Casa 212's), to drop lethal and non-lethal supplies (weapons and ammunition, uniforms and boots) into Nicaragua. The pilots were mostly from South Africa or Rhodesia and their bank accounts in the Cayman Islands indicated that they were making damn good money per flight, which routinely took off during the late afternoon and returned during the middle of the night. Lying in bed each evening, you knew the mission was successful when you heard the reverse roar of the engines as the planes landed on the runway. One evening one of the DC-6's did not return from its mission and we heard that it had been shot down inside of Nicaragua.

Three weeks later, one of the "kickers" aboard the aircraft returned to the island and told us how the aircraft had been struck by a surface to air missile. He had been the only one wearing a parachute that day and, therefore, was the only survivor after exiting the aircraft and landing safely amongst some trees in the jungle. Recounting his story, the "kicker" went on to tell us how it had taken him eight days to work his way back to the Rio Coco River bordering Honduras and Nicaragua with little or no food and water. What impressed me the most, however, was the fact that this young man still had the patience to remain on the Nicaraguan side of the river for an extra day avoiding Sandinista patrols knowing that Honduras and freedom were within eyesight on the other side of the river – an incredible survival story. I was so impressed by his story that I gave him a Penn State hat that I had. A year later, I ran into the same "kicker" in the airport in Miami and, much to my surprise, he was wearing the worn and frayed Penn State ball cap.

One day as we were constructing an outside shower, a young Honduran Navy Lieutenant informed us that a sailboat had docked at the island. As we ran to the dock, the first thing that I noticed was six beautiful girls in bikinis serving as the crew. The captain of the vessel, a tan young man of approximately 30 with long hair, claimed that his sailboat was having engine problems and, therefore, requested permission to come ashore, knowing from his map that he had entered Honduran "restricted space". Having been on the island for almost three months, seeing a female was a real treat; seeing six beautifully tanned women in bikinis was a dream come true. Because I had crewed on several sailboats while living in

Marblehead, Massachusetts, I immediately noticed how low the vessel was in the water and passed on my comments to the young Honduran Lieutenant. When I asked if I could conduct an inspection of the vessel, he smiled and said "of course." After conducting a thorough, methodical search, we eventually found several false compartments in the hull of the sailboat containing 180 kilos of cocaine – my first encounter with a drug smuggler. Several weeks later, while walking along the beach on the southern end of the island, we found eight to ten bundles, which had washed up on the beach and discovered another 30 kilos of cocaine. Most speculated that the cocaine had been dumped overboard by a "mother-ship" to be picked up by a smaller vessel or to avoid being discovered by the U.S. Coast Guard or Honduran Navy. In both instances, we reported our findings to Headquarters and sent a ton of photographs before burning the cocaine.

With the waters surrounding Swan Island containing a variety of species of fish, one afternoon when one of our logistics officers named Rick R. decided to go fishing in a 12-foot aluminum boat with one of the Nicaraguan carpenters assigned to the island, no one paid much attention until it started getting dark and they still had not returned. Getting worried, John notified the deputy chief of our office in Tegucigalpa, Steve M., who upon receiving the news, gave the order to launch several helicopters at daybreak along with our Twin Otter and Porter fixed wing aircraft if they did not show up. As daylight approached, and there was still no sign of Rick and the carpenter, the helicopter and planes headed to Swan Island (a 2 ½ hour flight), and began searching the waters surrounding the island using a "grid system." As one of the searchers, I can honestly say that it was like looking for a "needle in a haystack". There was so much to cover. Add the reflection of the sun off the water to the equation, and you can imagine the daunting task we had at hand. Hours later when there still was no sign of Rick and the carpenter, Steve M. called the U.S. Coast Guard in Miami, Florida who immediately dispatched a C-130 aircraft to assist in the search and rescue. Thank God, that the C-130 had the capacity to cover large swathes of water and, shortly upon their arrival, spotted Rick and the carpenter clinging to the overturned boat as it drifted in the current several miles from the island. Although sunburned and thirsty, Rick claimed that the boat had started leaking and taking on water within an hour after beginning to fish and eventually capsized. Although only ½ miles from shore, Rick had made the decision to remain with the carpenter who could not swim instead of swimming to shore himself and, therefore, clung to the carpenter for over 18 hours in the water until being rescued – a true act of bravery.

Following the 29 February 1988 deadline, I was asked to remain on the island for two more months as part of a five-man contingent to ensure that our interests were protected on the island while it remained in a "moth ball' mode. Living on Swan Island was an incredible experience. Even though we lived in Spartan quarters, slept in hammocks or makeshift beds, we ate like kings frequently dining on lobster, shrimp, fresh fish, or beef from one of the many steers that Spencer Bennett had on the island. Although we had a small water desalinization plant on the island, which was supposed to take the salt out of the ocean water, to this day I can still taste the salt in my mouth when I think of drinking desalinized water.

At night, we frequently played poker, read, or listened to music. The poker games were memorable in that we played "table stakes" and you would often see players writing checks, throwing down hundreds of dollars, or an expensive watch on the table if they thought that they had a good hand. I remember the evening one of our pilots by the name of Mike bluffed John W. during a poker game only to find out years later that Mike won the $3,000 pot with only a pair of threes in his hand.

One of the pilots even brought a baby raccoon to the island as a pet that everyone played with for weeks. As it grew older however, the raccoon became wilder and wilder and eventually it escaped. Following its escape, the raccoon was frequently spotted during the evenings wondering around the island scavenging for food. After it ended up biting several individuals who had to get a series of rabies shots in their stomachs, the medical officer assigned to the island put a bounty on the raccoon's head and "dead or alive wanted posters" all over the place in an effort to determine if the raccoon was indeed rabid. Sure enough, late one night, we all were awakened to a number of loud crashing and banging sounds as one of the pilots chased and eventually killed the 40 pound plus raccoon in the kitchen with a baseball bat as it was searching for food. The body of the raccoon was sent back to Tegucigalpa to test it for rabies, and much to the relief of everyone that was bitten, the tests came back negative.

* * *

On 7 April 1988, before returning to the United States, the Drug Enforcement Agency (DEA) snatched a Colombian drug lord by the name of Ramon Matta Ballesteros in Honduras and put him on an airplane to the United States although the U.S. did not have any formal extradition treaty with the Honduran government. Matta Ballesteros had set up a cocaine smuggling operation in Honduras and was somewhat of a "Robin Hood" to the local populace, employing hundreds of locals in cigar factories in the El Parriso province near Danli. He had also built numerous schools and churches with money that he had received from shipping cocaine from Colombia to the United States by way of Guatemala.

When the Honduran's heard that Matta Ballesteros had illegally been snatched by U.S. agents and put on a plane to the U.S., they were infuriated. Therefore, when hundreds of people from Danli boarded buses to march on the U.S. Embassy in Tegucigalpa and protest the illegal extradition of Matta Ballesteros, the Honduran security forces did nothing. When the protesters realized this, the demonstration became violent. By 7:00 p.m. that evening 800 to 1,000 people began overturning and burning vehicles as they departed a park in downtown Tegucigalpa, heading towards the U.S. Embassy. It was late in the day and Ambassador Briggs and the majority of the Embassy employees had already departed the Embassy compound. One officer, Jack K., the State Department Regional Security Officer, Sy D., and the 12-member U.S. Marine detachment were but a few that remained in the Embassy that evening as it was besieged. Time after time, the U.S. Marines asked permission to discharge tear gas as they watched the crowd throw stones and set fires to some 20 vehicles parked in the Embassy parking lot outside the walls, but Ambassador Briggs, who remained in his residence high on the mountain overlooking the city, repeatedly denied their requests. Because the hostile crowd could not penetrate the high walls of the U.S. Embassy compound, the crowd decided to set fire to the U.S. Embassy annex across the street. When Jack and Sy received reports that there were U.S. Embassy employees trapped inside the burning annex, they made the decision to discharge the tear gas on the crowd who, at the time, had also begun firing weapons into the air. As the Honduran security forces finally arrived to restore order, Jack and Sy covered their heads with towels and rushed out of the Embassy to the burning annex where they entered and rescued several U.S. AID employees trapped inside. Both would eventually receive awards for their heroism. Four demonstrators were killed from stray bullets fired into the air by the crowd that evening and several others were wounded. Total damage to U.S. Government property was estimated at over $4 million USD.

U.S. Embassy Annex Tegucigalpa, Honduras

I returned to the United States one week after the 7 April 1988 incident at the U.S. Embassy in time for my son Matthew to be born on 28 April 1988 and soon learned that I was being assigned to Tegucigalpa at the request of the chief of our office, Terry W. After ten weeks of language training – enough to order a cheeseburger, a beer, and get my face slapped (not necessarily in that order) – I asked Bill A. if he could hook me up with the chief of the paramilitary group within the Special Activities Division (SAD) – a crusty old veteran of the Vietnam war named Hank B. The purpose for meeting Hank was to see if I could attend several courses at the Farm being conducted under the auspices of SAD, which would prepare me for my new assignment in Honduras. With the "green light" from Hank, I drove to the Farm and joined an existing Career-Trainee course for DO case officers who had just started mapping and orientation, compass reading, and escape and evasion training.

The final exercise for the escape and evasion portion of this training involved being kidnapped from our room. With our hands tied behind our back and with a loosely fitting black hood placed over our heads, we were then taken to a small jail where we were stripped to our underwear. Then, during the course of the next 24 to 48 hours, we were interrogated by military interrogators using a variety of interrogation techniques such as sleep deprivation, temperature extremes, and standing for long periods with the loosely fitting black hood over our heads and our hands tied behind our backs. Occasionally, we were roughed up or punched in the stomach if we did not provide the appropriate answer or respond quickly enough. The cells were small and it was almost impossible to sleep. On top of that, the temperature kept changing and the cells either were freezing cold or hot as hell. During the entire time, we were being monitored to see how we would react and to see what we would say. All I know is that I never want to go through that type of training again. Even though I knew that it was only an exercise, if I ever find out who the interrogators were during this training, I swear that I would kick the living shit out of each and everyone one of them. After two days, my ankles were so swollen from standing that I could barely walk.

Later after surviving this ordeal, I asked Hank if I could become a firearms instructor since in those days only paramilitary officers served as Agency firearms and re-qualification instructors for Agency personnel. Only two other Agency officers, who were not from SAD, had ever be granted authority to be Agency firearm instructors at the time – one of these officers was serving in San Salvador, El Salvador; while the other was assigned to a country in South America. Because Hank knew that I had previously taken the "crash and bang" course, he introduced me to his firearms instructors at the Farm and told them that I would be assisting them with teaching the next "crash and bang" course under their tutelage. After becoming certified as a firearms instructor at the Farm, I was sent to a U.S. military base north of Washington, DC where I then spent the next few days re-qualifying Agency personnel at several ranges leased by the Agency under the direction of the SAD instructors. During this period, I also had the opportunity to take a course where I learned about a variety of automatic rifles, machine guns, and handguns. Part of this training included disassembling and assembling the weapons after firing them at the range. Little did I know that this would prove invaluable to me after being assigned to Honduras because a year later, I was put in charge of "arms interdiction" – a program intended to intercept arms, ammunition and explosives being shipped from Nicaragua across Honduras to El Salvador. One day before my departure, Hank arrived at the military base north of Washington, DC and called me into his office. I cannot tell you how proud I was to hear Hank say, "Richard, you have done an outstanding job over the past few weeks and are now one of us. Go help yourself to whatever equipment and gear that you may need in the warehouse to make your life easier in Honduras". One hell of a compliment for a person that was not a paramilitary officer, and one that I will never forget.

Chapter 7

"Honduras: Intercepting Arms, Ammunition, Explosives and Narcotics"

I arrived in Honduras in August 1988 with my wife, Karen, who had just given up a lucrative career as a Conference Planner with EDS; our 15-month-old daughter Kelly; and our three-month-old son, Matthew. Prior to our departure, Karen had to sell our townhouse, purchase a new house, pack and unpack – all of this while pregnant and working full time while I was TDY in Honduras or in language school. To make matters worse, Karen had never even been outside of the United States except for our honeymoon to Acapulco. When the plane landed in Tegucigalpa a host of support personnel from the Embassy met us, and I can still recall the look on Karen's face when she saw the city for the first time– the place we would be calling home for the next three years. Honduras was, and still is, the second most impoverished country in the Western Hemisphere behind Haiti, with an average national income of less than $300 per year. Ushered into several waiting vehicles, followed by a hoard of begging, shoeless children, we were transported to the Hotel Maya and provided with a one-room suite in the basement of the hotel.

Because we had two small children, Karen immediately asked for bottled water to make formula. Unbeknownst to us, the water bottles had been filled by a hose from an outside faucet and by the next day both Kelly and Matthew were sick with stomach cramps, fever, and diarrhea. After their stool was taken to a local clinic and examined, our worse nightmare became a reality – both had amoebas and parasites.

Although we were fortunate to have a medical officer and nurse assigned to our office in Tegucigalpa, a husband and wife team, both were on home-leave in the United States at the time. To make matters worse, the U.S. Embassy doctor, who had regional responsibility, lived in Panama. When the health of both children began to deteriorate I took it upon myself to drive them to the U.S. Military Air Base in Pomerola two hours north of Tegucigalpa. I made the trip with my pistol in my lap because the road to Pomerola had been put "off limits" by the embassy Regional Security Officer (RSO) due to the high number of terrorist and criminal acts against Americans at the time.

When we arrived at the Pomerola Air Base, Karen and I were met by a young military doctor who informed us that we would have to wait in the infirmary because he had to first deal with a gunshot wound and a broken femur. Three hours later, when the doctor finally arrived, I showed him the results of the stool samples from the lab in Tegucigalpa. After completing his exam on both children, we received some Pedialyte® (a dehydration fluid), some Flagyl (an antibiotic medicine used against bacteria and parasites like giardia and amoeba) and a host of other medications. With the help of the Pedialyte®, we were able to notice a slight improvement in both Kelly and Matthew on the way home to Tegucigalpa. However, for the next 10 days, both of them had bloody bowel movements as the Flagyl killed everything including the giardia and amoeba in their systems.

Two weeks after living in the Hotel Maya, we moved into a large residence on the outskirts of the capital, not far from the airport. As a guarded community, our house sat high on a mountain overlooking a large reservoir that served as the main water supply for the city. The house was enormous with 12 rooms, 30-foot ceilings, and 16 skylights on the roof. Since I was the only member of our office at the time to reside outside of the city, several security measures were installed: steel bars and additional locks on all of the doors and windows, an alarm system, and broken glass and nails installed on all of the ten-foot exterior walls. In addition to the guards that roamed the streets in the guarded community, we also had armed guards posted within the walls of our residential compound 24 hours a day. What a surrealistic setting to see Karen playing with Kelly and Matthew in the backyard with an armed guard watching their every movement.

Like all of my co-workers, I was issued an "official vehicle," a Motorola radio, a pistol, and a shotgun for our residence. After the chief of our office, Terry W. ordered a new armored vehicle I asked if I could have his "old" Toyota Land Cruiser, which had been damaged during the demonstration at the U.S. Embassy earlier in the year. (During the 7 April 1988 demonstration, demonstrators had broken into several cars in the parking lot of the U.S. Embassy and found the golf clubs belonging to Jack K., which were then used as clubs to destroy vehicles that evening. Jack used to say that he actually saw his five-iron flying through the air that night.) I was excited about getting Terry's vehicle since it was the only full size Toyota Land Cruiser in country at the time with a V-8 engine. To say the vehicle was damaged however was an understatement—it had to be repaired at a local auto repair shop before it was drivable.

At the time of our arrival, the Agency had a large number of employees assigned to Honduras. Half were assigned to a compound in the capital while the remaining half, were assigned to an operations base in the country on the outskirts of Tegucigalpa, and at a large warehouse north of the city. Some of our officers were also deployed to several forward bases co-located with Honduran military units along the border with Nicaragua. Each week these officers would report to these sites on Monday aboard one of our helicopters or fixed wing aircraft and then return to Tegucigalpa on Friday. I still smile when I think of the little thatched roof bar where we all hung out each Friday afternoon, which looked like a used car lot due to the number of Toyota Land Cruisers parked there. Many of us were designated as "military advisors" as a way of getting around the staffing issues. A portion of my time was spent working in the U.S. Embassy, and the embassy Regional Security Officer, at the time, Sy D., allowed me to be listed as a member of his staff.

To transport our officers, the Agency had a host of helicopters, old 1960 vintage Huey H and N models and fixed-wing aircraft to include a Porter, Twin Otter, and a Cessna 210 aircraft. All were ideal for short take-off and landing due to their powerful engines. Pilots were from one of the Agency proprietaries located in the United States. One day our Cessna crashed while landing at one of our forward bases and both the pilot, Dan, and one of our officers named Bob B., were knocked unconscious. When Bob came to, he grabbed an unconscious Dan from the plane shortly before it burst into flames. From that day on, each time we flew into this site, we had to fly over the charred remains of that Cessna.

Porter Aircraft

As the first Agency security officer assigned to Tegucigalpa, the majority of my time was spent securing the operations base and the forward sites. After conducting surveys at each of these locations, I followed up by implementing security measures, evacuation plans, and emergency destruction plans. Our main operations base in Tegucigalpa was located on a compound surrounded by a huge wall on the outskirts of the city. Several buildings on the compound served as warehouses and a motor pool. Because we could not rely on the local electricity, several, huge 250-kilowatt diesel generators were brought in to serve as back up power. One of the first things we constructed shortly after my arrival was a small operations and communications center that we manned by volunteer officers looking for some over-time. This served as the hub for messages dispatched or received from the U.S. Embassy, all of our forward bases, CIA Headquarters in McLean, Virginia, and any of our facilities in the world. The center also contained our weapons vault. We hired local guards to patrol the compound and to control visitor and vehicle access and at the main entrance, we installed an electronic sliding gate. Under my supervision, closed circuit television (CCTV) cameras where strategically placed throughout the compound and monitored from the operations and communications center. Many of the forward sites, with the exception of one location, were located on Honduran military bases, so additional security measures needed were minimal. When constructing this new forward site however, we had to fence the entire compound, construct living quarters, mess facilities, latrines, put up lighting, construct guard posts, and ensure that the facility had plenty of emergency power. After the construction was completed, I suggested that we purchase geese to serve as sentries, which were later placed between the exterior and interior fences.

Forward Site in Honduras 1988

Only three kilometers from the border of El Salvador, this site was chosen due to its proximity to the "Bolson"–an area in dispute with the International World Court in The Hague. The dispute arose as a result of "The Football War", as it is known, or (La guerra de fútbol, in Spanish). This was a six-day war fought by El Salvador and Honduras in July 1969. It had little to do with football (soccer), however, instead being caused by political differences between Hondurans and Salvadorans, including immigration from El Salvador to Honduras. The name derives from the timing of the war, which overlapped with rioting from a series of football matches during the second North American qualifying round for the 1970 FIFA World Cup. On 14 July 1969, the Salvadoran army launched an attack against Honduras. Six days later the Organization of American States negotiated a cease-fire, which took effect on 20 July, with the Salvadoran troops withdrawing in early August. Although the war only lasted six days, casualties on both sides were high with each country losing approximately 2,000 individuals each. Eleven years later the two nations signed a peace treaty on 30 October 1980 to put the border dispute before the International Court of Justice (ICJ) in The Hague. In 1992, the Court awarded most of the disputed territory to Honduras, and in 1998, Honduras and El Salvador signed a border demarcation treaty to implement the terms of the ICJ decree.

Our officers assigned to forward bases served as advisors to the Honduran military whose mission involved searching for Salvadoran guerillas in and around the "Bolson". One day while I was accompanying a Honduran team to search for Salvadoran guerillas in the mountainous "Bolson", we returned to a small village exhausted, hungry and thirsty. As we were entering a small cantina to get something to eat and drink, much to our surprise, a small band of Salvadoran guerillas rounded the corner from one of the small side streets on their way into the same cantina. As our Honduran captain slowly raised his arm in a "hold fire" truce gesture, without saying so much as a word, both parties entered the cantina and sat down at tables facing each other. To this day, I cannot believe that no one fired his weapon. Following our meals, each group slowly rose from their tables and departed. I was even more surprised when the Honduran captain gave the Salvadoran's a five-minute head start to escape – just enough time for them to disappear into the mountains prior to our pursuing them again; what a game of "cat and mouse".

Forward Site in Honduras in 1989

On another occasion, while I was visiting one of our officers by the name of "Chochi" at another forward site, we received a report informing us that Salvadoran guerillas had just attacked a Honduran police station at Nueva Ocotepeque along the border of El Salvador and Honduras killing several Honduran border guards. Chochi immediately notified the Honduran officer in charge at Cucuyagua and the next thing we knew, he and I along with 30 members of the Honduran Special Forces assigned to Cucuyagua were in several vehicles heading to the border. Arriving at the Neuva Ocotepeque border crossing 45 minutes later, we were told that the Salvadoran guerillas had just headed back across the border following the attack via a small blind pass (paseo ciego) known as Paseo El Conejo (the rabbit pass). The Honduran's, in the meantime, had opened up a dialogue with their Salvadoran military counterparts in an attempt to block the guerillas from returning to Salvadoran soil. Having grown up in the area, our Honduran Special Forces Lieutenant named Sevilla advised that he knew the area around Paseo El Conejo very well. So the decision was made to drive as far as we could adjacent to the pass and then walk on foot to an area where Chochi and Sevilla believed that the guerillas would be passing.

To not draw attention, the decision was made to dress in civilian clothing rather than in military fatigues. No sooner had we set up a perimeter, than 20 uniformed Honduran soldiers passed within 100 meters of our position searching for the same band of guerillas. At that point, our "pucker factor" was running high since we were dressed in civilian clothing and could easily have been mistaken for the Salvadoran guerillas. Somewhere around 4:00 a.m., several flares launched, followed by a steady series of 60 and 81-millimeter mortar rounds. At daybreak, a low flying Salvadoran reconnaissance aircraft flew directly over our position and then the Salvadoran and Honduran soldiers launched their attack on the guerillas. For the entire day, as we watched from our position high above in the blind pass as the battle raged below us, I can remember thinking, here it is the first day of deer season in Pennsylvania and I am in the mountains along the Honduran/Salvadoran border hunting humans. Although we remained in the pass the duration of the battle, hoping that the guerillas would be forced to retreat back to Honduran soil through our pass, this never happened. What amazed me the most, when I look back on that day, was the support the guerillas were receiving from the local people in the form of shelter, food, and water. Unfortunately, those living on the border had to be impartial to both sides in order to survive.

Upon returning to Tegucigalpa, I attended a staff meeting hosted by the chief of our office, Terry W. where the events from the past two days near Nueva Ocotepeque were discussed. When I told Terry after the meeting that I had been in the area, Terry's response was one that I will never forget. He said, "Richard, although it is important for us to gather intelligence, you should not have unnecessarily put yourself in harms way. You have a wife and two young children and could have been killed." Although Terry was right, information, which I provided pertaining to the events from those days, was written up and disseminated in several intelligence reports.

In addition to our forward sites, we maintained a small presence in the Gulf of de Fonseca, which bordered Nicaragua and El Salvador headed by Horst J., an old former U.S. Special Forces Sergeant Major and his deputy, Dave H. As advisors, both men were responsible for training members of the Honduran Navy in a program known as "Las Piraneas." This program used specially designed fast boats that had radar, dual 150 horsepower engines, and 50 caliber machine guns mounted on the bow to patrol the Gulf of de Fonseca for arms, drug, and contraband smugglers. Our office in El Salvador had a similar program across the Gulf in Salvadoran waters under the tutelage of an officer named Dean N. Horst was as tough as they come and although he was approaching 65 years of age, he used to lead the Honduran Navy recruits in swimming tests across the Gulf.

On one occasion, the Peace Corp assigned to this location, a young man who began growing marijuana. Upon discovering the field, Horst made the young man run behind his vehicle rather than give him a ride back to town. Another incident Horst was involved in occurred when several bandits placed a tree across the road in order to stop his vehicle to rob him along the dirt road from Jicaro Galan to Amapala. When confronted, Horst reportedly threw a hand grenade at them. When he approached the injured robbers, one of the bandits mentioned that they had been conducting this type of activity for years to which Horst replied, "Well, then consider yourself lucky because you are not very good." I had a similar incident in Jicaro Galan when an individual approached me and asked for my money while I was stopping to get gas in my Toyota Land Cruiser. When I asked the man why I would give him my money, he drew a knife. When I produced my pistol, the odds quickly changed to my favor. After putting the knife back in his pocket, it was comical that the man continued to beg for money after just trying to rob me.

During my first visit to Amapala, also known as "Tiger Island", I was met by Horst and Dave and asked if I would mind meeting a retired U.S. Army Colonel who was living on the island. When I agreed, I was driven to a waterfront residence and introduced to an American named "Chan." Upon entering the residence, I was asked to remain in the foyer and told that the Colonel would be meeting with me shortly. After twenty or so minutes of conversation, I was told that the Colonel was ready to see me and as I entered the study, which had been converted into a bar, much to my surprise I was introduced to a lifelike statue of the infamous Kentucky Fried Chicken Colonel Sanders. You can only imagine how many new people fell for the same stunt upon arriving on Amapala for the first time.

One time as I was driving back to Tegucigalpa from Amapala with a case officer named Dave L., who was with the Defense Intelligence Agency (DIA), we decided to stop at a small restaurant in the town of Jicaro Galan to grab a quick bite to eat. Shortly after sitting down and ordering our food, several U.S. military personnel in civilian clothes, who Dave recognized, entered, nodded, and sat down near us. As Dave and I were discussing our trip to Amapala, it quickly became apparent that the soldiers, for some reason, were trying to "eavesdrop" on our conversation, maybe because they knew that Dave belonged to the DIA. When it became obvious of their intentions, Dave began by saying to me in a voice louder than usual,

"Can you believe that a Soviet submarine was spotted in the Gulf of de Fonseca yesterday?" to which I replied, "Yes, but no one is supposed to know about it". Then for the next five minutes or so, he fabricated an incredulous story describing in detail where and how the submarine was spotted as our new neighbors took in every tidbit of information. Unbelievable, but true; the following day, knowing full well that Dave and I had just returned from Amapala, an irate Steve M., the chief of our office, called both of us in and threw a draft intelligence report down on his desk. The report had been prepared by the Military Attaché's office in the U.S. Embassy and they wanted to coordinate with the CIA prior to distributing it. Much to our surprise, the report detailed the sighting of a Soviet submarine in the Gulf of de Fonseca and claimed that the information had been received from "sources whose reporting to date had not yet been corroborated." After confessing that, yes, we were the sources, and after describing how the whole incident occurred, Steve shouted for us to get the hell of his office as he grabbed the phone and told his secretary to get the Military Attaché on the line in an effort to squelch the report.

Gulf of De Fonseca, Honduras in 1985

* * *

In December 1988, Karen and I returned to the United States with Kelly and Matthew to spend Christmas with our families. (I cannot tell you how angry and sad I was on 21 December 1988, when Pan Am Flight 103 from London to New York exploded over the small town of Lockerbie, Scotland killing all 259 people on board and 11 others on the ground. Two of my friends were aboard that flight – Matt G., and Daniel O., a security officer from the U.S. Embassy in

Nicosia, Cyprus. The State Department believed that the bombing of Pan Am 103 was an action authorized by the Libyan Government. In May 2000, the trial of two Libyan intelligence officers charged with planting the bomb started in The Netherlands. It ended in February 2001 with the conviction of defendant Abdelbaset Ali Mohmed al-Megrahi who received a life sentence. The other defendant, Al Amin Khalifa Fhimah, was acquitted and set free.)

After spending Christmas in the United States with our families, both Karen and I were eager to return to Honduras and to the new life, that we had started there. While Karen focused on getting the house in order and attending children playgroups, I concentrated on my work. Our residence was located near the Honduran First Battalion and the Honduran police and intelligence services, and my day usually began by visiting these sites before driving to the operations base or the U.S. Embassy. For entertainment, on weekends we would frequently visit several of the small villages surrounding the capital of Tegucigalpa such as Via de Los Angeles, Lake Yahoa north of the city, or to the northern beach town of Tela. Once, Karen, the kids, and I even rented an entire island off the coast of Honduras named Sandy Key for $52.00 per night and stayed for five days. On Wednesday evenings, we bowled on a U.S. Embassy bowling team; on Thursday evenings, we played darts in a U.S. Embassy dart league; and on weekends, we played golf at the local Country Club, or basketball and football at the American school. During periods of increased threat, we played golf with our pistols attached to our hips. These activities were eventually curtailed, however, when a walk-in to the U.S. Embassy advised that a leftist group was planning to attack the bowling ally and sure enough, it was determined that he was telling the truth.

Shortly after returning to Honduras, on 26 January 1989, only minutes from our house, members of the Cinchonero Popular Liberation Movement gunned down the former head of the Honduran Armed Forces, retired General Gustavo Alvarez Martinez and his bodyguard as they exited a church in Tegucigalpa after attending mass. The Cinchonero members had disguised themselves as street repair workers and escaped in stolen vans. General Alvarez had been ousted from his office by fellow officers who had accused him of corruption and authoritarian tendencies. His nephew, Oscar Alvarez, was a good friend of mine and eventually would become the Minister of Public Safety and Security under Honduran President Ricardo Maduro Joest in 2002.

One of the first assignments I was given after returning from vacation was to work with a team of local police officers that monitored leftist groups who were trying to harm the U.S. Embassy and American citizens in Honduras. The initial group consisted of an assortment of men and women of all ages. All were provided with names such as Tio (uncle), Tia (aunt), Abuelo (Grandfather), Abuela (grandmother), etc and all were very street savvy. The team was also comprised of analysts who analyzed the information collected by the police officers. Shortly thereafter, I was asked to deploy with this new team and members of the State Department Diplomatic Security Staff to San Pedro Sula, Honduras. On 28 February 1989, we were assigned to support U.S. Ambassador Briggs during the Fifth Ministerial Conference between Central American Countries, members of the European Economic Community, and the Contadora group where the decision to negotiate a free trade agreement would be discussed. Because the U.S. Embassy had received information that leftist groups planned to disrupt the conference (including several death threats against Ambassador Briggs), we decided to pre-stage this new counter surveillance team at the hotel where Ambassador Briggs and other conference members were staying, at the conference itself, which was going to be held in a conference center in downtown San Pedro Sula, and along the routes to and from the conference center. As we were heading to San Pedro Sula however, we received word that the hotel where the Ambassador and many other dignitaries were to stay had just been bombed. Upon receiving this information, one of the State Department security officers immediately called the head of the United Fruit Company, who graciously offered his residence, a large villa on the outskirts of San Pedro Sula, to Ambassador Briggs to stay as his guest during the conference. We were grateful to find out that this residence was much more secure than any hotel in the city.

On the day of the Fifth Ministerial Conference, it was hot as hell, with temperatures way above 100 degrees Fahrenheit. Sweltering, all I can remember saying to myself was what a day to wear a Kevlar bulletproof vest—one of the only times in my life that I thought it prudent to wear one. Departing the residence early in the morning, we proceeded to the conference center in downtown San Pedro Sula; our small motorcade transporting Ambassador Briggs with counter surveillance members pre-positioned all along the route. As we were pulling up to the conference, one of the counter surveillance members on motorcycle reported that a white Toyota double cab pick-up truck matching the description of a vehicle that was involved in the hotel bombing the night before was spotted heading our way. The counter surveillance member added that the vehicle had four occupants inside—three men and one woman, all armed with M-16 rifles. Trust me when I say that hearing this type of information will get your adrenaline pumping. As the report was passed to the Honduran police, they soon located the vehicle and ended up chasing it all over the city but by some miracle, the vehicle managed to escape.

Later that evening, as we were returning to the conference center with the Ambassador for a reception and dinner party, I was surprised to see that the Hondurans had permitted a small carnival and fair to take place in the park directly in front of the conference center. Exiting our vehicle, my heart almost stopped when several young Honduran boys ages 8 to 10 threw an assortment of firecrackers at our feet. While several of the State Department security officers quickly covered the Ambassador and whisked him into the conference center, I am happy to report that the security detail, me included, did not open fire on those young boys, whose stupid actions could have gotten them killed.

Shortly after attending this conference, I was sitting in the U.S. Embassy when suddenly I heard a loud gunshot. Running to the sound of where the shot came from, I entered an office used by members of the State Department security office, and immediately saw the head of the Ambassador's security detail lying on the floor screaming and bleeding as two officers tried to administer first aid. As one of the security officers moved his hand to get additional gauze from a first aid kit to cover the wound, I was shocked to see a stream of blood spew from the wound that almost hit the ceiling. There was no doubt in my mind that the bullet had hit his femoral artery. I soon learned that the officers had just returned from the firearms range after re-qualifying and were in the process of cleaning their weapons when one went off, wounding the officer. Incredibly, the security officer survived, thanks in part to the quick actions of his two colleagues. To commemorate the incident, the security officer's shoe was nailed to the wall above the door. Following weeks in a local hospital, the security officer returned to the United States and never came back to Honduras.

I can sadly say that I know what it is like to be shot. While hunting quail with several friends from the U.S. Embassy in the Zamorano area of Honduras, I was accidentally shot by a fellow hunter with number 7 bird shot from his shotgun at a distance of less than 25 to 30 feet as quail flushed in all directions. Although approximately 32 pellets hit my legs and stomach, penetrating the skin, fortunately, I was wearing heavy canvas hunting pants and a jacket. Still, by the time I was carried back to my vehicle, which was parked about a mile away from where the incident happened my socks and shoes were drenched in blood. All I can say is thank God I was not hit in the groin and that the pellets were steel shot versus lead shot (lead being a softer metal, deforms on impact, inflicting a larger wound). As for the fellow hunter, who will remain anonymous, following the incident he became very, very distraught knowing that he had accidentally shot someone. For the record, this was never reported.

* * *

As we approached the anniversary of the 7 April 1988 burning of the U.S. Consulate, the aforementioned countersurveillance team was deployed to find out whether leftists were planning to stage demonstrations against the U.S. Embassy again—this proved to be so. On the eve of 7 April 1989, 10,000 protestors gathered in a park in downtown Tegucigalpa and headed to the embassy, burning flags and destroying vehicles along the way. As the mob worked their way, the team provided crucial information to the State Department Regional Security Officer and his staff who were sitting on the roof of the embassy observing the entire situation with me. This time as the crowd got within two blocks of the embassy, Honduran police and military units put a blocking force in front of them to prevent them from reaching it.

Diplomatic Security Team at U.S. Embassy, 7 April 1989

On 16 April 1989, while dining on our terrace with my brother, Jim, who was visiting from the U.S., we heard a large explosion and I jumped into my car and headed downtown. As I was driving, I heard from the chief of our office, Terry that one of his guards had told him that the explosion had occurred at the U.S. Embassy warehouse one kilometer northwest of the embassy. Arriving at the scene, which had been secured by Honduran security officials, I was met by the head of the Honduran bomb-squad, Captain Salomon de Jesus Escoto Salinas. Noticing a heavily damaged motorcycle and the partial remains of a body at the scene, I was informed that one person was killed and another seriously injured when a powerful explosive, that they were attempting to hurl from their motorcycle at the warehouse, exploded before they could throw it. Some speculated that the bomb was to be thrown by members of the Honduran left to commemorate the 7 April 1988 burning of the U.S. Consulate.

Later that evening, after assisting the bomb-squad with their post-blast investigation, I accompanied another Honduran Captain by the name of Billy Joya Amendola to the Escuela Hospital where he tried in vain to interview the semiconscious man. Fortunately, at the hospital we were able to find the man's partially destroyed jacket that contained his wallet and identification.

The Honduran bomb-squad at the time was poorly equipped, so I wrote a cable to Headquarters the following day requesting funds for equipment and training. Shortly thereafter, we arranged to have several Agency instructors travel to Honduras to provide training.

When the military base in the village of Lapterique was chosen as the site to hold the training, I coordinated with the Hondurans to construct a training site that would mirror what we had in the United States. Several structures were built and target vehicles, several cars and a bus, were purchased and transported to the site. At the conclusion of this training, we were able to hold similar training for bomb-squad members from the rest of the Central American countries at the Lapaterique facility under a new program known as Regional Intelligence Coordination Centers (RICC).

Explosive Training Site

Later when the building housing the Honduran bomb-squad, which was located less than 1.5 miles from the U.S. Embassy, began to deteriorate, Captain Billy Joya was advanced $54,000 dollars, and turned it into $324,000 USD on the black market in that the official exchange rate at the time was 2 to 1 and the black market rate was 6 to 1. This money was used to construct a new two-story bomb-squad building, and new kennels to house ten canines, which were purchased in New York and flown to Honduras. Labrador retrievers were the dogs of choice. A new canine training facility was built on the compound and, like with the bomb-squad training program, we ended up training canines and handlers from all of the RICC Central American countries in Honduras.

Canine Training Facility

The new bomb-squad building was beautiful. In addition to the living and sleeping quarters, money was used to construct and supply a new kitchen and photo lab. My present to them was a new pool table and television set. You cannot imagine how proud I was during the grand opening when I learned that the Honduran's wanted to name the building after me in my honor. Unfortunately, prior to my departure from Honduras, the chief of our office at the time, Jack G., made the Hondurans remove the small plaque with my name on it, which had been placed above the main entrance to the facility.

Due to my special relationship with the Honduran bomb-squad, I was immediately notified anytime a bomb was discovered or exploded. I was most interested when the U.S. Embassy, the American School, one of the U.S. companies, a residence housing Americans, or the Peace Corps (which was bombed on 19 December 1988) was involved. You would think that bombings were uncommon, but in Honduras in 1989, bombings were very common. It was not unusual for two or three bombs to detonate in the capital of Tegucigalpa or the northern cities of La Ceiba and San Pedro Sula in one night. Restaurants, banks, shopping centers, and supermarkets were favorite targets of the Honduran left. One evening I remember five separate explosive devices were discovered in five different supermarkets in Tegucigalpa. As I raced from one scene to the next with the Honduran bomb-squad, as they x-rayed and deactivated the devices with their water cannons/pan disrupters, the Hondurans ended up capturing two individuals who were placing the small devices in boxes. Both were wearing identical Casio wristwatches as those used in the devices found in the small boxes. You cannot believe how lucky several of the bomb-squad members were that evening when one of the bombs exploded only seconds after x-raying it in the last supermarket we visited. Fortunately, no one was injured.

In April 1989, ARENA's Alfredo Cristiani Burkhard won the Salvadoran presidential election with 54% of the vote replacing Christian Democrat Napoleon Duarte's administration. Shortly after the 1989 Salvadoran Presidential elections, I received a call from chief of our office, Terry W., instructing me to visit El Salvador to meet with the chief of our office there, Bob H., and the newly elected President Cristiani. While visiting one of our forward sites, I boarded a helicopter and shortly was enroute to the capital, San Salvador. As we touched down at a military base housing the Salvadoran General Staff in downtown San Salvador, the chief of our office, Bob H., and an officer named Frank M., met me. Minutes later, we were being driven to the Presidential Palace. Bob H. told me along the way that President Cristiani was looking for ways to improve his security because his newly appointed Attorney General, Roberto Garcia, had been killed the day before (on 19 April 1989) when an explosive device was placed on the roof of the Attorney General's armored vehicle by two men on a motorcycle. After listening intently to Bob, I explained how I thought we could assist President Cristiani. Upon meeting President Cristiani (a Georgetown University graduate who spoke perfect English), and his top Advisor Tony Tona, Cristiani began the conversation by saying that I had come highly recommended. During the course of our conversation, I was astonished to learn that he was still living in his personal residence and had not yet moved into the Presidential Palace. I was even more shocked to learn that his wife was still driving their children to and from school and other activities. Choosing my words carefully, I responded by saying something along the lines of *"Mr. President, the people of El Salvador have elected you to lead and serve this nation, therefore, you have a responsibility to the people who elected you to stay alive."* After making several recommendations, he paid me one of the highest compliments that I have ever received in my life. "Richard," he said, "I am the student and you are the teacher. Tell me what I need to do, and I will do it."

Upon returning to Honduras, I wrote a detailed cable to the Counterterrorism Center (CTC) requesting that they send a team of instructors to El Salvador. Of note, when Duarte's daughter, Ines Duarte Duran and her friend, were kidnapped by Salvadoran leftist rebels in 1985, President Duarte personally asked for an officer named Danny B. to assist in the negotiations for her release along with two Roman Catholic priests – Father Ellacuria and Monsignor Riveras Damas. Danny, a former Dade County Florida police officer, had been in charge of training Duarte's security detail and had made quite an impression on the President of El Salvador. More so, after he assisted in successfully negotiating the release of Duarte's kidnapped daughter.

President Cristiani's inauguration on 1 June1989 marked the first time that power had passed peacefully from one freely elected civilian leader to another in El Salvador. During his inauguration, Cristiani called for direct dialogue to end the decade of conflict between the government and guerrillas in which 75,000 people would die between 1980 and 1992. An unmediated dialogue process involving monthly meetings between the two sides was initiated in September 1989, lasting until the FMLN launched a bloody, nationwide offensive in November that year.

* * *

On 13 June 1989, Vice-President Dan Quayle visited Honduras during a trip to Latin America, which included stops in Guatemala, El Salvador, and Costa Rica from 11 to 14 June. (Before his arrival, I can still remember meeting with members of VP Quayle's staff, the U.S. Secret Service, and Honduran police and intelligence services at the airport in Tegucigalpa to discuss the details of the trip.)

A young officer from the VP's staff (who was serving as the "White House advance person" for this portion of the trip), began by giving a ten minute overview on where the VP's plane would park, where the press would be located, and where the motorcade vehicles would be staged. Afterwards, I politely reminded the young man that, as Americans, we were guests in Honduras. Instead of "telling" the Hondurans what to do, he might want to consider asking their opinion to determine what works best for them since this was not the first visit by a dignitary to Honduras. Much to my delight, Honduran police Captain Billy Joya politely spoke up and remarked, "No, it is best to park the plane here, place the press over there, and stage the motorcade vehicles here." Lastly, the Hondurans advised that they would be placing several snipers on the roof of the airport for additional security measures. The only thing that the head of the USSS advance team asked for was to ensure that the snipers did not point their rifles and scopes at the VP upon his arrival. The USSS further requested that Honduran helicopters not fly over the motorcade as it was proceeding from one point to another.

On the day of the visit, the first comical incident occurred when one of the USSS drivers, who had a bad case of diarrhea, had to quickly exit the VP's armored limousine prior to the VP's arrival and accidentally locked the vehicle before handing it over to one of his colleagues as he sped to the bathroom. After trying in vain to open the limousine and without a spare set of keys on hand, I politely informed the USSS that the Hondurans had a person on their staff that was skilled at breaking into automobiles. Although the USSS repeatedly declined our offer, as the VP's plane landed, the Honduran was given the "green light" to attempt to break in and within minutes had the limousine open. As Vice-President Quayle began his decent of the portable stairs from the plane, my radio started squawking and all I could hear was the head of the USSS counterassault team screaming something about the Hondurans having their rifles and scopes on the VP. As you can imagine, when I looked up on the roof, sure enough, all eight of the Honduran snipers were pointing their rifles at Vice-President Quayle in an attempt to get a better look at him via their scopes. This led to the USSS counter assault team snipers pointing their rifles at the Honduran snipers until my Honduran counterpart, Captain Billy Joya, calmly radioed to the Honduran snipers to "get their rifles off" the Vice-President.

Prior to the motorcade departing the airport via one of the main gates in the rear of the airfield, we noticed that someone had placed a large chain with a new padlock on it. As everyone began scrambling for a key, I calmly produced a large bolt cutter that I carried with me in my Toyota Land Cruiser and cut the padlock just as the motorcade began to leave. Lastly, much to the displeasure of the USSS, Honduran helicopters constantly flew directly over the motorcade as it worked its way to the presidential palace in downtown Tegucigalpa where Vice-President Quayle was scheduled to meet with President, Jose Simen Azcona del Hoyo.

Vice-President Quayle was scheduled to stay as a guest of U.S. Ambassador Everett Briggs in the Ambassador's villa on top of a mountain overlooking Tegucigalpa during his visit. Several days earlier I had accompanied the USSS and several U.S. military aides to the Ambassador's compound to conduct a survey of potential helicopter landing zones (HLZs) in the event that the USSS needed to evacuate the VP from the compound. Due to the number of trees on the compound and antennas on the roof of the residence, neither the USSS nor the military aides believed it possible to safely land a helicopter in the compound and therefore, a small field approximately one mile north of the compound was identified as the HLZ to use in an emergency evacuation. Pointing out that this would require the VP being driven in his motorcade to this location, I offered to have one of our Agency pilots survey the compound to see if he could land a helicopter there. Receiving permission to do so, I radioed our air operations office and requested that one of our pilots conduct a fly over to determine if he could land. As one of our Agency helicopters arrived 30 minutes later, our pilot, "Big Mike", after surveying the compound, simply replied that he could land his Huey helicopter on the tennis court if we took the net down. With the USSS and the military aides saying that was impossible, I dropped the net to the tennis court and we all watched in amazement as Mike slowly descended and landed within the fenced court. As he exited the helicopter alone, dressed in blue jeans and a Hawaiian shirt, the USSS and the military aid replied that we could use our pilot and helicopter for emergency evacuation–but only if Mike agreed to fly with a co-pilot and a crew chief, to which he agreed to.

Prior to Ambassador Everett Briggs' departure from Honduras on 15 June 1989, I was asked by the deputy chief of our office, Steve M., to accompany him to a ceremony in Yamales that the Contras wanted to host for the Ambassador. What a sight it was, to see 18,000 Contras assembled to pay tribute to the Ambassador who had supported them throughout much of this conflict. After his departure, Ambassador Briggs was replaced by Ambassador Cresencio Arcos. One afternoon, shortly after Ambassador Arcos' arrival, I remember being called by the Embassy RSO, Sy D., after a package was dropped off by two men in a vehicle at one of the guard posts outside the U.S. Embassy. The package was wrapped in brown wrapping paper, similar to that of a paper bag, and addressed in magic marker to the U.S. Ambassador, Criscencio Arcos. The men who dropped off the package did not tell the guards what was inside, and Ambassador Arcos' name was misspelled, so the guards decided to bring the package into the U.S. Embassy and x-ray it—not a smart idea. When Sy asked me to look at the x-ray, I immediately called the Honduran bomb-squad—the x-ray revealed a box with tubes and what appeared to be wires inside. When the bomb-squad arrived and looked at the x-ray, they concurred that it could be an explosive device and the decision was made to deactivate the device in place using a water cannon/pan disrupter. You could have heard a pin drop when we all realized that the package contained specially wrapped Honduran cigars for Ambassador Arcos; each one individually, wrapped and placed in a tube with his name monogrammed on the side. I can still recall trying to explain to Ambassador Arcos, before he threw me out of his office, why we blew up his cigars. Looking back on the incident, I probably would have made the same call again.

* * *

In late June 1989, I was sitting in a staff meeting hosted by our chief, Terry W., when he held up a report and began to rant and rave about the amount of weapons, ammunition and explosives crossing Honduras from Nicaragua to El Salvador.

"Intelligence!" Terry screamed, *"without intelligence we have no idea where the weapons are originating from, how they are being concealed and transported, where they are entering Honduras, and where they are entering El Salvador".* After Terry completed his tirade, I calmly raised my hand and remarked *"Terry, I am confident that if we can get the Honduran Government re-focused on this issue, within six months you will see the largest seizure in the history of Central America."* When everyone in the room continued to remain silent, some snickering under their breath, Terry calmly asked me to describe how we could get the Honduran Government re-focused. I began by saying that in talking to my Honduran counterpart, Captain Billy Joya, I learned that in 1983, the Honduran Government had embarked on an initiative to stem the flow of arms entering Honduras using Mobile Search Teams (MSTs). A training program was implemented to look for

false compartments, and the Hondurans purchased an assortment of equipment, gear, and vehicles (three 24-foot trucks similar to those used by U-Haul or Ryder rentals). But the MST's had, had only one success in six years (1983-1989) when an assortment of rifles and ammunition was found concealed in the ceiling of a tractor trailer after it had collided with a Lada along Central America (CA) Highway 1 near the town of Jicaro Galan in Honduras. Apparently, one of the major problems facing the MSTs, in those days, was the size of the trucks used to haul personnel and equipment in remote areas as well as the cost of fuel to operate them and thus, the 24-foot trucks remained parked with minimal mileage on them. At the conclusion of my remarks, I told Terry that with his concurrence, I would meet with Billy to see if the Hondurans would be interested in resurrecting their MST program.

The following day after my meeting with Billy, I reported to Terry that the Hondurans liked the idea of resurrecting the MST program due to the increased amount of arms, ammunition and explosives entering their country. Over the next several weeks, the Honduran Government began interviewing, vetting and selecting 36 individuals to compliment 12 of the original 1983 MST members for four new 12-member MST teams.

In that Honduras southern border with Nicaragua is marked by three major border crossings, the decision was made to deploy an MST to La Fraternidad/El Espino along the Honduran/Nicaraguan border where the Pan American Highway (also known as Central American (CA) Highway 1) crosses the border and continues across Honduras to El Amatillo where it enters El Salvador; another MST at El Amatillo along the Honduran/El Salvadoran border; one MST at the northernmost crossing at El Paraiso (also known as Los Manos) near Danli in the El Paraiso Department, where the highway continues to Tegucigalpa and Yuscurra; and one MST in Tegucigalpa on standby as a reactionary force in the event that the Hondurans developed information and had to depart quickly. A fifth MST was eventually deployed at the southernmost border crossing located at Guasaule in the Choluteca Department just east of El Triunfo to cover Guasaule and the Central American Highway 3 (CA-3), a southern excursion of the Pan American Highway that links Choluteca, Honduras with Puerto Corinto, Nicaragua and points southeast.

With funding from his government, Captain Billy Joya purchased 24 brand new Toyota Land Cruisers in Panama to transport personnel and equipment (mirrors, tools, drills, portable x-ray equipment, generators, and lights) to conduct inspections. In order to recognize these new teams throughout the country, the Hondurans purchased black special weapons assault team (SWAT) vests and hats so that they would stand apart from the normal Honduran police and military units wearing military fatigues.

When the 24 Toyota Land Cruisers and equipment arrived, I and several of my colleagues were invited to attend a ceremony where it was all laid out on the ground in front of the Head of the Honduran Armed Forces as the 48 new MST members looked on in uniform at full attention. During the ceremony, we were told that the new MST members would be taught to look for "indicators" that were out of place, did not belong, or factors which would lend someone to believe that there might be a false compartment of some kind; i.e. fresh paint; scratches; new linoleum, metal or wood on the floor, walls or ceilings; and new tires along side of old tires. More importantly, the MST members would be trained to tap on areas to determine if they sounded hollow or solid and would be inserting hoses into gas tanks and containers to see if they contained fuel or other liquids.

New MST Equipment

Several Honduran newspaper articles and television news reports (intended to educate the populace on the mission of the MSTs), accompanied the deployment of these new teams by the Honduran Government. In addition to resurrecting the MST program, the news reports claimed that the Honduran Government would be enhancing their legal border crossings by adding additional drop bars, access control areas, and search areas.

Honduran Border Crossing Construction

As part of this new initiative, buildings were constructed and remodeled by the Honduran Government to house personnel and computers so that they could begin registering vehicles and personnel entering and departing their country at each border crossing. When a vehicle entered or departed, a log would be kept on the type of vehicle, its contents, origin, destination, and information on the driver. According to the news reports, monthly reports would be issued, watch lists maintained, and reports would be sent to the other border crossings in the event that a vehicle or driver was suspicious.

From the outside, the structures were said to look very primitive but on the inside, it was said that it was not uncommon for them to have an assortment of computers, uninterrupted power supplies (UPS), fax machines, telephones, and air conditioning. The news also mentioned that kennels were being constructed to house several canines trained to sniff out explosives that were added to supplement the Mobile Search Teams.

Border Crossing

In addition to searching vehicles at the legal crossings, the newspaper articles and television reports outlined how the MSTs would be operating at the illegal crossings or "blind passes" known as Paseo Ciegos along the borders. Equipped with night vision goggles, the MST's intercepted and inspected any vehicle or individual who attempted to cross the border.

While most using illegal border crossings did so out of habit and were not involved in anything illicit, the reports indicated that still a large amount of contraband (coffee, cigarettes, liquor, sneakers, clothing, medicine, cosmetics, and toiletries) was routinely found and confiscated.

I found it comical that on one occasion an MST member reportedly opened up several sacks in the back of a pick-up truck late one night only to find that they were filled with iguanas and armadillos—both delicacies in Honduras, although armadillo meat is a carrier of the deadly disease, leprosy.

The news reports continued that most of the time the MSTs set up during the day or evenings directly on the border or a half mile or so inland—preferably at a curve in the road to add the element of surprise. By day and night, the MSTs were careful to display signs that read that these were "official Honduran check points" (Puesto de Registro). For vehicles that tried to ignore the signs and the MST members trying to flag them down, a chain with nails was laid across the road in serpentine intervals that would flatten tires.

Honduran MST Deployment

In addition, the Hondurans were careful to ensure that each MST deployed with a Honduran Immigration officer specially trained to spot and identify false documents and to question individuals. In order to ensure their safety and security as they searched the vehicles and questioned the occupants, several MST members, armed with machine guns, rifles, and grenade launchers, served as sentries. It was an impressive sight to see film footage on the television and photographs in the newspapers of these new teams deployed around Tegucigalpa, along the Pan American Highway, and along the Honduran borders.

Shortly after the first Honduran MSTs were deployed, a Central American Summit was held in Tela, Honduras during the first week of August 1989. With Presidents from each of the five Central American countries on hand, the governments of these countries entered into a series of accords to promote peace and democracy in the region. On 7 August 1989, the "Tela Accord" was signed condemning the actions by Nicaraguan President Daniel Ortega to end the cease-fire with the Nicaraguan Resistance and to commence offensive military operations again.

The accord further called on Ortega to reverse that decision and for both the Government of Nicaragua and the Nicaraguan Resistance to abide by the cease-fire. Part of this accord, without U.S. input, produced a new schedule for Contra demobilization with a deadline of 5 December 1989. Although the Organization of American States (OAS) agreed to supervise the process and the U.S. Government expressed disapproval of the new agreement, the United States Congress approved $49.7 million in humanitarian aid to the Contras to be given through February 1990. The White House and Congress further agreed that the Contra aid would be cut off, however, if the Nicaraguan rebels failed to disband.

On 18 October 1989, several of the Honduran newspapers reported that a MST assigned to La Fraternidad/El Espino hit pay dirt less than six months after the program was resurrected, when the largest seizure of weapons, ammunition, and explosives in the history of Central America was discovered inside the walls and floors of a truck coming from Nicaragua enroute to the FMLN in El Salvador. During a routine inspection, one of the MST Officers discovered several hundred Soviet, East German, Polish, Hungarian, Czechoslovakian, Danish and U.S. manufactured rifles, ammunition, rifle propelled grenades, rocket propelled grenades and launchers, explosives, detonation cord, timing devices, blasting caps, claymore mines, radios, and an assortment of FLMN training material cleverly concealed in the walls. In addition, several hundred mortars were discovered in the floor.

FURGON UTILIZADO PARA TRANSPORTAR LAS ARMAS
CON DESTINO AL SALVADOR, EN LA FRONTERA DE
LA FRATERNIDAD, SAN MARCOS DE COLON, DEPTO.
DE CHOLUTECA.
18 DE OCTUBRE, 1989

The vehicle had been a refrigerated cargo truck (pictured above) that was hauling furniture. When inspecting the rear of the truck, an MST Lieutenant noticed corrugated steel panels had been welded to the floor and walls. After removing the furniture and inspecting the vehicle further, the Lieutenant began to tap on the walls and noticed that some sections sounded hollow. Suspecting false compartments, the Lieutenant gave the order to tear into the walls.

Two hours later, after removing the steel corrugated panels, which were even more difficult to remove because spot welds had been placed on top of the screws securing the panels, the MST members discovered hundreds of rifles, ammunition, and explosives embedded in the walls. As several MST members pounded on the floor with steel pry bars trying to peel back the steel corrugated panels on the floor, the MST Lieutenant had to scream at them to stop because they did not know what was beneath the floor.

Their worst suspicions were confirmed when the MST members discovered that the floor was lined with over one thousand 60 and 81 mm mortar rounds primed and ready to go.

Mobile Search Team (MST) Arms Seizure-La Fraternidad, Honduras 1989

Honduras MST arms seizure in 1989

Following the international release of this news, I can still recall seeing the U.S. Ambassador to the United Nations, on television, holding up a Soviet AK-47 rifle from this seizure in front of the United Nations while condemning Nicaraguan President Ortega.

Much to the Hondurans delight, they also found the codes to the radios. While tracing the weapons, the Hondurans discovered that some had originated in Russia, were sent to Cuba, and ended up in Nicaragua.

Several of the articles highlighted that the seizure demonstrated that the Sandinista Government, headed by Daniel Ortega, was not interested in promoting peace and democracy in the region and was continuing to supply weapons, explosives, and ammunition to the FMLN despite the Tela Accord in August of that year.

After driving to La Fraternidad/El Espino, a three-hour drive from Tegucigalpa, to see first hand the enormous amount of seized weapons and ammunition which had been publicly displayed on the Pan American highway for reporters and news crews to document, I returned to my residence four days later at 4:00 a.m. With only four hours sleep, my radio went off on the morning of 22 October 1989 at approximately 8:00 a.m. with the sound of my radio code name being repeated over and over by one of my fellow officer's. When I finally responded, Charlie W., reported that a TAN (Transportes Aereos Nacionales)/SAHSA (Servicíos Aereos de Honduras S.A.) Boeing 727-200 (N88705), after drifting from its VOR/DME to Runway 01 at 7:45 a.m had crashed into a 6,000-foot mountain near Cerro de Hules (Translated into "rubber hill"); some 5,000 feet from the runway at Toncontin International Airport in Tegucigalpa. As

Charlie was talking to me, our medical services officer, Tom M., was busy assembling the rest of our emergency rescue team that had been organized shortly after his arrival in August 1989. At weekly meetings, each one of the all-volunteer team were trained by Tom in fundamental first aid and the use of specialized emergency medical gear. As a unit, this six-man team had practiced rescue techniques including rappelling from helicopters from as high as 300 feet and using special rescue gear.

In addition to medical officer Tom M. and branch chief Charlie W., the remaining team consisted of myself, two operation officers, Larry W. and Pedro T., and a communications officer Dan S. Responsible for securing the site, I was always the first one down the rappel line. Organized to support Agency projects, the team was activated during the crash because local emergency resources were completely overwhelmed.

As I headed to the airport that morning, one of our helicopters, standing by for a planned mission, departed immediately to the crash site. Sighting survivors, our air operations personnel managed to land in the mountainous terrain, picked up three passengers that were badly injured, and transported them to ambulances waiting at the nearby Toncontin airport. Arriving at the airport, our team was met by Captain Billy Joya, who stated that he would accompany us. When we arrived at the crash site in a second helicopter, the scene was chaotic.

Ill equipped, unprepared, and disorganized, my first impression was that local authorities were unable to deal with the emergency and could not stop the looting that had begun. I am proud to say that our arrival immediately brought a sense of order and purpose to the scattered rescue efforts. Starting in the aircraft, we made a systematic search for survivors. Individual team members climbed into the still burning wreckage, maneuvered around pieces with razor sharp metal fragments, and pressed into sections that were precariously perched on the mountainside.

Afterwards, we quickly established a security perimeter around the aircraft and searched the remainder of the wreckage-strewn half-mile crash site. When all possibility of finding other survivors was exhausted, we returned to the fuselage where most of the bodies remained. Throughout the day, we battled the fire and slowly moved forward through the wreckage to remove the bodies before the intense heat destroyed the remains, collecting all personal items that might assist with identification.

Tans Sasha Airline Crash Tegucigalpa, Honduras 1989

This crashed killed 123 of the 138 passengers on board and half of the eight-member crew, including several RIGG and USAID employees from the U.S. Embassy. As a result, of our efforts, 70 victims were extricated and identified, including a U.S. Marine security guard watch stander from the U.S. Embassy in Managua who was aboard the flight. In addition, with some local assistance, we located and retrieved the black box as well as some official documents that were part of a classified pouch.

Looking back on that day, our team was the only organized, purposeful, and properly equipped rescue effort at the crash site that morning. Although we were organized for Agency support, we quickly mobilized in a lifesaving effort that was carried out with great courage. In the best tradition of Agency employees, we stepped into a disintegrating situation, took charge, and pressed forward at great risk. I believe that our response that day was a model of what the Agency is all about–anticipating problems, preparing collectively, and collaborating to achieve a common goal.

Upon returning to Tegucigalpa, exhausted after being at the crash site for the better part of ten hours, I took a long shower. I was preparing to take a nap when I was reminded by Karen that we had a dinner party to go to that evening at the residence of my good friend, Assistant Regional Security Officer (ARSO) Ray F. and his wife,

Elizabeth. I cannot describe how bizarre it was sitting around the table that evening discussing the events of that morning with no one in the room, other than Karen knowing that I had been at the crash scene the entire day. More bizarre was the fact that the U.S. Embassy brought in two psychiatrists for embassy employees to talk to due to the number of embassy employees that were killed on the flight. However, no one ever approached any of us on the rescue team to see how we were feeling or coping with the incident.

The following morning, much to my surprise, I was asked to return to the site by the new chief of our office, Steve M., who had just replaced Terry W., to continue sifting through the debris due to the number of classified documents that were on the plane including those from several diplomatic pouches.

Six months later a Tan Sasha cargo plane slammed into the same mountain killing the pilot, co-pilot and crew chief that were aboard. Déjà vu set in when several of us were again called to the scene while viewing the remnants of the first Tan Sasha plane crash as we landed in the helicopter to search for survivors from this second crash. As we were returning to the civilian side of the airport runway that morning from the crash scene, I noticed a large inbound helicopter that was flying low on the horizon towards the military side of the airport.

Sandinista MI-24 (Hind-D) Helicopter Defection-Tegucigalpa, Honduras 1989

This helicopter did not look like anything that I had ever seen in my life. It stopped in front of the military traffic control tower and began to descend; I quickly exited our helicopter, jumped in my Toyota Land Cruiser, and drove across the runway to see a Sandinista Mi-24 Hind-D helicopter parked in front of the control tower with the pilot in a Sandinista flight suit being escorted inside by two Honduran military officers. Knowing that the pilot was probably defecting after flying low to avoid the Honduran radar, I carefully opened up the door to the helicopter and began taking photo after photo of the control panel and the cockpit. After exiting it and starting on my second roll of 24 pictures, several Honduran security personnel–called upon to provide security for the helicopter, asked me who I was and what I was doing there.

Although I showed them my credentials, one of the security guards proceeded to open my camera and rip out the film. Luckily for me, I had just put the new roll of film in and, therefore, was able to keep the other roll of 24 which I had concealed in the inside pocket of my jacket. As I was escorted from the airport, I immediately drove to the U.S. Embassy to report that a Sandinista pilot had defected with his Mi-24 Hind-D helicopter and handed my film to a fellow officer who proceeded to develop it.

Inside of the Hind-D helicopter

Even in black and white, the photos were excellent and showed details of a Hind-D rarely ever seen outside the Soviet Union. The pilot, we were later told, claimed that he had defected after hearing reports that the Americans were willing to pay one million USD for anyone defecting with a Hind-D helicopter.

Unfortunately, for him, the editor of Soldier of Fortune magazine had made this promise and not the U.S. Government and he never received his payoff. After being debriefed for months by members of the Honduran and U.S. military, the pilot and the Mi-24 Hind-D helicopter were allowed to return to Managua shortly after Violeta Chamorro was elected President of Nicaragua in February 1990.

* * *

In late November 1989, I returned to San Salvador amid rumors of a large offensive being planned by the FMLN guerrillas. During my visit, the Salvadoran police captured a terrorist named Fausto Gallardo Valdez who, during interrogation, provided information that an American citizen named Jennifer Jean Casolo, who resided in the Miralvalle neighborhood of San Salvador, was storing weapons used for terrorist acts. In view of the confession by Valdez, the police requested the participation of representatives of the U.S. Embassy be present when they entered the residence on 24 November 1989. Searching the residence, the police found a large number of weapons buried in the yard (103 shells for 60mm mortars, 213 blocks of TNT, 405 electronic detonating caps, 150 feet of timing fuse, 15 knives, several AK-47 magazines, 12,510 AK-47 cartridges, 9,110 M-16 rifle cartridges, 325 G-3 rifle shells and an enormous amount of documents belonging to the FMLN-FDR); [Farabundo Marti National Liberations Front-Revolutionary Democratic Front.]

Arraigned for eight days after her arrest, Casolo was released by a judge "for lack of evidence". Clearly, as an American, there were political factors involved. Although Casolo claimed that she was subjected to physical and psychological torture during her detention, it is interesting to note that she was accompanied by a U.S. Embassy official the entire time. Later after Casolo returned to the United States, police arrested a woman named Aguilar Marroquin (alias Marina) as she was fleeing the scene after having placed a bomb on the engine of a bus. During questioning, Aguilar Marroquin admitted that she was an active member of the People's Revolutionary Army, that the person in charge of logistics for this organization was the American Casolo, and that she had obtained the explosive material from Casolo's residence in the Miravalle area of San Salvador.

The evening of 28 November 1989, while sitting in the bar of the Sheraton Hotel in downtown San Salvador with some of my co-workers, we began to hear several large explosions followed by gunfire. Without exchanging a word, all of us knew that the much-anticipated FMLN offensive had begun with the rebels entering the northern suburbs of San Salvador and being repelled by Salvadoran government troops with the support of the Salvadoran Air Force. As our radios began to crackle with information coming in dribs and drabs, we soon found out that the large explosions had occurred at the power plant while the smaller ones were from explosives being placed on the street transformers to knock out the power throughout the city.

U.S Embassy in El Salvador

While the guerrillas moved from street to street with the armed forces in pursuit, several decided to breach the wall of the residence belonging to the chief of our office, Bob H. Upon seeing them enter his yard, Bob and his wife retreated to their master bedroom. Although the guerillas knew that there was someone in the bedroom hiding, unable to breach the door, they decided to make themselves at home. For the next several hours, the guerrillas cooked, slept, and used the showers and bathroom. As Bob repeatedly called for assistance, no one was able to respond due to the fighting in the streets. Finally, when the guerillas decided to leave the house and set it on fire, one of our technical services officers, Al K., drove a group of Salvadoran soldiers to the residence and staged a heroic rescue for which he later would be awarded a medal.

Returning to Tegucigalpa shortly after the FLMN offensive, I learned that Rafael Callejas had won the Presidential election in

Honduras several days earlier on 26 November 1989. As was the case with President Cristiani in El Salvador, we offered to send a team of instructors from the Counterterrorism Center (CTC) to meet with the new Honduran President. Several weeks later, I received a call at 2:30 a.m. informing me that there had been a shooting in front of the Honduran President's residence.

Unlike President Cristiani, the new Honduran President had decided against living in the Presidential Palace in downtown Tegucigalpa. Arriving at the scene, I saw the body of a man who had been shot in the head approximately 100 yards from the President's compound. One of the soldiers who I had trained claimed the man had fired at the residence several times from his vehicle as it passed. After firing, the man then stopped at the end of the street, exited his vehicle with his weapon and proceeded towards the soldier who lowered his rifle, a 7.62 Fusil Automatique Léger (FAL), and shot the individual in the head. When I tried to comfort the soldier, he remarked that before shooting the man, the only thing that he could remember from the training was me repeatedly saying *"when confronted, shoot or otherwise you would be the one lying on the ground"*. While it is difficult to take someone's life, I told the soldier that he had done the right thing.

Thinking about the residence of the President of Honduras brings back several memories. One involves a member of the USSS detail by the name of Frank Y. throwing a football with the son of the Honduran President in the backyard of the residence during a trip by Vice-President Quayle as the President of Honduras and Vice-President Quayle both looked on with admiration as the President's son caught pass after pass.

On another occasion, one evening as Karen and I were driving home from a restaurant I hit a horse that was lying in the middle of the road near the residence of the President of Honduras. Since it was very dark and the road winding, I did not even have time to brake. The horse was killed instantly. Fortunately, we were driving the Toyota Land Cruiser instead of Karen's small Subaru. With the latter, we definitely would have been killed. Even with the front engine of the Toyota Land Cruiser heavily damaged, I was still able to pull the vehicle off the road before losing all of the fluid in the radiator. After walking the rest of the way to our residence, the following morning, I was awakened by a call from my friend Oscar Alvarez, who began the conversation by laughing and saying "Richard, last night as we were coming back from the Presidential

Palace with the President we had to avoid a horse lying in the road that some asshole hit and left lying there. The motorcade barely missed it." In response I replied, *"Oscar, I was the asshole that hit the horse and if you would have looked closely you would have seen my Land Cruiser parked alongside the road."*

To this day, we both laugh when discussing the incident although I know that Karen and I could easily have been killed. Total damage to the Toyota Land Cruiser was $12,000 USD. Unbelievably, several weeks after getting it back from the repair shop, I rounded another curve in the same road only to hit a donkey, which was tied to several other donkeys' carrying firewood on their backs. Fortunately, I was not driving very fast at the time so I barely hit the first donkey, which immediately fell to the ground, causing a domino effect with the rest. Looking in my rearview mirror, all I can recall seeing were donkey's bucking while trying to get back on their feet and firewood flying all over the place.

Shortly after the above incident, while driving back to Tegucigalpa along the Honduran/Salvadoran border north of El Amatillo, a Honduran MST stopped me just as it began to get dark. As I was being questioned, a U.S. military convoy came racing past me towards the checkpoint. Ignoring the MST officer trying to flag down the convoy, and the sign, which read that it was an official Honduran checkpoint, the convoy eventually came to a screeching halt when they noticed the chain of nails that had been placed across the road. Several more feet and the convoy probably would have been fired upon as they entered the MST secure zone reserved for inspections. As an irate U.S. Army Major descended his HUM-V vehicle swearing at the top of his lungs and demanding to know why a U.S. Army convoy was being stopped, one of the MST Lieutenants who spoke some English, calmly reminded the Major that this was an official Honduran checkpoint. The Honduran Lieutenant further wanted to know why the Major and his convoy had disobeyed the MST officer with the flag, ignored the signs, and had not stopped.

Seeing that the situation was escalating and on the verge of getting out of control, I walked over to the convoy. Seeing me, the U.S. Army Major immediately asked, "Who the f--- are you?" My response went something like this: *"Major, do you realize that it is dark and that you are driving along the border of Honduras and El Salvador although there is a prohibition for any American to be within ten kilometers of the border. On top of that, you purposely ignored signs saying that this was an official Honduran checkpoint and your convoy could easily have been fired upon. Your actions have put you and your men at risk and therefore, I will be speaking to your commanding officer at Pomerola/Soto Cano Air Base tomorrow. And, by the way, if you need to ask me who I am, then you are dumber than I initially thought."*

The Major, realizing the gravity of the situation and the fact that I might be CIA because CIA officers had special dispensation to operate along the borders, began to plead with me saying that he and his men were on their way back to Pomerola/Soto Cano and were running late. The Major added that he decided to try the road along the border rather than the highway through Tegucigalpa to save time. Before dismissing the Major, I asked him to apologize to the Honduran Lieutenant and reminded him that we, as Americans, were guests in Honduras. The next day, I phoned the Base Commander at Pomerola and had an interesting conversation with him concerning the Major and the incident.

Later, when driving along the Salvadoran/Honduran border with Captain Salomon Jesus Escoto and several of his colleagues early one morning, Captain Escoto decided to invite me to his parent's farm (finca) to rest since none of us had gotten much sleep during the past few days. As the sun was beginning to rise, I could barely keep my eyes open while driving and, suddenly, I realized that I had driven off the road. Salomon, who was in the front seat with me immediately awoke and asked me if everything was all right. Realizing where we were, Salomon offered to drive the remaining few miles to his parent's farm and I readily accepted. Jumping into the passenger seat, all I could think about was getting some much-needed sleep. Several minutes later, however, I awoke to realize that we had again driven off the road – this time with Salomon sound asleep at the wheel. All I can say is that with both incidents we were lucky to be alive.

Not wanting to take any more chances, I exited the vehicle and splashed water in my face. Finally, after what seemed like hours, we pulled into the farm and were warmly greeted by Captain Escoto's mother and father who graciously told us that we could rest without worrying. Within minutes, I strung my hammock up between two trees only to be awoken an hour or so later by the sound of gunshots. Half-dazed, I looked through bleary eyes to see several of the Captain's colleagues shooting at iguanas that were perched high up in the trees with their rifles—with the intent of cooking them for lunch. The rounds were passing right through the iguanas as they continued to cling to the branches. Knowing that I would not be able to get any additional sleep unless I intervened, I grabbed my pistol, aimed it at a large iguana high in the tree, and fired. It fell to the ground with a thud as one of the Hondurans inspected the small bullet hole on one side of the iguana and the large exit hole on the other.

Several iguanas later, I knew that I could finally return to my hammock as several Honduran's began to skin the iguanas and prepare lunch. Another hour or two later and I awoke to find a table carefully prepared with fried iguana that was cooked in hot oil after being soaked in coconut milk and rolled in battered eggs and breadcrumbs. In addition, we ate huge ripe mango fruit (which I recall got stuck in everyone's teeth) from several of the trees on the property. And, yes—the iguana tasted like chicken—and it was one of the best meals that I can remember eating in Honduras. Our normal meals while traveling, consisted of refried red beans (frijoles) and rice, red meat (carne asada), or fried chicken (pollo) with tortillas and warm Coca Cola.

* * *

The U.S. military presence in Honduras expanded in the late 1980s as a result of the civil war in neighboring Nicaragua (supported by the U.S. backed Contras, right-wing rebels fighting the Sandinista Government of Nicaragua). As U.S. military personnel arrived in the country to coordinate material support to the Contras and to conduct training maneuvers, more and more attacks against the Sandinista Government were launched from safe havens in Honduras. "Special Project" was the code name for the secret arming of the contra rebels from bases in Honduras in 1983.

Adolpho Calero addressing the Nicaraguan Resistance (Contras) 1986

Adolpho Calero with the Nicaraguan Resistance (Contras) 1986

Enrique Bermudez

Major General John Singlaub with
Nicaraguan Resistance (Contras) 1986

Nicaraguan Resistance Leader Jose Benito Bravo aka Comandante "Mack"

Nicaraguan "Comandantes"

Contras with redeye missiles supplied by the U.S.

To add fuel to the fire, during a June 1983 visit to Honduras, DCI William (Bill) Casey decided to provide the Nicaraguan rebels with training in psychological warfare, a step that led to the writing of a manual that caused a furor in the U.S. Congress. (To my knowledge, I am the only person that has an original copy of this manual.)

In May 1986, Casey returned to Honduras while I was TDY. He visited several of the Contra bases to include Yamales along with the chief of our office, Vince S., and the Chief of the Central American Task Force (CATF), Alan F., who was the CIA

Headquarters official most heavily involved with efforts to support the Contras notwithstanding the limits of the Boland Amendment upon Contra aid. Having my camera with me, I took photograph after photograph of Casey's meeting with the Contras that day (a visit that never officially took place). Five years later, on 9 July 1991, Alan F. plead guilty to two counts of withholding information from Congress while entering the plea as part of an agreement to cooperate with an Independent Counsel's investigation, and on 31 January 1992, he was sentenced to one hundred hours of community service to be performed within one year of his sentence. Alan F. was eventually pardoned by President George H. Bush on 24 December 1992.

DCI William (Bill) Casey during visit to Honduras in May 1986

DCI William (Bill) Casey's visit with the Contras in Honduras May 1986

DCI William (Bill) Casey's visit with the Contras in Honduras May 1986

* * *

The presence of Contra forces and American military personnel provoked considerable animosity for many Hondurans. In fact, several groups associated with the political left formed to combat their presence with terrorism. Thus, Honduras, which had largely been spared the extensive terrorism associated with long civil wars in other Central American countries, saw an increase in terrorist bombings and assassinations in the late 1980s.

These bombings were largely associated with the Contra crisis and the Frente Patriótico Morazanista (Morazanist Patriotic Front-FPM), a small, left wing terrorist organization responsible for a number of incidents in the late 1980s and early 1990s that was the most active group implicated in the upswing of these attacks.

The FPM was sometimes linked to the Honduran Communist Party, and its aims were usually described as "leftist." However, while the FPM repeatedly made public statements claiming responsibility for attacks, it did not articulate a detailed set of aims. While most of the group's attacks targeted Americans, both military and civilians alike, the FPM's target selection indicated that its primary goal was combating the U.S. presence in Honduras, not fighting for a Marxist state. Identifying and attacking CIA officers was their first choice, followed by U.S. Embassy and U.S. Military personnel. The FPM's first reported attack was in the fall of 1988 when they assassinated American expatriate Leo Mills, a private businessman, who was shot while jogging.

The group also claimed responsibility for an explosion at the U.S. Peace Corps office in December 1988, which resulted in no casualties but caused significant damage, and later targeted U.S. AID. The group's three most famous attacks, however, all involved American servicemen. On 11 April 1989, a bomb detonated underneath a U.S. convoy that was carrying supplies in the northern part of Honduras, although no one was injured. A similar attack targeted a U.S. convoy in February 1989 in the same area. Later in July 1989, seven U.S. soldiers were wounded when FPM terrorists in the northern port city of La Ceiba threw a homemade explosive device at them as they left a nightclub around midnight. Seven more U.S. military personnel were wounded when the bus they were riding in from Pomerola/Soto Cano Air Base to the beach was ambushed by snipers northwest of Tegucigalpa at approximately 1:00 p.m. on 11 March 1990.

When there was a huge parade in front of the airport during the morning of 11 March, many speculated that the FPM changed their plans and decided to wait in hiding along the highway from Tegucigalpa to San Pedro Sula for a target of opportunity to pass by. In this case, it was the U.S. Air Force bus carrying the 28 off-duty airmen.

HIGHWAY 1: 10K NORTH OF TEGUCIGALPA, HONDURAS
1:00 P.M.   March 31, 1990

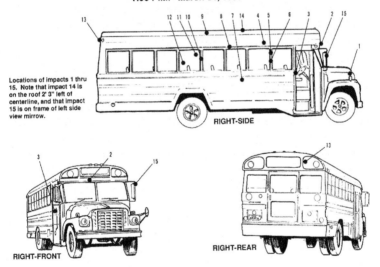

Locations of impacts 1 thru 15. Note that impact 14 is on the roof 2' 3" left of centerline, and that impact 15 is on frame of left side view mirrow.

RIGHT-SIDE

RIGHT-FRONT

RIGHT-REAR

According to the news reports, although the bus was riddled with bullets and one was later found lodged in the headrest behind the bus driver's head, the driver was not injured during the attack and continued driving the bus to the nearest hospital in Tegucigalpa. When the bus arrived, the Honduran police found an armed and obviously shaken military policeman standing in the doorway. Upon entering to assist in evacuating the injured, the Honduran police reported that the scene was horrific with blood everywhere and several U.S. soldiers wounded. Apparently, additional police officers had to be called to the scene to keep reporters from boarding the bus to take pictures and to keep them from trying to remove some of the 15 bullets that had struck the bus as the passengers were being transported inside the hospital for medical treatment.

Because two of the U.S. Airmen were in critical condition, one with a gunshot to the head and one with multiple gunshots to the abdomen, helicopters were called from the Pomerola/Soto Cano U.S. Air Base to transport the two servicemen to the U.S. medical facility there. I can still recall seeing on television a young woman reporter and a cameraman slipping under the flimsy makeshift rope line that the Honduran security personnel had set up as a perimeter, as one of the injured U.S. servicemen on a gurney was being placed in the back of a pickup truck to take him to one of the waiting helicopters. As the reporter and cameraman approached to take pictures of the injured servicemen, the cameraman bumped into the gurney and the intravenous (IV) bag almost fell. Eventually, amid the chaos, both servicemen were transported via the helicopters to Pomerola/Soto Cano Air Base and, fortunately, both survived.

On 25 February 1990, the Contras finally began departing Honduras after the Sandinista government, under massive pressure, staged an election in an attempt to prove their "democratic" stripes. However, the Sandinista leadership fundamentally misjudged the mindset of the Nicaraguan people and, as a result, the Ortega-led Sandinistas were embarrassingly ousted from power by the victory of the Coalition of Nicaraguan Opposition Parties headed by Violeta Chamorro. While most of the Honduran terrorist organizations put down their arms after the Contras left, the FPM continued its terrorist attacks for several years and was implicated in a rocket attack against a United Nations site in June 1991 on the outskirts of Tegucigalpa and an assassination in February 1992. The group's last attack occurred in April 1995 when a leaflet bomb exploded near the offices of several foreign press agencies although no one was injured. Today the FPM is no longer considered an active terrorist group.

* * *

When I departed Honduras and returned to the United States after serving several years, I had over 20 commendations in my file, including two from the President of Honduras; two from the former

Chief of Staff of the Honduran Armed Forces; two from the former Director of the Honduran Intelligence Service; and one from the Chief of Operations of the Salvadoran Army General Staff. In my last performance evaluation, it was noted, "my talents had been applied to meeting objectives far beyond that expected of a security officer" and that "my performance, although lacking any formalized training as such, was of a very high caliber."

Chapter 8

"Back Home and the Move to the Directorate of Operations (DO)"

After serving in Honduras, Karen, Kelly, Matthew, I returned to the United States to re-acquaint ourselves with our parents, family and friends. Kelly was only 4 ½ years old while Matthew was 3 years old. Neither of them could remember anything about living in the U.S. so for them every day was new and exciting.

Upon settling into our residence in Fairfax Station, Virginia, which had been rented for several years while we were away, and after taking my "home-leave", I reported to the Stafford Building to meet with the new Director of Security, Frank R., only to find out that I had no job lined up. Although I had notified the Office of Security six months previously that I would be returning to Washington and had filled out a "dream sheet" naming my top three choices for assignment, no one had taken any action.

When meeting Frank R. and his deputy Ray R., I was shocked to learn that they had not even focused on the fact that I had returned and was ready to begin a new assignment. I later learned that months earlier I had been approved by the career board to become the head of a new program involving a worldwide personal protection program but did not get the position when the person who had selected me, Ty H., was transferred and his replacement, Tony D., selected another security officer instead. As fate would have it, the individual put into that position was later dismissed for misappropriating funds. As I began to protest to Ray R. that it was not fair that I did not have an assignment, he told me, "The new Research and Analysis Division in the Gloucester Building is looking for people. Why don't you go over and see Kathy P." Arriving in the Gloucester Building, you cannot imagine the pain I was experiencing to be placed in a sterile vault with no windows after my time in Central America. More depressing was the fact that I soon learned that I would be supervising several analysts that the Office of Security had just hired to form this new division and that my branch was going to focus on Africa, Central and South America.

Unfortunately, the Research and Analysis Division was new, and the Directorate of Operations (DO) did not even know that we existed. Although we all had brand new computers on our desks, the phones remained silent. The only redeeming feature was that I was reunited with an old friend of mine from the Overseas Security

Support Branch (OSSB), Charlie P., who was the group chief in charge of the branch that I was in. Charlie eventually would work his way up the ranks to become the Director of the Office of Security in 2007. I can still remember as if it were yesterday, my first day walking around and meeting all of the analysts in my branch. Trust me when I say that it did not take me long to realize that what motivated an analyst did not necessarily motivate me. I had this one analyst assigned to my branch and every day he came in and worked for eight hours typing information into his computer. When I asked him what he was working on, he simply replied that he was conducting a study of all of the alarm activations that were occurring in Africa, Central and South America. I was shocked to learn that for the past six months, he would sit there each day and type all of this information into a database although no customer had requested this analysis. When I asked him to provide me with an update of what he had compiled to date, he gave me a long report with hundreds of alarm activations that could not be explained and had no hypothesis or explanation as to what might have been the cause of the alarms.

Shortly after my arrival in the Research and Analysis Division, one of the first projects that I was asked to work on involved writing a paper for the DCI Designee Robert (Bob) Gates. In conducting research, I soon realized that Bob Gates had received several death threats and an unusual amount of hate mail and phone calls when he was the Acting Director following Casey's death in 1987. More of a shock was that CIA employees were actually suspected of writing some of the hate mail and death threats. When we presented the paper to Bob Gates, which included an overview of the various terrorist groups that would consider him a target as well, I was pleased to see that he was very interested in the analysis pertaining to the unusual number of death threats, hate mail and threatening phone calls that he had received. One person in particular had written Bob Gates several letters from California expressing his dislike for him and eventually showed up at the CIA Headquarters main gate at Route 123 asking to speak to him. As I explained, it is one thing to write a letter, but quite another to drive across country to try to carry out the threat. Based upon our analysis, DCI Designee Bob Gates allowed the Office of Security to provide security at his residence.

Due to the fact that I had just returned from Central America, had traveled extensively throughout South America and Africa, and was well known in the DO, I took it upon myself to try and convince the DO that this new Research and Analysis Division was a great idea and could be beneficial. To help our cause, with the blessing of a new supervisor by the name of Ward M., we resurrected a program that I had implemented in Honduras referred to as a "Personal Protection Survey." This survey looked at the daily patterns and routines of our CIA officers living overseas. The second portion of the survey involved writing and implementing emergency and evacuation plans concentrating on rally points/staging areas, safe havens, emergency communications, and emergency supplies such as food and water. After these plans were written, we made sure that they were integrated into all existing plans. Having successfully implemented this program in Honduras while serving there, I was asked by the support chief in the Latin American Division at the time, to conduct similar surveys throughout Central and South America. In addition, after briefing my idea to the former support chief in Tegucigalpa, Jack K., who had just been appointed as the support chief in the Africa Division, I was asked to TDY to a high threat post in Africa for several weeks in February 1992 to conduct the Personal Protection Survey there. Interestingly, during my trip, Osama Bin Ladin was frequently spotted driving around town in his white Mercedes.

Upon returning, one day while sitting in the Agency library and reading a Honduran newspaper, I saw an article about the Honduran MST program that piqued my interest. According to the article, with the success of the 18 October 1989 arms seizure at La Fraternidad, the Hondurans were eager for a second success and therefore, word was sent to all of the MST members that it was important to try to develop a network of personnel who could report on arms or narcotics shipments. The Hondurans were particularly interested in knowing if any of the MST members knew of anyone affiliated with the Salvadoran FLMN. Shortly, thereafter, one of the MST members in Santa Rosa de Copan claimed that he had grown up with an individual who was affiliated with the FMLN. However, when the MST member approached him, he was informed that this person no longer was associated with the FLMN or their cause. When asked if he knew of anyone still part of the organization, the individual provided the name of his cousin who, when approached, provided information involving an impending arms shipment that was going to cross the border from Honduras into El Salvador near the town of La Virtud sometime during Easter week – "Semana Santa", the holiest week of the year in Central America. With this information in hand, the Hondurans took a MST into the remote area near La Virtud and set up roadblocks during the day and evening hours.

For the next seven days, the Hondurans only encountered seven vehicles but during the morning of 7 April 1990, the MST stopped a small truck carrying fruits and vegetables. In the course of their routine inspection, the Honduran MST was just about to let the driver continue when one of the MST members began inspecting the undercarriage and noticed that the support beams were metal instead of wooden. After drilling into one of them, the MST member discovered that it was hollow. Tearing off the wooden side panel, the MST member discovered 24 AK-47 assault rifles from North Korea and Hungary, 76 ammunition magazines for the AK-47 assault rifle, 16 blocks of TNT, 60 pounds of the explosive Flex X, five rolls of detonating cord, and a small bag containing detonators hidden in the hollow support beams. Further inspection revealed a second false compartment in the ceiling of the cab containing an assortment of false documents and FLMN propaganda material.

La Virtud seizure

During interrogation, the Hondurans quickly discovered that the driver and passenger were Salvadoran citizens using Honduran fake identification. When questioned, the two advised that they were instructed to pick up the vehicle, which had already been loaded with the weapons and explosives at a gas station in San Pedro Sula. They further claimed that the keys were in the ignition when they got to the gas station as well as payment for their services, which had been hidden in the false compartment located in the ceiling of the vehicle. The two Salvadorans were then instructed to drive to the Salvadoran border where they would be met. The arms, ammunition, and explosives were to have been removed from the false compartments and shipped across the border on mules near the town of La Virtud. Although the two admitted that the entire operation was very compartmentalized and claimed that they did not have any additional information, the Hondurans were able to extract the location of a safe house where they were to rendezvous before crossing the border. With this information in hand, the Hondurans raided the safe house and discovered an assortment of medical supplies, FLMN propaganda, additional weapons, false passports, a printing press, money, and some communications equipment and gear.

La Virtud seizure

La Virtud safehouse

La Virtud safehouse

The next day the Hondurans set up surveillance at the gas station in San Pedro Sula and one month later a truck similar to the one seized near La Virtud, showed up and parked. Following the driver back to a warehouse on the outskirts of San Pedro Sula, the Hondurans discovered that the building was dedicated to constructing false compartments in vehicles used to smuggle arms, ammunition, and explosives. Hollow metal support tubes similar to that found in the bed of the truck that had been seized near La Virtud on the morning of 7 April 1990, were also found at the scene.

Warehouse – San Pedro Sula

Hollow Metal Tubes Used to Hide Weapons, Ammunition and Explosives Found in the Warehouse at San Pedro Sula

San Pedro Sula seizure

San Pedro Sula seizure

In that the only remaining piece of the puzzle involved where the arms, ammunition and explosives where being stored prior to being inserted into the false compartments, as luck would have it, on 18 May 1990, this piece was found after a "compasino" walked into a police station in San Pedro Sula claiming that he had discovered a hand grenade in a sugar cane field near Poterillos (a small village about 25 kilometers south of San Pedro Sula). Arriving at the scene with a MST team and some canines, the Hondurans soon uncovered in the woods on the outskirts of a sugarcane field, fifty nine 81MM mortar rounds, 39 RPG-7 rounds, forty five 57MM mortar rounds, sixty five 60MM mortar rounds, 39 propellant charges for the RPG's, seventy half blocks of TNT, 41 rolls of time fuse and detonating cord, 15 AK-47 ammunition magazines, 8 ammunition belts for a 50 caliber machinegun, one RPG-7 and one AK-47.

Seizure near Poterillos

Two weeks earlier, at the same time this case was unfolding, the newspaper article claimed that the Hondurans had received word from an informant that one of the former Contra Comandante's, known as Comandante "Danto", was selling arms, ammunition, and explosives to the FMLN.

Arenales seizure

After learning that Comandante Danto was living near the small town of Arenales in the Choluteca Region in Southern Honduras, the Hondurans decided to conduct a raid on his residence using one of the MST teams during the evening of 4 May 1990. As they burst into the residence, which was nothing more than a five-room house with dirt floors in four of the five rooms, they soon discovered, after talking to the Comandante's wife and son, that he was in Nicaragua and was not expected back for several weeks. Because the only wooden floor in the residence looked somewhat new, the Honduran Lieutenant gave the order to rip it up and subsequently discovered seventy-nine 60MM mortar rounds, thirty 81MM mortar rounds, one Soviet bloc 12.7MM DSHK-38 machinegun, one 81MM mortar tripod, one 81MM mortar, one tripod for the 12.7 machine gun, one 7.63 Soviet bloc PK machinegun, one 81MM mortar base plate, and several ruck sacks.

According to the newspaper article, several weeks later, on 8 June 1990, an irate Comandante Danto walked into the Choluteca police station shouting that he wanted to know who had the balls to raid his residence. The police officer called a Honduran Major who also happened to be in charge of the MSTs in the region. When the police officer asked what he should do with the Comandante, he was told to interrogate him until the Major arrived to see if he had any other weapons of interest.

Shortly after the Honduran Major arrived at the police station, several MST members were provided with information from the interrogation, which led to their digging up three Redeye missiles, which the Comandante had buried on his property in Arenales. During questioning, the Comandante admitted that he was going to sell the missiles to the FMLN for $70,000 per missile. Thus within five weeks of the 7 April 1990 discovery near La Virtud, the Hondurans were able to put several key FLMN arms trafficking networks completely out of business.

Mobile Search Team unearthing three Redeye missiles

* * *

Following these events, the Central American Regional Intelligence Coordination Center (RICC) decided to host their semi-annual conference in Guatemala. Upon receiving the agenda, I realized that one of the main topics to be discussed at the conference involved shoulder fired surface to air missiles, so I asked permission to travel to Honduras to see if the Hondurans were willing to bring one of the Redeye missiles, that they had just uncovered, to the conference.

After describing my plan to do so, much to my surprise, I was granted permission to fly to Honduras to meet with the Hondurans in an attempt to see if we could transport one of the Redeye missiles to Guatemala for display purposes at the RICC conference. You cannot imagine the looks we received from other passengers when police Captain Salomon de Jesus Escoto and I boarded a Honduran Tans Sasha airline enroute to Guatemala City, and placed the missile, which was in a large, green plastic container, in the overhead compartment bin. Fortunately, I was traveling with Captain Escoto, so we boarded the plane directly from a side door at the airport in Tegucigalpa and did not have to go through Honduran security.

The same was true when arriving in El Salvador and Guatemala. In both instances, as was the case in Honduras, we did not have to go through security, immigration or customs control. Arriving in San Salvador, we were met by Salvadoran officials who were going to join us at the RICC conference and upon our arrival in Guatemala City where we were met at the airport by our Guatemalan RICC hosts. Much to the amazement of everyone at the conference, Captain Escoto and I produced a Redeye missile for everyone's inspection.

Several years later when I visited Costa Rica in the spring of 2001, I ran into an old friend of mine, Colonel Miguel Torres, from the Costa Rican police who was at the RICC conference in Guatemala that year. The first thing he said to me when I saw him was, "Richard, do you remember hand carrying that Redeye missile aboard a civilian aircraft from Honduras with Captain Escoto through El Salvador to Guatemala for the RICC conference?" to which I replied, "Of course!"

Costa Rica 2001

* * *

Later during the afternoon of 27 August 1990, while watching the evening news, I learned that a white Volkswagen mini-van with Belgian license plates had approached a Honduran border crossing from Nicaragua. The driver of the vehicle, a French woman with the last name of Demaziere, appeared nervous and agitated during questioning by one of the MST officers because it was nearing 6:00 p.m. and the border was about to close for the day. Due to her responses, and noticing that the van had an antenna for a citizen band radio, which was illegal in Honduras, the MST officer decided to question Demaziere further. In the interim, the MST officer asked his fellow officers to conduct a more thorough inspection of the vehicle. The van was sitting low to the ground, so one of the MST officers brought a canine to the scene and, after a brief inspection, the canine went on alert indicating the possibilities of explosives. Upon dismantling the van, the Hondurans discovered hundreds of homemade mortars and explosive increments for the mortars hidden in the floor and walls of the vehicle. In addition, the Honduran MST found plans to attack military compounds in El Salvador; several radios, radio codes, FLMN propaganda material, and an assortment of false documents, passports, and identification belonging to Demaziere hidden in false compartments. According to the news report, in several of the documents Demaziere had different names, different addresses, and dates and places of birth. In addition, several of the photographs depicted her with different hairstyles – both long and short. The news report went on to say that the Honduran MST officers became suspicious that something was hidden in the floor of the van after noticing new linoleum, freshly painted walls, and pre-fabricated furniture in the rear of the van – items not common in vehicles in Central America. Not only were the mortars and explosive increments found in the floor but also in the side interior walls of the van and in the pre-fabricated furniture.

Honduran MST Seizure of Van with Belgian License Plates at a Fraternidad, Honduras August 1990

During questioning, the only information that Demaziere provided was that she was working for one of the world refugee organizations based in Brussels, Belgium; was on her way to El Salvador to meet some friends; and did not have any knowledge of how the mortars and explosive increments got into the floor, walls and furniture of her van. Furthermore, Demaziere stated that she could not explain the false documents and passports that she had in her possession. Lastly, the report mentioned that the Hondurans shared the information with their Salvadoran counterparts including the plans to attack San Miguel and Usulatan.

I later learned that although Demaziere ended up being convicted by a Honduran court for arms smuggling and was confined to a prison near Jicaro Galan where temperatures during the summer exceed 120 degrees, she was eventually released, after a year of imprisonment due to pressure from the French Government and, in particular, the wife of the French President. The entire time she was imprisoned Demaziere claimed her innocence and never divulged any information – definitely hard-core.

One of the last successful arms seizures by the Honduran MSTs that I can remember reading about occurred on 22 February 1991 near the town of Dificultades along the Honduran/Nicaraguan border. In this incident, the Honduran press reported that after conducting MST operations along the border for three days without success, one morning as daylight was approaching and the Honduran MST had begun their journey back to Tegucigalpa, they noticed a small red truck, which had stalled while trying to cross a small stream along the border. The hood of the vehicle was up and the young driver appeared nervous as the Hondurans approached him in their military fatigues.

As one of the MST officers began to question the driver (a 19 year-old Honduran), the press reported that a second MST officer began to look under the hood to see if he could get the vehicle started again. When a third officer began to conduct a cursory inspection of the burlap bags filled with bananas and platinos (a type of banana) in the rear of the vehicle, while inspecting the burlap sacks, the officer found 24 Russian rocket propelled grenades, an assortment of explosives, electrical blasting caps, and radios.

Stalled red truck

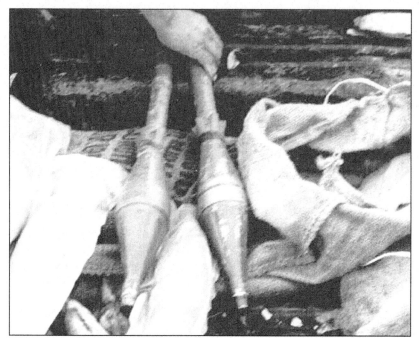

RPG rounds found in back of stalled truck by Honduran MST in Dificultades, Honduras February 1991

Documents and RPG rounds seized by Honduran MST in Dificultades, Honduras in February 1991

The Honduran press continued that although during interrogation, the young driver claimed ignorance; he provided the name and address of the individual whom he received the burlap bags from in Nicaragua and the name and address of the individual who he was to deliver the burlap bags to in Tegucigalpa. Later that evening, the Hondurans conducted a raid on the residence in Tegucigalpa and found that it belonged to a senior official of the Honduran terrorist group known as the Chincineros. Following the raid, interrogation of several of the individuals revealed that the rocket propelled grenades and explosives were to be used in a plot to attack the U.S. Embassy in Tegucigalpa later that month.

According to the article, the Hondurans further received word that a former Sandinista official was looking to sell arms and ammunition to the FMLN in El Salvador. Upon receipt of this information, the Hondurans decided to send someone to meet with them posing as a member of the FLMN in an attempt to entice the official to deliver the weapons to a member in Honduras. After making a small deposit, the individual, posing as the FLMN member, provided detailed instructions to the Sandinista official as well as a map with the date and time the delivery was to be made. In that the Sandinista official was supposed to cross a small stream in his vehicle with the weapons from Nicaragua into Honduras via an illegal border crossing at 3:00 a.m. near the town of Guasale, the Hondurans decided to pre-position one of their MSTs on the Honduran side several hours earlier. After establishing communications with Tegucigalpa, the Honduran MST settled back to wait in the darkness for the Sandinista official to arrive. Once the vehicle crossed the stream from Nicaragua into Honduras, their plan called for starting two generators to illuminate the entire area with light from 1,000-watt lamps pointing at the vehicle. Once the lights went on, the MST Captain was going to get on a bullhorn and let the driver and passengers know that they had five seconds to exit the vehicle with their hands over their heads or the vehicle would be fired upon.

According to the press report, as everything was going as planned, at 2:45 a.m. all of a sudden the silence was shattered by a blood-curdling scream coming from the direction of one of the MST officers who was sitting with his back against a tree. As the MST Captain, rushed to his side and shoved his hand over his mouth, he quickly realized that the MST officer was being attacked by huge fire ants that were ravaging his body. As the Captain repeatedly whispered into the individual's ear "to take the pain", lest they be discovered, they began to tear off the MST officer's clothing and rinse his body with water from their canteens. Minutes later the Hondurans were able to calm down the officer with the help of some rubbing alcohol, a sedative, and some pain medication although his body was completely covered with huge welts from the fire ants that had stung him. Literally, seconds after finishing with the MST officer, the Hondurans saw headlights coming their way from far off in the distance and no sooner had the vehicle crossed the stream than the lights went on and the driver and his 15-year-old son were ordered to exit their vehicle. This time their efforts produced 25 Kalashnikov assault rifles hidden in the rear of the Sandinista official's pick up truck and a small amount of ammunition, explosives, and detonation cord.

In a subsequent Honduran news report, I learned that with the election of Nicaraguan President Violeta Chamorro and peace accords being signed throughout Central America, it was interesting to see that many of the traffickers that had been involved in selling arms, ammunition and explosives for years had changed to drugs– literally overnight – using the same vehicles, false compartments, and routes from Nicaragua across Honduras to El Salvador and Guatemala. According to the news report, although trafficking in arms was still lucrative, shipping drugs appeared to be even more rewarding. A by-product of the Honduran arms interdiction program was an inordinate amount of narcotics, which the Hondurans confiscated during their routine arms inspections.

In an April 1990, a Honduran news story reported that President Callejas had visited Washington, DC and was severely criticized by members of Congress for not doing enough to stem the flow of drugs from Central and South America through Honduras to the United States. Shortly after his return to Honduras, the news reported that an MST team discovered 250 kilos of cocaine hidden inside two 55-gallon drums strapped underneath a tractor-trailer truck, which had crossed the Los Manos Border checkpoint between Honduras and Nicaragua on 24 April 1990. As the driver of the vehicle arrived at the border crossing, he tried to bribe one of the MST officials by giving him $200 to let him pass the checkpoint without being inspected. Accepting the $200, the MST official radioed an MST team that was conducting routine inspections two kilometers from the border crossing. When the tractor-trailer was stopped, one of the MST members noticed welding marks around both of the 55-gallon fuel drums and when he inserted a hose inside quickly realized that only a portion of the drum contained diesel fuel. During further inspection, 250 kilos of cocaine was found stuffed in both drums.

Truck seized by the Honduran MST at La Fraternidad in 1990 with 250 kilograms of cocaine inside

Close up of drum

Honduran MST seizure of 250 kilograms of cocaine in April 1990 at La Fraternidad, Honduras

Two days later, a similar tractor-trailer was abandoned on the Nicaraguan side of the Los Manos border-crossing checkpoint at the same time the Hondurans held a press conference announcing the 24 April cocaine seizure. The following morning after the Hondurans notified the Nicaraguan Government; a delegation arrived at the border crossing consisting of the newly elected President of Nicaragua, Violeta Chamorro, and the Head of the Nicaraguan Defense Forces, Humberto Ortega. When the Hondurans approached the tractor-trailer from the Honduran side with a similar delegation, the two 55-gallon drums were removed and inspected and an additional 159 kilos of cocaine was discovered.

These two discoveries were followed by an additional seizure on 10 May 1990 when 300 kilos of cocaine was discovered hidden in false compartments inside the inner wall of a tractor-trailer loaded with 500 one hundred pound sacks of corn as the vehicle crossed from Nicaragua into Honduras at the El Espino/La Fraternidad border crossing. The driver of the vehicle (a Guatemalan) owned four additional tractor-trailers that were in convoy at the time of the seizure. The vehicle contained 35 false compartments to hide cocaine. In light of the negative press that he had received in Washington, DC, the press report claimed that President Callejas was ecstatic with these three cocaine seizures and, in several well publicized press announcements, thumbed his nose at Washington for accusing him of not doing anything to combat drug trafficking.

Honduran MST members inspecting a tractor trailer containing false compartments

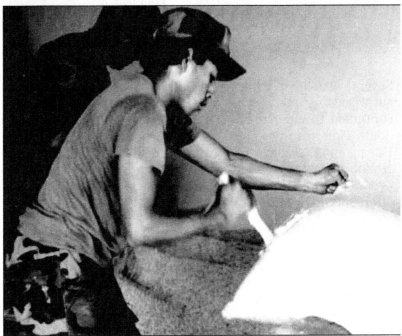

Honduran MST member searching for cocaine inside of the sacks of corn

In late May 1990, my good friend, Oscar Alvarez, called me to say that President Callejas had decided to present me with the highest Honduran civilian award the country provided. This was a special day for me and I got to return to Honduras with my wife, Karen, and my brother, Jim, to attend the ceremony.

Receiving the Highest Honduran Civilian Award from President Rafael Callejas

* * *

Several years later, while sitting in the library in Headquarters, I was surprised to read in a Honduran newspaper that Honduras continued to emerge as an increasingly important land bridge for South American-produced cocaine destined for the United States. During 1992, seizures of cocaine smuggled via land routes through Honduras increased significantly in both frequency and volume with over 1,422 kilos of cocaine seized in eight operations due to the efforts of the Honduran MST program.

The article went on to say that on 3 June 1992, a Honduran MST assigned to Guasuale discovered 670 kilos of cocaine concealed in the false floor of a tractor trailer being driven from Nicaragua to Guatemala as it crossed into Honduras from Nicaragua along an illegal border crossing near Guasuale.

A month later, on 29 July 1992, a Honduran MST at El Espino/La Fraternidad seized 23 kilos of cocaine concealed in the false floor of a tractor-trailer enroute from Costa Rica to Guatemala as it crossed into Honduras from Nicaragua at the border crossing of El Espino/La Fraternidad. On 7 August 1992, a Honduran MST at El Espino/La Fraternidad seized an additional 104 kilos of cocaine concealed in a tractor-trailer being driven from Costa Rica to El Salvador as it crossed into Honduras from Nicaragua at the El Espino/La Fraternidad border crossing. And on 1 September 1992, 68 kilos of cocaine was discovered at Guasuale by the Gausaule MST concealed in a tractor-trailer being driven from Costa Rica to El Salvador after it crossed an illegal border crossing.

Later that month, according to the Honduran newspaper article, a retired Honduran Army Colonel was arrested in San Pedro Sula following the seizure of 69 kilos of cocaine at the San Pedro Sula Airport. During interrogation, the Colonel admitted to participating in numerous trans-shipments of cocaine over a period of five years and stated that their primary method was via maritime vessels into Honduras' north coast and then tractor-trailers across the Honduran/Nicaraguan border.

The article continued that on 29 November 1992, a Honduran MST assigned to El Espino/La Fraternidad discovered 212 kilos of cocaine concealed in the false floor of a tractor-trailer being driven from Nicaragua to El Salvador and onto Guatemala. A similar tractor-trailer was believed to have remained on the Nicaraguan side of border. In addition, on 4 December 1992, 276 kilos of cocaine was seized at El Espino/La Fraternidad, concealed in altered frames of a tractor-trailer being driven from Nicaragua to Guatemala.

A side product of this seizure was the discovery of 178 kilos of heroin (pictured on the following page) by a Honduran MST assigned to El Espino/La Fraternidad on 31 July 1992 carefully concealed in the floor of a tractor-trailer carrying huge cargo containers on a flat bed truck destined for the U.S. via Guatemala – according to the article, the largest seizure of Colombian heroin destined for the U.S. discovered to date. The newspaper reported that a Honduran MST officer became suspicious of the tractor-trailer after an initial inspection revealed several broken spot-welds in the undercarriage of the flat bed trailer and new tires along side of worn tires.

178 kilos of heroin

Lastly, the Honduran newspaper article revealed that since the Hondurans resurrected the MST program in 1989, additional Honduran MSTs were placed along the Honduran/Guatemalan border crossings at Nueva Ocotepeque and Santa Rosa de Copan, the southern border crossing of Guasuale along the Honduran/Nicaraguan border, and in the northern city of San Pedro Sula to operate along the north coast. In three years, the Honduran MST program had grown from 48 to 144 members with some individual teams expanding from 12 to 24 members. In addition, it had expanded from four teams to eight wherein, the Hondurans had 32 major arms and narcotics seizures during this period.

* * *

One day while sitting in the Research and Analysis Division in the Gloucester Building, I thought of my old chief in Honduras, Steve M., who had just been transferred to El Salvador. The Government of El Salvador had just signed a "Peace Accord/Cease-Fire" with the FMLN guerrillas and the newspaper was reporting that the Salvadoran Government was eager to demonstrate to the world that the FMLN was not honoring their side of the bargain by disarming. Earlier in the year, on 2 January 1991, the FMLN downed a U.S. helicopter in the San Miguel department carrying three U.S. military advisors who were enroute to Honduras. Two of them Lt. Colonel David Pickett and crew chief PFC Earnest Dawson, were brutally executed after surviving the crash. The third, Chief Warrant Officer Daniel Scott, died of injuries suffered in the shootdown. The U.S. Government was enraged that the FMLN had refused to turn over the two individuals responsible.

According to the newspaper article, over the years, the Salvadoran MSTs had been hampered because of their inability to operate in hostile areas controlled by the FMLN due to the vulnerability of an FLMN attack. It continued that with the cease-fire, the Salvadoran MSTs, with additional refresher training, appeared ready for success. Following their refresher training, the article claimed that the MSTs had deployed all over the country in areas that no Salvadoran military units had been in years due to the FMLN control. Whenever they set up at one location for more than an hour or so, they would move so that the FLMN would not be able to discover their exact location – a reminder of their name, Mobile Search Teams (MSTs). Although the MSTs had found an inordinate amount of contraband (clothing, shoes, tobacco, liquor, cosmetics, and a few personal weapons and ammunition), unfortunately, according to the article, they did not find the large shipment that the Salvadoran Government was hoping that they would discover. After reading the article, I wondered if the Salvadoran MSTs had come across such a shipment, what type of firefight they would have gotten into. I am confident that the individuals transporting the shipment were not going to want to surrender without a fight.

* * *

In late May 1992, I was glad to hear that Bill A. had asked the Director of Security for me to work on a special program he had been assigned to in the Directorate of Operations (DO), Special Activities Division (SAD) for a period of 90 days. When I left Gloucester Building, I knew in my heart that not only would I never return, but knew it was time to try and transfer from the Office of Security to the DO.

On my first day in SAD with Bill, I learned that for the past several months he had been supervising a sensitive program whose mission was to provide direct support to the United Nations Special Commission (UNSCOM) implementation and enforcement of United Nations Security Council Resolutions (UNSCR) 687 resulting from the cessation of hostilities following the 1990-1991 First Gulf War. I also learned that Bill had been asked to serve on a promotion panel for two weeks and, therefore, wanted me to head the program in his absence. His parting words that first day were, "Richard, you better come up to speed quickly on this program in that we are flying to New York City tomorrow morning to brief the Head of UNSCOM, Rolfe Ekeus." As background, the U.N. Security Council passed Resolution 687 on 3 April 1991 as part of the cease-fire arrangements ending operation Desert Storm. The resolution, among other things, required Iraq to rid itself permanently and unconditionally of all nuclear, biological, and chemical weapons capabilities and allow U.N. inspectors full access to verify and monitor compliance. The resolution further called for the "destruction, removal, or rendering harmless" of its weapons of mass destruction and ballistic missiles with a range over 150 kilometers and required Iraq to make a declaration, within 15 days, of the location, amounts, and types of all such items. The resolution established a monitoring and inspection mechanism UNSCOM to ensure Iraqi compliance. Resolution 687 also linked a decision to lift sanctions with Iraq's fulfillment of the disarmament provisions. The resolution was passed under Chapter 7 of the U.N. Charter, meaning that military force could be used to enforce compliance.

Baghdad was obligated to make full declarations about its weapons programs and accept monitoring and verification activity as determined necessary by UNSCOM and the International Atomic Energy Agency (IAEA). The U.N. inspectors were supposed to verify the Iraqi declarations and report their evaluations to the Security Council, which would then make decisions on sanctions. The inspections were not originally intended as a mechanism for discovering concealed weapons. On 10 April 1991, Iraq accepted Resolution 687 and on 18 April 1991 provided initial declaration required under Resolution 687. This declaration included some chemical weapons and materials and 53 Al-Hussein and Scud type surface-to-surface ballistic missiles. Iraq claimed it had no biological weapons program. On 16 May 1991, Iraq submitted a revised declaration covering additional chemical weapons and a refinement of its missile declaration. Later, in May 1991, through an exchange of letters between U.N. Secretary General Boutros Boutros-Ghali and Iraqi Foreign Minister Tariq Aziz, Iraq accepted the privileges and immunities of the Special Commission (UNSCOM) and its personnel. These guarantees included the right of "unrestricted freedom of entry and exit, without delay or hindrance of its personnel, property, supplies, and equipment". On 9 June 1991, UNSCOM conducted its first chemical weapons inspection, and on 17 June 1991, the Security Council adopted Resolution 699 which confirmed that the Special Commission and the IAEA had the authority to conduct activities under section C of Resolution 687. The first missile inspection was conducted by UNSCOM on 30 June 1991 and the first biological inspection on 2 August 1991.

In August 1991, Bill was called to the seventh floor by the Deputy Director of Operations (DDO) at the time, Ted P., and asked if he would put together a group of Agency and U.S. Special Operations Command (USSOCOM) personnel to support UNSCOM. Prior to this time, the State Department had been responsible for coordinating the U.S. involvement in these missions to include the target selection, mission planning, and security. Bill was told that the Agency was being brought into the equation after an Iraqi defector reported that several of the U.N. inspection books naming the locations of all of the proposed inspection sites was left in a hotel room by one of the U.N. inspectors during a recent inspection. This was found by the Iraqis – and the inspectors wondered why all of the sites where empty when they arrived.

Following his appointment, the first thing Bill did was visit USSOCOM and ask for several of their top operators and analysts to support this initiative. He then integrated the personnel with a group of specialized Agency officers. Their mission was to gather as much intelligence as possible on the Iraqi WMD program so that sites that supported these efforts could be recommended to UNSCOM for inspection. Once the sites were selected, the analysts would make a detailed target study of the site. The operators then devised a training program for the UNSCOM team members, under the direction of Chief Inspector David Kay, to learn about how to conduct a thorough, methodical search of a site, building, or room to look for items of an intelligence value.

On 15 August 1991, the Security Council adopted Resolution 707, demanding that Iraq immediately provide full, final, and complete disclosures (FFCDs), as required by Resolution 687. On 6 September 1991, Iraqi officials blocked the first heliborne UNSCOM inspection team. During this same IAEA inspection, inspectors found large amounts of documentation relating to Iraq's efforts to acquire nuclear weapons. Although the Iraqi officials confiscated some documents from the inspectors, the inspectors refused to yield a second set of documents. In response, the Iraqis refused to allow the team to leave the site with these documents and a four-day standoff ensued, during which the team remained in the parking lot of the site. Fortunately, Iraq finally permitted the team to leave with the documents after a statement from the Security Council threatened enforcement actions.

Prior to this inspection, it was customary for the inspectors to give a list of the sites to be inspected each day to the Iraqis as they departed the hotel in the morning. It was no great surprise therefore, that the sites had been cleaned out of documents prior to their arrival. With the addition of several new inspectors, each morning the Iraqis were simply told, for example, to head north, then east, and then south before arriving at a pre-determined site. When the Iraqis would say they did not have authorization to enter or did not have a key to the site, a special locksmith on the team always magically appeared to assist them. Using this new methodology, on the first day of the inspection in September 1991, the inspection team hit pay dirt and found over 18,000 documents pertaining to the Iraqi WMD program that led to the aforementioned 4-day parking lot stand off.

On 11 October 1991, the Security Council adopted Resolution 715 that approved joint UNSCOM and IAEA plans for ongoing monitoring and verification. UNSCOM's plan established that Iraq would "accept unconditionally the inspectors and all other personnel designated by the Special Commission." In response, the Iraqis stated that they considered the Ongoing Monitoring and Verification Plans adopted by Resolution 715 to be unlawful and, therefore, were not ready to comply. Later, in February 1992, Iraq refused to comply with a UNSCOM/IAEA decision to destroy certain facilities used in proscribed programs and related items. In response, the Security Council condemned Iraq's failure to comply with its obligations and Iraq finally agreed to the destruction of those facilities and items. On 19 March 1992, Iraq declared the existence of 89 previously undeclared ballistic missiles, chemical weapons, associated material, and claimed that it unilaterally destroyed most of these undeclared items in the summer of 1991, in violation of Resolution 687. In April 1992, Iraq called for a halt to UNSCOM's aerial surveillance flights, stating that the aircraft and its pilot might be endangered. In response, the President of the Security Council issued a statement reaffirming UNSCOM's right to conduct such flights and Iraq acquiesced saying that it did not intend to carry out any military action aimed at UNSCOM's aerial flights.

* * *

In May 1992, shortly upon my arrival in SAD, Iraq provided its first full, final and complete disclosures (FFCD's) for its prohibited biological and missile programs while adding that they only had a defensive biological weapons program. Then in June 1992, Iraq provided its first FFCD for its prohibited chemical weapons program. In July 1992, several inspectors on an UNSCOM inspection team began destroying large quantities of Iraq's chemical weapons and their related production facilities. During a 6-29 July 1992 UNSCOM Inspection, Iraq refused an inspection team access to the Iraqi Ministry of Agriculture although UNSCOM had reliable information that the site contained archives related to proscribed activities. Inspectors eventually gained access only after members of the Council threatened enforcement action.

During an after action briefing at the Pentagon, to say that Bill and I were proud is an understatement when the J-3 at the time, General Brantner, told several of the USSOCOM members that "we knew where you guys were and were prepared to go in and get you if necessary." In late July 1992, I finally transferred to the DO from the DA but only after the Chief SAD at the time, George H., sponsored me along with the Chief CTC, Fred T., and the Chief LA Division, Vince S. Ironically, even with the endorsement of three DO Division Chiefs, my application was denied. When George was informed of the decision, he told me not to worry. He immediately grabbed the application, marched to the seventh floor, and returned several minutes later with the approval signature from the Chief of Human Resources, Dick C. I was, and still am, very appreciative to George for making my transfer from the DA to the DO happen.

Following my transfer to the DO, in addition to managing the USSOCOM operators, analysts and the specialized Agency officer's, I was made a branch chief in a newly formed group within SAD under Bill's auspices. I was 37 years old and was as happy as I could be now that I was finally out of the Office of Security and embarking on a new career in the DO. Although the two other branch chiefs in this group were in their late 50's, along with the majority of the branch chiefs in SAD, I was accepted into the ranks because of the backing I had from Bill, George H., and the Deputy Chief of SAD, Bill R. Since my branch was brand new, we were asked to design training programs to support the Counterterrorism Center (CTC) and the newly formed Counternarcotics Center (CNC). Relying on my past experience in Central America and the new mission of the USSOCOM operators, analysts and specialized Agency officer's, we helped design a program that uses a thorough methodology to search for items of an intelligence and law enforcement value. This methodology ensures that discovered items are recorded and logged so that the "chain of evidence" is not broken when dealing with items of a law enforcement value, which can be used, in a court of law; and items of an intelligence value, which can be used to expand the amount of information and knowledge known about the participants. With the success of the course, my branch developed several additional courses and by the time that I departed the group, we had a stable of independent contractor instructors who were providing this training worldwide to the DO. In addition, with the success of this group, my branch was called upon to plan and support several counterterrorism and counternarcotic raids and "takedown" operations. One such operation in South America involved taking down a "Kingpin" narcotics trafficker in 1992, while another one involved a sensitive counterterrorism operation in Central Eurasia.

In 1991, Bill A. attended a Hostage Negotiation Course presented by Scotland Yard, and was impressed by the lead instructor, Norm B., a British Metropolitan Police official. After retiring from the police force, he contacted Bill and eventually came to work for the Agency as a consultant. Married to an American, Norm had acquired a "green card". Although Norm did not speak any Spanish, Bill recommended Norm assist the Latin American Division. A year later, I read an article entitled, *"The Sendero File, Abimael Guzman's Capture: A Turning Point in the War"* in a Peruvian newspaper which detailed how the Peruvian Government had captured Abimael Guzman, the head of the "Shining Path" or "Sendero Luminoso". According to the article, an elite counterterrorist unit of the National Directorate Against Terrorism (DINCOTE), under its new commander, General Antonio Vidal, raided a residence in the middle-class Lima neighborhood of Surco, Peru on 12 September 1992, and captured Guzman. Several weeks earlier, the DINCOTE had placed the aforementioned residence, operating as a dance studio, under surveillance after learning that the residence was serving as a "Shining Path" safe house.

The article described how DINCOTE members provided around the clock surveillance on the dance studio from a residence across the street, while additional members, in disguise, set up temporary fruit and vegetable stands on the street in front of the dance studio. A third group, as part of the surveillance, reportedly dressed as medical personnel, providing free blood pressure tests from a temporary stand. After several days, the outline of a large figure was observed walking back and forth in front of the curtained window on the second floor of the dance studio one evening. This was much to the delight of General Vidal since Abimael Guzman was known to be an enormous figure weighing close to 300 pounds.

The following day, the DINCOTE members, dressed as garbage men, collected the garbage from the residence and found French cigarettes and Absolut vodka – two favorites of Abimael Guzman. On 12 September 1992, suspecting that Guzman may indeed be in the residence, General Vidal gave the order to raid the residence and, on the second floor, DINCOTE members found a bearded, casually dressed man with a distinct air of a university professor. As fortune would have it, he was indeed the supreme leader of the "Shining Path" and the most wanted man in Peru for more than a decade.

In addition to Abimael Guzman, the DINCOTE captured nine people at the safe house, including two well-known activists, a prominent metropolitan Lima leader, and the companion of the "Shining Path" leader. Following the operation on the safe house, the DINCOTE also raided two other safe houses, arresting 30 more people and, in the days that followed, police units swept up the "Shining Path" National Coordinator responsible for liaison with the Regional Committees and the "Shining Path" Coordinator of the northern Lima zone. During all of the raids, a cache of documents, notes, and computer disks were obtained and exploited by the Peruvians.

The article claimed that General Vidal had handpicked the members of this new unit and had every member polygraphed. To ensure the unit's integrity, the DINCOTE members were placed in seclusion for days at a time, without any contact with their family or friends so that nothing would be leaked in the event that they were provided an order to move on a suspect target. To guarantee the secrecy of these operations, not even President Fujimori was notified. On 27 September 1992, the Peruvian Navy took over the custody of Abimael Guzman, placing him on the San Lorenzo Island submarine base, offshore from the port of Callao.

The morning of 22 December 1992, I walked into the front office of the Special Activities Division (SAD) to find everyone in a very somber mood. When I asked Paul F. what was going on, he slowly replied that we had just received word that one of our officers, Larry F., had been killed in East Africa. Larry, a former 1st Special Forces Operational Detachment-Delta (1st SFOD-D) member came to work for the Agency's SAD after retiring from the U.S. Army. In early December 1992, Larry and several other SAD Officers, including my deputy at the time, John H., were chosen for an assignment under the deputy chief of SAD's paramilitary group, Leon W. The mission of the small SAD team was to gather intelligence before the arrival of U.S. troops in this African country and, later when the troops arrived in country, to serve as a liaison with the U.S. military forces. On 22 December 1992, the vehicle in which Larry was riding drove over a Russian-built mine on the outskirts of a small village and he was killed. Three other U.S. Army soldiers were wounded in the incident and one of them later died. I was later informed that when Larry and my deputy, John, arrived in this small village that day, they were met by the local warlord who asked them which way they had come into the village. Larry and John replied that upon arriving at the fork in the road at the entrance to the village they had taken the road to the right. The warlord in turn told them that they both had been lucky because the road they had chosen was heavily mined. As John was continuing his discussions with the warlord, Larry decided to check out the other road with several of the U.S. Army soldiers and no sooner had they begun their journey when they hit the landmine and Larry was killed instantly. He was later buried at Arlington National Cemetery. On 31 December 1992, CIA Director Robert M. Gates awarded him a posthumous Intelligence Star for exceptional service. The citation recognized his "superior performance under hazardous combat conditions with the Central Intelligence Agency." As a sniper, Larry was nearly without peer. I remember one time at the Farm, during a session in which he and I got to test the ballistic resistant capabilities of various pieces of armor. Larry calmly loaded a sniper rifle that he had checked out from the gun vault and his first round and all subsequent rounds cut through an armored door like butter as everyone's face changed from one of delight to one of "oh shit, back to the drawing board".

* * *

Monday morning, 25 January 1993, was a normal, cold winter day. I arrived at work at 7:30 a.m. versus my normal 7:00 a.m. arrival after running into traffic on Interstate 495. Minutes after arriving, rumors began circulating around the halls of CIA Headquarters that there had been a shooting at the Route 123 entrance near the main visitor center.

Although I was no longer in the Office of Security, I immediately ran to the scene to see if I could lend some assistance. The first thing I saw was the body of CIA employee Frank Darling slumped over the seat in his vehicle and was shocked by the amount of confusion in that people were walking all over the crime scene although the Agency security protective officers had begun to cordon off the area while awaiting the arrival of Fairfax County Police.

When the FBI finally arrived, there was a heated discussion as to who would have jurisdiction in the case. Fairfax County Police claimed that they had jurisdiction because the incident did not occur on U.S. Government property; while the FBI countered that the murders took place immediately outside of a U.S. Government installation adjacent to U.S. Government property and involved U.S. government employees. Eventually calmer heads prevailed and the FBI and Fairfax County Police decided that it would be a joint investigation. Virginia State Police also arrived at the scene in that they have jurisdiction on adjoining Route 193. Most of the witnesses at the scene interviewed said that they thought the shooting was part of a CIA training exercise rather than a "real" incident in that many had their windows up on this cold morning with their radios on and, therefore, did not use any defensive maneuvers. The only person who reportedly used some type of defense action when the shooting began was a seasoned DO case officer named Mike K. who had been through the Agency's "crash and bang" course at the Farm and had just returned to Headquarters after serving overseas. To make matters worse, the traffic light at Route 123 and the main entrance to the CIA at the time was set at over 2 ½ minutes. It since has been changed to less then 45 seconds.

From what we were able to gather, at approximately 8:00 a.m., a single assailant, later identified as Mir Aimal Kasi, emerged from his vehicle behind a row of cars that were stopped at the traffic light waiting to make a left turn from Route 123 into the main entrance to the CIA compound. Armed with an AK-47 assault rifle, Kasi opened fire as he walked down the rows of automobiles and, within seconds, murdered Frank Darling and Lasing Bennett; wounded Nicholas Starr, Calvin Morgan, and Stephan Williams – all CIA employees. Several witnesses reported that Kasi exited his car with the rifle and, before shooting, actually discharged his weapon into the ground to see if it was functioning. Others reported that after firing into the first vehicle occupied by Frank Darling and his wife, he then moved to a second vehicle where he saw a female employee, looked her directly in the face, and moved on without firing his weapon at her. After killing several of the occupants, Kasi proceeded to return to his vehicle firing into many of the vehicles for a second time prior to departing the scene. Kasi, who lived in

Reston, Virginia with his friend, Zahed Mir, calmly fled the scene. A day after the shooting, he boarded a plane and escaped to Pakistan. Mir reported Kasi as a missing person two days later and Kasi remained the subject of a manhunt for more than four years.

The morning of 15 June 1997, sources provided information to the CIA that Kasi was in a hotel room in Pakistan. With this in hand, FBI agents stormed the room, handcuffed him, threw a hood over his head, and transported him to a jail in Pakistan, which later consented to Kasi's extradition to the Commonwealth of Virginia. During the flight back to Fairfax, Virginia, Kasi provided an oral and written confession claiming that he shot approximately 10 rounds while shooting five people that day in front of CIA Headquarters. Kasi also claimed that several days before the shooting he had narrowed his choice between the CIA and the Israeli Embassy in Washington, DC and stated that the reason why he had stopped shooting that day in front of the CIA was because "there wasn't anybody left to shoot." He also reportedly told the FBI that he only shot males because it was against his religion to shoot females.

Upon his arrival back in the United States, Kasi was tuned over to Fairfax County, Virginia for prosecution. Judith Darling, a CIA Logistics Officer, who had been a front seat passenger in the vehicle with her husband, Frank, the morning that her husband was killed, testified during Kasi's trial. Although there was no provision for the death penalty for a defendant charged with a Federal crime, on 4 February 1998, after three post-trial hearings, Kasi was sentenced to death for capital murder and was executed on 14 November 2002. Today, situated on the hillside near the entrance to Route 123 is a small memorial commemorating those that lost their lives that morning.

* * *

Less than a week after this incident, I attended a course at the Farm consisting of several men and a woman who were going overseas. The course was designed to see how you reacted and handled yourself when tired or completely exhausted in that you were in training 12 to 15 hours per day.

During the next three weeks, including the weekends, we woke up at 6:00 a.m. each day and had two hours of physical fitness. This was followed by an exhaustive regime of training which included heading to the range and shooting combat style courses or practicing our driving skills on a specialized track. In addition to shooting on the standard firearm ranges, we also practiced in a "shoot house" recently constructed at the Farm where your actions could be videotaped and later critiqued. I remember one such exercise where we were supposed to meet an agent. When meeting the agent, suddenly without warning a pop-up target would appear of a man with a shotgun. The purpose of the exercise was to draw your weapon from the holster on your hip and shoot the target prior to slowly departing the scene, as various other targets would suddenly appear. The only female student in our class shot the agent and when asked why she had shot the agent (the first student to ever do so), her reply was simple "I thought that I was being set up." This same farm girl by the name of Ellen B. grew up hunting pheasant and out shot everyone on the shotgun course.

Although I consider myself an avid hunter as well and not a bad shot with a shotgun, I received a zero in this particular course after one of the students decided to play a prank on me and loosened the cap on the shotgun's pump slide which ejects the shells. When I shot my first shot and tried to eject the first shell, the ejector slide, spring, and everything else came apart in my hands. When I tried to protest, the instructor told me that I should have checked my weapon first to make sure that it was in good condition prior to proceeding to the firing line – a lesson well learned.

When we were not shooting during this course, we were learning a variety of defensive driving maneuvers. At nighttime after cleaning our weapons and eating dinner, we were taught survival first aid for hours at a time. We were rated and scored following each exercise and I was delighted to learn that at the end of the course I had won the "Top Gun" award, which was presented, to the top student in the class at the graduation.

* * *

After finishing this training, I decided to spend several days in the mountains in Northern Pennsylvania with my friends Chuck Doelp, Paul Evanko, Sunny Snyder, Mike Brown, and George Wenschoff – an annual event that, when I was in the country, we would get together in the wintertime to shoot handguns, snowshoe, eat, drink, and relax.

The cabin that Sunny was a member of was built in the 1930s as part of President Roosevelt's Conservation Corp Program. Located in Potter County, the cabin had no running water, plumbing, or electricity. To say that it was rustic was an understatement. It was almost impossible to get a vehicle up the three-mile logging road in the wintertime due to the amount of snow, so we always brought a toboggan along and filled it with our provisions that included our clothing, guns, ammunition, food, beer, wine, and even a little bourbon for Sunny. Then, for the better part of a day, we dragged the toboggan up the mountain until we reached the cabin – a ritual that I am glad that I only had to perform once per year.

Waking up in the morning, we were always greeted by an inch or so of fresh snow and Sunny with a half of cup of bourbon, which we had to consume before we left our sleeping bags. It was during such a trip that all of us huddled around a small transistor radio one evening and heard that a massive explosion occurred in the public parking garage of the World Trade Center in New York City earlier in the day on 26 February 1993. We later learned that for two months prior to the bombing, the conspirators gathered materials needed for the terrorist act while residing in New Jersey. After renting storage space, the 1,500-pound urea-nitrate bomb, when completed, was loaded into a Ryder rental van and driven into the basement of the World Trade Center where the timer was set prior to the conspirators departing the area. Upon detonating, the explosion rocked the World Trade Center killing six people and injuring over a thousand others. The men that committed this heinous crime were linked to several terrorist groups including the Islamic Jihad, Hamas, and the Sudanese National Islamic Front.

In December 1993, Sheikh Abdullah Rahman and 14 followers were indicted in the U.S. for the bombing of the World Trade Center. They were also accused of conspiracy to blow up the Holland and Lincoln Tunnels under the Hudson River; the George Washington Bridge; the United Nations Building; and for planning assassinations of prominent Americans to include Senator Alfonso D'Amato.

On 4 March 1994, a jury also found Mohammed Salameh, Ahmad Ajaj, Mohammed Abuhalima, and Nidal Ayyad guilty of the World Trade Center bombing. All were sentenced to 240 years in prison. The masterminds for this plot, Eyad Ismoil and Ramzi Yousef, however, were not caught until later. Prosecutors believed Eyad helped Ramzi load the bomb into the truck and then drove it to the World Trade Center basement where he parked the vehicle and departed the area. Eyad was sentenced to 240 years in prison and ordered to pay a $10 million dollar fine. Yousef received life in prison plus 240 years and a $4.5 million dollar fine. He was also ordered to pay $250 million dollars in restitution. The fines were given to insure that these men would never profit from their actions. The judge further recommended that Yousef spend his sentence in solitary confinement. Federal prosecutors are still looking for Adul Rahmin Yasin in connection with the bombing. He is believed to have fled to Iraq.

* * *

As noted in "Jihad in America" by famed author, Steve Emerson, three years earlier, in November 1990, an Egyptian immigrant, El Sayyid Nosair, was arrested by NYC police for the murder of militant Rabbi Amir Kahane. Although Nosair had ties to a radical international network, NYC police never investigated the possibility of a larger conspiracy, believing that he was a lone gunman in the homicide.

After Nosair's arrest, detectives searched his Manhattan apartment and found 47 boxes of personal possessions and papers but dismissed these papers as irrelevant religious materials. It was only after the World Trade Center bombing three years later in 1993 that law enforcement officials re-examined Nosair's papers and realized that they had overlooked one of the largest collection of terrorist materials ever found in the U.S. These papers included plans to blow up American skyscrapers and revealed that Nosair was at the head of a worldwide terrorist organization headquartered right here in the U.S. The boxes included formulas for bomb making, detailed instructions for attacking aircraft, assassination targets, and classified U.S. military documents. One such quote found in a spiral notebook in the apartment of El Sayyid Nosair by New York City law enforcement officials, spells out Nosair's plans for the destruction of the enemies of Allah, *"We have to thoroughly demoralize the enemies of God by means of destroying and blowing up their towers that constitute the pillars of their civilization such as the tourist attractions they are so proud of and the high buildings they are so proud of."*

I always liked the way Steve Emerson put it when he said that he, *"...found it interesting to note, that anti-western militants find the United States the easiest place to raise funds, disseminate propaganda, and build up their political organizations. The United States gives them a platform that they can use for the rest of the world to produce their films and distribute their propaganda to support their global movement. Due to our Constitutional rights to*

"Freedom of Religion" and "Freedom of Speech" in the United States, many statements made by these groups go largely unnoticed. It is ironic, however, that the very freedoms, which allow these groups to function and operate in the United States, are what they despise. From an American viewpoint, it is difficult to comprehend why people that we allow to benefit from our system and our protections would turn around and, in essence, hate us for it."

* * *

During a civil war to conquer Somalia in 1993, Islamic terrorists created widespread famine by attacking the United Nation's (UN) humanitarian efforts. Acting as part of the UN's Peacekeeping Forces, American soldiers were sent to Somalia to restore order so that international aid could be distributed.

During the period of 3 to 4 October 1993, eighteen American servicemen were killed in a 15 hour gun battle which included shooting down five U.S. helicopters, two of which were "Black Hawks", with rocket propelled grenades and machine guns. In a victory parade, the naked bodies of the U.S. soldiers were dragged by ropes through the streets of Mogadishu amid cheers of the Islamic Extremists. An al-Qaeda defector, Jamal Ahmed al-Fadl, implicated both Osama Bin Ladin and Mohammed Atef in planning the killings that were carried out under the leadership of Mohammed Farah Aideed. Two soldiers killed during the fighting, Sergeant First Class Randall Shugart and Master Sergeant Gary Gordon, were individuals that I had trained with at one of our explosive training facilities. Both would receive the Medal of Honor posthumously for their actions. Gordon's sniper team provided fire from the lead helicopter at the two crash sites and when he learned ground forces were not available to secure one of the sites, he and Shughart volunteered to be inserted to protect four wounded personnel. After receiving permission to perform this mission, he and Shughart were inserted 100 meters south of the crash site. With only his sniper rifle and pistol, Gordon and Shughart fought through a maze of shanties and shacks to reach the injured crew. Gordon pulled the pilot and the other crew from the aircraft, establishing a perimeter, which placed him and Shughart in the most vulnerable position. Gordon then used his long-range rifle and side arm to kill an undetermined number of attackers and, afterwards, went to the wreckage to recover some of the crew's weapons. Though low on ammunition, he gave it to the dazed pilot and radioed for help. After Shughart was fatally wounded and his own ammunition exhausted, Gordon returned to the wreckage, recovered a rifle with the last five rounds of ammunition and gave it to the pilot with the words, "good luck." Armed only with his pistol, he continued to fight until he was fatally wounded. His actions saved the pilot's life.

* * *

During the late 1980's and early 1990's, Pablo Escobar was one of the most violent criminals as well as one of the richest men in the world. He began his criminal record in Medellin as a car thief and tomb pillager but later turned to drug smuggling, eventually forming the Medellin Cartel with the Ochoa Brothers (Jorge, Juan David and Fabio), Carlos Lehder and Gonzalo Rodriguez Gacha (aka El Mexicano) which, at its height, was responsible for 80% of cocaine "exports" to the U.S.

During his reign of terror, Escobar and his followers assassinated policemen, government ministers and, in 1989, the popular Liberal Party presidential candidate, Luis Galan. In 1991, the Colombian government struck a deal with Escobar who volunteered to serve time only if he was confined to a prison, which he built himself known as "La Catedral" which contained a soccer field, a Jacuzzi, gym, and a luxurious office. A year later, in July 1992, the Colombian government decided to send Escobar to a high security prison but he escaped before the arrival of the police. Shortly thereafter, the U.S. started providing special military advisers from Delta Force and an Army intelligence unit known as "Centra Spike" to train a group of special police units known as the Colombian Search Bloc in Medellin under the command of Colonel Hugo Martinez who was called back to Colombia from Madrid. Colombian Search Bloc was established to study Escobar's idiosyncrasies, unique personal style, and to recognize his voice in an attempt to hunt him down.

As was the case with the special counterterrorist unit in Peru, Colonel Martinez handpicked the members of the Colombian Search Bloc and had every member polygraphed. To ensure the unit's integrity, like the Peruvian counterterrorist unit, Colombian Search Bloc members were placed in seclusion for days at a time, without any contact with their family or friends so that nothing would be leaked in the event that they were provided an order to move on a suspect target. One day in February 1993, while flying in a Beechcraft aircraft over Medellin, one of the Centra Spike electronic surveillance operators monitoring the airwaves was stunned to hear a brief radio transmission from Pablo Escobar who was irate that the U.S. Embassy in Bogotá refused to issue visas for his wife and children to flee to the United States. After plotting the coordinates, the intercept was sent to the Search Bloc headquarters where Colonel Martinez shared the information with his top officers. The transmissions were linked to the apartment building that housed Pablo Escobar's wife and family in Medellin.

On the night of 26 November 1993, the U.S. Embassy in Bogotá learned that Pablo Escobar's wife and children were planning once more to flee Colombia, this time aboard a Lufthansa flight to Germany. When the plane carrying the family of Escobar finally landed in Frankfurt, Germany, it was forced to taxi to a remote spot on an alternate runway, out of the view of press waiting in the terminal, where it was then sent back to Colombia. When Escobar's son reported the incident to his father from a telephone, Escobar became irate.

As luck would have it, this communication was intercepted by the "Centra Spike" operators scanning the communications in the area where Escobar was supposed to be hiding out in Medellin and traced it to a neighborhood and the exact location of Escobar. As Colonel Martinez's unit raided the residence on 2 December 1993, Escobar opened fire and was met by volleys of return fire from some of the dozen special police unit members. Escobar was eventually shot and killed as he and his bodyguards tried to elude police by climbing onto a rooftop of the safe house where they were hiding.

The following day, the local Colombian newspapers reported that the Colombian authorities in Medellin had traced Escobar when he telephoned a radio station over the weekend to protest official treatment of his wife and children whose attempt to leave the country was rebuffed. Escobar reportedly eluded police by frequently shifting from one safe house to another and paying weekly bribes to corrupt officials. The United States and Colombia had offered $8.7 million for his capture.

Burning cocaine in South America

Chapter 9

"Life at its Best: My First European Post"

In August 1993, the Deputy Chief of the Special Activities Division (SAD), Bill R., was selected to be the next chief in one of our European posts and wanted me to accompany him as one of his branch chiefs. Several days later, when the Chief of SAD, George H., was selected to head our office in another European post, Bill was trumped and George asked me to accompany him as one of his branch chiefs. Shortly thereafter, in September 1993, I returned to language training in preparation for my PCS. The highlight of this ten-month language-training program involved a one-month immersion with George in this European country where I lived with a local family and even played in several rugby games.

I arrived in my first European post with my family on 12 July 1994. This time, instead of two children, we had three children following the birth of our youngest daughter, Kathleen, who was born on 16 September 1993. One month to the day of our arrival, "Carlos the Jackal," the celebrated international terrorist was tracked down and apprehended in Khartoum, Sudan by the Sudanese government. He was turned over to the French Direction del la Surveillance (DST) based on an international arrest warrant for killing two unarmed DST police officers who had visited his apartment in Paris in the 1970's. After being transported to a prison in Paris, France, Carlos appeared before Jean-Louis Bruguiere, France's top anti-terrorist judge on 16 August 1994. While the French and the rest of the world savored the capture of the most dangerous terrorist in the world. Little did anyone know that Billy W., a retired, legendary Special Forces Command Sergeant Major, under the direction of the chief of our office, Cofer Black, was the individual who first spotted and photographed Carlos several months earlier on 8 February 1994. Since the United States did not have any active arrest warrants against Carlos, the decision was to have the Sudanese take Carlos into custody and turn him over to the DST.

Carlos, whose real name is Illich Ramirez Sanchez, is a Venezuelan born Marxist who at an early age allied himself with the Palestinian cause. Although Carlos is believed to have played a role in the kidnapping and murder of the Israeli athletes during the 1972 summer Olympics in Munich, his first murder occurred on 30 December 1973 when he entered the residence of a prominent

London businessman, who was also a leading fund raiser for Jewish charities, shot and killed him.

Carlos is most noted for orchestrating the attack on the Organization of Petroleum Exporting Countries (OPEC) meeting in December 1975, kidnapping 11 Middle East Ministers and killing three of them. Following the attack, Carlos and the kidnappers commandeered a plane and flew to Algiers where they released the hostages after receiving $20 million in ransom. They then surrendered only to be released shortly thereafter, due to a sympathetic government. Carlos again made headlines with his involvement in the Palestinian hijacking of a French airliner headed for Entebbe, Uganda, which ended in the famous raid by Israeli commandos. Later in 1982, a team led by Carlos tried to blow up a nuclear reactor in France but the attempt failed. Also in 1982, after the French arrested two of Carlos' accomplices, Magdalena Kopp and Bruno Breguet, Carlos went on a killing spree that resulted in 125 injuries and 12 deaths, which led to the French releasing Kopp and Breguet. Kopp eventually joined Carlos in Damascus, Syria and they married in 1985. Prior to ending up in Khartoum, Sudan in August 1993 under the protection of President Al-Bashir and his Vice-President Hassan al-Turabi, Carlos is believed to have spent time in the Bekaa Valley in Lebanon, Syria, Yemen, and Jordan. It was in Jordan that Carlos married his second wife, a young Jordanian Arab by the name of Lana, who was with him at the time of his arrest.

* * *

Although promised a branch chief position before I arrived in country, I was stunned to find that the previous chief had just promoted an officer currently assigned to our office to this position without first checking with George H. When informed of this decision, George asked me if I was interested in setting up and managing a new counternarcotics program for a year before taking over the branch chief position. According to George, the Counternarcotics Center (CNC) was interested in developing a counternarcotics program in the country where we were assigned because, it and one of its neighbors, were increasingly becoming the gateway into Europe for Latin American based cocaine.

In the mid 1980s, Colombian drug lords had to flee Colombia due to pressure being put on them for the first time in their history. Two of these drug lords, Jorge Luis Ochoa and Gilberto Rodríguez-Orejuela, fled to Europe where they had already established some friendships and had strong economic interests. Carlos Lehder, another drug lord, had already been in Europe for some time. All three of these drug lords felt that they could operate freely in Europe without being harassed by the Drug Enforcement Agency (DEA) although DEA had just opened its first office there. An additional plus for them was the fact that many of the recently elected socialist government's in Europe were reluctant to collaborate with the United States Government. Since each of these men thought that their stay would be a long-term one, their fellow Colombian traffickers began to organize new markets for cocaine shipments to Europe. Ironically, in 1986, both Jorge Luis Ochoa and Gilberto Rodríguez-Orejuela were arrested in Europe and extradited to Colombia where they continued using their contacts in prison to ship cocaine to Europe prior to being released by the Colombian Government. By 1989, the country where I had been assigned became the main point of entry for cocaine in Europe and the principal receptor of money laundering for Colombian traffickers.

As the counternarcotics program manager, George wanted me to work with the two police services, one civilian and one military and in close coordination/cooperation with U.S. law enforcement representatives in the U.S. Embassy there, including the DEA and FBI. Our goal for establishing this program was to provide the host country with intelligence from the Counternarcotics Center (CNC), other Headquarters components, Latin America, and European sister offices, as well as technical equipment and training. We started by providing "lead" information, notably from Latin America due to the increased amount of cocaine shipped to and through Europe, and convinced the civilian and military police counternarcotic services that it was more important to focus on disrupting entire networks rather than individual traffickers.

To demonstrate the effectiveness of the success of this government over the three years that I was in this European post, you need to look at the number of organizations dismantled and the number of successful seizures this country had between 1994 and 1996. According to European Police Office (Europol) and European Drug Office (Eurodrug) reports, during the first two years of my assignment (1994-1996), this country doubled the amount of cocaine, heroin and hashish seized during the previous years ranking them near the top in Europe for the first time. In addition, hundreds of individuals were incarcerated on drug trafficking charges, over 100 narcotics trafficking groups were dismantled, and a handful of cocaine conversion laboratories were dismantled. Information obtained during one of their "takedown" operations in 1995 was passed to several Latin American countries, which led to the dismantlement of a major Colombian trafficker in April 1996.

According to Europol and Eurodrug reports, of the cocaine seized in Europe in 1995, 42 percent originated in Colombia, 21 percent in Brazil and Venezuela, and seven percent in Panama and Bolivia. The majority of the cocaine shipped from South America was aboard maritime vessels and in containers. Air service was used to a lesser extent. Of the heroin seized in Europe during 1995, 85-90 percent originated in Turkey and Southwest Asia (Afghanistan and Pakistan), while 10-15 percent originated in Southeastern Asia (Laos and Thailand). Most of this heroin arrived in small trucks and vehicles via the "Balkans Route" through Romania, Bulgaria, and Hungary and, to a lesser extent, Italy and Greece. Almost all of the hashish originated in Morocco.

During my third year (1996-1997), the European country where I was assigned again doubled the amount of cocaine, heroin and hashish seized during the previous year, ranking them at the top in European seizures for the third straight year. The highlight of 1996 was the seizure of over 1,100 kilograms of cocaine following a one-year investigation by the police. In addition to the cocaine, numerous arrests were made, residences and companies were raided, and several bank accounts were frozen. This was one of the largest and most important narcotics trafficking organization dismantlement's in this country's history.

1,100 kilograms of Cocaine

While public credit was given to several services, according to the press reports, the equipment and training provided proved invaluable in carrying out this operation. The press reported that H/F intercept equipment was crucial in locating and tracking the vessel while cellular telephone intercept systems used to monitor the mobile telephone conversations of the head of the organization eventually led to his capture and arrest. Although we cannot assume all the credit for this success, I am confident that our assistance clearly enhanced their efforts to combat narcotics trafficking and organized crime during my three-year tour. There is no doubt in my mind that the lead information, equipment, and training we provided produced solid results and enabled this country to develop their own follow-on capabilities. In February 1996, our office was recognized for outstanding achievement through training and, at the time of my departure in the summer of 1997, the counternarcotics program in this country was responsible for more than sixty percent of the office's intelligence reporting.

Another highlight of the counternarcotics program, in 1996, involved the military police rather than the civilian police. In August of that year, the military police asked for assistance in intercepting shipments of hashish and marijuana transported from Northern Africa using fast boats equipped with large engines. Upon reaching the coast, these boats would quickly unload their cargo of hashish and marijuana and then turn around to head back to North Africa. The military police claimed they had a source that worked at a marina in North Africa, who was willing to assist in identifying the boats that were transporting these shipments. After identifying one or more of the boats, the military police wanted to put tracking devices on them to see where the boats were delivering their merchandise. More importantly, the military police were interested in identifying who was picking up the shipment on the other end after it reached landfall to find out where they were transporting the drugs. After our initial meeting, I drafted a cable and sent it back to the Counternarcotics Center (CNC) requesting permission to support this operation. Receiving approval for such an operation requires the signature of not only the Director of the Counternarcotics Center, but also the Deputy Director of Operations (DDO) because it involved an operation with another government. Instead of the approval to proceed that we were looking for, however, we received a cable from Headquarters requesting additional information to demonstrate that we could conduct the operation securely and safely without compromising the operation or the source. In most instances, when a source is compromised the local traffickers would kill him or her. Finally, in early December, George sent a cable back to Washington starting with the phrase, "Let's review the bidding", and went on to say that if we did not begin the operation immediately, the hashish and cannabis cultivation in North Africa would be over and hurricane season would be upon us. Lo and behold, the next day George walked into my office and handed me an "Eyes Only" cable with DDO approval to proceed.

Over the Mediterranean Sea 1996

Shortly thereafter, Headquarters sent a team of technicians to assist us in the effort. On their arrival, we met with our military police counterparts, then drove down to the coast and settled in a small town where the military police had several helicopters and fixed wing aircraft at a nearby airfield. Unfortunately, as we began to test some of our equipment the weather turned nasty and the water became very rough with nine to twelve foot swells. The first night I was on board the military police vessel the swells began to make me and the majority of the crew seasick. After watching one after another of us vomiting overboard, the Captain, an old seasoned veteran of the seas, finally said "enough". He ordered two long loaves of bread similar to French baguettes, a package of twelve year old Manchego cheese soaked in olive oil, and several bottles of wine be brought top side and ordered everyone to eat the bread and cheese and then drink the wine. Unbelievably, within a half hour, we were no longer seasick. The Captain explained that the bread soaked up the acid in our stomach, the cheese made us feel like we had something in our stomach so we did not dry heave or throw-up, and lastly the wine calmed our nerves. After two days on these seas, we decided to abort the operation and return to land until the weather cleared. Finally, thirty-six hours after returning to port the weather began to improve and the seas began to calm but, by this time, the moon was full and everyone knew that nobody would risk transporting a shipment of drugs when they could easily be spotted.

During the next several days, while waiting for cover of darkness, we decided to take a drive along the coast. As evening approached and the moon began to fade, taken to a beach, we watched as a host of boats appeared, unloaded cargo, and vanished as quickly as they had arrived. What a "cat and mouse" game to see the traffickers on cell phones waiting for the "all clear" signal from their friends on the beach as the patrol boats went by. Inspecting some of the fast boats with their 250 horsepower engines at one of the marinas, it was no great surprise to see that some of them had bullet holes—some patched, some not. Having waned, with no moon, we hoped that word would come that one of the vessel's carrying drugs would cross the water. Eager for success, we returned to the helicopter, the military police vessel, and the vehicles.

On 21 December 1996, as the 56 foot military police vessel was departing, they received word that a boat with drugs on board was heading their way. Locating the vessel, we were later told that the military police vessel pulled along side of the boat, boarded it, and found hashish hidden in a false compartment in the floor. As the military police handcuffed and transported the boat Captain and the four-member crew to their vessel, the military police Captain remained below deck as the second in command, a young police Lieutenant, walked up to the Captain of the boat seated nearby with his hands handcuffed behind his back shivering from the cold. When the Lieutenant asked the Captain of the boat whom he was transporting the drugs to, the Captain spat in his face and told him to f--- himself. He repeated the question and again received the same answer.

As he was about to ask the boat Captain a third time whom he was transporting the drugs to, the Captain of the military police vessel came out from below deck and calmly approached the Captain of the drug smuggling boat. Nearing him the individual immediately began by saying, "Don't you know who I am? I'm so and so, and you all are going to be in deep f---ing trouble for having stopped me and confiscated my cargo." We were told that the military police Captain politely asked the boat Captain if he would like a cigarette to which the boat Captain replied, "Of course." The military police Captain then asked the boat Captain if he would like a blanket and then placed one over his shivering shoulders. Next, the military police Captain offered the boat Captain a cup of coffee and surprisingly took off his handcuffs. As the man stood face to face with the military police Captain obviously feeling quite a bit better, we were told that the military police Captain slowly asked the boat Captain whom he was going to deliver the drugs to. As the boat Captain turned to spit in the face of the military police Captain and say "f--- you", the military police Captain promptly pushed the man overboard and said, "Well, maybe after a few hours in the sea, you will remember". The military police Captain asked his crew to take coordinates and then sped away into the darkness. An hour or so later, the military police vessel returned to the spot where the boat Captain had been thrown overboard and found him bobbing in the waves clinging to a small piece of wood as a life preserver. As the crew hauled him back on board, the military police Captain approached the boat Captain and very politely asked him if he would like a cup of coffee, a cigarette, and a blanket to which the boat Captain eagerly agreed. This time when the military police Captain asked the boat Captain, who he was delivering the hashish to, the boat Captain began singing like a canary providing information on everything he knew about the delivery and the organization behind it.

* * *

I would love to say that we had more success than this one incident but Christmas was rapidly approaching and even narcotics traffickers take time off during the Christmas holidays. The following day we returned home with only this one small seizure of about 5,000 kilos of hashish to claim as success.

Arriving back at our office on Christmas Eve, 24 December 1996, I was surprised to read about an incident, which had occurred at CIA Headquarters the night before on 23 December 1996. At 8:58 p.m. guards at the CIA's main entrance noticed a 1996 Ford pick up truck bearing a Virginia license plate approaching the gate at a high rate of speed. Instead of slowing down to show identification, the vehicle continued through the gate despite the guard's efforts to stop it. Entering the compound, the vehicle continued to the front doors and eventually came to a stop after attempting to drive up the steps into the main Headquarters building with security personnel in pursuit. As the vehicle came to a stop, the security protective officers, with weapons drawn, asked the occupant to exit the vehicle. Acting irrational, the driver repeatedly replied, "Shoot me. Please shoot me." After a standoff of several minutes, the security protective officers convinced the driver, identified as David O.

Crump, to exit the vehicle and he was immediately taken into custody. During his interrogation, Mr. Crump advised that he had intended to crash his vehicle into the main entrance of the CIA. This incident immediately brought about a number of changes in the security posture at the compound entrances, which I cannot go into detail about or discuss.

* * *

During my tour in this European post, in addition to focusing on counternarcotics, we decided to add organized crime to our charter. So, in addition to targeting Italian organized crime, we decided to target Russian organized crime as well which was rapidly expanding outside of the borders of Russia.

In the early 1990s, Sergei "Mikhas" Mikhailov, the leader of Moscow's Solntsevo organization, the largest and most powerful Russian Crime Group and many of his fellow Russian Organized Crime figures, including Semion Mogilevich, fled Moscow to avoid the then widespread gangland wars in the capital. In addition to operating in Moscow, the Solntsevo organization, which reportedly had grown to 4,000 members worldwide, had substantial interests in Belgium, the United States, and in South America. Working with Colombian traffickers, the Solntsevo organization started supplying cocaine to Russia for domestic consumption, transporting the drug through Russian to European markets, and smuggling Afghan heroin through Russia to Europe. After departing Russia, Mogilevich and his top henchmen settled in Israel where Mogilevich received Israeli citizenship. After marrying a Hungarian national, Mogilevich legally immigrated to Budapest, Hungary where he began to build the foundation of his global criminal empire in the mode of a traditional American mafia family. Shortly thereafter, Mogilevich bought a string of nightclubs in Prague, Riga, and Kiev called the "Black and White Clubs" that went on to become one of the world's foremost centers of prostitution with the Black and White Club in Budapest becoming the hub of Mogilevich's operations which, at the height of the organization, consisted of approximately 250 members – mostly relatives.

During the same period (the early 1990s), the United States Government learned that a major Russian mafia figure in New York City, named Riccardo Fanchini, who was operating from the "Little Odessa" neighborhood of Brooklyn, was involved in smuggling cocaine to the United States from Europe. Because he had close connections to the inner circle of Russian President Boris Yeltsin,

Fanchini facilitated a legitimate deal to export vodka to Russia under a partnership with Moscow's National Sports Foundation, which received a royalty from every bottle sold. In 1992, the Kremlyovskaya Group was formed in Brussels, Belgium under Fanchini and began producing Belgium vodka that was transported tax-free into Russia with the tax going to sports associations such as the Monaco Grand Prix, which he sponsored. Several years later, he and his friends negotiated for the company to merge into a NASDAQ-listed "shell" company, Asia Media Communications (AMC), and reportedly received $89 million in AMC shares. In the interim, like many other Russian organized crime figures, Fanchini selected southern Europe as his base of operation for laundering money generated in businesses stemming from drug trafficking, arms trafficking, extortion, and kidnapping. Operating from a small town along the coast, he and two of his business partners, Roman Frumson and Harry Peralta created a company named Global Regal Yachting Service, which specialized in selling luxury yachts to enable them to operate virtually unnoticed.

One of the yachts that Global Regal Yachting Service was trying to sell was named the "Kremlin Princess" (the second largest private yacht in the world). The 175 foot, 6 inch "Kremlin Princess" was built by Oceanfast in Fremantle, Australia in 1994 as the "Oceana C". The yacht's name changed to "Kremlin Princess" after Fanchini purchased it in 1996 –reportedly for $45 million. The yacht changed its name in 1998 to the "Merlin" and later to "Lil Sis" before adopting its current name the "Bakhshish". In December 1995, Russian President Boris Yeltsin repealed the decree allowing the import of liquor duty free in Russia with the tax going to sports associations, and in April 1996, the Kremlyovskaya Group filed for bankruptcy.

Several months later, in November 1996, Fanchini lost his liquor import/export company. To further complicate matters for him, the Belgium government had opened an investigation on him for laundering Moscow mafia money through Geneva to Antwerp for investment in residential real estate. Fanchini was eventually arrested and convicted in Antwerp of bankruptcy fraud in relation to the Kremlyovskaya Group Company's collapse and although he was only given a two-year prison sentence, most of it was suspended. The second member of this group, Harry Peralta, was arrested on cocaine charges in the Caribbean while the third member of this group, Roman Frumson was found dead in his home with two gun shot wounds to the back of his head. Apparently, he had been cheating on his wife who ordered him killed. The wife was later arrested and charged with murder. Thus, a little over a year after beginning their operation, the police in this European country were able to have Fanchini and his top associates jailed and all of their assets frozen which lead to the dismantlement of the entire organization.

* * *

During the morning of 29 July 1994, a loud explosion rocked the U.S. Embassy. As reports trickled in that a large car bomb had detonated near the Plaza de Ramales in Madrid, the Spanish civilian and Madrid metropolitan police had cordoned off the scene. I subsequently learned that three people, including General Francisco Veguillas from the Spanish Ministry of Defense, had been killed and fifteen others injured in the blast.

This was my first association with ETA, the "Basque Fatherland and Liberty" leftist group that uses terrorism with the goal of forming an independent Basque state in parts of northern Spain and southwest France. Since killing its first Spanish victim in 1968 in San Sebastian, ETA has killed over eight hundred individuals, mostly senior Spanish government officials, regional officials, journalists, and civilians while targeting government and military institutions in Basque regions. One of their more brazen acts occurred in 1973, when ETA operatives killed the aging dictator Francisco Franco's apparent successor, Admiral Luis Carrero Blanco, in retaliation for the government's execution of Basque militants by planting an underground bomb below his habitual parking spot outside a Madrid church across the street from the U.S. Embassy. The State Department lists ETA as a foreign terrorist group. Following the 29 July 1994 assassination of General Francisco Veguillas, the Spanish National Police bomb-squad began an intensive refresher training program, although they and their counterpart in the military police were considered two of the finest bomb-squads in the world.

On 19 April 1995, I learned that a car bomb had detonated along side the armored Audi belonging to the leader of the Spanish opposition conservative Popular Party, Jose Maria Aznar, who later served as Spain's Prime Minister. Although one of the female attackers died and 19 people were injured, Aznar survived along with his bodyguard and driver thanks in part to the vehicles airbag deploying. After learning, that Aznar departed his residence at the same time every morning and used the same route to work, the following day we learned that the Spanish National Police immediately began providing personal protection training to Aznar's security detail. It was during this training that we learned that Spanish investigators disrupted an ETA plot to assassinate King Juan Carlos of Spain.

I had briefly met King Juan Carlos and his wife Queen Sofia during a National Police Day celebration in Retiro Park during a visit to Madrid shortly after my arrival in Europe. Following the ceremony, the Spanish National Police held a small reception for invited guests, many of whom stood in line to meet the King and Queen. I was not comfortable meeting with the King and Queen, in that I was particularly concerned that somehow my CIA affiliation would be divulged. My worst nightmare became a reality when the head of the Spanish National Police grabbed me by the hand as the greeting line was beginning to break up and presented me to the King and Queen by saying, "Your Highness, Queen Sofia, may I introduce Richard Irwin from the Central Intelligence Agency". With my mouth open and my heart skipping a beat, the Queen politely informed me that her mother had once worked for the Office of Strategic Services under William (Bill) Donovan as part of the Greek resistance movement following World War II and then went on to talk about it in some detail. Afterwards, the King called one of his aides and presented me with a tie clip with the Royal Crown insignia upon it – a gift that I wear frequently and treasure to this day.

* * *

While I was working closely with my counterparts to combat terrorism in Europe, one of the most horrendous acts of terrorism occurred on U.S. soil in 1995.

On the morning of 19 April 1995, most employees of the Murrah Federal Building in Oklahoma City, Oklahoma had already arrived at work and children been dropped off at the daycare center when a huge explosion tore through the building at 9:02 a.m. Pulverized, nearly the entire north face of the nine-story building was now dust and rubble.

In all, 168 people were killed in the explosion, including 19 children, and it took two weeks of sorting through debris to find the victims. After hearing the news on television, I was immediately convinced that this act, like that of the World Trade Center bombing in 1993, was the result of Islamic extremists. Boy was I wrong, especially after seeing the face of a tall, clean cut, white suspect who had been arrested shortly after the bombing. To this day, it is difficult for me to believe that an American could commit such an act against other Americans. Two years earlier, on 19 April 1993, the standoff between the FBI and the Branch Davidian cult (led by David Koresh) at the Davidian compound in Waco, Texas ended in a fiery tragedy. When the FBI tried to end the standoff by gassing the complex, the entire compound went up in fire, claiming the lives of 75 followers, including many young children. The death toll at the Davidian compound was high and many people blamed the U.S. government for the tragedy. One such person was Timothy McVeigh. Angered by the Waco tragedy, McVeigh decided to enact retribution on those he felt responsible–the Federal Government, especially the FBI and the Bureau of Alcohol, Tobacco, and Firearms (ATF). In downtown Oklahoma City, the Alfred P. Murrah Federal Building held numerous Federal agency offices, including those of the ATF.

Planning his revenge for the second anniversary of the Waco disaster, McVeigh enlisted his friend, Terry Nichols, and several others to help him pull off his plan. In September 1994, McVeigh purchased large amounts of fertilizer (ammonium nitrate–the main ingredient for the bomb) and then stored it in a rented shed in Herington, Kansas. McVeigh and Nichols stole other supplies needed to complete the bomb from a quarry in Marion, Kansas. On 17 April 1995, McVeigh rented a Ryder truck and with the assistance of Nichols loaded it with approximately 5,000 pounds of ammonium nitrate fertilizer. McVeigh drove the Ryder truck to the Murrah Federal Building on the morning of 19 April, parked it in front of the building, lit the bomb's fuse, left the keys inside the truck, and locked the door. Afterwards, he calmly walked across the parking lot to an alley and started to jog.

Ninety minutes after the explosion, McVeigh was pulled over by a highway patrol officer for driving without a license plate, but when the officer discovered that McVeigh had an unregistered gun, he arrested him on a firearms charge. Before McVeigh was released, his ties to the explosion were discovered. Unfortunately, for McVeigh, almost all his purchases and rental agreements relating to the bombing were traced back to him after the explosion. On 3 June 1997, McVeigh was convicted of murder and conspiracy, and on 15 August 1997, he was sentenced to death by lethal injection. McVeigh was executed on 11 June 2001. Nichols was brought in for questioning two days after the blast and then arrested for his role in McVeigh's plan. On 24 December 1997, a federal jury found Nichols guilty and on 5 June 1998, Nichols was sentenced to life in prison. In

March 2004, Nichols went on trial for murder charges by the State of Oklahoma. A third accomplice, Michael Fortier, who testified against McVeigh and Nichols, received a 12-year prison sentence and was fined $200,000 on 27 May 1998 for knowing about the plan but not informing authorities before the explosion. What little remained of the Murrah Federal Building was demolished on 23 May 1995. In 2000, a memorial was built on the location to remember the tragedy of the Oklahoma City Bombing.

* * *

Serving overseas meant that we frequently received an enormous number of invitations to attend receptions and special events at various Embassies. Since it was impossible to attend all of the events, we always carefully chose which ones we would have the greatest chance of meeting targets of opportunities for possible recruitment.

Getting an invitation to the Russian Embassy, for example, was almost impossible because the U.S Ambassador and only a few key figures would get invitations. Therefore, when the chief of our office, George H., called me into his office and told me that he wanted me to attend a function at the Russian Embassy in his absence, I was elated. Arriving early, as was my custom, I was introduced to a variety of Russian diplomats and military personnel as I made my way through the reception line. The Russian Embassy had just been built several years earlier and was truly magnificent.

After making small talk to a variety of other embassy officials in the room, whom I recognized from other events, and as the guestroom began to get crowded, I decided to put my back against a wall and carefully observe my surroundings. Much to my surprise, a Russian who I had briefly met earlier appeared to being doing the same thing so I quietly walked up behind him and said, *"By the way that you are scanning the crowd and the room it is obvious that you must have been a bodyguard at one time,"* to which he shockingly replied, *"Why yes, how did you know?"* When I told him that I had read his file, I thought that he was going to have a heart attack. I then extended my hand, reintroduced myself by presenting my business card, and told him that I had been a bodyguard too, at one time. The Russian, who I will refer to as Alex, at first greeted me with suspicion but then warmed up after he realized that I was kidding. I immediately liked Alex and we talked for the next hour or so about a variety of topics including fishing and hunting–two of my favorite pastimes. Unlike the majority of the other individuals in the room, I purposely never talked about work, politics, or current events during a social outing such as this. As the evening was winding down, I casually mentioned to Alex that I had a zodiac with a 25 horsepower engine and frequently fished in several of the lakes northeast of the capital where we lived. When I asked him if he wanted to join me one day, he gave me his personal cell phone number and I, in turn, gave him mine.

The following day, after reporting my encounter with Alex to Headquarters and asking for traces, I learned that, like me, Alex was an Intelligence Officer – in his case a KGB Officer. After receiving permission to see him again, I called Alex but before asking him if he wanted to go fishing, Alex invited me to have drinks with him that evening. As I jumped in a cab to the bar where we would meet, the skies opened up and it began to rain heavily. When I arrived, much to my surprise, there was Alex standing outside in the rain under an awning in front of the bar, leaning against a wall smoking a cigarette, wearing a black trench coat with his collar up and a black fedora hat on his head. As I exited the cab and approached him I told Alex that he looked liked a character right out of an old "Humphrey Bogart" movie to which he replied, *"Richard, that is exactly how I planned it."* As we were seated at a table, the bar, I soon realized, was a call girl service establishment with red velvet couches, thick drapes, mirrors, and beautiful young girls on the arms of older men everywhere in the room. Ordering vodka and tonics, we both settled into a game of questions such as *"Where were you born?" "How many brothers and sisters do you have?" "What do your parents do for a living?" "Where did you go to school?" "Are you married?" "Do you have any children?" "Do you like living here?" "Is this your first post?"* and *"Where did you serve before?"* Like Alex, I was taking everything in so that I could write it up the following day. I am confident that he was doing the same thing. As the evening continued, every now and then Alex asked the server for a shot of vodka and we toasted everything from "our mothers and fathers" to "world peace." If you never have drunk vodka with a Russian, it is a real experience. They never appear to get drunk. As the evening concluded, and not being in any condition to drive, I hailed a cab. Before doing so however, I managed to get Alex to agree to go fishing with me the coming Saturday. Instead of giving me his address though, Alex asked that I pick him up at 6 a.m. at the same bar where we were.

As I arrived with my zodiac strapped to the roof of my Jeep Cherokee that Saturday morning a little before 6:00 a.m., there was

Alex waiting in front of the bar. The lakes where we were going to fish were located one hour north. Shortly after putting the boat in the water and making our first casts of the morning, both of us had nice pike on our lines, which we released after taking photographs.

After catching a dozen or so pike, we decided to have lunch at the base of the remains of a 12th century castle that overlooked the lake. While I took out my sandwich and some beers, Alex produced an array of Russian delicacies to include smoked salmon, caviar, red beets, fresh bread, hardboiled eggs and, of course, a bottle of cold vodka; what a perfect fall day. As it was approaching 3:00 p.m., we decided to head back to my vehicle, which was approximately seven miles from where we were fishing.

Gliding across the water, suddenly we both heard a large noise and turned to see that my 25 horsepower engine had been ripped from the transom and was beginning to sink in the water. Thank goodness that I had secured it with a safety line. Because the water in the lake was low during the fall, I had accidentally hit an underwater stump. Pulling the soaking wet engine back in the boat, I looked at Alex and remarked, *"Boy, are we f---ed."* Alex remained calm as the "Rock of Gibraltar." Taking the spark plug out, and using his lighter, Alex dried and replaced it, then pulled and pulled on the cord trying to get the engine started but to no avail.

For the next hour or so, we repeated this process while drinking shots of vodka in between attempts to get the engine started until suddenly the engine roared and we headed back to our vehicle. Thank God in that there were only a few boats on the lake that day and no one in site of us. Arriving back at the car as darkness settled in, we took one last swig of vodka from his bottle and quietly drove the two hours back to Madrid hardly saying a word to each other along the way. As I dropped Alex off at the bar, I was hoping that we would be able to repeat our fishing expedition again one day. On Monday morning, I wrote the entire episode up in a cable to Headquarters knowing that some people back there would think that I was crazy. The good news was that Alex and I were becoming friends, knowing full well that each of us worked as Intelligence Officers. I am confident that when he conducted his traces they revealed that I was CIA.

Two weeks later, Alex called my cell phone and the next thing I knew we were at the lake fishing again. On the third occasion, after Alex lost yet another of my favorite fishing lures, I received permission from Headquarters to purchase a brand new rod and reel for Alex, an assortment of fishing lures, and a brand new tackle box from Cabelas. At first, Alex told me that he could not accept my gift, but after using the rod and reel, he relinquished, especially after I reminded him that he kept losing several of my favorite lures. To my surprise, as I was ready to drop him off at the bar, he told me to take him to his residence where he ran upstairs with his new fishing gear and tackle. Returning several minutes later, Alex presented me with a box containing a beautiful "matryoshka" doll as a token of his appreciation, which I readily accepted.

We continued fishing together throughout the winter and into the spring time and even spent some time together with our families at dinners and visiting the countryside. Quite a sight—me translating to English for Karen and Alex translating to Russian for his wife. On two occasions when we were about to go fishing, Alex asked if he could bring along a Russian friend. The first individual was a huge Russian whom Alex referred to as "the Bear", and was visiting from Moscow. His friend's hands were as big as a baseball catcher's glove and I took him to be some sort technical service officer that was visiting TDY. You could definitely tell that Alex and "the Bear" had known each other for a long time and were good friends. On the second occasion, I learned that the elder person that Alex brought with him was the new Russian Federal Security Service (FSB) officer assigned to the Russian Embassy. When we all went for a swim and were trying to get back into the boat that day, the FSB Officer remarked how old he was getting. Trying to be polite, I remarked, *"Sir, you are not old"* to which the FSB officer calmly replied, *"Richard, I was a Colonel in the KGB when you were still shitting yellow"*, to which we all had a good laugh.

As our relationship was coming up on one year, a few in Headquarters were becoming concerned that, with the introduction of the FSB Officer into the equation, Alex was getting ready to "pitch (attempt to recruit) me" and that the FSB Officer had come with us to provide Alex with a second assessment. I told Headquarters that if this was the case, I was prepared to politely decline his offer and then counter-pitch Alex. Then one day, unexpectedly, Alex called me to say that he was being reassigned to Moscow. Prior to hanging up, Alex paid me one of the highest compliments that an Intelligence Officer can receive by saying, "Richard, you have been a good friend and someone I know that I can trust. In the event that anything happens in my country and it begins to go to "shit," I know that I will be able to count on you." I never saw Alex again. Although I knew from the beginning that I would never have been able to recruit Alex and vice versa and maybe I am naïve, but I truly believe that if all hell broke loose in his country, Alex knew in his heart that I was someone he could turn to who would try and get him and his family out of Russia. What a nice recruitment that would have been!

* * *

Speaking of Russians, in the spring of 1997, the country where I was serving hosted a counternarcotics conference attended, by a host of nations from around the world. That evening following an elaborate opening dinner at a beautiful castle overlooking the ocean, as I was leaving the event after talking to several of my counterparts who were the hosts for this conference, I was approached by a representative from Russia. He asked me in perfect English if I would be willing to introduce the head of the Russian counternarcotics service to the host delegation, to which I readily agreed. Following this brief introduction and exchange, I formally introduced myself to the Russians and gave them my business card. Later that evening when it was approaching midnight and I was sitting with my colleagues in the hotel bar having a "nightcap," the Russian delegation stopped by our table and the interpreter told me that the head of the Russian counternarcotics service wanted to invite me to his room for a drink, to which I accepted.

Not wanting to be rude to my colleagues, I had another drink and then excused myself wondering if the Russians were still awake since it was nearing 1:00 a.m. Knocking on their door, I was warmly greeted and pleasantly surprised to see that the Russian's had prepared an entire table of delicacies that they had brought with them from Russia–the finest smoked salmon and white fish, pickled eggs, red and black caviar, homemade bread, sweet sausage, and red beets. Of course, there were bottles of ice-cold vodka, and I mean bottles.

In addition to the head of the Russian counternarcotics service, I was introduced to a gentleman whom the Russian interpreter referred to as the head of the Ukrainian counternarcotics service and one of his aides. Then for the next two hours, we toasted everything that you can imagine drinking tumbler-size glasses filled with an inch or so of vodka each time. When I got up to leave, I could barely see straight, but the Head of the Ukrainian delegation produced a bottle of ice-cold yellow vodka from his country that he insisted we try. As I finally crawled out of their room and into mine somewhere past 3:30 a.m., I stuck my finger down my throat in front of the toilet and vomited for the better part of two minutes, heaving up everything in my stomach so the room would quit spinning when I tried to sleep that night.

The next morning, hung over like a "son of a bitch", I crawled out of bed, showered and walked down to breakfast only to find my new Russian and Ukrainian acquaintances eating as if they had slept for eight hours or more. As they waved me over to their table, they must have thought that I was some sort of "light weight" because I barely had a thing to eat. Well, for the rest of the day, I swore that I was not going to touch another drop of alcohol and was pleased with myself during a great seafood lunch that I did not even have any wine. As evening approached and we had dinner, again I was on my best behavior avoiding alcohol. Unfortunately, as I was on my way to my room and my nice comfortable bed as it neared midnight, I passed the hotel bar where the Irish delegation was having a pint of beer or two. By the looks of it, they had been there for some time. As I waved goodnight and told them I was heading to my room, the head of the Irish counternarcotics service pleaded with me to have one beer with him. Being Irish myself and not wanting to offend my Irish colleague, I accepted—what a mistake. After more beers than I can remember, several hours later, I again crawled to my room near 3:00 a.m. very inebriated, and once again, repeated the purging process before getting into bed. To this day, I do not know which is worse, trying to keep up with Russians and Ukrainians drinking vodka—or Irishmen drinking beer. They both damn near killed me.

* * *

Looking back, I am fortunate to say that the chief of our office, George H., his wife, Vivian, Karen and I probably have seen more parts of Spain than anyone we know and probably have been to more bull fights that anyone we have ever met.

For the entire month of May each year, George, Vivian, Karen and I would be guests at a bull fight every single day not only in the Plaza de Toros in Madrid but also in many of the smaller towns and villages surrounding Madrid where each little village had their own bullfighting rings or plazas. Many times, we ate the bulls testicles (Juevos de Toro) thinly sliced and cooked in olive oil as an appetizer while drinking red wine only hours after the bull had been killed.

I can still recall the first bullfight that Karen and I went to as guests of a colonel in a small town outside of the capital. The first bull to emerge into the small plaza to face one of the best matadors in the world, Cesar Rincon from Colombia, was enormous. As the bull raced around the plaza striking out at anything in his way, Cesar Rincon and his peones, (assistants) used their capes to manoeuvre the bull to charge one of the picador's on horseback positioned on either side of the ring, outside a white circle marked in the sand. The job of the picador is to strike the bull with his lance or pike (known as a vara) and try to severe the tendon in the bull's upper neck so that the bull cannot raise his head entirely.

Upon striking the horse below the enormous padding, everyone in the plaza gasped as the bull lifted the horse and the rider into the air as the picador repeatedly kept driving his lance into the bull's enormous neck muscle. As blood began to flow from the horse's underbelly, it suddenly fell to the ground with the picador still in the stirrups, slowly breathing its last few breaths due to the puncture wounds it had received from the bull's horns. While the peones tried in vain to get the bull's attention, the bull suddenly turned and raced across the plaza to the back-up picador astride his mount. Again, the bull lunged at the horse, goring it below the padding as the picador plunged his lance into the neck of the bull. Within minutes, two horses were dead and the dazed and injured picadors were hauled away in shock.

As the bull stood motionless in the middle of the plaza, the signal was given for a banderillero to approach the bull with his banderillas – a pair of sticks the length of a man's arm with vicious, harpoon-like points. As the matador and the peones manoeuvred the bull, the banderillero slowly began to use his body and voice to coax the bull into charging. Then, without notice, he drove both banderillas into the bull's upper back as the bull charged past him. As he slowly walked away, a second banderillero repeated this process followed by a third. With six banderillas in his back, the bull was bleeding profusely as it charged one of the peones directly in front of our first row seats and splattered all of us with blood as he swung his head from side to side. To this day, I can still see Karen's face and white sweater smeared with the blood from this bull. As Cesar Rincon motioned the bull towards him with his cape, the bull headed directly towards him in a fit of rage and lashed out. As the crowd looked on in silence, the bull lifted Cesar Rincon high on his horns goring his inner thigh in the process. As the peones raced to his aid, Cesar Rincon was thrown from the bull and lay motionless in the middle of the plaza as the bull continued to strike out at everything in his sight.

Eventually, Cesar Rincon was hauled to the side where paramedics immediately began to bandage his severely bleeding leg. Within seconds, an ambulance arrived on the scene and Cesar Rincon was placed on a gurney. As the paramedics began to place him in the ambulance, Cesar Rincon raised his hand and asked for his sword. He then sat up and wearily got to his feet. With the bull, still standing motionless in the middle of the plaza bleeding profusely, Cesar Rincon limped slowly towards the bull with his sword in his hand until both he and the bull stood eye to eye.

With the size of the blood stain on his inner thigh becoming larger by the second, Cesar Rincon slowly raised his sword and drove the blade between the bull's shoulder blades and down into its heart with a ferocious blow dropping the bull to the ground instantly. As if on cue, Cesar Rincon also fell to the ground as the crowd applauded in frenzy. When the peones rushed to his side to transfer him to the gurney and waiting ambulance, our host, the colonel looked at me and softly said; "That, my friend, is why Cesar Rincon receives $100,000 every time he steps into the ring".

On many occasions during these bullfights, we were fortunate to see the matador show his or her art. I say his or her since while we were in Madrid there was a female matador named Cristina Sanchez who debuted as a bullfighter in the Plaza de Toros in Madrid on 3 February 1993 and went on to become one of the most prominent female matadoras in the sport. To describe the spectacle I will begin by saying that after the bull has repeatedly been tested and weakened, the bullfighter will take off his/her hat to dedicate the life of the bull to someone. The matador will then begin to use his/her small red cape, known as a muleta, to get the bull to charge in a controlled manner using a variety of passes. If the matador is fortunate to string a set of passes together in a sequence and can finish a series with a spectacular move that brings the bull to a screeching halt, the matador will usually end the sequence by slowly walking away from the bull leaving his/her back unprotected.

When this sequence, known as a faena, is particularly smooth and elegant, the band will strike up a musical number known as a pasodoble (except in Madrid). Although the bullfight may last only 10 to 12 minutes, the well renowned matadors may try to extend the number of passes to show their "stuff" although they know that the crowd might boo them if they go to long. From time to time, though, with great passes, the crowd will applaud with a striking series of "olé's." Eventually, the time will come for the bull to die, and as the trumpets sound announcing the death of the bull (known as the "suerte suprema"), the matador will use his/her cape to square the bull so that they can be in a position to insert their sword between the bull's shoulder blades and kill it. With the bull in position, head down, attention fixed on the muleta, the matador will line up his/her sword for the kill as the bull takes his final charge. As the matador thrusts their sword deeply into the bulls back and into its heart, on most occasions, the bull will die instantly. If the matador is sloppy, misses the heart and strikes a lung, the death will be slow and agonizing with blood frequently oozing from the bulls mouth as it waits for its death. On these occasions, the crowd will not only whistle and boo but often times will throw their seat cushions at the matador in a sign of disgust. When the bull eventually falls to the ground, the peones will move in quickly with their capes to distract the bull so that the matador can strike a final blow to the back of the bulls' neck using a small dagger known as a puntilla. If the death of the bull is swift and artistic, then the crowd will show their appreciation by standing and clapping. For the matador, the ultimate triumph is to be carried out of the plaza on the shoulders of the crowd. For the bull, if it is exceptional and makes numerous passes in sequence prior to its death, the crowd may ask the President of the Plaza for one of the bull's ears as a trophy in its honor. Two ears are a rare occasion and two ears and a tail is almost unheard of.

I only saw this happen once in the small town of Chinchon during a bullfight where the famous matador, Jose Miguel Arroyo Delgado aka Joselito, fought six bulls all by himself one evening while also serving as the banderillero placing all six banderillas in each of the six bulls.

In addition to seeing numerous bullfights, I also got to run with the bulls in Pamplona; visit the Fair (Feria) in Seville; attend the Las Falles celebration in Valencia where the locals burn large papier-mâché statues in every town plaza; and observe the "Good Friday" processions in Toledo and Valladolid.

God, I loved Spain!

Chapter 10

"When I Didn't Think Life Could Get Any Better: My Second European Post"

In the spring of 1997, during a visit to Madrid, the Chief of our European Division, Hollis H., asked me if I was interested in being a branch chief in another European post.

Before accepting the assignment, I asked Hollis if I could do my language study in country instead of returning to the United States for a year with my family and then transferring back to Europe. Since studying abroad in this fashion was not the norm, much to my surprise, Hollis suggested that I visit the country, select a language school, and then provide an idea of how much the whole thing was going to cost. He reminded me, that I would be the "guinea pig" for such a program and, therefore, could not fail if the program was to continue following my immersion. After visiting the country and finding a language school, I put together a program where I would study in the capital for two months and then do two to three week immersions in cities all over the country. In between immersions, I thought it best to return to the capital to study there.

In August of 1997, I moved my family to my second European post, settled in a beautiful villa outside of the capital, and began my language immersion. Although I was authorized a full year to learn the language, after ten months I tested at the three level in speaking, reading, and writing and, decided to forgo the last two months in order to begin working. The cost of the ten-month program was $25,000–less than the cost of a full time language student at our language school in Washington, DC. In addition to visiting different areas and learning about the history, art, and culture, during the immersions I had the opportunity to read the local newspapers and listen to local news every day as well as view local television and some 52 movies in the host language. I also went to wine tasting classes and even took several cooking classes. I used to say to myself, "Where else can you eat a five course homemade meal while on TDY for less than $25?"

In early July 1998, after completing my language training and testing in Washington, DC, I reported to work ready to assume a branch whose focus was to spot, assess, develop, recruit, and/or handle targets unilaterally and with liaison. Although our relationship with our counterparts at this time was tenuous at best, my goal was to outline a plan similar to that which I had developed at my previous post to offer training in an effort to establish close ties with them, which was no small task thanks to Rick Ames, the infamous CIA spy. As I as was being introduced to my counterparts, on 7 August 1998, less than a month after starting my new assignment, two U.S. Embassies in East Africa were bombed. The first explosion in Nairobi, Kenya killed 213 people and injured 5,000; the second in Dar, Es Salaam, Tanzania, occurred five minutes after the blast in Nairobi, killing 11 and wounding 85. Trucks carrying explosives carried out both acts. After learning of the incidents, I immediately drafted a cable to CTC requesting permission to travel to Nairobi or Dar es Salaam since I was a former security officer, had post-blast investigation training, and was a trained paramedic. I also suggested that our support chief, Robert Y., and our security officer, Doug S., accompany me. Much to my surprise, our request was denied, although we could have arrived within hours. We later learned that the FEST did not arrive until three days after the incident because the 707 aircraft that they were traveling on had engine problems and was forced to land in Rota, Spain. This event later led to the U.S. Government purchasing several G-5 Gulfstream jets to transport the FEST.

Because al-Qaeda was immediately suspected of both bombings, the following day I visited my civilian police counterterrorism counterpart, and asked him if his service had any reporting on al-Qaeda. Surprisingly, I was handed a detailed al-Qaeda report that his section had recently prepared and then afterwards we discussed, during the better part of two hours, how our two organizations could work together in combating terrorism. As part of these discussions, I talked about several of the training courses, which we could offer and two weeks later, we were running our first three-week course. Special operations and personal protection training followed this course. My son Matthew still reminds me of the times that we used to sneak into soccer matches in the back of one of the bomb-squad vehicles along with several other bomb-squad members following this training.

In response to the East Africa bombings, on 20 August 1998, 79 Tomahawk cruise missiles fired from U.S. Navy ships in the Arabian Sea pounded training camps near Khost, Afghanistan and Al Shifa, a pharmaceutical plant in Khartoum, Sudan, which the U.S. Government had suspected was being used by Bin Ladin to produce deadly VX nerve gas. Unfortunately, some 20 to 30 locals were killed in this subsequent raid. Shortly after the cruise missile attack, the news reported that soil samples were taken at the pharmaceutical plant in Khartoum to determine if VX was present, but no evidence of it was ever found.

No sooner had we finished the training than we received a cable from our office in London informing us that an al-Qaeda cell in Ireland had called a telephone number in the country where I was serving. We later learned that the cell was believed to be affiliated with a plot to blow up the U.S. Embassy in Tirana, Albania. After I brought this to the attention of the FBI Legatt and the head of the civilian police counterterrorism section, the police were able to identify the residence and immediately placed it under surveillance. After receiving authorization, a wiretap was placed on the telephone and shortly thereafter on 2 October 1998, the police raided the residence and arrested several Yemeni and Egyptian Islamic Jihad members. Indeed, they were part of a plan to blow up the U.S. Embassy in Tirana, Albania. Following the raid, all of the local newspapers and television channels reported that the police searched the apartment and found beards, wigs, weapons, gold bullion, contact numbers, and mobile phones, which the police were able to exploit. Within hours of the raid, a whole slew of FBI agents and a U.S. Attorney from NYC arrived in to assist the police with their investigation.

In November 1998, Abdullah Öcalan was expelled from Syria where he had been living and leading the Kurdistan Workers Party (PKK) for some 18 years. Öcalan and other former student activists in Ankara, Turkey founded the PKK in 1978 as a Marxist-Leninist organization with the aim to achieve an independent Kurdish state by armed struggle. Turkey's predominantly Kurdish southeast provinces were the main theatre of this bitter conflict in the course of which around 3,000 settlements were evacuated and/or burned, and up to three million people were internally displaced and tens of thousands killed. The Turkish media claimed that Öcalan was responsible for the deaths of about 29,000 people. On 12 November 1998, Öcalan arrived in Italy, applied for asylum, and was detained by the Italian civilian police based on an international arrest warrant issued by Germany. Italian Prime Minister Massimo D'Alema rejected a request by Turkey for the extradition of Öcalan because the charges brought against him carried the death penalty. During the next several weeks, Öcalan remained confined to a small safe house near Fumicino.

On 16 December, an Italian Appeal Court in Rome lifted the detention order after Germany withdrew its arrest warrant claiming that the Italian court had no grounds for detaining Öcalan further inflaming the Turks and renewing threats of economic retaliation against the Italians. Following the Italian Appeal Court's decision, Prime Minister D'Alema asserted that Öcalan would be kept under police surveillance until a decision could be made on what to do with him or where to send him. Although the Italian Government indicated that they were exploring the possibilities of bringing Öcalan to trial before a national or international court, in January 1999, with the knowledge of the Italian government, Öcalan left Italy for an unknown destination (found to be Russia). On 15 February 1999, Öcalan was taken into the custody of Turkish security forces as he left the Greek Embassy in Nairobi, Kenya and brought to Turkey where he was detained on the island of Imral2 in the Marmara Sea, which can only be reached by boat from Mudanya.

According to the indictment against Öcalan, 4,472 civilians and 5,346 members of the security forces (including 1,225 village guards and 247 police officers) were killed during the PKK's struggle to become an independent Kurdish state. After a lengthy, well-publicized trial, Öcalan was sentenced to death on 29 June 1999, after a State Security Court found him guilty of the charges of "treason and separatism" under Article 125 of the Turkish Penal Code (TPC).

Earlier in February 1999, we received a cable that the Agency had reliable information that Bin Ladin was spending a lot of time at a camp near Kandahar, Afghanistan. Surrounded by desert, Bin Ladin had lived 12 miles outside of Kandahar in a secluded compound comprised of 80 or so mud huts and concrete buildings, which included apartments, a mosque, and a medical facility known as Tarnak Farm. Armed guards and a 10-foot wall protected the compound. On 11 February 1999, information was obtained that Bin Ladin would be falcon hunting with an Emirate prince after a United Arab Emirates aircraft was spotted near the camp. Although a military strike was prepared, it was never launched for fear of killing the Emirate prince. The following day, 12 February 1999, Bin Ladin was gone and an opportunity was squandered.

* * *

On 12 March 1999, Iranian President Mohammad Khatami launched the first state visit by an Iranian leader to a Western nation in two decades when he visited Rome and the Vatican for three days. Italian Foreign Minister Lamberto Dini, the main architect who paved the way for Khatami's visit, along with a high-ranking Vatican representative, welcomed the Iranian leader at the airport, while thousands of police deployed in a massive security operation, tangling Rome's traffic for much of the day.

In the shadow of the Coliseum, thousands of Iranian exiles and their Italian supporters protested the visit, carrying banners, torches and pictures of executed loved ones alleging that more than 300 people had been publicly executed, nine people stoned to death, and 28 dissidents assassinated abroad since Khatami came to power 21 months earlier. During a state dinner hosted by Italian President Oscar Luigi Scalfaro, Khatami claimed that although Iran had "no intentions of hostility with any country, Iran demanded rational, healthy relations based on mutual respect and non-interference".

During the early evening of 24 March 1999, as the chief of our office, Jack O. was departing for the day at his regular time of 5:00 p.m., he waved goodbye to his deputy, Ed L., our reports officer, Susan F., and myself, reminding us to give him a call if anything occurred. Shortly thereafter, the NATO bombing campaign began in Kosovo involving up to 1,000 aircraft operating from bases in Italy, including the U.S. Air Force base in Aviano, and aircraft carriers stationed in the Adriatic. Tomahawk cruise missiles were also extensively used, fired from aircraft, ships, and submarines. All of the NATO members were involved to some degree, even Greece, despite publicly opposing the war. Within minutes, a crowd of approximately 5,000 angry protestors gathered in front of the facility where we were working with the local security forces, composed of the civilian and military police units, straining to hold them back.

With all of the focus on the mob centered on the front gate of the facility, a pizza deliveryman calmly delivered a pizza to me at the back gate since the three of us knew that it was going to be a long night. Over the next ten weeks of the conflict, NATO aircraft flew over 38,000 combat missions. In addition to airpower, one battalion from the U.S. Army's 82nd Airborne Division deployed to help combat missions. NATO's goal was to replace Yugoslav troops with international peacekeepers in order to ensure that the Albanian refugees could return to their homes. The campaign was designed to destroy Yugoslav air defenses and high-value military targets in an attempt to end the conflict as quickly as possible.

It soon became evident however, that NATO had seriously underestimated Milošević's will to resist. On the ground, the ethnic cleansing campaign by the Serbians was stepped up and within a week of the war starting, over 300,000 Kosovo Albanians had fled into neighboring Albania and Macedonia, with many thousands more displaced within Kosovo. By April 1999, the United Nations was reporting that 850,000 people, the vast majority of them Albanians, had fled their homes. The television pictures of thousands of refugees streaming across the border were an invaluable morale boost for NATO, making it much easier for the alliance to argue that Serbian ethnic cleansing was a greater evil than NATO bombardment.

Several days into the bombing campaign, NATO military operations switched to attacking Yugoslav units on the ground, hitting targets as small as individual tanks and artillery pieces, as well as "dual-use" targets of use to both civilians and the military, which included bridges across the Danube River, factories, power stations, telecommunications facilities, the headquarters of Yugoslavian leftists, and state television broadcasting towers. This activity was heavily constrained by politics as each target needed to be approved by nineteen member states.

On 31 March 1999, Yugoslav forces captured three U.S. soldiers who eventually were released in part due to the efforts of an unofficial delegation of U.S. religious leaders including the Reverend Jessie Jackson. On 7 May 1999, NATO bombs hit the Chinese Embassy in Belgrade killing three Chinese journalists and outraging the Chinese. NATO claimed they were firing at Yugoslav positions. Although the U.S. and NATO later apologized for the bombing saying that it occurred because of an outdated map provided by the CIA, this was challenged by several reports that claimed that NATO intentionally bombed the embassy because it was being used as a relay station for Yugoslav army radio signals. Shortly thereafter, the senior CIA official who was responsible for this bombing proudly stepped forward and resigned saying, "I was responsible and the buck stops with me", one of the true remaining leaders that was left in the Agency at the time.

When the NATO bombing campaign ended on 11 June 1999, Kosovo was in chaos and the future of Yugoslavia remained unknown. The war had inflicted many casualties and the combination of fighting and the targeting of civilians had left an estimated 1,500 to 2,000 civilians and combatants dead. Yugoslavia claimed that NATO attacks caused between 1,200 and 5,700 civilian casualties while NATO acknowledged killing at most 1,500 civilians. Although the exact number of Albanian civilians killed is unclear, the total number of Albanian dead is generally claimed to be around 10,000. Military casualties on the NATO side were light and, according to official reports, the alliance suffered no fatalities from combat operations. In the early hours of 5 May 1999, an American military AH-63 Apache helicopter crashed not far from the border between Kosovo and Albania and the two American pilots died in that crash. They were the only NATO casualties during the war according to NATO official statements. In Yugoslavia there were up to 5,000 military casualties according to NATO estimates, while the Yugoslav authorities claim 169 soldiers were killed and 299 wounded. KLA losses are difficult to analyze and reports range from less than 1,000 to more than 10,000. Within three weeks, over 500,000 Albanian refugees had returned home. Shortly before the end of the bombing, Yugoslav President Slobodan Milošević, along with Milan Milutinovic, Nikola Sainvic, Dragoljub Ojdanic, and Vlajko Stojilkovic were charged by the International Criminal Tribunal for the Former Yugoslavia (ICTY) with crimes against humanity including murder, forcible transfer, deportation and "persecution on political, racial or religious grounds".

Following the start of the bombing campaign, I was sent to one of our U.S. Air Force Base's to ensure that the U.S. Military was getting the intelligence they needed. Upon arriving, the first thing that I noticed was that it had been transformed into something resembling a U.S. base in Vietnam during the Vietnam war. Thick strands of concertina wire had been strung all around the base and at night, fires were burning in 55-gallon drums sending plumes of black smoke into the night sky. The most amazing sight was the non-stop take off and landing activity involving an array of aircraft including the B-117 Stealth Fighter Bomber.

Prior to returning home, I decided to take several of my military counterparts to dinner at a local restaurant on the outside of town. In many of these small villages, it is customary for the waiter to bring you whatever the chef is cooking that evening so in our case, we started our meal with an appetizer of tomatoes and mozzarella cheese made from buffalo milk, a plate of pasta with mushrooms, and for the main course, thick, two-inch steaks. When the owner brought several bottles of red wine without labels and opened them for us, I immediately told him that the wine was the best I had tasted in the three years that I had been in country, to which he proudly replied, "Thank you, I make it myself". After a dessert of Tiramisu, as I was paying the bill which had been scrawled on a paper napkin, I asked the owner of the restaurant if I could purchase several bottles of his wine to take back home with me. Within minutes, the owner returned with an old World War II jerry can (used during the war for hauling water and fuel), filled with several gallons of his homemade wine. When I tried to pay him, the owner politely refused payment informing me that it was a gift. After driving to the airport and returning my rental car, I proceeded to the airline counter with my luggage and the jerry can filled with wine. When the attendant behind the counter asked me if I had any luggage to check, I promptly replied that I had one piece of luggage to check and the jerry can, which I was planning to hand, carry on the plane. When the attendant calmly asked me what I had in the can I, in turn, remarked, *"Wine."* Minutes later, I was on my way with my ticket and jerry can filled with wine to the security-screening checkpoint. When I was about to continue through security, I was again questioned about the contents of the jerry can to which I again replied that it was filled with wine and I was told to proceed. As I boarded the flight back home, I was approached by a flight attendant who, without even bothering to ask me the contents of the jerry can, offered to place the can in a closet behind the pilot and co-pilot where they keep their coats saying that it would not fit in the overhead compartment. Although I know that this trip occurred prior to 9/11, looking back, it is still astonishing that I carried a jerry can filled with wine through airport security and onto an aircraft without anyone actually opening the container and determining/verifying its contents – unbelievable.

* * *

Back home, one morning while sitting in my office, I received a phone call from the Embassy Regional Security Officer, Rich G., asking me to come to his office.

On arriving, he handed me a letter poorly written in English. The author claimed that he was a member of the Russian security services, would be visiting Rome on a specific date, and wanted to meet with someone from the CIA to talk about the possibility of defecting. It stated that the Russian would be standing on a specific corner several blocks from the U.S. Embassy at a specific time and would have a green book in his right hand. When receiving such a letter, our first impression is that it is a "set up" or a way for the Russians to try to identify CIA officers that are in-country. But, in the event that the individual was indeed a member of the Russian security services and wanted to defect, the decision was made that it was worth the risk to meet with him.

On the date that the Russian provided, I departed my office several hours early, conducted through surveillance detection to ensure that I was not being followed, put on a disguise at a safe house, and then conducted additional surveillance detection to the location where the Russian claimed he would be waiting. For security purposes and in an effort to determine if our meeting was monitored, I had several members of my staff, both male and female, pre-positioned near the site. As I approached the rendezvous point at the appropriate time, there on the corner was a Slavic looking individual with a green colored book in his right hand. Cautiously approaching the individual, without introducing myself, I calmly motioned for him to follow me. Seconds later we were on our way to a café several blocks away which I had identified earlier, with members of my staff closely in tow and others already pre-positioned in close proximity in and around the café.

After introductions, it became evident that the Russian's English was not very good. To make matters worse, my ability to speak and understand Russian is minimal. From what I could glean, the Russian claimed to be a member of the Federal Security Service of the Russian Federation (FSB) and had been planning this visit to Rome for over five years to discuss defecting. I was further able to gather that he was visiting Rome with his wife and two friends, and had told them that he would be gone for a while in an attempt to find some antique books. Following this exchange, I asked the Russian if I could have his passport and any other pocket litter which he had in his wallet and on his person to which he reluctantly agreed, protesting that he was fearful of wandering around the city without any documentation. I then promised to meet him in an hour and provided the name of a second café in another portion of town to meet.

Departing the area, I conducted a "brush pass" with one of my colleagues who immediately went to our office to run traces on the Russian, make copies of every page in his passport and all of his documentation, and write the entire incident up in a cable. Less than an hour later, I met with my colleague who reported that although the Agency had no trace information on him, Headquarters had decided it was worthwhile to try to have a follow-up meeting with the Russian. Meeting at the second café, I returned the documents and passport to the Russian and asked him if he could slip away from his wife and friends for a few hours the following day, to which he agreed. I then gave him information on the time and place where we would be having our follow-up meeting.

After removing my disguise, I returned to my office where I wrote a more detailed cable on our discussions and at the conclusion of the cable requested a native Russian speaker for the follow-up meeting. The next morning, a young woman from one of our European offices who spoke fluent Russian, arrived to translate during the meeting. After conducting thorough surveillance detection, I arrived at the pre-determined location in disguise with the young Russian linguist at my side. As the Russian entered our vehicle, she immediately introduced herself and greeted him warmly in Russian. I then proceeded to conduct surveillance detection enroute to a secluded park 45 minutes north of the capital. With the assistance of the Russian linguist, I was able to debrief the Russian for the better part of an hour and although I had purchased a variety of Russian delicacies, the Russian was too nervous to eat. As the Russian began to get comfortable and talk, we soon learned that he was a Non-Official Cover Officer (NOC) who had established a business on behalf of the FSB to meet with targets of opportunity and gather intelligence without any association to the Russian government. During our discussions, he explained how he was recruited, the training he had received, and how his business worked, all of which was later written up and disseminated in several intelligence reports.

Two days later, we repeated the debriefing process. This time, at the conclusion of our meeting as the Russian was thanking both of us profusely for ensuring his safety, and with a slight impish smile upon his face, he told the interpreter to tell me that the next time we meet, it would not be necessary for me to wear my disguise. Without saying another word, I carefully removed my hairpiece, glasses, and mustache at which time the Russian extended his hand and said in his native tongue, "Thank you." Although I tried to provide the Russian with some money, he emphatically replied that he would not accept any adding that he was not looking to defect for money but rather to be able to give his wife and nine-year old daughter the opportunity for a better life outside of Russia. I then handed him a phone number that he could use in the event that he was ready to defect or to trigger another meeting if he could break away one more time before he returned to Russia. Our last meeting was to take place on the day before he was to return home to his native country, but for reasons not known, he never showed up.

* * *

During the period of 20 to 21 November 1999, President Clinton attended a conference on "Progressive Governance for the 21st Century" in Florence, Italy, along with five other world leaders – British Prime Minister Tony Blair; Brazilian President Fernando Cardoso; Italian Prime Minister Massimo D'Alema; French Prime Minister Lionel Jospin; and German Chancellor Gerhard Schroeder. The conference, held in the Palazzo Vecchio, was co-sponsored by the New York University through its Law School's Global Law School Program and the European University Institute of Florence. My job was to be the interface between the USSS and the local intelligence services as well as the conduit of intelligence and threat information for the USSS. Assigned to a USSS agent from the USSS Intelligence Division, I rode in the motorcade with the agent and a member of the Italian internal intelligence service everywhere the President went. If we received threat information or anything that would affect the route or motorcade involving protestors or demonstrators my job would be to pass the information to the USSS Intelligence Division agent who, in turn, would pass it on to the Lead USSS agent. That agent would make a decision as to whether we needed to take evasive measures or change routes. On several occasions during Presidential visits, that I had been involved in when stationed in Latin America, protesters had tried to block our route and even threw eggs and rocks at the motorcade as it went by.

The night before President Clinton's arrival, as several members of the USSS advance team arrived, the Regional Security officer at the U.S. Embassy, Rich G., and I invited the USSS intelligence chief, Jack J. and 20 members of the hostage rescue team to eat with us at a small restaurant in Florence. Although it was cold, wet, and miserable outside, the owner of the restaurant lit a huge fire in the fireplace upon our arrival and soon we were all dining on some of the thickest steaks I have ever eaten in my life–a two-inch piece of meat known as "Florintina" along with some great pasta and wine. The following evening as we were waiting at the airport in the cold and rain for the President and his staff to land, I can still remember Prime Minister Tony Blair and his entourage arriving in a small Gulf Stream jet and being whisked away in an armored Mercedes with a lead and follow car and a motorcycle police escort. On the other hand, we knew that President Clinton was traveling with a large delegation arriving on the heels of a visit to Athens, Greece where he had been met by thousands of left wing protestors chanting anti-American slogans.

Several months earlier, in preparation for President Clinton's visit to Italy, the U.S. Embassy in Rome had booked a large number of rooms in several of the top hotels in Florence. When the British admin officer called his counterpart in the U.S. Embassy asking if the U.S. Embassy could relinquish several rooms to the British, the U.S. admin officer's first response was that it was impossible due to the large delegation traveling with President Clinton. But when the admin Officer changed his mind and asked his British counterpart how many rooms the British would need, the British admin officer sheepishly replied, "Eight". In order to transport the large number of staff and press traveling with President Clinton during the visit, we had arranged for a number of vans and buses to be inserted into the Presidential motorcade, which incredibly had grown to 67 vehicles. As Air Force One arrived along with several other 747 aircraft during the evening of 20 November 1999, the enormous motorcade resembling a huge snake worked its way through the narrow streets of Florence to an ancient villa owned by the University of New York – the co-host of the "Progressive Governance for the 21st Century" conference. Suddenly, as the motorcade turned to enter through the large wrought iron gates at the entrance to the villa, the Presidential limousine smashed into the 1,000-year-old gate and wall as it tried to maneuver its way into the compound and down the narrow tree lined path to the main villa. When the motorcade finally came to stop, President Clinton exited the limousine and glanced at the damage on the driver's side prior to entering the villa. The damaged limousine was immediately replaced with the spare limousine and returned to the airport to be placed aboard one of the 747's.

During the evening, famed Italian opera tenor Andrea Bocelli serenaded the audience; what an incredible, beautiful voice. Following dinner, as the motorcade departed, a green camouflaged Italian ambulance resembling a 1945 Mobile Army Surgical Hospital (MASH) ambulance with its lights and sirens blaring worked its way in between several vehicles in the motorcade in front of us much to the disdain of the USSS agent who was driving our car – a real "no no" for USSS protocol. Following this ambulance with a number of vehicles behind it, unbeknownst to all of us, the ambulance had broken off from the motorcade and was heading back to its base instead of the hotel where President Clinton was staying. Hearing the Presidential motorcade sirens several blocks away, we were very, very fortunate since security officials blocked none of the intersections as our vehicles passed through them while following the Italian ambulance back to its base rather than the hotel. As our driver broke away to return to the hotel, I looked at my counterpart and could not resist a small smile – much to the displeasure of the USSS agent who was in the vehicle along with us that evening.

If the two events were not enough, the following day the Presidential limousine accidentally ran over the foot of the Mayor of Florence after arriving at the Palazzo Vecchio as the Mayor ran up to the limousine to meet President Clinton. Then as we were returning to the airport for the President to depart that afternoon, an Italian moped entered from a side street adjacent to the Presidential limousine with a young woman, sitting sidesaddle on the back. When the young woman spread her legs, you could easily see that she was not wearing any panties much to the delight of President Clinton and much to the displeasure of the First Lady, Hilary Rodham Clinton. As we turned the final corner to enter the airport, we passed a school where several teenage Italian boys were playing basketball. As the boys ran to the fence to see who was in the motorcade, suddenly all dropped their pants and flashed the Presidential motorcade a "moon." Trust me when I say that the Italians were glad to see the Americans depart.

* * *

In late November 1999, the chief of our office, Jack O., returned to Headquarters and was replaced by a new chief by the name of Jeff C. who had just completed several months of language refresher training. As the new chief was being handed the reins, on 30 November 1999, the Jordanian's intercepted a call between Abu Zubaydah and Khadr Abu Hoshar, a Palestinian militant, in which Zubaida says "The training is over", and "The grooms are ready for the big wedding".

Believing that an attack was imminent, the Jordanians arrested Hoshar while he was still on the phone talking to Zubaida. During a raid on his residence they discovered several maps of the proposed bomb sites targeted by suicide bombers around the start of the millennium on 1 January 2001 to include the Radisson Hotel in Jordan, two border crossings with Israel, and the settlement of John the Baptist (where Christians believe that Jesus was baptized on the Jordan River), Mount Nebu near Madaba, Jerash and Petra. An additional plan called for an attack using chemical/biological agents at Saint Peter's Square at the Vatican in Rome, Italy. To perpetrate these acts, the plotters had stockpiled the equivalent of 16 tons of TNT, enough to flatten "entire neighborhoods." Following the raids by the Jordanians, 27 other suspects were charged and 22 eventually convicted by a Jordanian military court for participating in the planned attacks; six were sentenced to death. Key alleged plotters included Raed Hijazi, a U.S. citizen who was part of a Boston al-Qaeda cell; and another U.S. Citizen, Khalil Deek, who was part of an Anaheim, California al-Qaeda cell. Hijazi was arrested and convicted in late 2000, while Deek was later arrested in Pakistan in 2001, deported to Jordan, but was released without ever going to trial. Abu Zubaydah was sentenced to death *in absentia* by a Jordanian court for his role in the plots. He was eventually captured on 28 March 2002 in a two-story apartment safe house in Faisalabad, Pakistan and is currently in U.S. custody in Guantanamo Bay, Cuba.

During this same period, the Jordanian government claimed that the Al Taqwa Bank in Switzerland and the Al Barakaat financial network based in Dubai, United Arab Emirates were raising funds for al-Qaeda and helping to finance the network of operatives who planned the attack. In early December 1999, Swiss authorities raided Al Taqwa-related businesses and the homes of bank leaders Youssef Nada, Ali Himmat, and Ahmad Huber, while Italian police raided Youssef Nada's villa in Lugano, Italy. Although no arrests were made, these raids led to the closure of the Al Taqwa Bank and the Al Barakaat financial network after 100 nations began cooperating with efforts to block the funds of these two groups.

On 8 December 1999, the U.S. Government learned about the al-Qaeda millennium-bombing plot from the Jordanian government as well as the fact that the Jordanians concluded more attacks were likely pending, including some inside the U.S. With this information in hand, the U.S. Government decided to implement a plan to neutralize the threat which focused on harassing and disrupting al-Qaeda members throughout the world. As part of the plan, the FBI was placed on heightened alert, counterterrorism teams were dispatched overseas, and a formal ultimatum was given to the Taliban to keep al-Qaeda under control. Friendly intelligence agencies were asked to help, Cabinet-level meetings were held every day at the White House to discuss the threat, and all U.S. embassies, military bases, police departments, and other agencies were given a warning to be on the lookout for signs of an al-Qaeda millennium attack. On 14 December 1999, just a few days before the 2000 millennium, an alert U.S. immigration pre-clearance agent became mildly suspicious of the occupant of a vehicle as he was departing a ferry from Victoria, British Colombia to Port Angeles, Washington near Seattle.

Presenting a fake Canadian passport, the computer check turned up no previous convictions or warrants in the name of Benni Noris. Further inspection of the vehicle, however, revealed 100 pounds of explosives stashed in the wheel bed of the trunk of his rental car, which the U.S. immigration officials first believed, were drugs. Algerian-born Ahmed Ressam, the true identity of the driver, was caught and arrested as he tried to flee the vehicle. Unfortunately, after questioning, it still was unclear, whether the explosive material was intended for four different targets or whether they were intended to be set off in rapid succession in or around the Los Angeles International Airport. Following a four-week trial in U.S. District Court in Los Angeles, on 6 April 2001, Ressam was convicted of nine counts, including conspiracy to commit an international terrorist act, explosives smuggling, and lying to customs officials. In addition to conspiracy, the court found him guilty of placing explosives close to a ferry terminal, using false identification documents, and several other related explosives-handling charges. Facing up to 130 years in prison, Ressam finally agreed to cooperate with prosecutors and provided information about his activities and those of his terrorist network. He claimed that he had received training in Afghanistan where he "learned how to blow up the infrastructure of a country" including electric power plants, gas plants, airports, railroads, large corporations, and hotels where conferences were held. Ressam also claimed that he was taught surveillance techniques to include disguising himself as a tourist taking pictures while surveilling a site.

As the millennium approached, information about possible attacks was coming into the U.S. Government at a furious pace and, several of the leads had a connection to Italy and the Vatican. Troubling was the fact that for the Great Jubilee of 2000, the Holy Father, Pope John Paul II was going to open the Holy Door at all four Roman Basilicas: on Christmas Eve the Holy Door of Saint Peter's Basilica; on Christmas Day that of Saint John Lateran, the Cathedral of Rome; on 1 January 2000 the Solemnity of Mary, Mother of God, that of Saint Mary Major; and on 18 January 2000, the beginning of the Week of Prayer for Christian Unity, that of Saint Paul's Outside the Walls. According to the description given in 1450 by Giovanni Ruccellai of Viterbo, Pope Martin V opened the Holy Door for the first time in the history of the Jubilee. In those days, Holy Years were celebrated every 33 years. In the Vatican Basilica, the opening of the Holy Door is first mentioned at Christmas 1499. On that occasion, Pope Alexander VI desired the Holy Door to be opened not only at Saint John Lateran, but in the other Roman

Basilicas as well – Saint Peter's, Saint Mary Major and Saint Paul's Outside the Walls. According to press reports, after being provided with the details of the potential plot to use chemical/biological agents at Saint Peter's Square during the millennium, the Pope reportedly slowly raised his head and almost in a whisper replied, "It is in God's hands." The Holy Father must have known nothing was going to happen since on Christmas Eve more than 100,000 people jammed into Saint Peter's Square waiting for hours to get a glance of the Pope as he gave mass and said Merry Christmas in numerous languages.

During the afternoon of 31 December 1999, as New Year's Eve was approaching, I was preparing to depart the office early to prepare for a huge New Year's Eve bash that the deputy chief of our office, Ed L., and his wife Glenda, were having on the rooftop terrace of their apartment overlooking the city that evening. As I was leaving, we received word from our counterparts that one of their sources claimed that he had information pertaining to a plot to set off a bomb in Times Square in New York City that evening as the clock hit the stroke of 12 midnight. Although we did not have much information about the source nor had a chance to vet him, I was told to send an immediate cable to Headquarters requesting a polygraph operator be dispatched to polygraph the source. The closest polygraph operator however, was in another European city, so I called a good friend of mine, Chris G. who was already at home getting ready for the nights' festivities with his family. I can still remember Chris' wife and children crying in the background as I heard Chris say that he would have to jump on a plane and would be gone for several days. At 8:00 p.m., I picked up Chris at the airport, along with Emil F. from my branch, and drove him to meet with our counterparts and the source but when we went to polygraph the source, his response was, "F--- you – I am not going to be polygraphed unless you deposit $10,000 into my bank account in the Middle East".

Being New Year's Eve, nothing was open – not even Western Union. Therefore, as the clock approached midnight and the source would still not agree to the polygraph, we were at a standstill. Suddenly, the senior official in the room, Colonel Humberto B., leaned over the source and told him that if one American was killed because of him, he would personally ensure that the source remained in a local jail and would never see daylight again. As I departed their headquarters that evening with Emil and Chris and headed to the party arriving shortly before midnight, I cannot tell you what a relief it was to learn that nothing happened in Times Square (which had been secured by over 50,000 law enforcement officials) in New York City that evening. For the next two hours as we brought in the new millennium, we watched the most incredible display of fire works from the rooftop terrace overlooking the city. The following day, as we returned to the source, we discovered that he had fabricated the entire story. As he was released, I was pleased to see Colonel Humberto B. quietly informing the source that he was going to put the word out on the street that he was a government "snitch", which normally was not a very good sign.

* * *

Looking back on my three-year tenure in this European country, I am proud to say that we doubled our repertoire of liaison contacts and used these contacts to open doors to several services not previously met, particularly in the areas of law enforcement. These efforts paid huge dividends in that prior to my departure we enjoyed strong relationships with three intelligence services and three law enforcement services targeting counterterrorism, organized crime, and counternarcotics. In addition, while I was stationed there, we increased the intelligence production and quadrupled the number of counterterrorism intelligence disseminations to the point where we ranked third in the DO in 1998; and ranked second in the DO in 1999. More importantly, we increased the number of recruitments. Lastly, I am most proud of the fact that shortly after my arrival in October 1998 we orchestrated the takedown of the aforementioned Yemeni and Egyptian Islamic Jihad members.

Chapter 11

"Drugs and Thugs; the Creation of the Counternarcotics Center"

As I arrived back in Washington, DC during the summer of 2000 after being overseas for the better part of six years, I was shocked to see how bad morale in the Agency had plummeted during the Clinton Administration. Not only because of the Aldrich Ames scandal–the experienced counterintelligence officer who turned out to be a Soviet mole, resulting in the deaths of 10 Soviets working for the Agency–but also due to the appointments of two very unpopular DCI's.

From 1993 to 1995, there was the short, unhappy tenure of James Woolsey who had spent a quarter of a century working as an attorney and as an influential counsel to the Senate Armed Services Committee. Woolsey had served on a number of government commissions, had no hands-on intelligence gathering experience, and repeatedly clashed with Dennis DeConconi who, at the time, was head of the Senate Intelligence Committee. John Deutch, who replaced Woolsey, turned out to be an even more unpopular DCI from 1995 to 1996. When Deutch came to the Agency, he vowed that he was going to stay for the "long haul" and wanted to re-vamp the way the Agency conducted business. In order to accomplish his goal, Deutch brought with him a woman by the name of Nora Slatkin who served as the Executive Director and was disdained by the Agency. At the time, morale was at its lowest point and with a "buy out" program initiated throughout the Federal government to downsize departments and agencies such as the CIA, Deutch and his staff thought that they were going to get rid of the "dead wood".

Unfortunately, instead of getting rid of the so-called "dead wood", what happened was that the Agency lost many of its senior officers in the 40 to 50 year old age group who could no longer stand the bureaucracy. Thus, a whole generation of the Agency's best and brightest departed leaving a huge void and hardly anyone with any institutional memory. Although Deutch was famous for several reasons during his tenure, one of the worst included prohibiting case officers from using "dirty assets" with questionable backgrounds, which further limited the Agency's ability to gather "Humint" or human intelligence. On one occasion before his resignation, the first few rows of senior Agency employees actually turned their back on Deutch while he was speaking during a town hall meeting and eventually walked out of the auditorium. After Deutch's resignation, several security officers reportedly went to his residence to retrieve some government items and found reams of classified information in his home office and on his personal computer, which led to the Agency revoking his clearances.

With the resignation of Deutch in 1997, President Clinton appointed George Tenet DCI. The son of Greek immigrants, Tenet was well respected within the Intelligence Community and within Congress, having served on both sides of the Senate – first on the staff of Republican John Heinz, and then on the staff of Democrat Patrick Leahy before becoming staff director of the Senate Select Committee on Intelligence referred to as the S.S.C.I. Tenet had also served for a period on Clinton's National Security Transition Team, which led to a senior position on the National Security Council (NSC) before his appointment as Deputy DCI in 1995 under Deutch. Tenet was very approachable, enjoyed slapping his colleagues on the back, talking sports, and sucking on cigars, although he gave up smoking in the early 1990's after suffering a mild heart attack. One of the first assignments Tenet made was hiring Jack Downing, as the Deputy Director of Operations (D.O.). Jack, a Harvard graduate and a veteran of the CIA, had served as the chief of our office in both Moscow and Beijing. During Tenet's term at the Agency, his deputy, Jim Pavitt, eventually replaced Jack.

* * *

I arrived in the Counternarcotics Center (CNC) in September 2000. Although the Director of CNC, Joe D., promised me a group chief position during an overseas visit earlier in the year, the day I arrived, Joe told me that it was his last day and that he was being reassigned as the Chief of the Far East Division. When I met with his replacement, Terry H., I was shocked to hear her say that she did not feel obligated to stand by the commitment made by Joe and was appointing her own group chief. I was then offered the deputy group chief position which I accepted since I did not have a choice.

The group where I was assigned had a huge budget and was divided into three branches consisting of Agency officers from all four directorates and one FBI detailee, Ladi C. One of my first assignments after assuming my new position was to travel to Central America in an attempt to convince a country to target a major money-laundering group with ties to one of the largest narcotics trafficking families there. In order to support this initiative and others, I developed a training program for CNC officers who needed to know how to support and conduct counternarcotics and organized crime operations. After returning, I was called to a staff meeting hosted by the Deputy Director of CNC, Sue B., who, during the meeting, was ranting and raving about not being able to provide statistics on the amount of opium being grown in Colombia. When I raised my hand and asked why we did not just send in a news crew to find out first hand how much opium was being cultivated, you would have thought that I had seven heads. Responding that the Revolutionary Armed Forces of Colombia, known as the Fuerzas Armadas Revolucionarias de Colombia (FARC), controlled most of the area, I was politely told that it was much too dangerous. In response, I told her that I still thought it a good idea because even poppy farmers like to talk about themselves. I further added that several years earlier, a Honduran Mobile Search Team (MST) had intercepted the largest amount of Colombian produced heroin destined for the United States to date along the Honduran/Nicaraguan border – 178 kilograms on 31 July 1992. In early January 2001, I returned to Central American in an effort to convince another government to resurrect their MST program after receiving information that the Colombian FARC was trading cocaine for weapons and explosives, which had been buried along their border during the Sandinista regime.

"Operation Linchpin" was established in May 1999, to facilitate the sharing of information and operational leads involving Italian, Eurasian, and Asian criminal groups both domestically and overseas. Since then, several law enforcement and intelligence departments and agencies, including the FBI, have been sharing information at regularly scheduled "Linchpin" meetings. In addition to organized crime targets, this group also targets illegal alien smugglers. Prior to the 1990s, prosecution of alien smuggling and other immigration offenses was not perceived, on a national level, to be a high law enforcement priority, unfortunately, criminal enforcement of immigration laws took a back seat to other concerns, including organized crime and racketeering, narcotics, public corruption, and white-collar crime.

Even with mass migration incidents involving Cuba and Haiti, such as the 1980 Cuban "Mariel Boatlift," creating major immigration enforcement problems, it was not until a series of high-profile maritime smuggling episodes involving migrants from the People's Republic of China (PRC) that captured the attention of both the U.S. government and the general public, which led to at least a dozen federal criminal prosecutions. The one incident that most focused the attention of the Department of Justice (DOJ) on alien smuggling as a major criminal law enforcement problem occurred on 6 June 1993 when the M/V Golden Venture, carrying approximately 300 illegal Chinese migrants, ran aground near a beach in Queens, New York, and ten migrants drowned as they attempted to swim ashore. One day later, in a separate incident, New York City Police rescued thirteen illegal migrants from China who were being held captive by suspected gang members, pending payment of smuggling fees.

The key figure behind both of these incidents was an individual named Cheng Chiu Ping, also known as "Sister Ping." Sister Ping was one of the first and, ultimately, most successful alien smugglers of all time, growing from a one-woman smuggling shop to become the leader of a multi-national smuggling empire. Beginning her career in the early 1980s, Sister Ping began smuggling handfuls of fellow villagers from China into the United States by airplane with fake identification documents. By April 2000, at the time of her arrest, Sister Ping had reached the pinnacle of her criminal trade and had smuggled more than one thousand aliens into the United States, sometimes hundreds at a time. Graduating from using a few seats on a commercial airplane, Sister Ping also began using cargo ships where her "customers" were imprisoned below deck for months at a time with little food and sometimes only two sips of water per day. To ensure her "customers" paid their smuggling fees, Sister Ping hired scores of people from several different countries, including armed thugs from the Fuk Ching, Chinatown's most vicious and feared gang, to move human cargo for her and to hold them hostage until their smuggling fees were paid.

The presence of these gang members guaranteed that Sister Ping was paid the $25,000 to $45,000 she demanded for the trip. Sometimes her "customers" were lucky and arrived safely in the United States where they promptly paid the exorbitant fees she charged and were released. Sometimes, these "customers" were not so fortunate. On at least one occasion, one of the rickety boats Sister Ping used to smuggle her "customers" capsized while offloading a larger vessel and fourteen of her "customers" drowned. On another occasion, her "customers" had the misfortune to be aboard the aforementioned "Golden Venture" which was intentionally grounded off the coast of Rockaway, Queens in early June 1993 when the offloading vessel failed to meet it in the open sea. The aliens on the "Golden Venture", many of whom could not swim, were forced into the frigid spring Atlantic waters and expected to make their own way to shore. Ten of them drowned. Following her arrest, Sister Ping was convicted in June 2005 and sentenced to 35 years in prison for her role in leading an international alien smuggling ring.

A key figure in the Sister Ping organization, Kenny Fang, was a Taiwanese snakehead whose organization assisted in smuggling United States-bound, undocumented Chinese migrants through Latin America by boat. Fang, in affiliation with other smugglers, transported migrants from China to the coast of Guatemala where the human cargo was offloaded and held in Guatemalan safe houses/sweathouses pending payment of smuggling fees. Those who paid the fee were referred to other smugglers who specialized in overland travel to the United States; and those who did not pay were severely punished. For example, the family of one female migrant paid $15,000 to have her smuggled into the United States. In 1998, upon her arrival in Guatemala, the woman learned that her fee had skyrocketed to $40,000 and when the woman could not pay, Kenny Fang held the woman in Guatemala for more than fifteen months. When she still could not pay the higher fee, the woman was sold to Mexican smugglers who brought her into Texas. From there, she was delivered to another Taiwanese smuggler named Chen Yung Ming. Still unable to pay the full $40,000, the woman learned that she was to be sold yet again, this time to smugglers in New York City. In June 1999, while living in Houston, the victim broke her back while attempting to escape through a second story window. Her cooperation from a hospital bed quickly led to the arrest of Chen Yung Ming and two cohorts who were indicted on charges of alien smuggling and hostage taking. Chen Yung Ming was convicted of hostage taking and sentenced to twenty-seven years, while his two codefendants were convicted of alien smuggling and received lesser sentences. In June 2001, Kenny Fang was arrested in Central America and eventually pled guilty to conspiracy to commit hostage taking as well.

* * *

In March 2001, nine months after arriving in CNC, I was asked by the Chief of Operations, Jay B., if I wanted to work for him and be in charge of special operations in CNC. In this capacity, I was asked to formulate operational plans to disrupt and dismantle illegal alien, organized crime, and narcotics organizations using a surge team concept.

Shortly thereafter, while accompanying Jay to a meeting with the FBI, I was informed that the law enforcement and Intelligence Community had been pursuing a key figure for five years who was under indictment in the U.S. When informed of this during the meeting, I calmly raised my hand and announced that if provided with the appropriate funds and equipment I would find this individual in less than six months and have him brought to justice in the U.S. To everyone's surprise, except me, following the meeting, I was asked to provide an operations plan. Although I was initially told that the Latin America Division was not interested in pursuing this target, soon after, I received funding and was granted permission to put together a surge team to visit Central America where the target was believed to be operating. Before departure, I asked several departments and agencies for all of their files on this target and then proceeded to record everything that I could find out about him. After compiling all of this data, I had a pretty good idea which Central American country this target might be operating in.

On 4 March 2001, I arrived in this Central American country with an analyst, a telephone intercept specialist, and a former operations officer who was back on contract with the Agency. Making sure that we stayed away from our office as much as possible, we decided to rent a safe house in the downtown section of the capital and the central market close to one of the locations that the target was suspected of using. Unfortunately, it (a small shop with a second floor apartment) was strategically located directly across from a police station making it almost impossible to remain for long periods to observe anyone entering or exiting the shop without drawing attention. Trying to be creative, I returned to the shop one day and sat on a wall near a fountain directly in front the police station with an artist sketchpad, charcoal, and pastels that I had purchased the night before. In order to blend into the environment, I purposely had not bathed or shaved, and wore torn blue jeans, a t-shirt, and sandals. Having my hair a little longer than usual did not hurt either. For the next hour or so, I began to sketch people, the street and surrounding buildings while focusing on everyone entering and exiting the shop. When a policemen came up to me to see what I was doing, he looked at my drawings, calmly shook his head, and walked away muttering under his breath that he hoped that I didn't expect to make a living from my drawings.

One day during a meeting with the local U.S. Customs attaché, I was informed that he might have a source that knew our target. The attaché then arranged for me to meet with the individual at which time I told him that I would pay him cash if he could get the target on a certain corner in front of a certain hotel at 10:00 a.m. within one weeks' time. When Headquarters found out that I had met the source and made the promise without their approval, they went ballistic worrying that somehow the Agency might have to divulge details of the operation in the event that the target was brought to justice and had to stand trial; which was totally ridiculous. The following day, after I told the source to cancel trying to get our target to the hotel, he provided me with information that in addition to a wife from his home country, the target was married to a local woman who was residing in a nearby Central American country with their eight-year old daughter and fifteen-year old son. After paying the source handsomely, and with the address of our target's wife in hand, I visited the neighboring Central American country on 20 April 2001 and rented a townhouse in the guarded community next door to the townhouse where our target was living. I also identified a local family with an eight-year old girl and a fifteen-year old boy to live in our newly rented townhouse hoping that the woman, young girl or boy would be able to extract from our target's wife or children where our target was or when he was coming to town. As luck would have it, less than a month and a half later, one Sunday morning our target's wife departed her residence dressed in her best Sunday dress and returned one-half hour later with groceries and fresh flowers. Several minutes later, a taxi arrived and out stepped our target. He was arrested, eventually pled guilty to the charges that were facing him, and currently is incarcerated in the U.S.

Shortly upon my return to the United States, I learned that the Italians were trying to locate Bernardo Provenzano, the 68-year-old head of the Italian Mafia or "Cosa Nostra". Specifically, the Italians had asked for a team of specialists to assist them to clandestinely photograph and video several suspect farmhouses in the area where Provenzano was believed to be hiding. The Italians claimed that over the years and on several occasions, they had been very close to capturing the elusive "Don" who had been in hiding for 38 years and was reportedly living in one safe house or another in the mountains outside of Palermo, Sicily. But Provenzano had always seemed to escape minutes before their arrival via a system of intricate underground tunnels leading from farmhouse to farmhouse in the rural mountainside. Hiding with the protection of local residents and some powerful politicians in the regions, on one or two occasions, Italian authorities reportedly found his plate of pasta still warm. Provenzano's personal fortune had been estimated at $600 million. Cameras and video equipment installed in the area near several suspicious farmhouses allegedly led to Provenzano's eventual capture in April 2006. After narrowing the search of the Mafia chief to several farmhouses in the rural countryside outside of Palermo, Provenzano was eventually found by Italian authorities hiding in a farmhouse in Corleone, Sicily, (made famous by the "Godfather" films of the 1970's), after tracking a parcel of freshly laundered socks and underwear. Although the small stucco farmhouse where the "Don" had been hiding was supposed to have been deserted, with the assistance of a camera in the area, the police became suspicious after they observed someone installing a television antenna. Shortly thereafter, the police watched a local shepherd deliver fresh ricotta cheese to the house where a man's arm and hand were observed reaching out to receive it. Finally, the police felt confident that Provenzano was in the residence after observing a parcel of laundry being delivered to the farmhouse that Provenzano's wife had given to a courier. The parcel had been passed from one farmhouse to another 10 times in the course of 48 hours before arriving at the suspect farmhouse. As the police rushed in, Provenzano tried to bar the door, and then finally surrendered. "You don't know the mistake you are making" was all he said.

* * *

In June 2001, we learned that the Italians were targeting Rosario Spadaro who owned the Sonesto Maho Beach Resort in the Dutch half of the island of St. Marten shared by the Netherlands and France. In addition to the Sonesto Maho Beach Resort, Spadaro also reportedly owned four casinos on the island – the Royal Islander; the La Terrasse; the Great Bay Beach Resort; and the Aquamarina.

Spadaro, who was from Santa de Riva, Messina, Italy, was reportedly using Italian "Cosa Nostra" Mafia money and reinvesting the profits abroad to buy casinos and finance other criminal transactions in casinos. Spadaro was also believed to have sent hundreds of millions of dollars all over the world to build airports and harbors, and to invest in real estate and arms sales to the Middle East, Afghanistan, Latin America, and North Africa. Spadaro had been arrested by French authorities on 19 November 1993 while on his yacht in St. Barts. Held in Guadeloupe for a year pending extradition to the Antilles in connection with the St. Marten airport scandal in which he was accused of allegedly diverting $13 million from airport and seaport expansion projects on St. Marten, he was eventually acquitted. Four years later, Spadaro was arrested again on 9 May 2005 in Rome's Fiumicino airport after landing in Italy on a flight from Caracas, Venezuela following a 12-year Italian investigation termed "Game of Chance" where he was charged with money laundering and being part of a criminal organization.

I can still vividly remember one of my trips to a Caribbean island when asked to locate and surveil a target. After reviewing every bit of information that we had on the target, I arrived on the island on 12 June 2001 with an analyst and a specialist. Met by one of our officers from a nearby island, we arranged to meet with our counterparts to brief them on our intent to target this figure. Much to everyone's surprise, our counterparts were excellent hosts and readily agreed to assist us in targeting this figure. Several officials back at Headquarters assumed that the service must have seen my name and read a file discussing a successful operation that I had worked with them back in 1987. During the next few weeks, we gathered as much information as we could against the target and his operation. Luckily, having just spent three years in Europe, my language skills were still good. Although all of the information collected was sent back to Headquarters for further analysis, after months of collecting information against the target without finding the "smoking gun" that, everyone was hoping to find, the operation was shut down.

Chapter 12

"Taking the Fight to al-Qaeda on Their Own Turf in Afghanistan"

On 7 August 2001 at 5:00 p.m., a fire erupted in the original Headquarters building at the CIA when sparks from welders working on the roof went down one of the airshafts igniting some paper. Almost all of the employees had departed for the day when dark, thick clouds of black smoke descended on the seventh floor forcing the evacuation of all of the senior Agency management and the entire Directorate of Operations (DO) Center. Soon several fire engines from Fairfax County arrived on the scene looking for a place to stage their personnel and equipment and trying to find, without much success, who was in charge.

After being informed that the firefighters had to be escorted in the building, the Battalion Chief was not pleased that none of the Agency security protective officers assigned to escort the firefighters had the appropriate protective clothing or air packs since all of their equipment was locked in a closet on the same floor of the fire, which by then was engulfed in thick black smoke. Unescorted, the firefighters raced from room to room not knowing the layout of the building. Their worst nightmare became a reality when the firefighters discovered the majority of the offices locked, after employees had spun the dials on the combination locks on the outer doors prior to departing which, at the time, was a common practice. Many of the firefighters feared that they were going to discover dead bodies behind the locked doors the following day. To make matters worse, the Battalion Chief was unable to communicate with any of his firefighters on the inside of the building because the Headquarters building construction prohibits electronic emanations entering or leaving the building.

The following day, I was called to the Executive Director's office on the seventh floor and was asked by A. B. "Buzzy" Krongard to serve as the Agency's Emergency Preparedness Program Manager responsible for developing and implementing contingency plans to ensure Continuity of Operations (COOP) and Continuity of Government (COG). For the next few weeks, I tried to get my hands on every Agency emergency plan ever written. What shocked me was the fact that there were volumes of plans but no one had ever taken the time to implement them or, more importantly, test them. I therefore, took it upon myself to re-write several of the plans and design a system to implement and test them. The first project was developing emergency preparedness plans and ensuring that we had the proper equipment and radios on hand to respond to, mitigate, and recover from a major incident. Unknown to everyone however, the clock was running, 9/11 was approaching, and we were running out of time.

* * *

At CIA headquarters on the morning of 11 September 2001, it was a clear day and the skies were crystal blue. At 8:46 a.m., I was standing in the vestibule of the Office of Security talking to several of my co-workers when out of the corner of my eye, images on the television screen showed the north tower of the World Trade Center (WTC) burning after being hit by American Airlines Flight 11.

My first reaction, along with that of many of my co-workers, was that a small plane had hit the building and I immediately recalled my mother telling me that a B-25 bomber had struck the Empire State Building on a foggy morning in late 1944 while she had worked as a secretary there. Fortunately, my mother had been on an errand that morning and although the building had suffered extensive damage, the building itself withstood the impact and fire. To this day, I can still recall my mother telling me that she remembered people jumping and landing on cars in the streets rather than face the flames and smoke from the burning building. Little did I know that within an hour I would be viewing similar desperate acts. My mind also quickly raced to 26 February 1993, when a van packed with high explosives detonated in the underground parking garage of the WTC killing six people and injuring more than a thousand. Ramzi Yousef, the nephew of Khalid Sheikh Mohammed (KSM), had claimed responsibility for the 1993 WTC attack, promising that more would follow unless the United States stopped supporting Israel.

On the morning of 11 September, Director of Central Intelligence (DCI) George Tenet was having breakfast at the St. Regis Hotel in Washington, DC, with David Boren, an old friend and mentor who had served as the Chairman of the Senate Intelligence Committee. At 9:03 a.m. when United Airlines Flight 175 smashed into the south tower, I ran to the DCI suite on the seventh floor along with Charlie P., who was in charge of security on the CIA Headquarters compound, where we were met by the DDCI, John McLaughlin, the DDO Jim Pavitt, the Deputy Executive Director, John Brennan, and a host of other senior Agency officials.. Buzzy Krongard, the spirited Executive Director, quickly gave the order to evacuate both the new and old Headquarters buildings while adding that the 25 or so of us in front of him would remain in the building and, if need be, "go down with the ship". Among all of the senior officials in front of him that morning, I was the only one with enough courage to say "Sir, we will not be doing anyone any good if we perish and, we need to evacuate as well", to which he agreed.

Although both buildings on the compound had public address systems, the decision was made by Buzzy to go door to door and tell everyone to evacuate to prevent people from panicking. Security protective officers were summoned to assist with this task. As the evacuation began, the decision was also quickly made by Buzzy to keep a small skeleton staff in CTC (after the Chief CTC, Cofer Black, refused to evacuate) in the DO Global Response Center, and the Security Operations Center. All other personnel were to evacuate immediately only to find a massive traffic jam as thousands of employees tried to depart the compound. Unfortunately, when the buildings were evacuated, everyone stood outside with nowhere to go since Route 123, Route 193, and the George Washington Parkway were impassable.

At 9:37 a.m., we received additional information that a third plane, American Flight 77, which had taken off from Dulles International Airport, crashed into the Pentagon. At 9:50 a.m., I met with the senior staff in a small conference room that the Office of Security had established for such an occasion. Tenet, who earlier had arrived on the compound, was being briefed that two commercial passenger airlines had already struck both World Trade Center towers and that a third plane had hit the Pentagon. During the briefing, Tenet was handed yet another report that a fourth hijacked plane, over Pennsylvania, was apparently heading for the Washington, DC area and that the intended target could be the CIA, the White House, the Capitol, or the State Department. Recalling that Ramzi Yousef, who was responsible for the first World Trade Center attack in 1993, had devised a plan to fly a plane packed with explosives into the CIA headquarters building, someone suggested that we all move to the printing and photography building on the compound which was used as temporary office space following the 7 August 2001 fire.

When our party of 25 eventually reached the printing and photography building, the chief of the facility Dave F. met us. When Tenet asked how many secure voice telephones we had at our disposal, Dave stepped up to say three; only to receive an elbow in his side from a junior officer reminding him that two were not working. Tenet then asked if the facility had a "red phone" to the White House to which Dave quietly answered, "no". Eyeing Tenet, I thought he was going to have apoplexy as the veins on the side of his neck began to appear. The entire group, of 25 or so senior officials, including Tenet, was then ushered into a small conference room where Tenet received an additional briefing from the Chief of the Counterterrorist Center, Cofer Black, on the events thus far that morning.

In the midst of the briefing, I was summoned to a small room across the hall from the conference room where Tenet's secretary and several of his senior staff had set up residence. Entering the room, I noticed two of my colleagues, Chris K. and Ken L, and an irate Charlie Allen, the Head of the National Intelligence Council (NIC), who was on the phone speaking to NSA. When the NSA officer on the other end of the line asked Charlie if they could "go secure" a reference to inserting a secure key for secure communications, Charlie told the NSA officer who he was and replied that he did not have a secure phone. Charlie then asked the officer to relay the information to him to which the officer declined. In response, I heard Charlie shout into the phone and say; *"Son, if you do not give me the God damn information, I will ensure that you never work for the U.S. Government again. Do I make myself clear?"* Hearing this, the NSA officer on the other end of the phone informed Charlie that United Airlines Flight 93 had crashed into a field in western Pennsylvania. The NSA officer further provided information that six commercial flights may have been hijacked that morning since there were still several planes unaccounted for.

In the interim, Tenet was summoned to the small office to speak to the Vice President who wanted to know if we could anticipate further attacks. When Tenet hung up the phone and was briefed by Charlie about the unaccounted aircraft, Tenet asked his secretary to phone his British counterpart in MI-6 to let the British know of the events of that morning and the unaccounted aircraft. As he hung up the phone, Tenet, who rarely swears, was heard shouting, *"F--- this. I cannot operate under these conditions. We are all going back into the main Headquarters building."* As we began to trickle out of the old printing and photography building, I remember standing with the Deputy Director of Security, John T., and looking up at the sky as two U.S. Air Force F-16's streaked low overhead and thinking, it was my 25th anniversary with the Agency.

After racing around for most of the morning, I finally was able to call my wife, Karen, and reassure her that I was all right. I was one of the few employees that had a Government Emergency Telecommunications Service (GETS) card from the National Communications System. The GETS card provides National Security/Emergency Preparedness personnel a high probability of completion for their phone calls when normal calling methods are unsuccessful. GETS is in a constant state of readiness and is designed for periods of severe network congestion or disruption working through a series of enhancements to the Public Switched Telephone Network. Users receive a GETS "calling card" to access this service and the card provides access phone numbers via a Personal Identification Number (PIN).

Unfortunately, the rest of the afternoon of 9/11 remains a blur as the senior Agency leadership continued to huddle in the DCI conference room on the seventh floor. It took a long time to evacuate all the employees from the compound because we have only three entrances and exits into the CIA compound and the roads were still at a standstill (Route 123, Route 193, and the George Washington Parkway). Still, a small truck carrying several Vietnamese caterers somehow managed to pull up to the main entrance with a huge assortment of sandwiches for us all.

Later that evening, Tenet was summoned to the White House to meet with the President and the National Security Council (NSC) in the President's Emergency Operations Center (PEOC) following the President's address to the nation at 8:30 p.m. from the Oval Office. When Tenet returned to the CIA Headquarters at around 11:00 p.m., he looked exhausted. As he gathered the remaining members of his senior staff in his conference room on the seventh floor, he began to recall how his meeting with the President and NSC went. He started by saying that he had been asked if the morning events had been an intelligence failure, to which Tenet said that he replied, *"Ladies and Gentlemen, I submit to you that the FBI New York field office has more agents than I have clandestine service case officers overseas and, no, it was not an intelligence failure."*

Although all of us were prepared to stay through the night, Tenet told all of us to go home to get some rest, adding that the next few weeks would be a "marathon not a sprint." The only other personnel that were allowed to remain in the building that night was Cofer Black and elements of the Counterterrorist Center, the DO Global Response Center, and the Security Operations Center. That evening as I departed the compound shortly after midnight, I decided to drive down the George Washington Parkway towards Washington, DC. The Parkway was empty and there was not a car in sight. As I entered Washington, I purposely drove past the White House and stopped in awe to see the increased security in and around the ellipse including armored personnel carriers. The whole scene seemed like something out of the "War of the Worlds" movie. It was eerily quiet and deserted, with paper cluttering the streets and floating in the wind. As I proceeded along Constitutional Avenue towards the Memorial Bridge, it made me sick and angry to see smoke still billowing from the Pentagon. The Memorial Bridge and Highway 110 were both closed, so I did a U-turn to get onto Interstate 395. Driving along I-395 that evening, with red flashing lights and fire trucks at work continuing to extinguish the flames, I (like many) can close my eyes and still smell the smoke. Arriving at home at close to 1:30 a.m., I checked in on all the kids and crawled into bed with Karen. The next thing I knew, my alarm was going off and it was 4:30 a.m. Still tired, I got into my Jeep and headed back to Headquarters to arrive there by 6:00 a.m.

* * *

Ramzi Yousef's instant notoriety as the mastermind of the 1993 World Trade Center (WTC) bombing inspired Khalid Sheikh Mohammed (KSM) to become involved in planning attacks against the United States. KSM applied his imagination, technical aptitude, and managerial skills to hatch and plan an extraordinary array of terrorist schemes to include conventional car bombings, political assassinations, aircraft bombings, hijackings, reservoir poisonings, and, ultimately, the use of aircraft as missiles guided by suicide operatives.

Following the 1993 WTC attack, Yousef and KSM traveled to Manila in 1994 where they helped a group of Afghanistan war veterans with ties to Osama Bin Ladin in a plot to simultaneously explode bombs on 12 U.S. commercial jumbo jets over the Pacific Ocean during a two-day span in a plot known as "Bojinka" – Arab slang for "explosion". While sharing an apartment in Manila during the summer of 1994, KSM and Yousef acquired chemicals and other materials necessary to construct bombs and timers. They also cased target flights to Hong Kong and Seoul that would have onward legs to the United States.

During this same period, KSM and Yousef also developed plans to assassinate the Pope when he visited Manila and President

Clinton during a visit to the Philippines during his November 1994 trip to Manila. The two also plotted to bomb U.S. bound cargo carriers by smuggling jackets containing nitrocellulose onboard.

KSM and Yousef are believed to have started thinking about using aircraft as weapons while working on the Manila Air/Bojinka plot, and speculated about striking the World Trade Center and CIA Headquarters as early as 1995. KSM's original plan called for a total of ten aircraft to be hijacked – nine of which would crash into targets on both coasts, including those eventually hit on 11 September, plus the CIA and the FBI Headquarters, nuclear power plants, and the tallest buildings in California and the State of Washington. KSM, himself, wanted to land the tenth plane at a U.S. airport and, after killing all adult male passengers on board, planned on delivering a speech to the media excoriating U.S. support for Israel, the Philippines, and repressive governments in the Arab world.

In mid-1996, as Bin Ladin and his colleagues were completing their migration from Sudan to Afghanistan, KSM arranged a meeting with Bin Ladin in Tora Bora, Afghanistan through Mohammed Atef. It was at this meeting that KSM presented a proposal for an operation that would involve training pilots who would crash planes into buildings in the United States, which eventually would become the 9/11 operations. On 23 February 1998, KSM joined Bin Ladin, along with his chief Lieutenant, Ayman Zawahiri in signing the "fatwa", or religious ruling, that declared "jihad against Jews and Crusaders" proclaiming *The ruling to kill the Americans and their allies, civilians and military was an individual duty for every Muslim who could do it in any country in which it was possible to do it."*

In April 1999, following the U.S. Embassy bombings in Nairobi and Dar es Salaam; KSM was summoned by Bin Ladin to Kandahar, Afghanistan and given the green light to proceed with his proposal to attack the United States using commercial airplanes as weapons. The plot was now referred to within al-Qaeda as the "planes operation". No one but KSM, Bin Ladin, and Atef were involved in the initial selection of targets.

In the aftermath of the 11 September 2001 terrorist attacks in New York City and Washington, DC, the President of the United States ordered Tenet to launch a covert war against those responsible – the al-Qaeda terrorist organization and its Taliban supporters in Afghanistan – conveying unique and specific authorities to the CIA, via a Presidential Finding. This order was in response to a proposal submitted four days after the attacks to President Bush by the Chief of the Counterterrorist Center (CTC), Cofer Black, calling for unilateral CIA covert action in Afghanistan. In response to this proposal, President Bush's message was clear and simple, *"Find al-Qaeda and destroy them."* The President reinforced this message during a visit to CIA Headquarters on 26 September 2001, and his speech inside the auditorium that day, where the press was allowed to film for one of the first times in the history of the Agency, was powerful. After thanking everyone for their hard work, President Bush began by saying, *"You know George and I have been spending a lot of quality time together. There is a reason. I have a lot of confidence in him, and in the CIA, and so should America. It is important for America to realize that there are men and women who are spending hours on the task of making sure our country remain free. Men and women of the CIA who are sleeping on the floor, eating cold pizza, calling their kids on the phone saying, 'well, I won't be able to tuck you in tonight', because they love America. And I'm here to thank everybody who loves America in this building. And I want to thank you for what you're doing."* After hearing the President's remarks that day, I thought Tenet was going to cry. It was as if several tons of weight had been lifted off his shoulders to hear the President make this announcement in front of everyone in the audience and millions of viewers on television. Later, as the President's entourage departed the compound, Tenet came back into the main lobby, crossed the seal of the CIA with an unlighted cigar in his mouth, shoved his fist in the air, and shouted, *"Yes!"*

Following the President's speech in the CIA auditorium, the following day, 27 September 2001, a CIA Northern Alliance Liaison Team (NALT) headed by CIA officer Gary Schroen, a fluent Dari and Farsi speaker, was heading to the Panjshir Valley inside of Afghanistan. This was followed by six more teams between 27 September and 19 November 2001. Before 11 September 2001, the CIA had no infrastructure within Afghanistan to launch a major operation of this complexity and the Agency had to rely heavily on the DO's Special Activities Division (SAD) to carry out its mission using Soviet MI-17 helicopters and fixed wing aircraft flown by SAD pilots from Tashkent. As an SAD officer myself, I am proud to say that as an organization, SAD, like our technical services office, has a reputation of deploying their officers anywhere in the world, at anytime, and at a moment's notice.

The majority of the paramilitary officers in SAD are former members of the U.S. Special Operations community who have been cross-trained by the Agency in a variety of disciplines and skill sets to collect intelligence, handle agents, and run successful operations. Some come to the Agency and SAD with unique language skills. With Agency logistics officers purchasing and packing equipment, gear and weapons in Tashkent, during the course of the next few months, SAD would go on to serve as the mainframe for the CIA teams deploying into Afghanistan. With their pilots and aircraft, flying in all types of weather and combat conditions SAD ensured that the teams within Afghanistan were properly supplied.

During the morning of 22 October 2001, while sitting at my desk, I received a phone call from an old friend by the name of John C. who had replaced George H. as the chief of our office at my first European post. John had just been named as the chief of a new operational element within CTC responsible for tracking down Taliban and al-Qaeda members and transporting them to prison. Following our brief telephone conversation, John asked me if I could stop by his office. Upon arriving, I received a quick overview of this new group and, afterwards, was told that the Agency was looking at sites to hold captured Taliban and al-Qaeda members. Although the U.S. military base at Guantanamo Bay, Cuba was being considered, I was told that the Agency wanted me to visit an island in the Caribbean and conduct a survey on whether it could be used to house the prisoners since I was only one of a few employees still working for the Agency with an intimate knowledge of the island. The following day I departed with a member of this new operational group under the guise of conducting a survey of this Caribbean island to support a counternarcotics initiative using my previous position as the chief of special operations for the Counternarcotics Center as cover.

No sooner had I arrived at the airport in one of the Central American countries, than I immediately ran into several individuals who used to work with me back in the late 1980's and who were now assigned to the airport. After briefing the chief of our office, we visited his counterpart and asked if we could visit the island to see if it could support a counternarcotics initiative that the Counternarcotics Center was exploring. Fortunately, the head of the service remembered me and shortly thereafter, the four of us boarded a plane for the two-hour flight to the island. As we were making our approach to land on the enormous runway on the island, I could not believe the damage that Hurricane Mitch, a Category 5 storm, had inflicted almost three years earlier to the day in 1998. In an awesome display of power and destruction, Hurricane Mitch was at that time the deadliest hurricane to strike the Western Hemisphere in the last two centuries with maximum sustained winds of 180 mph. Mitch struck Central America with such viciousness that it was nearly a week before the magnitude of the disaster began to reach the outside world as the death toll rose to 11,000, with thousands of others missing and more than three million people homeless. Total damage from the storm was estimated at $5 billion. The President of Honduras, Carlos Flores Facusse, claimed the storm destroyed 50 years of progress. The island had severely been damaged by the hurricane, the tops of every tree were severed like tooth picks, and all of the buildings on the island were destroyed except for the one hurricane shelter which was built in the early 1960's to withstand a Category 5 storm. The runway that we had landed on was also in ill repair. What déjà vu to return to the island where I had spent so much of my time during the late 1980's. Conducting our survey and taking 100 or so digital photos, on the way back home, I asked our pilot if we could land at one of the U.S. airbases in-country. At that base, I then conducted a similar survey in the event that CTC wanted to use this facility instead as the site for prisoners that were captured under this new program. Returning to Headquarters several days later I turned in my report, complete with photos, suggesting that if CTC could convince the host government, both sites could be used to construct secure detention facilities. Weeks later, I learned that CTC had made the decision to use Guantanamo Bay, Cuba to house prisoners under this program instead of the island or the U.S. airbase.

* * *

From 19 to 21 October 2001, four postal workers at the Brentwood Mail Processing and Distribution Center in the District of Columbia were hospitalized with inhalation anthrax. Two of the workers later died.

The Mail Processing and Distribution Center was believed to have been contaminated by a letter sent to the Hart Senate Office Building containing Bacillus anthraces spores, commonly known as anthrax that had passed through the postal facility on 12 October 2001. When subsequent investigation by the Center for Disease Control and Prevention (CDC) showed widespread contamination of the center, the decision was made on 21 October 2001 to close all of the affected postal facilities, the U.S. Senate office buildings, as well as several government buildings until further testing could be conducted. In that the Agency routinely received mail from the Brentwood Mail Processing and Distribution Center, the main mail receiving facility on the CIA compound was closed for testing and traces of *Bacillus* anthraces were discovered. After weeks of cleaning and sterilizing the mail receiving facility and all of the mail screening equipment inside, the decision was made that from this time forward, all mail and packages received at CIA Headquarters would undergo new, improved screening measures. Following the incident at the Brentwood Mail Processing and Distribution Center, a second contaminated letter, addressed to another U.S. Senator and which was processed through the same mail sorter as the first letter, was discovered a month later on 17 November 2001 thereby prolonging the sterilization process necessary to re-open the facilities.

* * *

On 28 November 2001, word arrived in the Special Activities Division (SAD) that Johnny "Mike" Spann was shot to death during an uprising by Taliban prisoners near Mazar-e-Sharif.

Mike was among those CIA officers dispatched to Afghanistan in the weeks following the 11 September attacks to track down Osama Bin Ladin. Accompanied by other CIA operatives and Special Forces soldiers, Mike joined with Northern Alliance troops in late November 2001 for the siege of Mazar-e-Sharif. During the siege, several hundred Taliban prisoners were taken and herded into a low-slung fort in nearby Qala-i-Jangi. Among the prisoners was John Walker Lindh, a young Northern California man who had traveled to the Middle East on a religious odyssey and ended up with the Taliban. On 25 November 2001, Mike went to the fort hoping to find captives with information about Bin Ladin. Later that morning, the prisoners revolted, killing Mike. After retrieving Mike's body, he was buried in Arlington National Cemetery on 10 December 2001 with full honors, including a horse-drawn caisson that carried the flag-draped casket, three volleys of rifle shots by seven Marines, and a procession led by a Marine band and honor guard. Mike's widow, Shannon, carried her infant son, wrapped in a white blanket, to the coffin draped in an American flag, as Mike's two young daughters and other family members stood nearby.

As I stood by Executive Director, Buzzy Krongard that day, tears welled up in my eyes as DCI George Tenet began his remarks about Mike by saying, *"Here today, in American soil, we lay to lasting rest an American hero. United in loss and in sorrow, we are* united, as well, in our reverence for the timeless virtues upon which Mike Spann shaped his life – virtues for which he ultimately gave his life. Dignity, decency, bravery, liberty. From his earliest days, Mike not only knew what was right, he worked to do what was right – at home and in school in Alabama; as a United States Marine; and as an officer of the Central Intelligence Agency; and moreover, as the head of his own, young family. And it was in the quest for right that Mike, at his country's call, went to Afghanistan. To that place of danger and terror, he sought to bring justice and freedom. And to our nation, which he held so close to his heart, he sought to bring a still greater measure of strength and security. For Mike understood that it is not enough simply to dream of a better, safer world. He understood that it has to be built, with passion and dedication, in the face of obstacles, in the face of evil. Those who took him from us will be neither deeply mourned nor long remembered. But Mike Spann will be forever part of the treasured legacy of free peoples everywhere as we each owe him an immense debt of honor and gratitude. His example is our inspiration. His sacrifice is our strength. For the men and women of the Central Intelligence Agency, he remains the rigorous and resolute colleague. The professional who took great pride in his difficult and demanding work. The patriot who knew that information saves lives, and that its collection is a risk worth taking. May God bless Mike Spann, an American of courage, and may God bless those who love and miss him, and all who carry on the noble work that he began." Speaking after Tenet, Shannon Spann told the mourners her husband "served his country by being good" and "that her heart was broken two weeks ago in a place far from here." She continued that, "My husband is a hero, but Mike is a hero not because of the way that he died but rather because of the way that he lived. Mike was prepared to give his life in Afghanistan because he already gave his life every day to us at home." A simple white headstone marks Mike's grave similar to the rows around it, and he was later memorialized with a star on the wall at CIA Headquarters that commemorates employees who died in the line of duty.

As the ceremony ended that day and everyone slowly walked away with their heads down, fighting back tears, I decided to visit the nearby grave of another SAD officer buried in Arlington who tragically lost his life while on a mission in East Africa in December 1992. As I bent over the grave to pay my respects that day, I quietly whispered that I was sorry that none of the SAD leadership bothered to take the time to stop by his gravesite to acknowledge another hero, tragically killed while on duty.

As outlined in Bob Woodward's book *"Bush at War"*, by the second week of December 2001, three months after the Presidential Finding, all major Afghan cities had fallen to U.S., allied, and Northern Alliance Forces. With 110 CIA and 316 U.S. Army Special Forces personnel, combined with scores of Joint Special Operations Command (JSOC) personnel, and U.S. airpower, much of the Taliban regime and al-Qaeda had been either destroyed or disrupted with approximately 25 per cent of their leaders killed or captured. More importantly, 5,000 to 10,000 enemies had been killed and more than 5,000 prisoners had been captured – many of whom provided critical intelligence, while U.S. casualties on the other hand remained low. During the same period, more than 20 al-Qaeda training camps and safe havens had been raided thereby providing hundreds of documents, videos, and items of an intelligence value.

* * *

On New Year's Eve, 31 December 2001, at 3:00 p.m., most of my coworkers had already departed the compound trying to get an early start on traffic to begin the New Year's Eve celebrations, when I received a call to report to the Executive Director's office on the seventh floor.

As I entered Buzzy Krongard's office, I was greeted warmly and seated at the small conference table in front of his desk. Buzzy informed me that he just left a meeting with the DCI who was deeply concerned about the safety and security of the CIA officers we had in Afghanistan. Tenet's comments to Buzzy were along the lines of, *"I just lost one officer (a reference to Mike Spann), and I don't want to lose anyone else."* Buzzy then came straight to the point, *"Richard, I want you to go to Afghanistan to provide force protection measures and harden our facilities. I am not looking for a survey but rather someone who can implement security measures in Kabul and several of our forward bases. Based on what I have observed from you over the past few weeks, you are the most qualified officer we have."* Although I knew that Karen would kill me for accepting this mission without first checking with her, I responded by saying of course I would go and then thanked Buzzy for his confidence in me. Before leaving, I asked him to ensure a cable went to the chief of our office in Kabul outlining my mission and authority. This was extremely important in that the cable had to be coordinated with NE Division, CTC, and SAD Division letting everyone know, that I had the backing of both Buzzy and Tenet in the event I got into any "pissing contests" – which I knew I would. I also asked Buzzy for

$100,000 to accomplish my mission and was told that additional funding would be available if needed – music to my ears. As I got up to leave, Buzzy thanked me and said that he would let Tenet know that I would be departing the next day – so much for New Year's Day. Gathering my thoughts, I knew I would have hell to pay trying to explain to Karen why I had accepted this assignment.

Following my discussions with Buzzy, I immediately went to Central Travel to book a flight to Frankfurt, Germany with an onward destination to Uzbekistan. I then checked in with the Near East Division so that they could draft a cable informing the chief of our office in Kabul of my mission and arrival information. During a meeting with the Chief NE Division, Jim H., NE support chief, Heidi P., and the Director of NE Security, George H., I asked if they wanted to send a security officer from their division along with me. I prefaced my remarks by saying that I thought the trip would be an invaluable experience for any of their officers since very few security officers had any experience in this arena. Although NE Division had several security officers, I could not get anyone to accompany me. The same was said for the Counterterrorist Center when I talked to the Director of CTC Security, Tim H., who had more Security officers than NE Division– this being New Year's Eve and all. My last stop was the Special Activities Division to meet with Rod S., the chief, and Mike W., his deputy. As a SAD officer detailed to the Office of Security, I wanted to let them know of my conversation with Buzzy and my imminent departure. Both gave me their blessing and told me that they would notify the senior SAD officer in Kabul of my mission and arrival.

As I was departing the CIA compound, I received $1,500 to purchase clothing and equipment to assist me in my trip. On my way home, my first stop was Galyan's Sporting Goods and Outdoor store where I proceeded to purchase the best cold weather hiking boots, thermal underwear, pants, shirts, gloves, and down coat that I could find. One of my best purchases was a Polarguard sleeping bag that offered protection down to 30 below zero. When I rolled up to the checkout counter, I even threw in several boxes of nutritional "power bars." That night as I celebrated New Year's Eve with Karen, my children, and some friends who had come over, I did not have the courage to spoil the evening by telling Karen or anyone else of my imminent departure.

The next day, 1 January 2002, while having brunch, I calmly informed Karen and the children that I was asked by the Executive

Director and the DCI to go into Afghanistan and would be departing at 7:00 p.m. that evening aboard a flight from Dulles International Airport. Although Karen, Kelly, Matthew and Kathleen initially thought that I was kidding, when I told them I was serious, the only thing that Karen kept repeating was *"Why you?"* Although I tried to explain to her that my mission was to harden our facilities in Afghanistan by providing anti-terrorism and force protection measures, which could save lives, she was visibly shaken and upset. As I bid farewell to Karen and my family at Dulles International Airport that evening, I boarded a United Airlines flight to Frankfurt, Germany. To my surprise, I saw two of my Agency colleagues Glenn Y. and Bob P. aboard this same flight who were also sitting in first class. Both were physical security officers who, unbeknownst to me, were going into Afghanistan as well to assist in opening up our offices. Boy was I glad to see them.

Arriving at the airport in Tashkent, Uzbekistan, we were met by a CIA support officer and an employee of a contract Uzbek travel firm responsible for assisting personnel through customs and immigration. As we loaded our gear into a van and headed to the Sheraton Hotel in downtown Tashkent, I remember the city looking like any other former Soviet Union capital with dull gray buildings under overcast skies. To our delight, when we arrived at the Sheraton Hotel, we were met by a host of young, attractive receptionists with the shortest mini-skirts I had ever seen.

The following day, 3 January 2002, we got up early, had breakfast and were driven to the airport to board an SAD aircraft to fly into Kabul. As I proceeded to throw my bags on the aircraft, I recognized the pilot, Dan, who had ferried me all around Honduras during the late 1980's. Dan was one of the best pilots that we had. As a former Annapolis U.S. Naval Academy graduate, Dan had landed jets on aircraft carriers in all types of conditions during the day and at night. In Honduras, Dan flew us all around the country aboard our Twin Otter and Porter aircrafts, which could take off and land in several hundred yards. I had put my life in Dan's hands on hundreds of occasions and in all types of weather and seeing him again instantly put a smile on my face. There were only eight of us on the flight that morning, including a senior U.S. State Department official, Zalmay Khalilzad, who later became the U.S. Ambassador to Iraq. The flight time would be two and a half hours and although the weather forecast was clear, we were told that there was a chance of light snow. As we crossed the snow capped Hindu Kush Mountains, sure enough, it began to snow and suddenly the weather became worse. All I could think about was that if we went down in this remote region, we could kiss our asses' good-bye. Nobody would ever be able to find us. Sure enough, it was not long before the co-pilot turned his head and told us that we were going to be diverted to Dushanbe, Tajikistan. As we landed in Dushanbe, it was great to see several vehicles waiting for us and, even better, when Jerry B., a support officer who I knew from my days playing rugby at the Western Suburbs Rugby Club, meet us. Jerry took us to a hotel in downtown Dushanbe where we ate a quick meal and went to bed knowing that we would have to try again the following day to cross the Hindu Kush Mountains.

The morning of 4 January 2002 was cold. The winds were relatively light, and we received authorization to continue our flight. After crossing the snow-capped 14,500-foot Hindu Kush Mountains via the Anjuman Pass from Dushanbe, the scenery changed dramatically from snow-covered mountains to bleak and brown. This flat, barren, and rocky terrain continued as we flew down through the Panjshir Valley over Bagram Air Base, and into Kabul while trying to avoid Taliban anti-aircraft defense systems and shoulder fired missiles. The only water I saw was that of the Panjshir River.

Hindu Kush Mountains

Panjshir River

As we flew over the base and into Kabul, I took picture after picture of the airport and the surrounding area, which had been littered with the wreckage of Russian military aircraft – twisted, burned, and broken airframes – a graphic reminder of the fierce fighting that had taken place over the years for control of the airfield. Russian Mig fighters, AN-12 transport aircraft, some old twin-engine aircraft, and even several IL-76 cargo aircraft lay alongside of the runway, battered, and blasted. The runway was in ruins with several large craters and the ground literally covered with debris, twisted pieces of metal and unexploded ordnance, for the aircraft had been shelled and bombed repeatedly over the years long after they had been abandoned. The main terminal building and several adjoining collapsed buildings were empty. Their exteriors pockmarked with windows blown out from twenty years of war.

Flying into Kabul International Airport

Crater in the middle of the runway at Kabul International Airport

Unexploded ordnance on the runway at Kabul International Airport

Plane wreckage at Kabul International Airport

Main terminal at Kabul International Airport

Exiting our aircraft, I kissed the ground and headed with my gear towards several awaiting Toyota Hilux double cab pickup trucks and were met by a contingent of Northern Alliance in their traditional white-and-black patterned Panjshir neck scarves, and the deputy support chief, Dwayne H. As we headed from the airport through the slums on the northern edge of the city, we came to a traffic circle and our first checkpoint manned by young Northern Alliance guards. Clearing the checkpoint, we passed the U.S. Embassy on our right – a white marble building that had turned gray due to neglect, surrounded by a tall black fence. Closed since 1988 as a statement to the Soviets who had invaded Afghanistan, and to the powerful Afghan Communist regime, the U.S. Embassy officially reopened on 15 December 2001, one month after the defeat of the Taliban. The Afghan staff that had worked at the Embassy in 1988 when the Embassy closed had remained on the payroll working to maintain the compound and keep the building from being occupied.

U.S. Embassy in Kabul

Continuing past the U.S. Embassy, we drove south to a small hotel, which the Agency had occupied since the early morning hours of 14 November 2001 when members of the Northern Alliance, accompanied by several Special Activities Division officers, liberated Kabul. The hotel, a large two-story structure that had served as a VIP guesthouse for the Northern Alliance from 1992 to 1996 and had previously housed the Taliban, was located one mile south of the U.S. Embassy.

During the trip from the airport to the hotel, I had noticed only two other vehicles on the street. Arriving at the hotel, the first image I saw was a huge flag of the Afghan Northern Alliance encircling the compound and a mural of Ahmad Shah Masood, the charismatic Tajik leader of the Afghan Northern Alliance who was assassinated on 9 September 2001 when two suicide bombers posing as journalists detonated a bomb concealed in a camera during an interview with him. Entering the compound, I immediately noticed several disheveled Afghan Northern Alliance soldiers who were providing security with only one or two rusted AK-47 assault rifles among them. Barbed wire, steel, and rocks had been haphazardly stacked some distance from the front of the gate on the inside of the compound, to prevent a suicide driver attack. A toothless Afghan soldier, who had to be approaching 70 years of age, sat behind several sandbags near the hotel's front door operating an old Soviet machine gun mounted on top of a table facing the gate. The rear gate had one Afghan soldier providing security. He was sitting in a chair with his AK-47 resting in his lap facing the compound as opposed to facing the gate, which had been secured with a chain and padlock. As I entered the hotel, my old friend Bob E. a communications officer who I had served with in Europe, greeted me. Bob gave me a warm embrace, grabbed my gear, and told me that I would be bunking with him. Bob had to be near the communications equipment at all times, in the event that an emergency message had to be sent or received so he had one of the largest and most comfortable rooms across the hall from the main Agency office. After providing me a quick overview of the security situation, I met several other officers, including the support chief Monty L., and his deputy Dwayne H., who had met us at the airport – both were great people who I immediately liked.

After unpacking my gear, I received an assault rifle and a pistol, which I signed for and placed near my bed. Not wanting to run out of ammunition if I was involved in a firefight, I proceeded to load several magazines for the assault rifle. Later, as we were sitting at the lunch table, I looked around and realized that I was surrounded by 68 of some of the best and brightest the Agency had to offer, including Gary Schroen, who led the initial Jawbreaker Team into Afghanistan on 26 September 2001, and Billy W., the legendary, Special Forces officer who, at 72 years of age, was the oldest at the table. Operations officers and various other officers came and went over the next hour and I was proud to be part of them. Lunch consisted of soup with tomatoes, onions, small hot peppers, carrots, and radishes, fresh flat bread, rice, and an assortment of beef, lamb, and chicken filled with lots of bone and gristle. For dessert, we had feta cheese and fruit.

That afternoon, I began conducting a vulnerability study of the hotel and the compound where we were staying, writing down in my notebook some of my observations. The exterior fence surrounding the compound offered little or no protection. The gates were made of tin, and exterior lighting was non-existent. To make matters worse, the rear of the compound was completely exposed and my first instinct was that it would be extremely easy to penetrate from the abandoned buildings in the rear. Although there were numerous mangy dogs roaming the compound, they appeared to be more of a nuisance than a deterrent. The following morning, after consuming a breakfast of one egg and some fresh bread, I got a chance to provide my vulnerability study and security plan to the chief of our office, Richard B., who recently had replaced Gary B. Rich and I had both begun our careers together at the same site in Northern Virginia as security guards back in the late 1970's. Following my briefing, Rich suggested that I meet with the Director of the Afghanistan Intelligence Organization, Engineer Aref who, on 14 November 2000 when the Northern Alliance force occupied Kabul, assumed control of the remnants of the previous national intelligence organization renaming it the National Directorate of Security (NDS). Rich also suggested that in addition to Engineer Aref, we meet with Amrullah Saleh, the Head of "Department One in the Afghanistan Intelligence Organization in charge of liaison with the CIA. Amrullah was a 30-year old Panjshiri Tajik and trusted protégé of Ahmad Shah Masood.

During our meeting as we were drinking hot tea and eating an assortment of dried fruits and nuts, I informed Engineer Aref and Amrullah Saleh that I had personally been sent by DCI Tenet to ensure that we did not lose any more officers in Afghanistan. I then produced the sketch, which I had drawn outlining how I wanted to secure the guesthouse where we were staying. Since the hotel had little or no security, Engineer Aref made a suggestion and much to my surprise, after twenty minutes of debate with Amrullah Saleh, mainly due to the disruption that these measures were going to generate, everyone agreed.

With their approval in hand, I departed the meeting and drove around for the better part of an hour or so with my interpreter and two Northern Alliance guards looking for materials which could be used to provide protective measures. Shortly after completing these protective measures, Engineer Aref and Amrullah Saleh asked if we could place concrete barriers in and around the Presidential palace, which we readily agreed to as a gesture of good faith. Five hundred concrete cisterns were purchased and installed (some pictured on the following page) much to the delight of the owner of the concrete cistern company, who is probably retired and living in Florida by now.

Concrete cisterns outside of the Presidential Palace

Afghan Public safety personnel painting the cisterns outside of the palace

Afghan Security personnel at the traffic circle outside of the Presidential Palace

Soviet tank outside of the wall of the Presidential Palace

Three days after my arrival, on 7 January 2002, a U.S. Special Forces soldier was killed by small-arms fire and one of our Special Activities Division officer's was wounded when the group they were traveling with tried to negotiate their way through a checkpoint near Gardez and Khowst in Eastern Afghanistan. Green Beret Sergeant 1st Class Nathan Ross Chapman, a member of the U.S. Army's 1st Special Forces Group based in Fort Lewis, Washington, was the first member of the U.S. military to die from hostile fire during the three-month-old conflict. Both men were on a mission coordinating with local tribal elements in an area where U.S. forces were working with Afghan forces to track down Taliban and al-Qaeda fighters trying to flee into Pakistan. As we picked up the chief of our office, Rich B., at the airport that evening, I could see in his face that he was visibly shaken by the incident. I could not blame him. I did not even know Sergeant Chapman and I was very distraught.

Over the next few weeks, with the assistance of ten Afghan foreign nationals we hired, and several of our officers, we began to harden the hotel making it a more difficult target. After introducing ourselves to interim Chief of Mission, Ryan Crocker, and the new State Department security officer at the U.S. Embassy, we were given permission to help ourselves to anything at the U.S. Embassy and the U.S. Embassy Commissary, which would assist in hardening the hotel and making our lives more comfortable. Thanks in part to the Construction Battalion of the United States Navy (known as "Seabees"), who were assigned to the U.S. Embassy, we received an array of emergency portable lighting, a five kilowatt portable generator, and a huge 750 kilowatt generator, which took an entire day to move one mile from the U.S. Embassy to the hotel because we did not have a truck with a "ball and hitch". Thanks to the U.S. Marine detachment at the U.S. Embassy we were able to trade packets of Starbucks coffee and cases of beer for concertina and razor wire, "pop ups", trip flares, and sandbags. Later, when one of our technicians installed a satellite dish on the roof of the hotel and we were able to receive the American Armed Forces Network Channel, we provided the Marines with tapes of the NFL playoff games and, eventually, the Super Bowl in exchange for many of the items.

Screening the local Afghan workers

750 kilowatt generator

Entering the U.S. Embassy for the first time since its closure in 1988, was like going back in time with calendars from that period still on the walls, along with photographs of President Ronald Reagan and Secretary of State George Shultz. As we entered one of the offices, I noticed an ashtray with a half smoked cigar in it that I carefully removed and presented as a gift to Gary Schroen for memory sake in that it was not against regulations to smoke in U.S. Government buildings back then. Entering the Post Communication Center (PCC), I took two steps back when I saw several posters and calendars of partially nude women, which would not be accepted in today's society.

Mortar damage inside of the U.S. Embassy

As we entered the U.S. Commissary for the first time since 1988, with the local caretaker who had been in charge of securing the compound located in downtown Kabul behind an enormous wall, similar to my experience entering the U.S. Embassy, I thought I had passed through some sort of "time warp". It was hard to believe that the shelves of the commissary were still filled with canned goods, peanut butter and jelly, cereal, mayonnaise, mustard, catsup, beer, wine, and alcohol. The beer tasted like formaldehyde and the wine like vinegar, but the whiskey, gin and vodka tasted just fine. As was the case with the U.S. Embassy, due to the efforts of the local caretaker who remained on the Embassy payroll, everything in the commissary compound remained much as it did when the Americans departed in 1988. Magazines, reel-to-reel films still in the projectors of the movie theater, costumes still on their racks in the theater, and brand new washers, dryers, refrigerators, and stoves covered by years of dust were everywhere we looked. It did not take us long to call for a truck to transport some of these items to the hotel where we were staying, especially some portable heaters, since it was freezing cold at night. After arriving at our guesthouse, the heaters were placed in the bathrooms connected to a portable generator to warm water placed in large plastic Gatorade containers so that we could sponge bathe in the morning.

Although a local guard force was assigned to the hotel, I asked Engineer Aref and Amrullah Saleh for additional guards and was pleased to receive a new compliment of Northern Alliance soldiers. The soldiers arrived with an assortment of weapons, many of which were rusted, limited ammunition, and little or no warm weather clothing. The following day I visited the "black market" with my interpreter and purchased brand new assault rifles, which were still packed in grease, ammunition, and an assortment of warm weather clothing, bedding, and tents to house the guard force. We also purchased several 55-gallon drums and firewood that were placed at each of the guard posts to provide lighting and warmth. When the chief, Rich B., returned to the compound after being up country for several days, he was shocked to see flames shooting twenty feet into the air emanating from the barrels burning the firewood (which previously had held diesel fuel). The place was also lit up like a "Christmas tree" due to the new perimeter lighting, which we had installed in and around the hotel compound. Upon exiting his vehicle, Rich's first comments were, "Richard, if the Taliban and al-Qaeda did not know where we were before, I am confident that they do now." In response, I added, "While we may never be invincible or be able to prevent a standoff attack, I promise you, Rich, that when I am done here, this hotel is going to be one of the best defended facilities in Kabul".

Kabul January 2002

One day we decided to clean up the compound and began by removing all of the garbage and debris littered everywhere we looked. Our next project involved constructing a kitchen and a latrine for the new members of the Northern Alliance who had arrived and would be serving as guards.

Afghan cook

Eating with the local Afghan workers

After purchasing an array of new cookware, one afternoon I proudly sat in a circle on the ground with my new Afghan comrades carefully using the correct hand to feast on a dish of fresh rice and lamb that the Afghan cooks had prepared. As for a latrine, using our ingenuity, we took a ten-foot aluminum ladder, placed one end of it on a set of stacked rocks, and the other end on another set of stacked rocks with large empty plastic buckets under each hole. Using plywood, we constructed a small building around the ladder, which provided private stalls where the Afghans could do their business. In order to entice them to use this new facility, we placed a few Playboy magazines and toilet paper inside. Although all of the guards were devout Muslims, suddenly they all began to spend a good amount of time in their new bathroom, which saved me and everyone else from stepping in shit all over the compound. The only downside was the fact that the buckets had to be removed daily and the contents set on fire with diesel fuel.

With the arrival of our new Northern Alliance guards, we developed Standard Operating Procedures to ensure that we had appropriate security coverage. Contingency plans and emergency destruction plans were also put in place to round out our new security measures. I was thankful that the carpenter skills that my brother, Jim, had taught me quickly came back when constructing several guard posts. With the assistance of several local nationals that we hired, we filled sandbags and placed them on all of the interior walls along with concertina and razor wire donated by the U.S. Marines at the U.S. Embassy. After installing "pop ups' and trip flares around the rear of the compound, it did not take us long to notice that the number of dogs roaming the compound quickly diminished after one dog tripped a "pop up" in the middle of the night.

Using the carpenter skills that my brother taught me

Because the rear of the compound was completely exposed, I arranged to meet with the Minister of Defense to purchase some steel plates, which had been sitting on the tarmac at the airport for years. After a short discussion, it was agreed that we would pay $500 for each steel plate. When I asked if there were any cranes in the country to transport the steel plates, I was told that the only one in the city was a crane attached to a 1954 Soviet truck sitting in a field on the outskirts of Kabul. When I asked the Minister of Defense and several members of his staff if anyone owned the truck, no one knew.

When I asked how long the truck had been sitting in the field, I was told for at least ten years. When I asked if there was anyone in the country who could fix the truck, I was informed that there was a mechanic who lived an hour or so north of Kabul that might be able to get it started. Minutes later after the meeting broke up, my interpreter, two Northern Alliance guards, and I were heading north in my Toyota Hilux to find the mechanic. It did not give me warm and fuzzy feelings to hear from my interpreter, that land mines buried throughout the countryside, claimed hundreds of lives each year, as we drove along the war-ravaged road, twisting through the high, rugged mountains away from Kabul.

Arriving at the humble home of the mechanic, his children immediately ran inside since none of them had ever seen an American. Through the interpreter, I asked the mechanic if he knew of the Russian crane mounted to the truck in Kabul and asked him if he felt confident that he could get it started. When he replied, "Yes", I told the interpreter to tell the mechanic that I would pay him $100 per day until he got the truck running. Several minutes later, the mechanic returned with an oil-stained brown paper bag full of tools, which I looked at skeptically. As we jumped into our vehicle, I knew it was going to be a long ride back to Kabul in the dark.

Mechanic's village north of Kabul

Mechanic's house

The following day, after inspecting the Russian truck, the mechanic purchased several automotive parts, filters and oil at a small shop in downtown Kabul. That evening I was shocked to see him pulling up to the gate of our compound in a truck with a crane attached to it that had a broken windshield and bald tires. Upon seeing the mechanic, I was so happy that I paid him his $100 fee and a $100 bonus. Over the next several days, the truck retrieved steel plate after steel plate from the airport and drove them to the hotel where they were unloaded, prior to returning to the airport. Eventually, with the assistance of the crane, we were able to double-stack enough steel plates to form a wall.

Kabul, Afghanistan January 2002

In addition to securing the hotel where we were staying, I also began a program to clean up all of the unexploded ordnance at the airport in preparation for reopening it. After hiring ten Afghan nationals, we went to the "black market" in downtown Kabul and purchased old Soviet bomb suits. All I can say is what a sight it was, the Afghan nationals dressed in the Soviet bomb suits, looking like the "Michelin Tire Man" or the "Pillsbury Doughboy", under the careful eye of several U.S. bomb disposal technicians, slowly walking in lines across the airport, carefully picking up unexploded ordnance which was then transported to the far end of the airport and destroyed.

To everyone's amazement, within two weeks, the airport ordnance was removed, the runway repaired and, thanks in part to the British who volunteered to operate the control tower, the airport was officially reopened and the first Afghan domestic airliners were able to take off and land. With the security measures underway at our guesthouse in Kabul, I also had the chance to travel to Khandahar, and Mazar-e-Sharif, to harden the facilities in these locations as well.

Prior to my departure from Afghanistan in early February 2002, Interim President Hamid Karzai removed Engineer Aref as Director of the NDS, promoting him to a newly created position as Special Advisor to the President on Intelligence Matters, and replacing him with Amrullah Saleh as the new Director of the NDS. Although the global war against al-Qaeda remained unfinished, many of us believed that the initial military campaign in Afghanistan had succeeded. The collapse of the Taliban enabled the Afghan people to begin reclaiming their country and provided the U.S. an opportunity to build partnerships with an emerging government.

Secretary of State Colin Powell at the U.S. Embassy

Soviet Mi-17 helicopter in Kabul, Afghanistan January 2002

Chapter 13

"Making America Safe Again: The Creation of the Office of Homeland Security"

Arriving back in the United States from Afghanistan in early February 2002, I soon learned that President Bush had just outlined his vision for "Securing the Homeland and Strengthening the Nation" in a document released by the White House.

In the document, President Bush announced that Pennsylvania Governor Tom Ridge, as the new Director for the Office of Homeland Security (OHS), would be responsible for developing a "National Strategy for Homeland Security." As outlined by the President, *"the process by which this document is generated will involve consultations with literally hundreds of people, including officials from all relevant Federal agencies, the Congress, State and local governments as well as the best experts in private industry and at institutions of higher learning."*

The President continued, *"The strategy would be a long term national plan and not just a Federal government strategy. It would be comprehensive; utilize all appropriate options for achieving a more secure homeland; seek opportunity out of adversity; set clear objectives towards which the Nation could strive; be supported by a multi-year, cross cutting Federal budget plan; and include benchmarks and other performances measures by which we could evaluate our progress and allocate resources."* As part of this plan President Bush submitted his budget to Congress for FY 2003 directing $37.7 Billion to Homeland Security – up from $19.5 Billion in FY 2002.

While briefing Executive Director Buzzy Krongard and DCI George Tenet on what I had accomplished during my trip to Afghanistan shortly after my return to the United States, both stated that they were proud of the fact that I had "hit the ground running" and believed "my efforts saved lives". In a cable, the chief of our office in Kabul, Rich B., had written to NE Division, he stated that, "the hotel where our officers are staying is now one of the most secure facilities in Kabul." When asked by Tenet how many Agency officers we had in Kabul and how much money I had spent, I told him the number of employees and that we had spent $68,000 of the $100,000 to which Tenet smiled and said, "I would say that was money pretty well spent, don't you agree, Buzzy?"

Tenet went on to say that he had just met Governor Tom Ridge who, following 9/11, had been appointed as the Homeland Security Advisor to the President on 8 October 2001 as part of Executive Order 13228, which established the Office of Homeland Security (OHS) and the Homeland Security Council (HSC). During this meeting, Governor Ridge told Tenet that he was looking for some CIA officers to assist him in establishing this new entity and, therefore, wanted to know if Tenet would be interested in detailing several officers from the Agency to OHS. Telling Tenet that I would be excited about working for Governor Ridge and supporting such an entity, especially in light of the fact that I was born and raised in Pennsylvania, the next day I traveled to the Eisenhower Executive Office Building (EEOB) on the White House compound. When confronted by a U.S. Secret Service Uniformed Division Protective Officer at the entrance to the EEOB, I told him that I had an appointment with the new Executive Secretary for OHS, Carl Buchholz. Meeting Carl, I informed him that I had been sent by the DCI to meet with Governor Ridge. An hour or so later and a few phone calls back to the Agency, I finally was able to convince Carl that I was legitimate and eventually got to meet Governor Ridge.

Hearing me discuss the reasons why I was there, and after a quick overview of my background to include my recent activities in Afghanistan, Governor Ridge told me that following 9/11, he had been summoned to Washington, DC by the President to be the first Homeland Security Advisor. During this initial meeting, President Bush had told Governor Ridge that on 9/11 he had received conflicting reports of what was happening in New York, Pennsylvania and Washington, DC from 40 different Federal, State, and Local officials. The President went on to say that from that day forward, he was going to look to Governor Ridge to keep him informed as his new Assistant to the President for Homeland Security. In this capacity, Governor Ridge was going to coordinate the domestic response efforts of all departments and agencies in the event of an imminent terrorist threat, during and in the immediate aftermath of a terrorist attack within the United States. The President added that as the Assistant to the President for Homeland Security, Governor Ridge would be the principal point of contact for and to, the various Federal, State and Local departments and agencies with respect to coordination efforts.

Following this story, Governor Ridge looked me directly in the eyes and said, *"From this day forward, I am going to look to you, Richard, to keep me informed as my new Director of Incident*

Management." My mission I was told would be simple. When dealing with major disasters, emergencies, terrorist attacks, terrorist threats, wildland and urban fires, floods, hazardous material spills, nuclear accidents, aircraft accidents, earthquakes, hurricanes, tornadoes, tropical storms, war related disasters, public health and medical emergencies, and other occurrences requiring an emergency response; I was to run every threat and incident "to the ground" to see if there was a terrorist nexus, especially during periods of increased threat, and to report my findings back to Governor Ridge.

Governor Tom Ridge during a visit to the CIA in February 2002

As I departed the meeting very ecstatic, I invited Carl Buchholz and several members of his staff to the Agency to meet with Buzzy Krongard, the newly appointed Executive Secretary, John E., and his deputy, Phil L. The following day, Carl Buchholz, two of his deputies, Tim Stout and Ken Hill, and one of the new Human Resource Managers at the White House, Jeb Mason, accompanied me to a meeting with Buzzy, John, and Phil. During introductions, I can still recall John E.'s comments to the effect of *"Carl, I know that you may not have known all the details of Richard being detailed to OHS from the Agency, but when the elephants dance* (a reference to Ridge and Tenet's conversation) *sometimes we* (the workers) *have to clean up afterwards"*. Following lunch in the Executive Dining Room, I am confident that both parties departed that day with a better understanding of each other's respective missions. I was elated that Governor Ridge had selected me to be his Director of Incident Management, but the only thing that kept running through my mind was how was a CIA officer who had served the majority of his career overseas going to be allowed to manage domestic incidents.

Although I thought that I would be spending most of my time at the White House and the EEOB, as each day went by, I started spending more and more time at the new OHS Headquarters at the Nebraska Avenue Complex (NAC) – one of eleven Naval installations that were part of the Naval District Washington. The NAC had been involved in many activities over the years, the most important of which was the recovery of the keys of the German's primary cipher system, "Enigma" which was broken in 1944.

On 8 October 2001, following the creation of the Office of Homeland Security (OHS) we were provided Building 3 on the NAC compound. The remaining 31 buildings on the base were eventually turned over to the Department of Homeland Security (DHS) on 1 March 2003 when the Department became operational. As part of my duties as the Director of Incident Management, I soon discovered that I would be co-chairing the National Special Security Events (NSSE) working group with a U.S. Secret Service agent and a working group for those events that did not meet NSSE standards.

In May of 1998, President Clinton issued Presidential Decision Directive 62 (PDD-62). In effect, this directive formalized and delineated the roles and responsibilities of Federal agencies in the development of security plans for major events. The clarifying of responsibilities served to focus the role of each agency and eliminate the duplication of efforts and resources. In 2000, the Presidential Protection Act of 2000 became public law.

To support a NSSE, as you can imagine, there is a tremendous amount of advance planning and coordination in preparation for these events, particularly in the areas of venue and motorcade route security, communications, credentialing, and training. On 3 February 2002, the Secret Service was placed in charge of overseeing the security at Super Bowl XXXVI in New Orleans, Louisiana–the first time a Super Bowl had ever been designated a NSSE. Several weeks later, the Secret Service oversaw the security at the 2002 Winter Olympics from 8 to 24 February 2002 in Salt Lake City, Utah as I was getting my feet on the ground as the new Director of Incident Management for the Office of Homeland Security (OHS) at the White House.

In addition to being the co-chair for the NSSE working group, I soon discovered that in my new role I would also be involved in Continuity of Government (COG). This refers to the coordinated effort within the Federal government's executive branch to ensure that National Essential Functions (NEFs) continue to be performed during a catastrophic emergency. As part of COG, I had to learn about Continuity of Operations Plans (COOP), which refers to the efforts within individual executive departments and agencies to ensure that Primary Mission-Essential Functions (PMEFs) continue to be performed during a wide range of emergencies, including localized acts of nature, accidents, and technological or attack-related emergencies. Lastly, I was told that I would be involved in the Enduring Constitutional Government (ECG) which refers to the cooperative effort among the executive, legislative, and judicial branches of the Federal government, coordinated by the President, as a matter of comity with respect to the legislative and judicial branches and with proper respect for the constitutional separation of powers among the branches, to preserve the constitutional framework under which the Nation is governed, and the capability of all three branches of government to execute constitutional responsibilities and provide for orderly succession, appropriate transition of leadership, and interoperability and support of the NEFs during a catastrophic emergency. Part of this function included rotating time at an undisclosed location, outside of Washington, DC, several times per month, hundreds of feet underground.

As part of this effort, I was asked to implement shelter in place plans, evacuation plans, and identify staging areas, rally points, and helicopter landing zones at the NAC. To support these new plans, I ordered emergency lighting, a huge portable generator, medical, and first aid equipment, and even defibrillators. I even went so far as to order cases of water, cases of freeze-dried dehydrated foods, blankets, cots, pillows, sheets, and towels, as well as gas masks and chemical and biological suits, which we stored in a huge closet on the second floor of Building 3 at the NAC. After I departed OHS, all of these supplies were discovered and, ironically, no one there knew of their origin. Every time I visit the NAC today, I still smile when I see the original emergency evacuation signs that we posted on every floor in Building 3. As part of these plans, we even provided small pocket size cards with a map and directions to the primary and secondary evacuation sites and COOP sites.

Knowing that I might need to transport personnel and emergency supplies during a crisis or incident, I went to Buzzy Krongard and asked if the Agency would assign me a vehicle and, shortly thereafter, was delighted to receive a new Ford Expedition equipped with a special police, light and siren package. In order to get through roadblocks and police barricades during a crisis or incident, I was presented with a special "Federal Response Officer" credential stating, "The bearer, whose photograph and signature that appears hereon, has essential emergency duties with the Federal government. Request full assistance and unrestricted movement be afforded the person to whom this card is issued." The credential was placed inside of a leather credential case that was purchased at a local police supply store along with a badge with the inscription "Federal Emergency Preparedness USA." During the few times that I had to present these credentials to get to the White House during a demonstration or parade, I was never questioned about the credentials authenticity although I had a ton of badges from every department and agency in town as a back up to present to authorities if need be including a CIA credential that stated, "The person whose photograph and signature appear hereon, is an accredited representative of the United States Government engaged in an official business for the Central Intelligence Agency."

In the early days of OHS, I worked for a former Special Forces Colonel named Joe Rozek who had just been appointed the Director of Counterterrorism at the White House. Our small team, under Joe's auspices, consisted of a Federal Emergency Management Agency (FEMA) detailee, Katie Packard; a Department of Defense (DOD) detailee, Joel Bagnal; a Department of Justice (DOJ) detailee, Stephen King; a CIA Directorate of Intelligence (DI) detailee, Dennis B.; and a young Department of Education detailee, Eric Walker. Together, each day we ran every incident to the ground, which meant every plane crash, train derailment, chemical spill, building collapse, shooting incident, and white powder incident. Little did any of us know that every day somewhere in the United States there are several small plane crashes and train derailments that do not even receive national press coverage.

If an incident occurred, our primary function was to find out what happened; the type, size, and effects of the incident; where the incident occurred and whether it was a domestic incident with international roots; when the incident occurred; the elapsed time; who was involved; whether it was terrorist or criminal in nature; and the level of the initial response identifying the on-scene commander, law enforcement agencies, and the amount of Federal assets needed. We also quickly had to decide whether the incident affected succession of government; whether the incident required implementation of Continuity of Operations Plans (COOP) and/or Continuity of Government (COG); were there any indications of follow-on incidents; and lastly what information needed to be disseminated to Federal, State, Local, private sector officials and the public.

At the White House as the Director of Incident Management February 2002

Since everyone in OHS was putting in long hours to ensure the success of this new entity, every now and then on a Friday afternoon, Mark Holman, the OHS Deputy Assistant to the President of Homeland Security, would arrange for a "spur of the moment happy hour" in his office in the EEOB, which had a beautiful balcony overlooking West Executive Drive on the White House compound. When word got out about these events, it was not uncommon for everyone in OHS, all 142 people at the time, to congregate in Mark's office and the foyer outside of Deputy Homeland Security Advisor, Vice Admiral Steve Abbot's office, to eat an assortment of chicken wings, chips and sauces, washed down by cold beers or frozen margaritas. Unfortunately, Mark was called into White House Chief of Staff, Secretary Andrew Card's office one Monday morning following a blue "frozen margarita" event, where Secretary Card suggested to Mark "he may want to tone down the happy hours just a bit."

Shortly after establishing OHS, Governor Ridge went to Admiral James Loy, who was the Commandant of the U.S. Coast

Guard at the time, and asked him if he could detail some Coast Guard personnel to OHS to staff a 24-hour, seven day per week, 365 day per year operations center at the NAC. The following day, 20 of some of the finest men I ever worked with arrived at OHS. They began to work around the clock answering the phones and taking messages in a large conference room which we designated, the OHS "Coordination Center" in Building 3 at the NAC, under the direction of a U.S. Army Colonel assigned to OHS, Len Blevins. As the Director of the new Coordination Center, Len's mission was to ensure that senior OHS and other U.S. government officials were informed of current threat information and incidents as well as appropriate intelligence, law enforcement and regulatory agencies. After Governor Ridge met with all of the newly appointed State Homeland Security Advisors, Len asked each of them to submit a daily report to the OHS Coordination Center detailing any incidents or threats that had occurred in their respective states during a 24-hour period. In this way, the Coordination Center was able to compile statistics on individual threats and incidents for analysis by a new entity within OHS' Intelligence Directorate known as the Threat Monitoring Center (TMC), under the auspices of a senior official detailed to OHS from the FBI named Ken Piernick.

The Intelligence Directorate eventually would become the Intelligence and Analysis, Infrastructure and Protection Directorate (IAIP) within the New Department of Homeland Security (DHS) when the Department became operational on 1 March 2003 under the direction of Lt. General Patrick Hughes, the former Director of the Defense Intelligence Agency (DIA).

The mission of OHS was to develop and coordinate a comprehensive national strategy to secure the United States from terrorist threats or attacks. The mission of the Intelligence Directorate and the new Threat Monitoring Center was to monitor the flow of domestic and foreign terrorist threat information. In establishing the Threat Monitoring Center, OHS wanted to create a 24/7/365 center to ensure that all intelligence and law enforcement terrorist threat information relating to Homeland Security was disseminated to Federal, State, and Local government agencies and private entities.

The eventual goal of the Threat Monitoring Center was to assist in establishing the standard for threat prioritization, warning and response, and to assume hosting the daily Secure Voice Telecommunications System (SVTS) threat review to track the CIA produced Threat Matrix. At the time, the White House was hosting the SVTS at 7:00 a.m. and 3:00 p.m. each day, and at 10:00 a.m. on every Saturday and during holidays.

The purpose of the SVTS, which could last more than an hour, was to have a forum to provide a 24/7/365 focal point for interagency threat monitoring, and an immediate reaction to fast breaking incidents. The SVTS also ensured that intelligence and law enforcement departments and agencies were prepared to provide threat information to policymakers, and to continuously coordinate and follow-up with the other departments and agencies to ensure the implementation of corrective measures to specific threats.

In order to prepare for these meetings, each day I would arrive at the White House or the NAC at 6:00 a.m. along with the members of Joe Rozek's staff, to collect intelligence and law enforcement information from the various departments and agencies to brief Governor Ridge and prepare him for his daily morning meeting with the President. Part of this preparation included framing courses of action and security measures for Governor Ridge to take to the President to combat each of these threats to the homeland. Following his morning meeting with the President, Governor Ridge would always return with actions that the President wanted implemented, which we would then coordinate with the other Federal departments and agencies, and try to have them in place by the 3:00 p.m. SVTS.

One day I was asked by Ken Piernick to assist in designing and staffing the new Threat Monitoring Center. Shortly thereafter, we established the center on the second floor of the NAC adjacent to a new Special Compartmented Information Facility (SCIF) built to house three CIA officers (myself, a CIA briefer from the Directorate of Intelligence, Laura M., and a newly arrived security officer, Randy V.). After rearranging furniture to make the place look like an operations center, we hung signs from the ceiling with the names of the various departments and agencies that would be assigned there.

The intention of the liaison officers assigned to the Threat Monitoring Center was to provide a direct link back to their home departments and agencies for the purpose of coordinating information; to ensure the unimpeded flow of terrorist threat related information from their home departments and agencies; and to provide access to material to identify, respond to, or prevent a terrorism threat or incident against the United States. In addition to the liaison officers, we eventually received several Intelligence

Community analysts from the CIA, DIA, and NSA to analyze and triage the domestic and foreign terrorist threats to the United States. These analysts were responsible for coordinating data and identifying trends; monitoring, tracking and following up on threat information; assisting in facilitating the institution of standardized processes and formats within the intelligence and law enforcement communities, and regulatory agencies, for reporting and monitoring terrorist threats to the United States; and lastly assisting in the establishment of standards of threat prioritization, warning and response to domestic and foreign terrorist threats.

A good example of the Threat Monitoring Center's first attempts to synthesize and fuse actionable intelligence (what is commonly referred to as "connecting the dots"), is the following simplified analogy. If several reports of "hoof and mouth" disease outbreaks in separate states with the United States were received in the Threat Monitoring Center, the analysts would check with the Intelligence Community to see if there was any intelligence indicating that a terrorist group or "rogue state" was planning on introducing "hoof and mouth" into the United States and, if so, they had "connected the dots."

In order to properly share information in the Threat Monitoring Center, the Intelligence Community System, known as (ICSIS), was installed which provided enterprise capabilities for the Threat Monitoring Center to transfer homeland security information via the Joint Intelligence Worldwide Communications System (JWICS). JWICS is a system of interconnected computer networks used by the U.S. Department of Defense and the U.S. Department of State to transmit classified information up to and including information classified Top Secret and Special Compartment Information known as SCI. Via JWICS, the Threat Monitoring Center was able to obtain Counterterrorist (CT) Link from the CIA to obtain domestic and foreign threat information from 74 intelligence and law enforcement agencies.

In the event that OHS needed to staff a 24/7 operations center at the NAC during periods of increased threat or incidents, the decision was made to establish a multi-agency Federal coordination entity known as the Incident Support Group (ISG) that would facilitate domestic incident management for Incidents of National Significance requiring Federal operational coordination and/or resource coordination. The ISG, comprised of senior representatives from OHS, other Federal departments and agencies, and non-governmental organizations, was set up in a large conference room on the first floor of Building 3 at the NAC next door to the Coordination Center. The mission of the ISG was to support Governor Ridge, as the Homeland Security Advisor, and President Bush in coordinating the domestic response efforts of departments and agencies in the event of an imminent terrorist threat, and during and in the immediate aftermath of a terrorist attack within the United States. After setting up the new OHS Coordination Center, Threat Monitoring Center, and Incident Support Group, on 21 May 2002, the Vice President of the United States, Dick Cheney, visited the NAC to receive briefings and see first hand the three new OHS entities responsible for protecting the homeland – a very proud day for all of us involved in these efforts.

Presidential Directive 3 created the Homeland Security Advisory System (HSAS) six months after the terror attacks of 11 September 2001 under the auspices of U.S. Army Lieutenant Colonel John Fenzel, who was detailed to OHS. The intention of the HSAS was to design a comprehensive and effective means to disseminate information regarding the risk of terrorist acts to Federal, State, and Local authorities and to the American people as part of a series of initiatives to improve coordination and communication among all levels of government, and the American public, in the fight against terrorism.

Although the HSAS was unveiled on 12 March 2002, initial responsibility for managing the system was placed under U.S. Attorney General John Ashcroft until January 2003 when the decision was made to have DHS begin administering the system after DHS became operational on 1 March 2003. After the HSAS was implemented, Governor Ridge became the brunt of many jokes by late night talk show hosts. Robert DeNiro even played the role of a Homeland Security spokesperson during a skit on Saturday Night Live claiming that OHS was pursuing leads on several terrorists including one named "I sheet-mdurz" and his two accomplices "Hous-bin-pharteen" and his brother "I-bin-pharteen".

One spoof included a photograph of Governor Ridge explaining the HSAS "in a manner that even President Bush could understand. Beginning with the first level, Denial--General Risk of Terrorist Attacks; followed by the second level, Status Quo--Significant Risk of Terrorist Attacks; followed by the third level, Duct Tape Run--High Risk of Terrorist Attacks; and lastly, the highest level of the HSAS, Holy Shit--Severe Risk of Terrorist

Attacks". Another involved a picture of Governor Ridge next to a dog described as a mix of Rottweiler, Pit bull, and Doberman with an article unveiling Governor Ridge's newest weapon in the fight against terrorism. "The deputation of Rufus, a big "ol mongrel" ornery enough to make Al-Qaeda think twice about carrying out attacks against the U.S." According to the article, *"The hijacker ain't been born that won't load up his overalls when ol' Rufus here up an come at him. And if they don't run, well, they gonna be explainin' to the Muslim St.Peter why they's got a hole in 'em big enough to throw an angry cat through."*

Shortly after the appearance of these articles, Governor Ridge assembled the members of his OHS staff in a building on the Nebraska Avenue Complex (NAC) that served as the cafeteria where a new Subway sandwich shop had just been opened. While addressing the crowd of approximately 142 employees, I can still recall the President Abraham Lincoln quote that Governor Ridge used from "The Inner Life of Abraham Lincoln; Six Months at the White House" by Francis B. Carpenter. *"If I were to read, much less answer, all of the attacks made on me, this shop might as well be closed for any other business. I do the best I know how, the very best I can; and I mean to keep doing so until the end. If the end brings me out all right, what is said against me will not amount to anything. If the end brings me out wrong, ten angels swearing I was right would make no difference."*

In May 2002, following this address, we learned during the 7:00 a.m. Secure Voice Telecommunications System (SVTS) threat review that U.S. officials arrested an American citizen named Jose Padilla at O'Hare International Airport in Chicago as he returned to the United States from Pakistan, charging him with being an enemy combatant and planning to use a "dirty bomb" (an explosive laced with radioactive material) in an attack against America. Although prior to his conviction, Padilla brought a case against the Federal government stating that he had been denied the writ of habeas corpus (the right of an individual to petition against his or her imprisonment), a civilian jury eventually found Padilla guilty after a three-month trial and a day and a half of deliberations.

Even though the White House had decided in February 2002 that it was time to evaluate the configuration of the Executive Branch and design a "National Strategy for Homeland Security", it was not until 18 June 2002, that the President introduced the creation of the Department of Homeland Security (DHS). On that day, during the President's message to the Congress of the United States he stated, *"Our Nation is facing a new and changing threat unlike any we have faced before—the global threat of terrorism. No nation is immune and all nations must act decisively to protect against this constantly evolving threat. We must recognize that the threat of terrorism is a permanent condition, and we must take action to protect America against the terrorists that seek to kill the innocent. Our Nation is stronger and better prepared today than it was on 11 September. Yet, we can do better and, therefore, I propose the most extensive reorganization of the Federal Government since the 1940s by creating a new Department of Homeland Security. For the first time, we will have a single Department whose primary mission is to secure the homeland."*

The President's bold plan called for a unified security structure with the sole mission of transforming and realigning the current confusing patchwork of government activities into a single department whose primary mission was to protect our Nation. Combining 22 departments and agencies and over 180,000 personnel, DHS was designed to make Americans safer by having one department whose primary mission was to protect the American homeland. It would have more security agents in the field to help to stop terrorism and less resources in Washington, DC managing duplicative and redundant activities that drain critical homeland security resources.

On 16 July 2002, Dr. Richard Falkenrath, the newly appointed Assistant to the President for Homeland Security and Senior Director for Policy and Plans at OHS who had been huddled in the President's Emergency Operations Center (PEOC) for six weeks with a small group of OHS employees, emerged with a strategic plan for the President known as the "National Strategy for Homeland Security". This plan would serve as the foundation for the new Department of Homeland Security and had three strategic objectives: to prevent terrorist attacks within the United States; to reduce America's vulnerability to terrorism; and to minimize the damage and recovery time from attacks that do occur. The "National Strategy for Homeland Security" helped prepare our Nation for the work ahead in several ways: first, by providing direction to the Federal departments and agencies that had a role in homeland security; second, by suggesting steps that State and Local governments, private companies, organizations, and individual Americans could take to improve our security while offering incentives for them to do so; and third, by recommending certain actions to the Congress.

Dr. Falkenrath, a former Harvard professor had joined the Bush-Cheney Transition Team in December 2000 where he was involved in preparing for the Presidential transition within the NSC. Prior to writing the "National Strategy for Homeland Security", Dr. Falkenrath had reviewed proposals from the Hart-Rudman Commission and from Senator Joseph Lieberman to create a much smaller Department of Homeland Security, but neither bill received much support in Congress. As the "National Strategy for Homeland Security" was rolled out, I completed work on a briefing that Joe Rozek had asked me to put together entitled "Planning for Terrorist Attacks" which looked at the methodology and modus operandi of al-Qaeda.

Although Joe, in his new role as the Director of Counterterrorism at OHS, could easily have requested such a paper from the new Intelligence Directorate at OHS, from the CIA's Counterterrorism Center, or the Directorate of Intelligence at the CIA, he wanted a paper, in his words *"from an operation officer's point of view and perspective."* Therefore, for the better part of four months, I worked on a briefing, which was eventually presented to Governor Ridge one evening in his office in the West Wing of the White House – some 20 feet from the Oval Office. After hearing the briefing, Governor Ridge was so excited that he got on the phone and set up a meeting to brief the Director of the FBI, Robert Mueller and the Attorney General, John Ashcroft, the following day. Shortly after Joe began presenting the briefing the next day, FBI Director Mueller interrupted him by saying, *"Joe, over the past year I have heard literally hundreds of briefings on al-Qaeda to include their methodology, modus operandi, and intentions. How do I know what you are about to tell us will be any different?"* Joe simply replied *"As a Special Forces Officer, sir, I have spent the better part of 25 years of my life putting together and implementing plans to conduct operations against combatant forces all over the world, much in the same way that these bastards are trying to attack us."* Without saying another word, Director Mueller looked at Attorney General Ashcroft, nodded, and then said, "Joe, please continue." Following the briefing, Governor Ridge, Joe, and I were elated to hear both men say it was one of the best briefings that they had heard to date on al-Qaeda.

The first time we activated a partial ISG was on 4 July 2002 with representatives from the CIA, FBI, USSS, FEMA, HHS, DOT, DOD and representatives from OHS' new Intelligence Directorate Threat Monitoring Center, Coordination Center, Office of State and Local Coordination, Private Sector Office, General Counsel, and Public Affairs Office. Little did any of us know that shortly after standing up the ISG, a gunman would open fire at Israel's El Al Airlines' ticket counter at Los Angeles International Airport (LAX), killing two people and wounding three others before an El Al Airlines' security guard shot him dead. Immediately following the incident, thousands were evacuated from the international terminal, although all domestic arrivals and departures continued to operate normally. In the aftermath of the incident, airport police detained and questioned a man who was acting suspiciously and, based upon his actions, fire officials deployed a team to check for hazardous materials. To compound the situation, shortly after the shooting, a small plane struggling after takeoff, crashed into a Fourth of July celebration at a suburban Los Angeles park.

Upon learning of these incidents, I immediately had our FBI representative in the ISG contact his counterpart at LAX, with the USSS agent assigned to the ISG doing the same, in an attempt to gather as much information as possible on what had transpired. Within minutes, we were also on the phone with Jay Vincent, the newly appointed California Homeland Security Advisor; Martin Pomeroy, the Acting Chief of Police in Los Angeles; and James Hahn, the Mayor of Los Angeles. Within a short period, the ISG was able to piece together that the shooting was an isolated incident, that the gunmen acted alone, and that there did not appear to be any terrorist nexus.

As we were gathering this information, the OHS Coordination Center received a phone call from the Governor of California, Gray Davis, requesting to speak with Governor Ridge who, at the time, was traveling to his residence in Erie, Pennsylvania. Governor Davis reported that he was ready to hold a news conference to report what he had learned about the incident and wanted to confer with Governor Ridge to see if the new Office of Homeland Security had any additional facts. When we connected Governor Davis and Governor Ridge on a conference call, (and after we had the opportunity to brief Governor Ridge on all of the details we had collected), Governor Ridge calmly relayed all of the information to a stunned Governor Davis who was amazed at how quickly we, in the ISG, had amassed the facts despite being thousands of miles from the incident. Within minutes after their conversation, we all stood and watched the television monitors in the OHS Coordination Center as Governor Davis approached the podium for his news conference and announced that he had just gotten off the phone with Governor Ridge, the newly appointed Homeland Security Advisor. Governor Davis went on to provide the details of the incident, much of which was relayed to him by Governor Ridge.

While I would like to say that this is a good example of how the system is expected to work, it did not always end up this way. Any way that you looked at it, though, we were proud to say that this was our first real success in OHS. Five hours after the shooting, most of the international terminals at Los Angeles International Airport had reopened and, after a long day, several of us raced down to the White House to attend the 4th of July barbecue and fireworks celebration on the South Lawn, which President Bush was hosting for members of the Executive Office of the President's staff. Unfortunately, most of the night, instead of enjoying the festivities and fireworks, Joe Rozek and I were constantly being interrupted by several "Noble Eagle" domestic conference calls hosted by the new U.S. Northern Command (Northcom) at Cheyenne Mountain in Colorado Springs, Colorado. This was due to the number of civilian airplanes that were accidentally penetrating the restricted airspace over Washington, DC in an attempt to get a better look at the fireworks display that evening.

As I went home that night to an empty house (my family was at the beach for a week without me because I had to remain in Washington, DC), all I could think was what a great opportunity it was to celebrate the 4th of July on the South Lawn of the White House but I had no one close to share it with me.

Several days later, we activated a partial ISG for the second time during the period from 12 to 15 July 2002, when 12,000 lightning strikes were reported in California and Oregon, resulting in 375 fires. Of these four fires, the Biscuit, Sour Biscuit, Florence, and West Florence, eventually burned together to form one large fire named the "Biscuit Fire". This fire alone burned nearly 500,000 acres and cost $153 million to fight. By the end of the year, fires had burned across 7.2 million acres in the U.S., costing over $1 billion to fight. Almost uniformly, the fires of 2002 were characterized as catastrophic, but in fact, each fire was unique in character, offering individual lessons for the future.

On 6 September 2002, five days before the first anniversary of 9/11, a partial ISG was activated for the third time to monitor the Amtrak train trip by members of the U.S. Senate and U.S. House of Representatives from Washington, DC to New York City to mark the anniversary of 9/11. It was the first time in over 200 years that Congress convened in New York City. Upon arriving in New York City, Congress met at Federal Hall before visiting "ground zero." Thanks in part to the U.S. Capitol Police officer assigned to the ISG that day, we were able to get timely and accurate reporting during every moment of the trip, which ended back in Washington, DC later in the day without incident.

Heading up the Incident Support Group for the Office of Homeland Security at the Nebraska Avenue Complex in September 2002

As I previously mentioned, the Homeland Security Advisory System (HSAS) was designed to provide a means to communicate threat information to the public as well as to encourage the coordination of protective measures and preparedness activities among all levels of the government, public, and private sectors, and between all levels of law enforcement and public safety officials. The HSAS was also created to provide a common vocabulary, context, and structure for an ongoing national discussion about the nature of the threats that confront the homeland, and to provide the appropriate measures that should be taken in response, by seeking to inform and facilitate decisions appropriate to different levels of the government and to private citizens at home and at work.

The first time the U.S. Government raised the HSAS to "Orange" (high) from "Yellow" (elevated) was on 10 September 2002, one day before the anniversary of 9/11, after the Intelligence Community received information based on debriefings of a senior al-Qaeda operative of possible terrorist attacks timed to coincide with the anniversary of the 11 September attacks on the United States. According to Intelligence reporting which later was released to the public, al-Qaeda cells had been established in several South Asian countries in order to conduct car bomb and other attacks on U.S. facilities, and that these cells had been accumulating explosives since January 2002 in preparation for the attacks". Minutes after the President made the decision to elevate the HSAS following a Principals Committee meeting at the White House; the various news networks began announcing that the nation was going to "Orange."

As we were convening the ISG, the news broke on every news network and within minutes, the Director of FEMA, Joe Allbaugh, called the OHS Coordination Center from New York City cursing, screaming, and wanting to know who the senior OHS official was on site. Although there was a Domestic Threat Response and Incident Management (DTRIM) meeting, taking place in the conference room across from the ISG with several OHS officials far more senior than me, I was summoned to answer the call. Not being born yesterday, I was smart enough to call Joe Rozek first, who was in the White House Situation Room and asked him who had attended the Principals Committee meeting in place of Joe Allbaugh that morning.

After Joe Rozek informed me that Mike Brown, the Deputy Director of FEMA, had represented Joe Allbaugh at the Principals Committee meeting, I proceeded to the Coordination Center, picked up the phone, and introduced myself as Richard Irwin, the Director of Incident Management for OHS. The reply I received was *"big f--- ing deal"*. *"Now why didn't you "bleeping bleeps" notify me that the HSAS was being elevated"* at which time I replied that as I understood it, his Deputy, Mike Brown, had attended the Principals Committee meeting at the White House in his stead and, therefore, it was probably best that he receive such news directly from his Deputy. Well, after several more "bleeps" Joe Allbaugh accepted this response and asked to speak to the FEMA Director of Response and Recovery, Eric Tolbert, who was listening on the speakerphone in the Coordination Center along with everyone else in the room. After this exchange, I called Joe Rozek to report what had happened, he in turn, called Governor Ridge. Five minutes later, Governor Ridge was on the line explaining to me that he had just gotten off the phone with Joe Allbaugh and had discussed the conversation that Joe had with me that morning. I cannot tell you how proud I was when Governor Ridge told me that I represented him and that in talking to me in that tone of voice, Joe Allbaugh, in essence, was talking to him. He added that as long as he was the Homeland Security Advisor, nobody was going to speak to one of his people like that.

The following day, 11 September 2002, Governor Ridge attended a 9/11 ceremony in Schwenksville, Pennsylvania. Upon returning to Washington later that evening, Governor Ridge came by the NAC to say thank you to the entire ISG staff that were standing shift. Afterwards, as we were walking down the hall together, I thanked him for sticking up for me the day before, but added that when Joe Allbaugh called, I did not think that he knew who he was talking to since I kept on referring to myself as "Richard Irwin", and Joe Allbaugh kept referring to me as "motherf---er" and "c--- sucker" to which Governor Ridge laughed and laughed.

Due to the increased amount of information that the Intelligence Community had received requiring the HSAS to be elevated to "Orange" (High), Governor Ridge decided to convene teleconference calls with all of the Governors, a separate conference call with all of the new Homeland Security Advisors in each State, and lastly, with a group known as the "Roundtable" consisting of executives of the top 50 private sector companies in the United States. The purpose of the conference calls was to provide suggested random anti-terrorism security measures, which several of us had prepared at the request of the Governor. Each conference call began with the Governor saying, "Although we do not have specific targeting information, the sequential release of recent statements by key al-Qaeda members, strengthens previous assessments that al-Qaeda continues to plan for major attacks against U.S. interests." Governor Ridge then provided an extensive list of "little or no cost actions" and "actions that might bear some cost" that we had prepared for him. These ranged from increasing the number of visible security personnel wherever possible and arranging for law enforcement vehicles to be parked randomly near entrances and exits, to conducting vulnerability studies focusing on physical security, structural engineering, infrastructure engineering, power, water, and air infiltration.

To say that we were busy operating the ISG 24/7 over this period was an understatement. On 9/11 alone, during one three-hour period, we were evaluating and "running to ground" nine separate incidents to include a reported hijacking, a school shooting, a white powder incident, a nine-story building collapse, and even a threat against the President which was passed to the USSS. The following day, on 12 September 2002 as President Bush was addressing the 57th Session of the United Nations in New York City, we carefully monitored the boarding of the German owned Palermo-Senator six miles outside New York Harbor after low-level radiation readings were detected the day before. As Navy Seals and Department of Energy technicians thoroughly inspected the 708-foot vessel and its more than 650 40-foot containers, the inspection was cut short due to high winds and choppy seas. Although inspections resumed the following day, no radioactive material was found and the vessel was allowed to continue on to New York Harbor.

Later during the evening of 12 September 2002 as I was sitting in the ISG, I received a call from the Homeland Security Advisor in Georgia, via the OHS Coordination Center, who stated that he had been contacted by a Sheriff in Calhoun County, Georgia who reported that a woman claimed that she overheard three men of Middle Eastern descent at a restaurant discussing their plans to attack a pre-arranged target. When I asked the Homeland Security Advisor for his opinion on what facilities in Georgia could be "potential targets", he replied that the only thing he could think of were the two nuclear power plants in the State – the Edwin I. Hatch facility and the Vogtle facility. Recalling that in his January 2002 State of the Union Address, President Bush made reference to the fact that U.S. forces had uncovered evidence of potential attacks against American nuclear facilities in Afghanistan after U.S. soldiers found diagrams of U.S. nuclear power plants there, I decided to call the Sheriff directly to hear what he had to say. Before calling I "Googled" the President's State of the Union Address and found out that President Bush had told Congress and the Nation that *"Our discoveries in Afghanistan confirmed our worst fears. We have found diagrams of public water facilities, instructions on how to make chemical arms, maps of U.S. cities and descriptions of U.S. landmarks, in addition to nuclear-plant plans."* Following the President's address, the U.S. Intelligence Community warned that members of al-Qaeda might be tapping into the U.S.-based Internet sites that included information about nuclear facilities. Among other things, U.S. intelligence had received information from a suspected

Bin Ladin operative in the fall of 2001 and early 2002 suggesting that potential U.S. targets included nuclear power facilities, dams and water reservoirs. On top of that, at the same time, the FBI was reporting a series of suspicious incidents, including the surveillance of U.S. nuclear plants.

After reaching the Sheriff on his cell phone, he related that earlier in the day, a woman named Eunice Stone and her son had reported that they were sitting in a Shoney's Restaurant in Calhoun, Georgia at approximately 11:00 a.m. on 12 September 2002, when they overheard three men, who appeared to be of Middle Eastern descent, sitting next to them watching the television and laughing about the attacks of 9/11. According to the Sheriff, Ms. Stone was quoted as saying *"At first, you know, I just went ahead with my breakfast...but they were laughing, and I have very good hearing."* Ms. Stone then heard one of the men say *"If they mourn 11 September, what will they think about 13 September."* Afterwards, another man asked *"Do you think that will bring it down?"* to which the third man replied, *"Well, if that doesn't bring it down, I have contacts to bring it down."* The Sheriff continued that Ms. Stone thought that they were planning to blow up some pre-arranged target, and was shocked to hear the three men speaking with perfect American accents. Based on these comments, Ms. Stone grabbed a crayon, followed the men out when they left, and wrote down descriptions of their cars, their license plate numbers, and called the local Sheriffs Department to tell what she had overheard.

Following this call, the Georgia Bureau of Investigation issued a nationwide alert for the two cars and three men. By early the next morning, on 13 September 2002, the men had traveled down I-75 into Naples, Florida where one of the two cars stopped at a tollbooth. A police officer chased this car and pulled it over after eight miles while the second car proceeded to stop accordingly. This caused a tremendous law enforcement response as more than 100 officers from Federal and Local authorities blocked off a large portion of I-75. While the three men were detained and interrogated, bomb-sniffing dogs exhaustively searched each car. Although the inside and outside surfaces of the cars were swabbed, no trace of explosive materials was found.

As it turned out, the three men advised that they were medical students from Illinois on their way to Larkin Community Hospital in Miami to receive training. Following questioning they were released without being charged. Law enforcement officials reported that one of the three men was a United States Citizen by birth, another was a naturalized citizen, and a third was a foreign national in the United States on a valid student visa. Although the authorities could not connect the men to any surveillance activities or terrorist plot, I still have my suspicions if what Ms. Stone reported was true.

The following day, 13 September 2002, during the 7:00 a.m. Secure Voice Telecommunications System (SVTS) threat review, we learned that the FBI arrested Sahim Alwan, Yahya Goba, Yasein Taher, Faysal Galab, Shafal Mosed, and Mukhtar al-Bakri, in the small Buffalo, New York suburb of Lackawanna for conspiring with terrorist groups and for providing support to al-Qaeda. The six American citizens were of Yemeni descent and five of the six had been born and raised in Lackawanna. During questioning, while all initially claimed that they had been in Pakistan to attend a religious training camp, all eventually admitted to attending an al-Qaeda "jihadist" camp. Later in the day at the 3:00 p.m. SVTS, we received word that Pakistani and U.S. Officials had captured Ramzi bin al Shibh in Pakistan – a key facilitator for the 9/11 attack and a lead operative in a plot to hijack aircrafts and crash them into London's Heathrow Airport.

One day after returning from a meeting with the President shortly after the anniversary of 9/11, Governor Ridge told us that President Bush informed him that he wanted a permanent 24/7/365 "Operations Center" set up and staffed at our new OHS headquarters at the NAC to monitor threats and incidents along the lines of what the ISG was doing during periods of increased threats and incidents. The "Operations Center", which eventually would morph into the Homeland Security Operations Center (HSOC), when DHS stood up on 1 March 2003 under former U.S. Marine Corps General Matthew Broderick, was to serve as the nation's nerve center for information and domestic incident management.

That was the good news. The bad news was that the Governor told us that we had three days to set up the new "Operations Center" because the President was planning to clear his calendar at the end of the week and would be visiting the NAC to inspect it that Thursday.

Briefing President George Bush on the Incident Support Group (ISG) at the Nebraska Avenue Complex in September 2002

For the next three days, we commandeered every conference table that we could find in Building 3 at the NAC and moved them into a large conference room, 3010, on the first floor where we had been staffing the ISG. With the assistance of James "Buck" Buchanan, the Deputy Director of Technology at OHS, we began the process of installing Top Secret phones and computers beside Secret phones and computers beside unclassified phones and computers ensuring that we met the security regulations for separation of space. Although we had cords and lines running everywhere, and although the "Operations Center" was not pretty, three days later we were up, running, and ready to brief the President who, upon visiting the NAC on 19 September 2002, was elated. Today, the Homeland Security Operations Center (HSOC) is known as the National Operations Center (NOC) and is staffed by over 100 representatives from Federal departments and agencies as well as State and Local police departments and private sector contractors.

* * *

With the ISG operating 24/7 while we remained at "Orange", Governor Ridge began to rely on this new entity more and more to provide him with situational awareness and courses of action to take to the President.

During one incident, while Governor Ridge was attending a funeral service in Erie, Pennsylvania, a large explosion occurred in New York City's harbor and within minutes, every major news network was carrying the story. After seeing the story reported on Fox News, we immediately got on the phone to the New York City police and fire departments, the New York City Port Authority, the New York State Police, the Governor of New York, the New York City Mayor's office, the New York Homeland Security Advisor, the U.S. Coast Guard, the FBI, and FEMA in an attempt to piece together what had happened. Five minutes later, we were able to ascertain that the explosion, an accident, occurred when a large vessel was transporting fuel to one of the oil refinery storage containers. We were also further able to determine with some confidence that there did not appear to be any "terrorist nexus." As we wrote up a small incident report and distributed it to the senior OHS and White House officials, I was glad to see, the "anxiety level" begin to come back down on the faces of everyone in the ISG. Knowing that Governor Ridge was in church in Erie, I immediately called the head of his USSS security detail requesting that the Governor call me as soon as the funeral service ended. Ten minutes later, before departing the church, Governor Ridge called and we provided him with a full account of the incident in the New York City harbor. Seconds later, as he exited the church, he was met by a host of local news reporters who asked him if he had any details on the incident in New York City to which he replied that he had just gotten off the phone with his "Operations Center" in Washington, DC. Governor Ridge then went on to describe the information, which we had reported to include the fact that the U.S. Government did not suspect any terrorist nexus; makes you proud when it comes together like that.

While staffing the ISG, it was not uncommon to receive requests from the likes of Governor Gray Davis of California, through Governor Ridge asking if we could have a Combat Air Patrol (CAP) placed over the Golden Gate Bridge due to some threat or have the Deputy Chief of Staff at the White House, Joe Hagin, call us from Air Force One, with a request for information for the President—but we always came through. In the case of Governor Davis, one Saturday afternoon after receiving information of a potential attack on the Golden Gate Bridge by al-Qaeda, Governor Davis called Governor Ridge who, in turn, had me added to the conference call. *"Richard,"* he said, *"see if it is possible to get a CAP over the Golden Gate for Governor Davis."* After replying that I would get on it right away, I immediately called Pete Verga, the

Principal Deputy Assistant Secretary of Defense for Homeland Defense and a fellow member of the Counterterrorism and Security Group (CSG) at his residence. When I asked Pete if he had a secure phone and whether we could go secure, he replied that, unfortunately, he did not and therefore, would have to drive to the Pentagon to speak to me on a secure line. Thirty minutes later, I was informing Pete of the information we had received pertaining to the Golden Gate Bridge and told him of the CAP that Governor Ridge was requesting on behalf of Governor Davis. While Pete acknowledged that the location of the CAPs were classified and not distributable, he stated that he would check to see if there was a CAP in the vicinity of San Francisco. Fifteen minutes later, I was back on the phone with Pete after he had identified a CAP that would cover the Golden Gate Bridge. I, in turn, passed the information on to Governor Ridge and Governor Davis, both of whom were delighted. Being the class act that Governor Ridge is, he then asked me to get Pete Verga back on the phone so that he could thank him personally, which I did.

In the case of Joe Hagin who frequently called with requests for information, one time he called while aboard Air Force One saying that he had just received information that the U.S. Capitol was being evacuated. I, in turn, called Terry Gainer, the Chief of the Capitol Police who informed me that they were indeed evacuating a portion of the Capitol due to a water main break. As I was reporting this information back to Joe Hagin, I could hear President Bush in the background saying, *"Is that my new Operations Center on the line that you are talking to?"*

Many of the Situation Reports, which we wrote, found their way to the President. With people like Duncan Campbell, Susan Neely, Josh Filler, Tom DiNanno, Vice Admiral Brian Peterman (USCG), Ron Colburn, Ken Hill, Bob Kadlec, Jim Miller, Mike Byrne, Barbara Chaffee, Tim Stout, Wayne Parent, Steve Rickman, Morgan Middlemas, John Herr and Chris Furlow from OHS staffing the ISG, I am still amazed at how much we accomplished with that small group, sometimes while sharing phones and computers, in comparison to the larger Inter-Agency Incident Management Group (IMMG), which later was established after the Department of Homeland Security became operational on 1 March 2003. Today the IIMG is known as the Inter-Agency Management Planning Team (IMPT) and the Crisis Action team (CAT).

After several weeks of having the ISG operating around the clock 24/7, on 24 September 2002, the Attorney General, in consultation with the Homeland Security Council, and Governor Ridge, made the decision to return the HSAS threat level from "Orange" to an elevated risk of terrorist attack "Yellow" status. This was based on "a review of intelligence, an assessment of the threats by the Intelligence Community pertaining to the disruption of potential terrorist operations in the United States and abroad, as well as the passing of the anniversary of the 11 September terrorist attacks."

Despite all of the hours that we worked at OHS, we always found time to attend an Orioles Baseball game or play basketball together on Wednesday evenings and enjoy some refreshments and appetizers in the Chief's Club at the NAC afterwards; usually venison, (if I was fortunate enough to shoot a deer – a Pennsylvania deer, of course), although some people always thought that I was serving "road kill". As Commissioner for Governor Ridge's basketball league at the NAC, I had two rules: first, when the Governor played, he always played on my team; and second, we only played zone defense so that the Governor would not have to show up on national television with a black eye. I recall at one of the first games, which Governor Ridge showed up to play, the USSS did not know any of us and did not know whether to be on the court or remain in the shadows. At that time, a huge red head named Eric Walker used to play with us. Eric had been a "walk-on" linebacker at Texas A&M. When Eric went up for a rebound that night, he accidentally got Governor Ridge in a headlock and fell to the floor. Not being shy to join in a brawl, I proceeded to run across the court and jump on Eric's back with the Governor beneath him and proceed to throw a bunch of fake punches at Eric's head while reminding Governor Ridge at the same time that I was the only one who had come to his aid. This, unfortunately, caused the USSS to come running out on the floor. When they found out that we were not actually fighting, they proceeded to lecture us for the next several minutes on why the stunt was not very funny. From that night forward, the USSS always remained out of sight off the court.

* * *

During the evening of 23 October 2002, after playing basketball at the NAC, Governor Ridge approached me and asked me my thoughts regarding the shootings that were paralyzing the Greater Washington DC Metropolitan area–a reference to the shootings that were taking place in the Mid-Atlantic States known as the Beltway sniper attacks. I replied that, in my opinion it was impossible that they were being conducted by one shooter and I felt that the white van had nothing to do with any of the shootings. The following day, after two men were arrested, we learned that the attacks were perpetrated by John Allen Muhammad and Lee Boyd Malvo, driving a blue Chevrolet Caprice sedan. Both had begun their shooting rampage the month before with murders and robberies in Louisiana, Alabama, and Georgia, which had resulted in three deaths. Later, during a three-week period in October 2002, ten people were killed and three others critically injured in and around Washington, DC, in various locations throughout the Baltimore-Washington Metropolitan Area and along Interstate 95 in Virginia. During this shooting spree, it was widely speculated that a single sniper was using the Capital Beltway for travel, possibly in a white van or truck.

On 25 November 2002, President Bush rolled out the Homeland Security Act of 2002, which introduced the creation of the Department of Homeland Security (DHS) – the largest government reorganization in 50 years (since the Department of Defense was created). Pursuant to the Homeland Security Act of 2002, the Secretary of DHS was identified as the person that would be responsible for coordinating Federal operations within the United States to prepare for, respond to, and recover from terrorist attacks, major disasters, and other emergencies. The new department, created by the 35-page Homeland Security Act, assumed a number of government functions previously conducted in other departments, with the primary mission "to prevent terrorist attacks within the United States, reduce the vulnerability of the United States to terrorism, minimize the damage, and assist in the recovery from terrorist attacks that occurred within the United States." Merging 22 departments and agencies together and over 180,000 federal employees was no small task because the U.S. Coast Guard and Transportation Security Administration (TSA), Customs, Immigration, FEMA and the USSS, for example, all reported through separate chains of command to the President. In addition, all had separate statutory authorities vested in separate Presidential appointees confirmed by the Senate with separate appropriations that had to be expended by law as appropriated, making it virtually impossible to get all of the different agencies acting in harmony and in concert.

In late November 2002, shortly after the Homeland Security Act of 2002, was rolled out, I traveled with my family to

Philadelphia, Pennsylvania to spend time with my parents, brothers and sisters for Thanksgiving. Shortly upon arriving, I found out that my mother, who was in a nursing home at the time, had been rushed to the hospital. As I entered the hospital, I saw a priest leaving my mother's room and immediately thought that she had just received communion. I was informed by the priest however, that he had just administered the Sacrament of "Last Rites" to my mother who was in a partial coma. As I stayed with my mother throughout the night, I kept whispering to her to *"hang in there"* since my brother Jim was on his way from California. Much to my surprise, the following morning as I awoke in my chair after dozing off, I was surprised to see my mother sitting up in bed looking at me and saying, *"Hello, Richard."* When I told her that Jim was on his way from California, I was shocked to hear her say, *"Yea, you told me that yesterday."* Returning to Washington, DC after deer hunting for several days, on 13 December 2002 I attended the first of many Senior Officials Exercises that I would be asked to attend over the next few years. This one involved a Liquid Petroleum Gas explosion in New York City moderated by OHS' Joel Bagnal at the NAC. To this day, I think that this first exercise was one of the best that I participated in, because it outlined to everyone in the room the role of OHS and the ISG.

Many perks came with working at the White House to include: invitations to watch when visiting dignitaries arrived at the White House; attending the annual Easter Egg Hunt on the White House lawn with your children or the 4th of July barbecue on the South Lawn of the White House and watching the fireworks; the use of the Presidential box at the Kennedy Center to attend concerts; meeting world champion football, baseball or basketball teams, or superstars such as Arnold Schwarzenegger; receiving a private tour of the White House when it was decorated during the Christmas holidays or attending the Christmas Pageant for Peace choral concert; and, lastly, getting your picture taken with the President during the Christmas holidays as a member of the Executive Office of the President Staff.

The first time my wife, Karen, and I got our pictures taken with the President and First Lady Laura Bush occurred on 17 December 2002, in the Blue Room of the White House. After the photograph session, we retreated to the Green Room along with several of my OHS colleagues to include Ken Hill, Jim Miller and their wives. Taking over a corner of the room, it was one of the few times that we got to sit on the furniture and eat and drink from the huge buffets and bars that had been set up. As Governor Ridge and his wife, Michelle, entered the Green Room that evening, the Governor immediately came over and warmly greeted Karen and I. After posing with him for several photographs, we soon noticed that everyone in line to get their picture taken with the President proceeded to a line that had formed in front of Governor Ridge to get their photograph taken with him. Since it is difficult to eat or drink under these circumstances, I purposely made several covert "brush passes" to slip a glass or two of Grey Goose vodka and ice to the Governor who kept telling everyone within earshot that it was water. Several hours later and long after the President and the First lady went to bed; two USSS Uniformed Division Protective Service Officers at the White House came by and were surprised to see us still in the Green room. As I was talking to Mrs. Ridge, one of the officers told us that it was getting late and that we would have to leave. When Governor Ridge asked me what was going on, I remarked, *"We are getting kicked out of here boss,"* to which Governor Ridge replied, *"I have never been kicked out of the White House before so I guess I will have to talk to the President first thing tomorrow morning and let him know that we were kicked out of his house."* As we departed that evening, several of us, including Governor Ridge and his wife, Michelle, continued for another hour or so at the rooftop bar in the Hotel Washington. The following morning as Governor Ridge arrived at the White House Situation Room for his morning briefing 15 minutes late, he shot me a glare, as if it was my fault, he stayed up half the night and was running late.

* * *

Several weeks later, on 13 January 2003, while I was sleeping at an undisclosed facility several hundred feet below the earth surface, I received a call from my sister, Regina, and my sister, Chris, informing me that my mother had passed away. I had known moments earlier that my mother had passed on when I felt her spirit pass through me. In that I was scheduled to fly to Florida the next day to support the Colombia shuttle mission, which was to take off on 16 January 2003, I called my father who told me to continue with my plans since most of the preparations for my mother's funeral had already been put into place while I was visiting my family during Thanksgiving after my mother had taken ill.

Nine months earlier, U.S. National Aeronautics and Space Administration (NASA) Administrator Sean O'Keefe had asked Governor Ridge and the new Office of Homeland Security (OHS) for assistance in securing the Columbia launch because with the presence of Ilan Ramon, the Israeli astronaut, many space agency officials feared his presence might make the shuttle more of a terrorist target. Because the shuttle is most vulnerable when it is sitting on the launch pad for several days leading up to launch fully fueled and ready to go, OHS convened a working group consisting of Federal, State, and Local departments and agencies to ensure the safety of the Colombia shuttle launch along the lines of a National Special Security Event (NSSE), although the launch was never deemed a NSSE. In addition to the normal security measures, DOD promised to provide a CAP over the Kennedy Space Center air space; the U.S. Coast Guard was asked to provide additional patrols in the waters surrounding the Cape; and U.S. Customs promised to place armed helicopters in the air to patrol the skies over the Cape.

NASA Administrator Sean O'Keefe with Amy Donahue, Joe Clancy and Mike Byrne the night before the Colombia Space Shuttle launch 2003

The following day, on 14 January 2003, I flew to Florida with Mike Byrne, the Director of OHS' Emergency Preparedness, and Joe Clancy, a USSS agent assigned to OHS who was heavily involved in coordinating NSSE's on behalf of the USSS. Met by the Director of Security for NASA, Dave Saleeba, we were told that in the event that something happened during the launch, we would be whisked to the NASA Operations Center to provide updates to Governor Ridge for the President. After two days of briefings, several countdown meetings, and a tour of the Kennedy Space Center, the night before the shuttle launch, we joined Sean O'Keefe and a small group of his staff at the shuttle launch site where we took picture after picture of the Colombia shuttle fully illuminated on the launch pad. Mike, Joe, and I also posed for pictures on top of a miniature shuttle, which we sent back to Governor Ridge, much to his chagrin.

On the day of the launch, the weather was gorgeous. As we sat in a VIP section three miles across the water from the launch pad with several VIP's and the families of the Colombia astronauts, counting down the final seconds, goose bumps went up the back of my neck as I overheard the youngest son of Ilan Ramon, the Israeli astronaut, say, *"Farewell, my father. I doubt that I will ever see you again"* just when there was nine seconds left to lift off. As the Colombia space shuttle roared into space, tears began to flow down my checks as I silently paid tribute to my mother who had just passed away. Following the launch, we all ate a NASA customary meal of beans, rice, and corn bread before I returned to Philadelphia, Pennsylvania on Friday, 18 January in time for my mother's funeral on Saturday, 19 January 2003.

During the morning of Saturday, 1 February 2003, as I was on a chair lift at 9:00 a.m. on my way to the top of the mountain at Canaan Valley, West Virginia for my first ski run of the day, a cell phone started ringing. The first thing I could think of was what asshole has a cell phone on while skiing on such a beautiful day. Realizing that it was my own cell phone, I can still remember the chills that went up and down my spine when Amy Donahue, the Senior Advisor to the Administrator for Homeland Security at NASA, told me that they had just *"lost the shuttle."* When I asked her to repeat what she had just said, Amy responded, *"Richard, we believe that the Colombia blew up as it was re-entering the atmosphere somewhere over Texas."* We would later learn that at take off, chunks of insulating foam had broken away and punched a hole in the skin of the shuttle. As the chair lift approached the top of the mountain and snow began falling ever so slightly, I tried to compose my thoughts on what actions would need to be taken. Since the Colombia was on a routine flight, and was going to be escorted by fighter jets upon entering the atmosphere on its way to the Kennedy Space Center, the decision had been made by the Counterterrorism and Security Group (CSG), in consultation with Governor Ridge, not to "stand-up" the ISG and, therefore, I felt a little guilty. My first phone call, following the call from Amy Donahue, was to Governor Ridge, who I was able to reach at approximately 9:16 a.m. Governor Ridge told me that he had just got off the phone with NASA Administrator Sean O'Keefe who told him that he had just informed the President, who was at the Presidential retreat in Camp David, Maryland that the shuttle did not land on schedule. According to Sean O'Keefe, the space shuttle Columbia lost contact with flight controllers in Mission Control, Houston, at about 9:00 a.m., 16 minutes before it was scheduled to land at the Kennedy Space Center, when it was 207,000 feet over the State of Texas. President Bush, in response, was said to have "offered full and immediate support."

As the snow began to fall more rapidly, for the next 30 minutes, from the top of a mountain in Canaan Valley, West Virginia via my cell phone, I was able to suggest several immediate courses of action to Governor Ridge who was on his way to the White House Situation Room along with several HSC and NASA officials to include Joel Bagnal. The first recommendation was to have NASA warn residents in Texas to be aware of any fallen objects and not to touch any debris they found. Shortly thereafter, NASA mission control in Houston, Texas issued the following statement, *"Any debris that is located in the Dallas-Forth Worth vicinity should be avoided and may be hazardous due to the toxic nature of propellants used on board the shuttle and should be reported to local law enforcement authorities."* Next, it was recommended that FEMA be the "Lead Federal Agency" to coordinate the shuttle disaster efforts on the ground and FEMA began scrambling rescue teams. Along with the assistance of military forces from Fort Hood, Texas, elements of the Texas National Guard, the Texas Forestry Service, and the Texas Rangers, the rescue teams began searching and collecting wreckage of the orbiter and its crew. Reports of charred debris had stretched from Corsicana, southeast of Dallas, into Louisiana, and would turn up as far east as Arkansas, and as far west as Arizona and New Mexico. After NASA Headquarters reported that, there had been no reported difficulties from the shuttle before it lost contact with ground control, the decision was made to announce that there was no immediate information to suggest that terrorism was involved with the disappearance of the space shuttle; that there was no threat made against the flight; that the shuttle was out of range of a surface-to-air missile; and that the FBI was not involved in the investigation.

The shuttle Colombia went into service in 1981 and was NASA's oldest shuttle. The incident came on its 28th flight. There were seven astronauts onboard the Columbia space shuttle, two females, and the first Israeli astronaut ever to enter space. Ilan Ramon -- 48, a Colonel in the Israeli Air Force, was a fighter pilot who was the only payload specialist on Columbia. Ramon received a

Bachelor of Science degree in electronics and computer engineering from the University of Tel Aviv, Israel, in 1987. Ramon was selected as a payload specialist by the Israeli Air Force in 1997 and approved by U.S. space agency NASA in 1998. He reported for training at the NASA Johnson Space Center in Houston in July 1998 and was making his first space flight. Rick D. Husband -- 45, a Colonel in the U.S. Air Force, was a test pilot and veteran of one space flight. He served as commander for Columbia. NASA selected him in December 1994; William C. McCool -- 41, a commander in the U.S. Navy, was a former test pilot. He served as pilot for Columbia. Selected by NASA in April 1996, McCool was making his first space flight; Michael P. Anderson -- 43, a Lieutenant Colonel in the U.S. Air Force, was a former instructor pilot and tactical officer, and a veteran of one space flight. He served as payload commander and mission specialist for Columbia. NASA selected him in December 1994; David M. Brown -- 46, a captain in the U.S. Navy, was a naval aviator and flight surgeon. He served as mission specialist for Columbia. Selected by NASA in April 1996, Brown was making his first space flight; Kalpana Chawla -- 41, was an aerospace engineer and a certified flight instructor. She was serving as flight engineer and mission specialist for Columbia. NASA selected her in December 1994; and Laurel Blair Salton Clark -- 41, a commander in the U.S. Navy and a naval flight surgeon, was mission specialist on Columbia. Selected by NASA in April 1996, Clark was making her first space flight.

Later that morning, as I was driving back to Washington, DC, NASA officials announced that the space shuttle Columbia was destroyed. *"Sadly, from the videos that are available, it does not appear that there were any survivors,"* reported Bill Readdy, Associate Administrator for space flight, who also reported that *"it was too early to speculate about what destroyed the shuttle"*. The loss of Columbia was the most serious shuttle incident since the Challenger exploded on 28 January 1986, shortly after liftoff, killing all seven astronauts onboard. It took NASA three years to return to space and launch the Discovery shuttle after the Challenger disaster. Shortly after returning to the White House from Camp David in Maryland, in a brief televised address from the White House, President Bush announced, *"The Columbia's lost. There are no survivors. These men and women assumed great risk in the service to all humanity."* Bush then slowly read the names of the six Americans and the first Israeli astronaut on board the space shuttle. *"Our entire Nation grieves with you and those you love will always have the respect and gratitude of this country. The cause in which they died will continue. Our journey into space will go on."* Before his address, President Bush telephoned the families of the astronauts to console them and ordered the flag on top of the White House lowered to half-staff. At a news conference at the Kennedy Space Center, NASA Administrator Sean O'Keefe announced that experts from the U.S. Air Force and Navy, which had five of the seven crew members, would join officials from the Transportation Department and other Federal agencies on an independent board to investigate the tragedy. Sean O'Keefe also said that the space agency would be conducting its own investigation into the disaster, adding that there was no indication that anything or anyone on the ground had caused the tragedy.

During the evening of 6 February 2003, I walked over to the gymnasium at the NAC to play basketball. Because there were rumors that we would be raising the HSAS from "Yellow" to "Orange", I was not confident that we would have a large turnout for our weekly game. I was correct. The only other player to show up to shoot some hoops that night was the NAC Base Commander, Al DeMedeiros. Shortly after 8:00 p.m., I looked up to see Governor Ridge enter and motion for me to shower and dress. As we departed the gym that night, Governor Ridge told me that with the long hours that I had been putting in, especially following the Colombia Shuttle disaster, he wanted to take me out to celebrate my birthday that evening. Arriving at a little Mexican restaurant that we often frequented named "Guapos" close to the NAC; we were met by Ken Hill, Duncan Campbell, Tommy DiNanno, and Al DeMedeiros. For the next few hours, we ate plate after plate of delicious Mexican appetizers and washed them down with frozen margaritas. Unfortunately, instead of heading home, I returned to the NAC to sleep in a barracks and would continue to do so until DHS became operational on 1 March 2003, often boasting that I had slept in those quarters more than any other OHS employee, with the exception of maybe James "Buck" Buchanan.

The following day, 7 February 2003, the Homeland Security threat condition was elevated from "Yellow" to "Orange" after intelligence reports suggested the possibility of terrorist attacks against "apartment buildings, hotels, and other soft or lightly secured targets." Shortly thereafter, the Counterterrorism and Security Group (CSG), in consultation with Governor Ridge, made the decision to stand up the ISG and Ray Mey, a senior FBI agent detailed to OHS and I split 12-hour shifts to ensure that we could keep the ISG operating 24/7.

A week later during the morning of 15 February 2003, I awoke at 4:30 a.m. to be at the NAC to replace Ray Mey by 6:00 a.m. After showering, shaving, and dressing I opened the garage and found a huge drift of fresh snow in my driveway. Although most of the roads, including the highways, had not been plowed, driving to work that morning in my four-wheel drive Jeep was not as bad as I had expected since I was one of only a few drivers on the road that morning. Driving down 17th Street in front of the Eisenhower Executive Office Building (EEOB) and the White House was eerily quiet, though, as there was no one, and I mean no one, in sight with snow up to a foot or two on the unplowed city streets. Arriving at the NAC, I told Ray Mey and the rest of the employees who had been working through the night to go home, get some needed rest, and not to even bother trying to come back until the storm subsided; our shift would cover for them. Little did any of us know that this snowstorm would be the beginning of what would be referred to as the Blizzard of 2003 or the President Day Storm of 2003, which by the time it was over, would dump from 15 to 30 inches of snow from Washington, DC to Boston.

Although it was snowing upwards to a half inch per hour, that afternoon, we received a surprise visit by Governor Ridge who said that he wanted to thank everyone in the Coordination Center and ISG for their hard work. As evening approached and after everyone had eaten the breakfast and lunches that they had packed and we were running out of food, I decided to break out the "Meals Ready to Eat" (MREs); packages of dehydrated food that we had stored at the NAC for just such emergencies. I smiled to myself when I overheard people saying, *"I'll trade you my hot dogs and beans for your meat loaf."* Dividing our shift up into two groups, half of the people slept on cots in the hallways while the other group maintained the watch. I knew it was going to be a long night.

In order to break up the monotony I broke out the Jenga and Trivial Pursuit games for anyone that was willing to play. Thank God that the gymnasium was open so that those who cared to shower, shave and brush their teeth had a place to do so. The downside was that you had to plow through the snowdrifts to get to the gym from Building 3. For breakfast, lunch, and dinner the following day we all dined on MRE'S again as the snow continued to fall. The following morning, on 17 February, after several ISG members came to me to complain that they could not eat another MRE, I asked for a volunteer to make a "food run". Although I was not very confident that any stores would be open because the snow was still falling heavily, Jim Kish, a former National Guard Colonel, raised his hand and said he would go. I then gave him the keys to the Ford Expedition that the Agency had loaned me as an emergency vehicle and he walked out the door. Two hours later, Jim returned with two shopping bags filled with orange juice, milk, bread, eggs, bacon and potatoes. When I asked him where he had been, Jim replied that for the better part of an hour and a half, he had been driving up and down Connecticut and Wisconsin Avenues trying to find a food store that was open. Finally, as he was about to give up, Jim said that he found a small grocery store operated by a Vietnamese family that had only a few items left on their shelves, which he was happy to purchase from them. For the next hour or so, I volunteered to cook breakfast for the 25 or so ISG members. This was no small task, since the only appliances we had at the NAC at the time were a small microwave and a toaster oven. When Governor Ridge walked into the ISG that morning, to see how everyone was holding up, much to his surprise everyone's spirits were quite high as we were dining on microwaved scrambled eggs, and toast, home fried potatoes and bacon that were made in a toaster oven. I even broke out some venison tender loins that I had brought with me. Finally, that afternoon as the snow stopped falling, one by one our replacements arrived and we finally went home some 48 hours later for some much-needed rest.

On 27 February 2003, the decision was made to lower the threat level from "Orange" to "Yellow". The lowering was based on a careful review of "how this specific intelligence had evolved and progressed over the past three weeks; counterterrorism actions taken to address specific aspects of the threat situation; and the passing of the time period in or around the end of the Hajj, a Muslim religious period ending mid-February 2003." The Counterterrorism and Security Group (CSG) and Governor Ridge decided however, to keep the ISG up and running for another few days, until DHS became operational on 1 March 2003.

One evening, shortly after the HSAS returned to "Yellow", as I was sitting with Dab Kern from the White House Military Office and the Deputy Chief of Staff of the White House, Josh Bolten, at an undisclosed facility several hundred feet below the earth surface, Josh asked me if I planned to go with Governor Ridge to the new Department of Homeland Security or if I would like to remain at the White House and continue as the Director of Incident Management with the Homeland Security Council, as opposed to Office of Homeland Security which was going to be dissolved. In response to his question I stated, *"The decision would most likely be made at a level a lot higher than mine"*, and much to my surprise, Josh Bolten replied, *"Well Richard, it won't be made at a level higher than mine. We want you to stay at the White House."* Later, when Governor Ridge asked me if I was interested in being the Director of Incident Management in DHS, I told him that I thought that I could better serve him as the Director of Incident Management at the White House from the Situation Room rather than at DHS until the Department got the Homeland Security Operations Center (HSOC) up and running. As the Secretary of DHS, he would continue to be the recipient of everything that I received and "ran to ground". Interestingly, I was also offered the Director of Security position at DHS by Governor Ridge, which I turned down because, in this instance, I would have had to resign from the Agency and become a DHS employee versus being detailed, as was the case with my assignment to OHS and the HSC.

The following day, on 28 February 2003, the President signed HSPD-5, designating the Secretary DHS, as the Principal Federal Official (PFO) for domestic incident management. HSPD-5's intent was to unify domestic incident management under the Secretary through the development and administration of a National Response Plan (NRP), which would eventually become enacted in November 2004. In these efforts, with regard to domestic incidents, I was glad to see that the U.S. Government, for the first time, was going to treat crisis management and consequence management as a single, integrated function, rather than as two separate functions.

Chapter 14

"Serving a President in the White House"

The 28th of February 2003 was our last day in OHS. As we were transferring the roles and responsibility of the Incident Support Group (ISG) to the Department of Homeland Security (DHS), Vice Admiral Steve Abbot, the Deputy Homeland Security Advisor (pictured at right), visited the Nebraska Avenue Compound (NAC) to congratulate everyone in the ISG on what a great job we all had done during the past year and a half. That afternoon, as we all walked out of the small operations center, in Room 3010 Building 3, I carefully removed a photograph of President Bush's

visit to the ISG on 19 September 2002. Because of the significance of that day, and what OHS had accomplished in such a short period, I thought it was only right to take the photograph with me to my new assignment as the Director of Incident Management at the Homeland Security Council (HSC) at the White House.

The following day, 1 March 2003, when DHS became operational, we learned during a specially convened 10:00 a.m. Secure Voice Telecommunications System (SVTS) threat review that the mastermind of 9/11, Khalil Sheikh Mohammed, was arrested in Rawalpindi, Pakistan–one of the most important breakthroughs in the fight against al-Qaeda. The two key factors leading to his arrest was a bribe to an al-Qaeda operative in the amount of $27 million, as well as information gained from the NSA. Although the arrest was solely a Pakistani operation, the FBI observed the arrest and was involved in the interrogation process. According to Pakistani officials, KSM remained in Pakistan for three days and was subsequently moved by U.S. officials to an undisclosed location.

Arriving in the HSC, I discovered that the council was created on 8 October 2001 after President Bush signed HSPD-1 to ensure coordination of all homeland security-related activities among executive departments and agencies and to promote the effective development and implementation of all homeland security policies. As Governor Ridge became the Secretary of DHS, Vice Admiral Abbot, who was serving as Ridge's deputy in OHS, became the Acting Homeland Security Advisor for the HSC at the White House. Admiral Abbot would serve in this capacity until 29 April 2003 when the White House issued a press release stating that President Bush had announced his intention to appoint General John Gordon to be the Assistant to the President for Homeland Security. Per HSPD-5, as the Homeland Security Advisor, General Gordon was responsible for interagency policy coordination regarding domestic incident management as directed by the President. General Gordon, at the time, was the Deputy Assistant to the President, National Director and Deputy National Security Advisor for Combating Terrorism, replacing General Wayne Downing as Director of the Office of Combating Terrorism, who had held that position since 9 October 2001. General Gordon had also been the Deputy Director at the CIA under DCI George Tenet. I was glad that I would be working for General Gordon having spent the last year with him as a member of the Counterterrorism and Security Group (CSG).

The Counterterrorism and Security Group (CSG) is a combined NSC and HSC Sub-Group of the Deputies Committee that coordinates the campaign against global terrorism, sensitive terrorism issues, threat information, crisis operations, incident management activities and all matters concerning foreign and domestic terrorism to deter, detect, disrupt and destroy terrorists and those who harbor, protect or support them.

The HSC Principals Committee is a senior interagency forum under the HSC for homeland security issues. The HSC/PC is convened at the request of the Assistant to the President for Homeland Security, in consultation with the regular attendees of the HSC/PC and determines the agenda. When global terrorism with domestic implications is on the agenda of the HSC/PC, the Assistant to the President for Homeland Security and the Assistant to the President for National Security Affairs perform these tasks in concert. The HSC Deputies Committee (HSC/DC) serves as the senior sub-Cabinet interagency forum for consideration of policy issues affecting homeland security and can task and review the work of the HSC interagency groups to ensure that issues brought before the HSC/PC or the HSC have been properly analyzed and prepared for action. The HSC/DC, chaired by the Deputy Director of the Office of Homeland Security, consists of the deputies of the departments and agencies as well as the Assistant to the President and Chief of

Staff to the Vice President. The Assistant to the President and Deputy National Security Advisor can be invited to attend all meetings of the HSC/DC as well as the deputies of the departments and agencies mentioned above on the invite list. The Special Advisor to the President for Cyberspace Security can also be invited as well as other senior officials, when appropriate.

HSC Policy Coordination Committees (HSC/PCCs) coordinate the development and implementation of homeland security policies by multiple departments and agencies throughout the Federal government, and coordinate those policies with State and Local government. The Chairman of each HSC/PCC, in consultation with its Executive Secretary, can invite representatives of other executive departments and agencies to attend meetings of the HSC/PCC when appropriate, and can establish subordinate working groups to assist the PCC in the performance of its duties. The Vice President can attend all meetings of any entity established by or under this directive.

The new Homeland Security Operations Center (HSOC), at DHS, which was set up in the same small conference room that held the ISG, was designed to serve as the nation's nerve center for information and domestic incident management. As the primary national hub for domestic incident management, operational coordination, situational awareness, and monitoring of the homeland, the HSOC became a standing 24/7/365 interagency organization, fusing law enforcement, national intelligence, emergency response, and private sector reporting.

The HSOC's multi-agency watch consisted of integrated elements of DHS' Border and Transportation Security, Customs and Border Protection, Immigration and Customs Enforcement, Emergency Preparedness and Response/FEMA, Federal Protective Service, Information Analysis and Infrastructure Protection, Office of the National Capital Region Coordination, Office of State and Local Government Coordination and Preparedness, Public Affairs, Science and Technology, Transportation Security Administration (TSA), U.S. Coast Guard and the USSS.

The new Intelligence and Analysis, Infrastructure and Protection Directorate (IAIP) at DHS, in partnership with the HSOC, was responsible for all intelligence collection requirements, analysis, production, and product dissemination for DHS. Part of this responsibility included providing the threat and intelligence portion of situational awareness for the HSOC, forecasting follow-on threat activities and incidents, and coordinating Request for Information (RFI) in support of the Inter-Agency Incident Management Group (IIMG).

Like its predecessor, the Incident Support Group (ISG), the Inter-Agency Management Group (IIMG), was established as a Federal headquarters-level, multi-agency coordination entity that facilitates Federal domestic incident management for Incidents of National Significance. Activated by the Secretary DHS, the IIMG is responsible for identifying the nature, severity, magnitude, and complicity of the threat or incident.

Although IIMG membership is flexible and can be tailored or task organized (to provide appropriate subject matter expertise for the specific threat at hand), it is primarily comprised of senior representatives from DHS components. For incident specific activities, the IIMG replaced the Catastrophic Disaster Response Group that served as the policy-level multi-agency coordination entity under the old Federal Response Plan (FRP).

Serving as the focal point for Federal strategic incident management planning and coordination, the IIMG, in partnership with the HSOC, maintains situational awareness of threat assessments and ongoing incident-related operations and activities, while melding intelligence with domestic incident management actions that provide a single incident picture for Federal, State and Local authorities and the private sector. To accomplish its mission, the IIMG provides decision-making support for threat or incident related prevention, preparedness, response, and recovery efforts. The IIMG synthesizes information, frames issues, and makes recommendations to the Secretary DHS, the CSG, the HSC and the NSC at the White House; coordinates the execution of the interagency communications plan; disseminates national level decisions; and prepares for relocation to alternate sites.

Actions taken in response to credible threats include changes in the HSAS alert level, policy issues, operational courses of action, and priorities for the use or allocation of Federal resources. The IIMG provides policy coordination and recommendations for the application of Federal resources in cooperation with existing agency and interagency resource management and private-sector entities. It assesses national impacts of the incidents as well as those associated with the actual or proposed Federal response and anticipates evolving Federal resource and operation requirements according to the specifics of the situation at hand. Lastly, the IIMG is prepared to assume CSG's mission to provide a seamless incident management system between the NSC and the HSC that coordinates immediate response efforts, makes recommendations to the Homeland Security Advisor, the National Security Advisor, White House leadership, and resolves interagency policy conflicts, if the White House is untenable for some reason.

At the same time DHS was creating the IIMG, FEMA was establishing its own multi-agency center to provide overall Federal response coordination for Incidents of National Significance and emergency management implementation known as the National Response Coordination Center (NRCC). Maintained by FEMA as a functional component of the HSOC/NOC in support of incident management operations, the NRCC monitors potential or developing Incidents of National Significance and supports the efforts of regional and field components. Lastly, the NRCC resolves Federal resource support conflicts and other implementation issues forwarded by the Joint Field Offices and those issues that cannot be resolved by the NRCC are referred to the IIMG. During an incident, the NRCC operates on a 24/7 basis or as required to provide notification to departments and agencies on the activation (or potential activation) of ESFs in coordination with the HSOC to support incident operations. More than 40 departments and agencies from activated Emergency Support Functions (ESF) provide representatives to augment the NRCC during an incident and additional interagency representatives can be requested based upon the situation at hand. FEMA and DHS' Emergency Preparedness and Response Directorate provide management and support staff for functions not filled by ESF personnel.

* * *

Being Irish, 17 March (Saint Patrick's Day) is my favorite holiday and, in my opinion, should be a "Holy Day of Obligation" for everyone – Catholic or not. Therefore, I always wear a kilt on Saint Patrick's Day. For lunch, I always try to find a good pub to eat corned beef and cabbage and before the end of the day, I always try to find a nice Irish bar to have a pint or two.

As I entered the White House during the morning of 17 March 2003, I was hoping that this Saint Patrick's Day would be no different. The day commenced with President Bush smiling and saying that I was probably the only person in the White House wearing at kilt that day; and Governor Ridge chuckling and saying, *"nice skirt"*. Unfortunately, 17 March 2003, turned out to be a very busy day and I never found time to eat my corned beef and cabbage nor have a pint that evening. At around 12:30 p.m., Dwight Ware Watson, a tobacco farmer from Whitakers, North Carolina, drove a John Deere tractor, towing two vehicles, into a pond in Constitution Gardens, near the Vietnam Veterans Memorial on the National Mall. Wearing a military helmet and displaying an upside down American flag, Watson said that he was protesting the cutting of Federal tobacco subsidies, on which he blamed his own farm's failure, and the government's treatment of Gulf War veterans. Watson claimed to have explosives that he would detonate if police approached him. In response to Watson's threats, the United States Park Police cordoned off a large area on the Mall extending from the Lincoln Memorial to the Washington Monument. Several nearby government offices were also evacuated and major traffic arteries in the area were closed, which caused massive traffic jams and paralyzed traffic across the Washington metropolitan area for hours. A SWAT team composed of approximately 200 FBI and U.S. Park Police officers kept the pond surrounded as Watson drove his tractor around in circles, dug up part of an island in the pond, and communicated with authorities and the media on a cell phone. On the third morning of the standoff, 19 March 2003, President Bush calmly approached FBI Director Robert Mueller before his morning Cabinet meeting and said, *"Put an end to this situation–it is becoming an embarrassment."* With a little extra persuasion by the FBI and law enforcement authorities, Watson finally surrendered after a 48-hour standoff and no explosives were found. Watson was sentenced to six years in prison but a Federal Judge later reduced sentencing to 16 months.

* * *

With DHS operational, one of the first initiatives the department rolled out on 17 March 2003 was Operation "Liberty Shield". This was a comprehensive national plan under the auspices of Vice Admiral Brian Peterman (USCG), designed to increase protection for America's citizens and infrastructure while maintaining the free flow of goods and people across the borders with minimal disruption to the economy and way of life. As a multi-department, multi-agency, national team effort, "Liberty Shield" included increased security at borders; stronger transportation protections; ongoing measures to disrupt threats against the Nation; greater protections for critical infrastructure and key assets; and increased public health preparedness and Federal response resources positioned and ready.

Last, but not least, as the day was ending on 17 March 2003, I was asked to write a COOP Plan for the HSC.

I can tell you from first hand experience that it is one thing to write a COOP plan and another to implement it, to include finding a primary and alternate COOP site in the event that the White House or Washington, DC are untenable, and to staff the sites with the appropriate equipment and personnel to carry out your mission's essential functions. In addition to the COOP plan, I knew that it was essential that once the sites were up and running I would have to develop emergency evacuation plans to include identifying rally points and an emergency notification recall system to get personnel to report to these sites. Bottom line, thanks in part to the U.S. Secret Service, we were able to identify a facility in Washington, DC as the primary COOP site in the event that the White House staff needed to be relocated, and a second facility northeast of Washington, DC in the event that Washington, DC was untenable. In the event of a chemical, biological, or nuclear event, we identified a third site at an underground, undisclosed location northwest of the city of Washington, DC. Shortly after establishing these plans, all sites were equipped with classified and unclassified phones, computers and fax machines as well as pertinent information and data to be able to resume our mission essential functions. With the success of the HSC COOP plan, I was then asked to write a similar plan for the NSC to include identifying and outfitting the space at both the primary and secondary HSC COOP sites to co-locate the NSC.

Although my goal was to try to sneak away to the Dubliner, my favorite Irish bar in Washington, DC, before it closed that evening on 17 March 2003 the decision was made to elevate the HSAS again from "Yellow" to "Orange". This was due to the beginning of U.S. and Coalition military action in Iraq after the Intelligence Community reported, *"they believed terrorists would attempt multiple attacks against U.S. and Coalition targets worldwide in the event of a U.S led military campaign against Saddam Hussein"*. According to the Intelligence Community information which was relayed to the public, *"a large volume of reporting, across a range of sources, some of which were highly reliable, indicated that al-Qaeda probably would attempt to launch terrorist attacks against U.S. interests claiming they were defending Muslims or the Iraqi people rather than Saddam Hussein's regime"*. This time, instead of the ISG, DHS activated the IIMG for the first time.

In early April 2003, because the HSAS was still at "Orange" Deputy Chief of Staff, Joe Hagin, asked for assistance in planning the annual Easter Egg Hunt at the White House, which was scheduled for Monday, 21 April 2003. After much deliberation, due to security concerns, it was decided in our working group that the event be closed to the public, and that a limited number of tickets would be issued, through the Department of Defense, to the children and families of personnel of the four branches of the military (Army, Navy, Air Force, Marines), and the U.S. Coast Guard. During the day of the event, the crowd that showed up was less than half the normal 40,000 and the event proceeded without incident.

That morning, as I was hand carrying General Gordon's briefing book to his office at 7:00 a.m., two men dressed in black suits stood up as I entered the Homeland Security Advisor's suite in the West Wing of the White House. Much to my surprise, Dan Aykroyd extended his hand to introduce himself, as well as Jeff "Skunk" Baxter, the former lead guitarist for Steely Dan and later the Doobie Brothers band. I almost chuckled to myself because Dan Aykroyd was wearing a suit very similar to the one he wore in the movie the "Blues Brothers" with John Belushi. The only thing missing were his sunglasses. As we were making small talk, General Gordon arrived and the three of them departed to the White House "Mess" facility to have breakfast. After returning an hour or so later, I could not resist asking General Gordon why Dan Aykroyd and Jeff Baxter were there to see him. General Gordon simply replied, *"Richard, the godmother of Dan Aykroyd's daughter was killed on one of the planes that hit the World Trade Center and he wanted to let me know that although he is a Canadian citizen, he was willing to do whatever it takes to combat terrorism and fight al-Qaeda to include raising money if necessary."* He added that Dan Aykroyd had been writing letters and calling the White House since 9/11 trying to get an audience with him or someone of his stature and finally used his good friend, Jeff Baxter, to make the introduction. According to General Gordon, Jeff Baxter is a missile defense systems expert with a Top Secret security clearance and has been consulting with DOD and the Intelligence Community since 1995 when he was nominated to Chair the Civilian Advisory Board for Ballistic Missile Defense. On the other hand, Dan Aykroyd's wife, Donna Dixon, the actor from the early 1980s television show, "Bosom Buddies" was born in Alexandria, Virginia, and was raised in Lorton, Virginia. Her father owned a local nightclub known as "Hillbilly Heaven" along Route 1, which I used to drive by it on my way home from work when I first started working for the Agency back in 1977. From what I can recall, the nightclub would have fit perfectly in the "Blues Brothers" movie. As I returned to my office that morning, I couldn't help thinking about the noble gesture that Dan Aykroyd had made and what a "class act" both he and Jeff Baxter were.

Following a review of the intelligence and an assessment of threats by the Intelligence Community, DHS, in consultation with the HSC, made the decision to lower the threat advisory level to "Yellow" on 16 April 2003. Several weeks later in early May 2003, we learned at the 7:00 a.m. Secure Voice Telecommunications System (SVTS) threat briefing that a naturalized U.S. citizen originally from Kashmir and living in Columbus, Ohio, Iyman Faris, was arrested for conspiring to commit a terrorist act after he was suspected of planning to use blowtorches to collapse the Brooklyn Bridge. Fortunately, the New York City Police Department had learned about the plot and increased police surveillance around the bridge and, with the additional security, Faris and his accomplices decided to cancel the attack. Faris later pled guilty to conspiracy and providing material support to al-Qaeda, and was sentenced to 20 years–the maximum allowed under his plea agreement.

On 12 May 2003 at 3:00 p.m., two months after becoming operational, DHS and the U.S. Department of State, in cooperation with Federal, State, Local, and Canadian partners, undertook a five-day, full-scale exercise and simulation known as the Top Officials Two Exercise, or TOPOFF 2. As a Congressionally mandated exercise, TOPOFF 2 was designed to strengthen the Nation's capacity to prevent, prepare for, respond to, and recover from large-scale terrorist attacks involving weapons of mass destruction (WMD) with the main goal of providing the opportunity to test the Nation's preparedness and, at the same time, identify ways to improve response in the future. At the time, the TOPOFF 2 Exercise Program was the most comprehensive terrorism response exercise ever conducted in the United States, following a two-year cycle of seminars, planning events and exercises culminating in a full-scale exercise.

In this exercise, simulated attacks were planned in the Chicago and Seattle metropolitan areas. The State of Washington, King County, and the City of Seattle would respond to a hypothetical explosion containing radioactive material, and in a separate incident the State of Illinois, Cook, Lake, DuPage and Kane Counties, and the City of Chicago would respond to a covert release of a biological agent. At the start of the exercise, Tom Ridge, as the new Secretary of DHS, opened with the following remarks, *"Protection against terrorism requires that organizations at every level of government and in the private sector work together in partnership to prepare for events and deal with their consequences. During the next five days of this exercise, Federal, State, Local, and Canadian participants will be engaged in unclassified and classified round-the-clock exercise play to improve the Nation's capacity to manage extreme events; create broader frameworks for the operation of expert crisis and consequence management systems; validate authorities, strategies, plans, policies, procedures, and protocols; and build a sustainable, systematic national exercise program to support the national strategy for homeland security."*

The TOPOFF 2 exercise series was overseen by DHS' Office of Domestic Preparedness, which provided training, equipment, exercises, and technical assistance to the Nation's first responders, in partnership with the U.S. Department of State, Office of the Coordinator for Counterterrorism. Nineteen Federal agencies and the American Red Cross became involved, including the District of Columbia, State of Maryland, and Commonwealth of Virginia. The Government of Canada, including the Province of British Columbia and the City of Vancouver, also engaged in exercise play as part of Canada's participation in TOPOFF 2 keeping with the commitment to conduct joint exercises as outlined in Point 30 of the Smart Border Declaration Action Plan.

In that DHS was less than two months old, I am proud to say that the HSC at the White House, operating from a small makeshift Operations Center that we had set up on the 4th Floor of the Eisenhower Executive Office Building (EEOB), carried most of the weight during TOPOFF 2 for DHS. Because the conference rooms in the White House Situation Room were reserved most of the time, with the assistance of several members of the Counterterrorism Directorate within the HSC, we decided to find a location in the EEOB to serve as a makeshift Operations Center during the exercise. We knew however, if we went through the normal White House bureaucracy of requesting such a room via a memo, it would never have been authorized in time, let alone be furnished and outfitted with phones and computers, so we decided to take it upon ourselves to find and set up the room to accommodate our needs during the exercise. After finding a room that the Office of Presidential Records was using to store dozens of boxes of documents on the fourth floor of the EEOB, we contacted Presidential Records, informed them of our situation, and asked them if they could find another location to store the documents, to which they agreed. Several days later when the room was finally empty, we asked some of the painters who were working on the floor if they would not mind putting a fresh coat of paint on the room, which they did, although we did not have a work order. Next came furnishing the room and since the EEOB was undergoing major renovations, many rooms on the 17th Street side of the building were vacant with some containing the remnants of various pieces of furniture. So one evening, we went on a "furniture run" and confiscated as many desks, tables and chairs as we could find and transported them to this new office. Much to our fortune, we even found a large conference table, some nice leather chairs, a photocopier, phones, and even some computers.

The following day, after working much of the night, we had a makeshift operations center up and running to support TOPOFF2—along the lines of what we had with the ISG. In this case, however, we planned to use personnel from the various directorates within the HSC. Although we decided to keep the make-shift operations center intact following TOPOFF 2, when Colleen Litkenhaus and the White House Deputy Chief of Staff, Joe Hagin, found out about it, I received a call from Joe with the simple instructions, *"Richard, shut it down"*. Even though it has been several years, I wouldn't be surprised if the room is exactly as we left it that day.

Several weeks after TOPOFF 2, the HSAS was again elevated from "Yellow" to "Orange" on 20 May 2003 after the Riyadh compound and Casablanca bombings. In a report that later became public, a U.S. Intelligence Community spokesperson advised, *"In the wake of the terrorist bombings in Saudi Arabia and Morocco, intelligence reporting indicates that terrorists might attempt attacks against targets in the United States."* Secretary Ridge added that, *"The U.S. Intelligence Community believed that al-Qaeda had entered an operational period worldwide, which might include terrorist attacks in the United States."* With this information in hand, over the course of the next ten days, the HSC and DHS were in constant contact monitoring the situation until 30 May 2003, when the HSAS was lowered from "Orange" to "Yellow" based upon a number of factors, including a review of the intelligence and an assessment of the threats by the Intelligence Community. The U.S. Intelligence Community had also concluded that the number of indications and warnings that led to raising the level had decreased along with the heightened vulnerability associated with the Memorial Day Holiday.

In early June 2003, we learned during the 3:00 p.m. Secure Voice Telecommunications Systems (SVTS) threat briefing that 11 men, who would become known as the "Virginia Jihad Network", were arrested in Alexandria, Virginia on weapons counts and for violating the Neutrality Act, which prohibits U.S. citizens and residents from attacking countries with which the United States is at peace. Of these 11 men, four pled guilty. The other seven members of the group were indicted on additional charges of conspiring to support terrorist organizations. All were found to have connections with al-Qaeda, the Taliban, and Lashkar-i-Taiba, a terrorist organization that targets the Indian government. The Virginia men had used paintball games as a form of training and preparation for battle and had acquired surveillance and night vision equipment and wireless video cameras. The spiritual leader of the group, Ali al-Timimi, was found guilty of soliciting individuals to assault the United States and was sentenced to life in prison. Ali Asad Chandia received 15 years for supporting Lashkar-i-Taiba. Randoll Todd Royer, Ibrahim al-Hamdi, Yong Ki Kwon, Khwaja Mahmoud Hasan, Muhammed Aatique, and Donald T. Surratt all pled guilty and were sentenced to prison terms. Masoud Khan, Seifullah Chapman, and Hammad Adur-Raheem were found guilty at trial.

On 14 August 2003, I was sitting in the White House Situation Room when I looked up on one of the many television monitors to see Fox News reporting a massive power outage occurring throughout parts of the Northeastern and Midwestern United States, and Ontario, Canada. Picking up the phone, I immediately called DHS, which by then, had only been in existence for a little over five months. Unfortunately, it was too early for DHS to ascertain the cause of the "black out" which all the news channels began referring it as the "Northeast Blackout". Remembering that there was a small agency known as the North American Electrical Reliability Commission or NERC whose mission was to monitor and improve the reliability and security of the bulk power system in North America, I looked up one of my contacts there and decided to give him a call. After reaching him, I was told that a large transformer had blown in Ohio resulting in a major power outage causing a cascading effect across much of the power grids in the Northeast United States and parts of Canada. Shortly thereafter, Dr. Richard Falkenrath, the Deputy Homeland Security Advisor, came into the Situation Room along with Fran Townsend who, at the time, was head of the Office of Combating Terrorism as part of the NSC. By 6:30 p.m., we were conducting a secure video teleconference with President Bush who was in Crawford, Texas at the time; Vice

President Cheney who was in Jackson Hole, Wyoming; and Secretary Andrew Card who was vacationing in Maine. General John Gordon, the Homeland Security Advisor, on his sailboat in the Chesapeake Bay off the coast of Maryland had to conference in via a secure telephone. After Dr. Falkenrath provided an overview on what we had learned from the NERC, the anxiety level immediately began to come way down and, following these initial discussions, we began to focus on how to mitigate the incident as well as the response and recovery efforts.

That evening we sent an FBI agent to the home of the NERC employee with a secure telephone and the NERC employee ended up briefing the Deputies Committee the following morning at 6:00 a.m., which I chaired. The blackout, which we soon discovered, was the largest blackout in North American history affecting an estimated 40 million people in eight U.S. states (about one-seventh of the population of the U.S.) and 10 million people in the Province of Ontario (about one-third of the population of Canada). Outage-related financial losses were estimated at $6 billion USD ($6.8 billion CDN).

From 25 to 27 August 2003, as Co-chair of the NSSE Working Group, I was asked to coordinate a three-day security seminar for the FIFA Women's World Cup Soccer organizers and venue participants along with my fellow Co-chair, Donnie Coyer, from the USSS in order to prepare the organizers and venue participants for the events. Earlier in the year, on 25 April 2003, after China decided to postpone the start of the season for their men and women's professional soccer leagues due to Severe Acute Respiratory Syndrome (SARS), the Federation of International Football (Soccer) Association (FIFA) abruptly decided to move the Women's World Cup 2003, which was scheduled in four cities in East-Central China, including Shanghai, from 23 September to 11 October 2003. Later, on 26 May 2003, the games were awarded to the United States. FIFA claimed that they chose the United States over Sweden, the only other country besides the USA to make a formal bid to host the tournament, because the United States had hosted the 1999 Women's Soccer World Cup, which the U.S. won over China in Pasadena, California. With the award to the United States, six venues and a 32-game tournament schedule was announced, with the tournament beginning in Philadelphia, Pennsylvania, and Columbus, Ohio on 20 September 2003 and ending with the finals at the Home Depot Center in Carson, California on 12 October 2003.

* * *

Hurricane Isabel was the costliest and deadliest hurricane in the 2003 Atlantic hurricane season. It was also the ninth tropical storm, fifth hurricane, and second major hurricane of the season.

Isabel formed from a tropical wave on 6 September 2003 in the tropical Atlantic Ocean. It moved northwestward and, within an environment of light wind shear and warm waters, it steadily strengthened to reach peak winds of 165 mph on 11 September 2003. After fluctuating in intensity for four days, Isabel gradually weakened and made landfall on the Outer Banks of North Carolina with winds of 105 mph on 18 September 2003. The next day it quickly weakened over land, and became a tropical storm over western Pennsylvania. In North Carolina, the storm surge from Isabel washed out a portion of Hatteras Island to form what was, unofficially known as Isabel Inlet. Damage was greatest along the Outer Banks where thousands of homes were damaged or destroyed. The worst of the effects of Isabel occurred in Virginia, which reported the most deaths and damage from the hurricane. About 64% of the damage and 68% of the deaths occurred in these two states alone. Moderate to severe damage extended up the Atlantic Coastline and as far inland as West Virginia. Roughly, 6 million people were left without power throughout the Eastern portion of the United States from the strong winds of Isabel; and rainfall from the storm extended from South Carolina to Maine, and westward to Michigan. Throughout the path of Isabel, damage totaled about $3.6 Billion USD. Sixteen deaths in seven states were directly related to the hurricane, with 35 deaths in six states and one province indirectly related to the hurricane.

As Hurricane Isabel was bearing down on Virginia and the District of Colombia, the decision was made to evacuate the White House with the exception of a small skeleton staff, including those serving in the White House Situation Room. In addition to me, and Joel Bagnal (the new Director of the Counterterrorism Directorate in the HSC), the only other senior officials to weather the storm were Joe Hagin, the Deputy Chief of Staff, and Homeland Security Advisor, General John Gordon. Fearing that we might lose communications, we contacted a company named InfraLynx, which staged a large 24-foot emergency communications vehicle outside the West Wing of the White House as a backup measure. That evening as Joel Bagnal and I tried to catch a few hours of sleep on cots in the Eisenhower Executive Officer Building (EEOB) after spending most of the day on video conferences with the National Weather Service, the National Hurricane Center, FEMA, DHS, and a variety of other Federal, State and Local departments and agencies, I can still recall hearing the winds and rain raging outside. Getting up in the middle of the night and looking out the window, it was raining so hard I could not even see across West Executive Drive to the White House. That night, as I finally began to doze off, we were suddenly awakened by a loud crashing sound only to discover that two exterior window air conditioning units had incredibly been ripped out of their support structures and crashed to the ground below. The following day, although ravaged, Washington, DC and Old Town Alexandria survived the storm, and both General Gordon and I were particularly happy to learn that his sailboat, which was moored in a small slip north of Annapolis, had not been damaged.

As we were fully engaged with the aftermath of Hurricane Isabel, the White House published a "Progress Report on the Global War on Terrorism" in early September 2003. According to this report, since 11 September 2001, the United States, with the help of its allies and partners, had dismantled the repressive Taliban, denied al-Qaeda a safe haven in Afghanistan, and defeated Saddam Hussein's regime. The report outlined actions at home and abroad, which produced the following results: of the senior al-Qaeda leaders, operational managers, and key facilitators that the U.S. government had been tracking, nearly two-thirds had been taken into custody or killed, and the Department of Justice had charged over 260 individuals, uncovered in the course of terrorist investigations, and convicted or secured guilty pleas from over 140 individuals. Furthermore, the U.S. Government had disrupted alleged terrorist cells in Buffalo, Seattle, Portland, Detroit, North Carolina and Tampa, and terror networks had lost access to nearly $200 million. The report claimed that the creation of the DHS and its work with other departments and agencies had expanded intelligence and law enforcement capabilities, improved information sharing, facilitated the quick dissemination of threat information to the front lines, and that the homeland was markedly more secure than it was two years ago due to these and other initiatives. As examples, the report stated that the Administration was working to create "Smart Borders" to facilitate the rapid flow of legitimate commerce and people while detecting terrorists and their weapons before they entered the United States and was working to establish a Terrorist Threat Integration Center to integrate and analyze terrorism threat related information collected domestically and abroad to ensure that intelligence and law enforcement entities were working in common purpose. The document reported that the USA Patriot Act would provide authorities that would strengthen law enforcement's abilities to prevent, investigate, and prosecute acts of terror, and facilitate the Department of Justice's efforts to thwart potential terrorist activity throughout the U.S. Lastly, the report claimed that over 170 nations were continuing to participate in the war on terrorism by taking terrorists into custody, freezing their assets, and providing military forces and other support.

* * *

During the period 24 to 29 October 2003, California recorded the state's deadliest wildfire blazes in more than a decade, with 13 wildfires raging from Simi Valley to San Diego, and both the HSC and DHS were heavily involved in monitoring and coordinating the Federal response.

During this four-day period, the number of homes destroyed surpassed 1,900, the charred land totaled more than 600,000 acres, the death toll reached 16, and firefighters were unable to bring most of the blazes to within even 20 percent containment. We eventually learned that at least two of the state's 13 fires were blamed on arson. With most of the wildfires burning out of control, President Bush declared a major disaster in affected parts of California, opening the way for Federal funding for governments, businesses and people affected by the fires. California Governor Gray Davis declared states of emergency in the affected counties, activated the National Guard to help with disaster relief, and sent 135 fire engines from other areas, including Nevada and Arizona, to San Diego County. From the Federal side, the U.S. Defense Department provided military assets to fight the wildfires at the request of the National Interagency Fire Center, and four C-130 aircraft configured to drop water and fire-retardant chemicals were sent to the area. Eight UH-60 helicopters equipped with water buckets from the California National Guard were deployed as FEMA and the Small Business Administration (SBA) made plans to open "one-stop" centers for residents and business owners to file paperwork for emergency loans allowed under the President's Disaster Declaration.

In the end, the Cedar Fire was perhaps the most devastating. After it ignited on 25 October 2003, it consumed 80,000 acres in about 10 hours, and by the second day had reached 206,000 acres; the largest fire in the State of California since a blaze scorched 220,000 acres of Ventura County in 1932.

* * *

Earlier, on 22 October 2003, an airport postal facility in Greenville, South Carolina closed after a suspicious letter, put aside several days earlier on 15 October 2003, was found to contain Ricin; a highly toxic substance that is relatively easy to make from castor beans. Although there is no known antidote, it is considered a far less effective weapon for causing mass casualties than anthrax, which was mailed to U.S. Senate offices in late 2001, because it is more difficult to make airborne and requires inhalation of large quantities to be fatal.

The Ricin at the postal facility in Greenville was found in a small metal container inside an envelope with a warning "Caution RICIN POISON" typed on the outside of the letter. A typewritten letter inside the envelope signed "Fallen Angel", said that the writer had large amounts of Ricin that would be dumped into the nation's reservoirs if new rules limiting how long truckers could drive without rest went into effect on 4 January 2004. The letter included claims that the author could make much more and would "start dumping" if the new regulations were not abolished. The envelope contained no delivery address and no postmark. Postal officials eventually reopened the postal facility in Greenville after no one had fallen ill as a result of the letter, and after it was determined that the letter posed no threat to public health.

Several weeks later, on 6 November 2003, eleven postal facilities in the Washington area were closed after the U.S. Postal Service reported one of eight air sampling monitors had indicated small amounts of biological pathogens at the Anacostia Naval Station which handles mail sent to the Washington Navy Yard and the Navy annex. Five workers at the Anacostia Naval Station were offered antibiotics as a precautionary measure and on 8 November 2003, the 11 Washington-area postal facilities were reopened after test results came up negative.

While the 22 October 2003 South Carolina letter's existence was made public shortly after it was found, for reasons that I am still not clear about, acknowledgment of the White House letter was delayed by nearly three months. The real reason for the 11 Washington-area postal facilities closure did not become public until 2 February 2004, when an intern found a powdery substance on a letter-opening machine in the mailroom of Senate Majority Leader Bill Frist's fourth floor office suite in the Dirksen Building. After initial enzyme assays reported the presence of Ricin in the powdery substance found on the letter-opening machine, the substance was immediately sent to a Laboratory Response Network (LRN) for Bio-Terrorism at the Center for Disease Control and Prevention (CDC) in Atlanta, Georgia, which, on 3 February 2004 announced that the tests had confirmed it was Ricin. Following the confirmation, the White House decided to go public with the fact that on 6 November 2003, Ricin was found in an envelope that was addressed to the White House. According to the FBI, the U.S. Secret Service intercepted the White House letter on 6 November 2003 at an off-site facility that processes mail for the White House and was similar to one that was addressed to the Transportation Department, and found at the airport mail facility in Greenville, South Carolina on 15 October 2003. Both had been signed "Fallen Angel" and said that more Ricin would be used unless new trucking regulations, which took effect on 4 January 2004 limiting how long truckers could drive without resting, was repealed. The 6 November 2003 letter claimed that the author owned a tanker-truck fleet company and demanded that hours of service rules for drivers remain unchanged. In his own words, the author wrote, *"If you change the hours of service on 4 January 2004 I will turn DC into a ghost town. The powder on the letter is RICIN. Have a nice day, Fallen Angel."* The letter directed to the White House had a Chattanooga, Tennessee postmark and a follow-up investigation revealed that it had been processed on 17 October 2003 at a postal facility in Chattanooga, Tennessee, although the Zip Code for the White House was incorrect.

Unfortunately, six days passed before a Laboratory Response Network (LRN) for Bio-Terrorism at the Centers for Disease Control and Prevention (CDC) in Atlanta, Georgia received final confirmation that the powdery substance tested probable for Ricin on 12 November 2003. Upon receipt of this information, the FBI and other agencies were notified and an impromptu inter-agency Secure Voice Telecommunications System (SVTS) video conference was hosted by the HSC on 13 November 2003, with the FBI, DHS, HHS, Centers for Disease Control and Prevention (CDC), U.S. Postal Service and other agencies to discuss what to do. Because the Ricin in the letter was deemed to be of a low grade and not a threat to public health, it was decided not to make a public announcement other than to the American Trucking Association, which sent several bulletins to its members urging them to be on the lookout for people "displaying aggressive behavior" or "engaging in suspicious activity." One association bulletin asked that members "be alert for a potential disgruntled trucking company employees, or person purporting to be from the trucking industry" who has made threats in the past against government agencies. Because the substance was identified as Ricin and that it was processed in Senate Majority Leader Bill Frist's home state of Tennessee, the FBI "opened an investigation" to determine if the individual who identified themselves as "Fallen Angel" and who sent two threatening letters containing Ricin on 15 October and 6 November 2003, was responsible for the Ricin-laced mail sent to Senate Majority Leader Bill Frist in the Senate on 2 February 2004.

Following the discovery of the powdery substance in the Senate Office Building on 2 February 2004, members from the FBI's Hazardous Materials Response Unit (HMRU), the U.S. Capitol Police, and the Marine Corps Chemical Biological Incident Response Force known as (CBIRF) from Indian Head, Maryland, dressed in protection suits, sifted through unopened mail from the office buildings for days. In addition to closing the Russell Senate Office Building, the Hart Building, and the Dirksen Building, where the Ricin was found, the Washington, DC postal facility, known as the "V Street", that processes Congressional mail was also closed on 2 February 2004 for precautionary measures. Although 132 samples were taken in the "V Street" facility, the building was later re-opened after officials found no signs of Ricin and no workers had reported symptoms of poisoning. The Russell Senate Office Building was then re-opened on 5 February 2004, the Hart Building re-opened on 6 February 2004, and the Dirksen Building, where the Ricin was found in Senate Majority Leader Bill Frist's office suite, re-opened on 9 February 2004. No illnesses were reported in connection with the episode. Although the FBI has offered a $100,000 reward for information leading to an arrest in the "Fallen Angel" case, despite the Tennessee link, authorities have not found a clear association between the "Fallen Angel" letters and the Ricin powder that was found on the letter-opening machine in the office of Senate Majority Leader Bill Frist on 2 February 2004.

Shortly after this incident, one evening as I had just departed the White House, I received a cell phone call from the Situation Room that the Department of Health and Human Service (HHS) Operations Center had reported an inbound aircraft, with an ill passenger on board that could possibly have viral hemorrhagic fever (the collective name given to the diseases caused by a group of viruses such as the Ebola virus, named for the river in Zaire where it was discovered, and the Marburg virus, named for the city in Germany where the disease was first diagnosed). When I asked why the passenger was suspected of having viral hemorrhagic fever, I was told that a physician on board the plane had suggested that it might be because the passenger, a young female from the Sudan, had a high fever, muscle aches and severe abdominal pain. The passenger was also reportedly vomiting, had diarrhea, and was bleeding profusely from her mouth and nose–all symptoms of the virus, especially the inability of blood to clot. I was further informed that the passenger had boarded a flight from Khartoum, Sudan the day before, had changed planes in London, and that the onward flight was expected to land in Atlanta, Georgia within the hour. As my mind was racing at a million miles an hour, I remembered that the Ebola virus spreads through close personal contact with a person who is acutely ill with the disease.

My first thought was whether the airport in Atlanta had a location to isolate the aircraft, establish a perimeter, make an entry, and perform a medical evaluation without endangering the health and safety of the entry team, the crew, the fellow passengers, or the public. My second thought was whether the Atlanta airport had an on-site facility to isolate someone who is potentially infectious. After running all of these thoughts through my head, I requested the Situation Room convene a conference call for me with HHS, DHS, and the Center for Disease Control and Prevention (CDC).

For the next few minutes, we discussed a variety of issues, to include: whether we should allow the plane to taxi to the terminal, and, if not, where a perimeter could be established, and, if so, by whom; who should make the entry into the aircraft and how would they evaluate the passengers' illness; who would evaluate the non-ill passengers and crew and when could they be released; if it was indeed viral hemorrhagic fever, should the passenger be moved to an isolation area or to an ambulance to be transported to a local hospital; and lastly, who would deal with the press.

Just to be on the safe side, I also thought it would be a good idea to check if there were any other airlines reporting sick passengers in the event that this was some type of terrorist act involving a self-infected human.

Prior to putting our plan into action, all I can say is thank God that during further questioning by the physician on board, before the plane landed, the physician was able to ascertain that the young women had just had a blood transfusion; had been flying for more than 20 hours with a layover in London; and should never had been permitted to board the plane in Khartoum in the first place. We were very fortunate that this was not viral hemorrhagic fever because there is no known treatment for the Ebola or Marburg viruses and no vaccine. To date, there have been only four known outbreaks of Ebola virus involving humans–two in Sudan (1976, 1979) and two in Zaire (1976, 1995). Two small outbreaks of Marburg virus in humans occurred in Germany and Yugoslavia in 1967 but were linked to sources of virus in Africa.

* * *

As we were approaching the holiday season, on 17 December 2003, as a follow-on to HSPD-5, President Bush signed HSPD-8, which established additional policies to strengthen the preparedness of the United States to prevent and respond to threatened, or actual domestic terrorist incidents, major disasters and other emergencies. The timing could not have been more critical in that HSPD-8 provided additional authority to the Secretary of DHS as the Principal Federal Official for coordinating the implementation of all-hazards preparedness in the United States. HSPD-8 further called for establishing and maintaining a comprehensive exercise program that met national preparedness goals and capitalized on lessons learned from 11 September 2001 and the TOPOFF exercises.

On 21 December 2003, the HSAS threat level was again raised from "Yellow" to "Orange" after the U.S. Intelligence Community had received a substantial increase in the volume of threat related intelligence reports. According to the Intelligence Community information, which was later, relayed to the public, *"reliable sources had suggested the possibility of attacks against the United States during the holiday season and into early 2004 that could possibly rival the terrorist attack of 11 September 2001 in scope and impact"*. Part of the intelligence reported al-Qaeda operatives crashing planes that had departed England, France and Mexico, into buildings in the U.S. With this information in hand, the decision was made, during one of the Secure Voice Telecommunications System (SVTS) video teleconferences hosted by the HSC/NSC, that if flights originating from these countries did not provide a manifest list to the United States Government to be reviewed by DHS and the Intelligence Community; did not conduct secondary screening of their passengers; or did not place U.S. trained Air Marshals on board, then the flights would not be allowed to enter U.S. airspace. These requirements became very controversial for British Air, Air France, and Air Mexico, but eventually, when these countries realized that the U.S. was not bluffing, they all conceded to the demands. Shortly, after the HSAS was elevated, an FBI Counterterrorism Division communication disseminated, via the National Law Enforcement Telecommunications System (NLETS), general guidelines and countermeasures that law enforcement agencies could adopt in response to the heightened threat condition. Law enforcement agencies were encouraged to remain alert to possible indicators of terrorist planning and to report suspicious activity immediately to the nearest FBI Joint Terrorism Task Force (JTTF).

Huddling in the White House Situation Room during the Christmas holidays, day after day, on Secure Voice Telecommunications System (SVTS) video teleconferences, I can still recall Secretary Ridge and General Gordon remarking as they looked at the same faces around the table that, *"We have an incredible "A" Team but no "B" or "C" Team."*

On Christmas Eve, as it was getting late, I had to ask Karen and the children to join me at midnight mass at Saint Dominic's Catholic Church near the White House. Following mass, I returned to the Situation Room for a few more hours prior to driving home at 3:00 a.m. only to return the following morning, Christmas Day, at 7:00 a.m. after getting only a few hours of sleep.

This routine would go on through 9 January 2004, when the HSAS was finally lowered from "Orange" to "Yellow". The decision to lower the HSAS was based "on a careful review of the available intelligence as well as the passing of the holidays and many large gatherings that occurred during this time." The Intelligence Community had concluded that, *"Although they were still concerned about the continued threats, the threat conditions that they had been following had diminished."*

During this period, I can still remember being on a Secure Voice Telecommunications System (SVTS) video teleconference all night at the undisclosed facility several hundred feet underground on New Year's Eve 2003 with Homeland Security Advisor, General John Gordon, Deputy Chief of Staff, Joe Hagin, and an assortment of other HSC employees. My wife, Karen, was not too happy with me that evening in that she was hosting a dinner party at our house for six of our closest friends and, had to set the table for seven, versus eight. The only good memory I have from that night is that while other officials from the various Federal departments and agencies (who were participating on the secure voice video teleconference throughout the night), were eating pizza or Chinese food, thanks in part to the cooks at this location, we were dining on steak and lobster–off screen, of course.

Homeland Security Advisor General John Gordon in the Roosevelt room at the White House in 2004

After HSPD-5 directed the Secretary of DHS to develop and administer a National Incident Management System (NIMS), on 1 March 2004, shortly after participating in an exercise known as Unified Defense, DHS rolled out NIMS, which established a common set of standards and incident management lexicon with multi-jurisdictional and multi-disciplinary applicability.

* * *

On 11 March 2004, word arrived in the Homeland Security Operations Center (HSOC) at DHS and at the White House Situation Room that ten bombs exploded on four packed early-morning commuter trains in Madrid, killing 191 people and leaving at least 1,800 injured. We also learned that Spanish police had carried out controlled explosions on three other unexploded devices, which were hidden in rucksacks.

Although in the immediate aftermath of the attacks the Spanish government believed the Basque separatist group, ETA, was the main suspect, evidence began to emerge that Islamic militants might be behind the attacks. This evidence included the discovery of a stolen van containing seven detonators and an Arabic language tape close to a Madrid train station, as well as a letter sent to a London-based Arabic newspaper claiming responsibility for the attacks on behalf of the Abu Hafs al-Masri Brigades–a group that aligned itself to Osama Bin Ladin's al-Qaeda network. After a HSC/NSC hosted Secure Voice Telecommunications System (SVTS) video teleconference, Secretary Ridge cornered me and said, "Richard, what do you think?" I calmly replied, *"Sir, these people are creatures of habit. After the bombings in Madrid, I believe that al-Qaeda will conduct similar attacks in London, and then my gut feeling is that al-Qaeda will focus on the United States using the same modus operandi."* Secretary Ridge, in turn replied, *"Although I know how strongly you rely on your instincts, Richard, in this instance, I hope to God that you are wrong."*

Following a briefing to the Homeland Security Deputies Committee on 13 April 2004, Secretary Ridge sent a memo to his senior leadership in DHS on 16 April 2004 saying, *"We are entering a period of increased risk of potential terrorist activity based on many factors, to include numerous high-profile public events – the 2004 Olympic games; the World War II Memorial dedication; the 4th of July celebrations; the 2004 Presidential campaign, general elections, and inaugurations among various others. This domestic backdrop is complicated by continued terrorist attacks on the U.S. and its allies abroad designed to weaken the resolve of the international coalition engaged in the Global War on Terror. The Madrid bombings and other recent events demonstrate a continuing ability of terrorist organizations to threaten U.S. and allied national interests and security. The planning process established in this order represents the continuations of our unified national effort to preserve our freedoms and secure our homeland from terrorist attack during this period of increased threat. I am announcing that DHS has been designated to lead an interagency effort to coordinate the development, validation, and implementation of an integrated security plan covering an increased period of risk beginning on or about 24 May 2004 and continuing through the U.S. Presidential Inauguration on 20 January 2005."*

This planning for this effort was to build upon and accelerate key initiatives associated with HSPD-5, 7, and 8 implementation currently being pursued by various DHS directorates and staff offices. Under this directive, DHS was tasked with developing and implementing an interagency plan that identified priorities and implemented sustainable policies, strategies, tactics, technologies, and resources to enable the United States Government to prevent, protect against, prepare for, respond to, and recover from terrorist attacks during this period of increased risk. The end state of this effort was intended to be an enhanced, sustainable, "Yellow" security threshold across mission areas. President Bush was briefed on 24 May 2004.

The final plan called for implementing over one hundred additional permanent security measures across the various sectors of the United States equivalent to those normally imposed when the threat level was raised to "Orange" (High), in order to maintain the HSAS at "Yellow" (Elevated), so that the threat level would not have to be raised each time there was an impending threat or a substantial increase in the volume of threat related intelligence reporting. Four days later, on 28 May 2004, the first official terrorism warnings were issued without raising the threat level above "Yellow" (Elevated) and again on 8 July 2004 after Intelligence Community reports cited "credible evidence" of terrorist intent to affect upcoming elections.

In that I co-chaired the National Special Security Events (NSSE) working group and a second working group for those events that did not meet NSSE standards, with this new directive from Secretary Ridge at DHS, we spent the next few months compiling a comprehensive list of special events occurring nationwide during this period of increased risk.

In these working groups, we also developed a general protective template based on event priority level and coordinated DHS and Federal support for select events that met priority criteria such as NSSE's and for those events that did not meet NSSE status. Part of this preparation called for detailed security plans outlining what every Federal department and agency would bring to bear for the following upcoming high profile events: the National WWII Memorial Dedication in Washington, DC from 27 to 29 May 2004; the G-8 Summit in Sea Island, Georgia from 8 to 10 June 2004 (a NSSE); the Independence Day celebrations on the 4th of July 2004; the Democratic National Convention in Boston, Massachusetts from 26 to 29 July 2004 (a NSSE); the Summer Olympic Games in Athens, Greece from 13-29 August 2004; the Republican National Convention in New York City, New York from 30 August to 3 September 2004 (a NSSE); the United Nations 59th General

Assembly in New York City, New York from 13 September to 31 October 2004; the Presidential Elections on 2 November 2004; the Winter holidays from 25 November 2004 to 1 January 2005; and the Presidential Inauguration in Washington, DC on 20 January 2005 (a NSSE).

Upon receipt, the NSSE working group evaluates the request, questionnaire, and any other supporting information submitted to determine whether an event should be an NSSE. In some cases, the group may obtain additional relevant information through interviews or on-site assessments. The working group then provides a consensus recommendation to the Secretary of DHS regarding NSSE designation. After determining that an event meets the criteria of a NSSE, a formal designation decision is transmitted to the governor of the host state by DHS. The USSS then contacts the relevant Federal, State, and Local officials to begin planning, coordinating, and implementing a comprehensive security plan for the event. If an event is not designated a NSSE, if requested, Federal agencies can provide advice, training, and consultation for the event.

Although the FBI and FEMA have the ability to designate Special Event Readiness Levels (SERL) within their respective agencies, DHS decided to designate Special Event Homeland Security Levels for those events that do not meet NSSE standards. A Level I, for example, is an event of such large magnitude and significant national and/or international importance that it warrants significant DHS support and situational awareness as well as the full support of the United States Government (USG). Level I designation generally is reserved for a select number of events with enormous national or international importance such as the Presidential Election, a United Nations General Assembly, the dedication of the National WWII Memorial, or even the Super Bowl.

A Level I event will likely necessitate substantial pre-deployment of USG counterterrorism response assets and some Federal assets may be warranted in addition to consultation, technical advice or support for a specific functional area when local agencies may lack expertise or key resources. A Level II event which, although not of such magnitude to justify Level I status, nonetheless warrants substantial support of the USG, and some advanced stages of preparedness through a limited pre-deployment of USG assets such as the Presidential Debates, the Masters Golf Tournament, or the Boston Marathon. A Level III event requires limited Federal support and/or assets such as the Sundance Film

Festival or the U.S. Open Golf Championship. Resources remain on stand-by with predetermined response time-lines closely monitored for such an event. Lastly, a Level IV event is normally an event that does not meet the criteria warranting DHS direct support and involvement other than being monitored by the Homeland Security Operations Center. An example would be the Rose Bowl, Pro Bowl, or the Kentucky Derby.

In addition to the Federal support, DHS can assist State and Local jurisdictions hosting Level I, II, III or IV events by providing training and exercise opportunities through existing and/or tailored programs and encourages the use of existing Federal assistance programs in preparation for such events. A Principal Federal Official (PFO) is pre-designated for all NSSE's responsible for coordinating all Federal assets and support through DHS. During a NSSE or an event that does not meet NSSE standards, the FBI serves as the lead Federal agency for intelligence, criminal investigation of terrorist acts and threats, hostage rescue and counterterrorism, while FEMA is the lead Federal Agency for planning and coordination of response to, and recovery from, terrorist attacks and emergencies. In order to achieve the highest level of readiness during the event, other Federal departments and agencies can be called upon to provide a full range of resources to support the USSS, FBI, and FEMA, pre-deployed or on standby.

* * *

In May 2004, I learned that General John Gordon was retiring as the Homeland Security Advisor to be replaced by Fran Townsend. Fran had previously replaced General Gordon as the Deputy Assistant to the President, National Director, and Deputy National Security Advisor for Combating Terrorism.

Shortly thereafter, I met with Secretary Ridge at the undisclosed, underground facility during a Command Post Exercise known as "Eligible Receiver", which tested the communication and coordination among Federal agencies in preparation for a TOPOFF 3 Command Post Exercise known as "Forward Challenge". During our discussions, Secretary Ridge asked me if I would like to be detailed from the Agency to DHS as the Director of Incident Management since I had already served in this role with the Office of Homeland Security (OHS) and the Homeland Security Council (HSC). I was told that part of my responsibilities would be to create an Incident Management Division in DHS and, along with Bob Stephan, direct the Inter-Agency Incident Management Group (IIMG).

Jim Looney and Secretary Tom Ridge in 2004

Upon saying yes, the only request I had for Secretary Ridge was that I would need people to staff the Incident Management Division and assist in running the IIMG. After taking my plea to Bob Stephan, who had just created the Integration Staff (I-Staff) at DHS, Bob informed me that an Alaskan Native Corporation (ANC) named Alutiiq had just signed a $50 million Indefinite Delivery/Indefinite Quality (IDIQ) contract with DHS along with a company named Plexus to assist in the establishment of the I-Staff.

Upon my arrival in DHS, I was therefore, fortunate to hire several key employees, through Alutiiq and Plexus, who would assist me in developing Standard Operating Procedures for the IIMG, as well as emergency notification recall procedures. The Incident Management Division (IMD), which we established, provided the DHS leadership senior team with an immediate operational incident management capability that ensured, in coordination with the Homeland Security Operations Center (HSOC), the seamless integration of threat monitoring and strategic cross organizational element operational response activities. The IMD orchestrated incident management in the absence of an activated IIMG and, in the event the IIMG was activated, the IMD transitioned to the IIMG Executive Staff. The Executive Staff provided support to me and Bob Stephan, as the IIMG Director's, and facilitated, managed, and supervised IIMG activities at our direction or the direction of our designee.

During my first day in DHS, on 7 June 2004, I was directed to stand up the IIMG because President Bush was hosting the 30th G-8 Summit at Sea Island, Georgia from 8 to10 June 2004, and President Ronald Reagan had just passed away on 5 June–both events had been designated NSSE's. To complicate matters, Bob Stephan was on a much-needed vacation in Mexico. The USSS Special Agent in Charge of the Atlanta Field Office, Dave Wilkerson was designated the PFO for the G-8; USSS Senior Special Agent, Jim McDermond was named the PFO for the President Reagan funeral in Washington DC; and USSS Special Agent in Charge of the Los Angeles Field Office, Anthony Chapa was named the PFO in California where President Reagan was laid to rest.

Incredibly, in the midst of running the IIMG for both events, the following day, on 8 June 2004, I was tasked with identifying members of my staff to evaluate a Nuclear Regulatory Commission Indian Point Nuclear Power Plant Exercise along with members from FEMA. Thank goodness, Bob Shea, a senior FEMA officer, who was splitting 12 hour IIMG shifts with me, volunteered to head the team to evaluate this exercise.

After the United States assumed the Presidency of the G-8 from France at the beginning of 2004, President Bush, Chairman of the 2004 G-8 Summit, decided to meet with the G-8 leaders in the informal and relaxed setting of Sea Island, located on the southern portion of the Georgia coastline, 80 miles from Savannah, Georgia. Sitting in the IIMG at the Nebraska Avenue Complex (NAC), I was amazed that with the installation of several cameras installed to monitor the event, we could observe every building and movement made during the Summit. The G-8 Summit at Sea Island brought together the leaders of the world's major industrial democracies–Canada, France, Germany, Italy, Japan, Russia, the United Kingdom, and the United States. The European Union also attended the G-8 Summit, represented by the President of the European Commission and the leader of the country holding the Presidency of the European Council.

* * *

Ronald Reagan was the 40th President of the United States from 1981 to 1989. He had been suffering from Alzheimer's disease since 1994 and died on 5 June 2004 at his home in Bel-Air, Los Angeles, California, at age 93.

After Reagan's death, his casket was taken to the Kingsley and Gates Funeral Home in Santa Monica, California. On 7 June 2004, the casket was transported by hearse and displayed at the Ronald Reagan Presidential Library in Simi Valley, California prior to being flown to Washington, DC on 9 June 2004 for a public viewing and tribute at the U.S. Capitol Building. After lying in state for thirty-four hours in the Capitol Rotunda, a state funeral service was conducted at the Washington, DC National Cathedral on 11 June 2004, a day in which President Bush declared a national day of mourning.

The state funeral that was executed by the Military District of Washington (MDW) at the Washington, DC National Cathedral on 11 June 2004 was the first since Lyndon B. Johnson in 1973. After the state funeral service, President Reagan's casket was transported back to California for interment at the Reagan Presidential Library at dusk.

Forty minutes before Reagan's body arrived in Washington, DC, Capitol Hill Chief of Police Terry Gainer gave the order to evacuate the U.S. Capitol after a small plane had violated the restricted airspace around Washington, DC. As the plane was entering the restricted airspace, I received a call from the White House Situation Room to participate in an inter-agency emergency teleconference for this type of incident known as "NOBLE EAGLE" hosted by the U.S. Northern Command (Northcom) based out of Cheyenne Mountain in Colorado Springs, Colorado.

In the interim, I had the Homeland Security Operations Center (HSOC) call the new Transportation Security Administration Operations Center (TSOC) in Herndon, Virginia to find out what was going on. Fortunately, it did not take long to determine that the plane was carrying the Governor of Kentucky, Ernie Fletcher, to the Reagan funeral. Despite a malfunctioning transponder, air traffic controllers had told the pilot of the Governor's plane to proceed on its designated route from Cincinnati to Reagan National Airport outside the U.S. Capitol, but by then a special command post set up to monitor air traffic around the Capitol picked up an unidentified plane about 43 miles west of the city. Unable to identify the plane, the command post called Air Traffic Control and had two Air Force jets diverted to verify that the unidentified plane and the Governor's plane were the same. Fortunately, minutes later, after the Air Force pilots had verified the plane's identity, the Governor of Kentucky's plane was forced to land, and the "all clear" signal was given, but not before the U.S. Capitol was evacuated.

Several weeks later, during the first week of July 2004, Secretary Ridge walked into my office late one afternoon, threw his feet up on my desk and said, *"Richard, I want to host a Special Events Integrated Security Seminar for all of the sports organizations in the United States, the purpose of which is to provide a forum to engage the heads of the sporting organizations on homeland security issues and challenges, specifically focusing on security planning for high-profile sporting events. I hope that after the seminar each official will depart with a better understanding of what Federal assets the U.S. Government can bring to these type of high-profile sporting events." "Fine Sir"*, I replied, *"and when do you want to host such an event?"* Secretary Ridge's reply was before the end of July, which left less than three weeks to organize the event.

After identifying the participants that the Secretary wanted to attend, invitations in his name on behalf of DHS were sent on 15 July 2004 requesting their participation in this seminar.

Thanks to the able assistance of Amy Bockhop from DHS' Integration Staff and intern Tara Rooney, on 23 July 2004, senior officials from each of the sports organizations to include Paul Tagliabue, the Commissioner of the NFL; Sandy Alderson, the Executive Vice President for Operations of MLB; Russ Granik, the Deputy Commissioner of the NBA; Gary Bettman, the Commissioner of the NHL; Ivan Gazidis, the Deputy Commissioner of MLS; Henry Hughes, the Senior VP and Chief of Operations for the PGA; Mike Helton, the President of NASCAR; and Greg Shaheen, VP for men's basketball for the NCAA, were in attendance at the Transportation Security Administration, Operations Center in Herndon, Virginia.

With Former NFL Commissioner Paul Tagliabue and NHL Commissioner Gary Bettman at the TSA Operations Center 2004

Bob Stephan and Secretary Tom Ridge at the TSA Operations Center 2004

As I introduced Secretary Ridge to the audience that day simply by announcing, *"Ladies and Gentlemen, Secretary Tom Ridge"*, I can still recall the Secretary's follow-on comments, *"That was a good introduction. Well done. Thanks very much. That's how we work, a very efficient guy. Give him a mission and he gets it done, pure and simple. It's the mindset. Thanks, Rich, for that glorious, wonderful, expansive introduction. And more importantly, thanks for your friendship and your leadership. I've been working with Rich for nearly three years, when I first started at the White House, and he has been a valuable member of my team. Thanks. Welcome. We weren't quite sure what the response would be when we sent out the invitations and, happily, it's exceeded our expectations because I hoped everybody would show up, and you have, just about everybody has, and we thank you for that."* Governor Ridge then went on speaking for an additional 25 minutes on what he hoped to accomplish by bringing everyone together that day.

* * *

The 2004 Democratic National Convention (DNC) was a United States presidential nominating convention that took place from 26 to 29 July 2004 at the TD Banknorth Garden, then called FleetCenter, in Boston, Massachusetts.

The convention was one of a series of historic quadrennial meetings of the Democratic Party with the primary focus of officially nominating a candidate for President and adopting a party platform. New Mexico Governor Bill Richardson served as Chairman while former Presidential Advisor to Bill Clinton, Lottie Shackelford, served as Vice-Chairman. Counterterrorism measures included regulation of transportation in and out of the city, closure of several major arteries, and random baggage checks for the metropolitan train system. Manhole covers were welded shut, while garbage receptacles and postal boxes were removed from the streets for fear they would become tempting hiding places for explosives. One of the most controversial counterterrorism measures was the declaration of a designated free speech zone for protesters, limiting where and when protesters could exercise their First Amendment rights. Following this declaration, protesters, through the American Civil Liberties Union, mounted an unsuccessful lawsuit for the right to protest outside of the designated free speech zone, which the group claimed was unconstitutional but their petition was denied. FleetCenter access promulgated tight security measures that frustrated even the news media after the decision was made that reporters with credentials could no longer borrow or share their passes–a common practice for the major media outlets in the past. Due to the fact that the DNC was designated a NSSE, we activated the IIMG 24/7 until the conclusion of the convention and designated the USSS Special Agent in Charge of the Boston Field office, Steve Riccardi, as the Principal Federal Official (PFO).

On 1 August 2004, several days after the Democratic National Convention and the "standing down" of the IIMG, I was summoned to the DHS Executive Secretary's office and asked by Executive Secretary Ken Hill, if I ever heard of a classified document known as a "Red Stripper" that DHS had just received a document from the Agency and had passed it to the Under Secretary of Border and Transportation Security, Asa Hutchinson, since Secretary Ridge was on vacation in Florida and Deputy Secretary Admiral Jim Loy was on a trip outside of Washington, DC. Entering Asa's office, I was met by the Director of Operations for Border and Transportation Security, Randy Beardsworth, his Deputy, Wayne Parent, and Bob Stephan, the Director of DHS' Integration Staff. The document I was handed, the contents of which later became public, discussed the late July 2004 police raid on a house belonging to an individual named Dhiren Barot in Pakistan where the police discovered a number of incriminating documents in files on a laptop computer that included instructions for building car and truck bombs. The files on the laptop named specific financial institutions and buildings as possible targets in northern New Jersey, York City, and Washington DC to include the New York Stock Exchange. The report also mentioned that Dhiren was accused of planning attacks in England in plots, which were referred to as a "memorable black day of terror" with the employment of a "dirty bomb." After reading the document, I was asked to accompany Asa to a Principals Committee meeting being hosted at the White House and got to "back bench" him in the meeting that day.

During the Principal's Committee meeting, a Senior Intelligence Official provided an overview of the threat information that the Intelligence Community had received to that point, which eventually was released to the public.

The official began by saying, *"Several weeks ago, we had a meeting regarding the information that we had received about al-Qaeda's plans to carry out an attack in the homeland this year and what we had were pieces of a jigsaw puzzle. Now we have some very specific and credible information regarding al-Qaeda's plans to carry out attacks here in the United States. This new information is chilling in its scope, in its detail, in its breadth. It gives one a sense of the same feeling one would have if one found out that somebody broke into your house and, over the past several months, was taking a lot of details about your place of residence and looking for ways to attack you. The type of information that has been acquired about the targets here in the United States demonstrates that al-Qaeda is meticulous in its efforts, is patient in its efforts and, since 9/11, demonstrates that there has been an effort on their part to ensure that they have the information that they need in order to carry out attacks. What we have now is extensive information about the activities that have taken place from a reconnaissance standpoint in terms of collecting information, also in terms of casing and surveillance as far as the types of targets to be attacked, the vulnerabilities, the perceived vulnerabilities, as well as the possible optimal ways to carry out attacks to bring down buildings. There is detail now available regarding the types of security procedures at some specific buildings, the security checks that are required, the types of security personal at different posts, whether or not these individuals are armed or not, the presence of security officers at these posts at different times of the day, the types of uniforms that they wear, the number of pedestrians in the area, the number of employees in the buildings, information regarding potential escape routes for perpetrators of attacks, different points of reconnaissance in order to ensure that they have the full breadth of information regarding the targets, and different types of shops that are nearby. There is also extensive intelligence now available on the information they have been able to acquire regarding other facilities in the area, whether they are religious establishments, schools, libraries, hospitals, police departments, or fire departments. The information which we have been able to gather talks about the different access measures, as far as whether or not there's a physical desk or intercom systems; types of surveillance activities or counter-surveillance activities such as cameras; good places to go to meet employees; good places to go to acquire additional information; the types of traffic patterns that are near buildings; the different types of vehicles that in fact, can enter different types of parking facilities; the incline that is used; the exits as one enters an underground parking facility; the different types of materials that in fact should be brought into different types of vehicles and to address whether or not certain materials can, if detonated, cause, in fact, buildings to collapse; and the placement of such devices and bombs to maximize the damage to the architecture of the building. The information also identifies the disadvantages of certain types of plans in terms of the possible dissipation of the force in terms of the size, the height of the building, the height of a ceiling where in fact a vehicle might in fact be detonated. It talks about different means of ingress and egress and how one can get inside buildings; about the configurations of parking lots; about whether or not the parking garages and facilities are close to the core of the buildings and near certain offices; about the different types of shops nearby that can provide cover for additional types of acquisition of information; about the number of cars passing different types of targets at particular times of the day; and about the many types of procedures that employees themselves have to use for access to buildings. The information obtained thus far, recommends the type of material to be used; about the types of techniques; and about the types of trucks, vehicles, other types of means of bringing in and bringing close to the targets, explosive devices. Lastly, it refers to the extensive detail that individuals, who have been involved in these types of efforts, have been able to acquire from publicly available sites; from various types of information that is available; as well as the types of personal reconnaissance and surveillance and casing that goes on. So again, from the standpoint of intelligence availability on the different types of targets and the amount of detail available here, this information provides tremendous insight into what al-Qaeda is contemplating and what they already have identified in terms of means of attack."*

Upon returning to DHS from the White House, the decision was made to raise the HSAS from "Yellow" to "Orange" specifically for the financial services sectors in New York City, northern New Jersey, and Washington, DC "citing intelligence pointing to the possibility of a car or truck bomb attack, naming specific buildings as possible targets." That evening, after Secretary Ridge and Admiral Loy returned to DHS, they hosted a meeting for 35 of their top DHS officials, including myself as the Director of Incident Management, to discuss the threat. The meeting was then reduced to 25 and then eventually to the five DHS Under Secretaries plus Bob Stephan, as the Director of the Integration Staff, and myself.

Following the meeting, Bob Stephan and I, with the assistance of Chris Abbott, Danley Cornyn, Christiana Briggs, Bob Shea and Rear Admiral Tim Sullivan (USCG) from the Integration Staff, stayed up all night putting together a briefing for Secretary

Ridge to take to the President for an 8:00 a.m. Principal Committee meeting the following morning. The briefing focused on three parts: Part I provided an overview of the security measures currently in place at the financial institutions and buildings in Northern New Jersey, New York, and Washington, DC outlined in this threat; Part II provided an overview of what security measures the Federal government could bring to bear, to protect these institutions and buildings within the first 24 to 48 hours; and Part III provided an overview of what security measures the Federal government could bring to bear after 48 hours as well as a plan to sustain these measures for an extended period, to include through the Presidential elections in November 2004 and all the way to the Presidential Inauguration on 20 January 2005, if necessary.

At 4:00 a.m., after putting the final changes on the briefing, I decided to try to catch some sleep and headed to my office. Rolling up a classified "burn bag" as a pillow and using my suit jacket as a blanket, I lay down on the floor and passed out. Fifteen minutes later, I was awakened by a loud knock on the door. Disoriented from being in the dark, I ended up knocking several items off my desk as I scrambled to the door and opened it only to find Chris Abbott from my staff standing there saying that there was a General from the Pentagon on the line screaming that he wanted to speak to the senior DHS official on site. Since Bob Stephan had gone home to catch an hour's sleep, I ended up being that senior official. Having been through this drill once before, I started by politely introducing myself and then asked what I could do for the General who, in turn, introduced himself and wanted to know why he was not notified of the threat by DHS. In response, I mentioned that there had been a Principal Committee meeting at the White House earlier in the day hosted by the President and attended by Secretary of Defense, Donald Rumsfeld. I added that shortly after the meeting ended, DHS made a public announcement that the HSAS was being raised from "Yellow" to "Orange" so, with that as background, I told the General that it was 4:00 in the morning and I could not tell him why no one had notified him of the threat. I then politely hung up the phone and returned to re-reading the briefing that we had prepared for Secretary Ridge knowing full well that I would not be getting any more sleep.

At 7:00 a.m., Secretary Ridge arrived and Admiral Loy, Bob Stephan, and I proceeded to walk him through the briefing. Although Secretary Ridge looked very tired, we were all elated to see him return from the White House an hour later after briefing the

President totally re-energized. We were even more pleased to hear the Secretary remark that after briefing President Bush, the President slammed the report down on the table and told him *"the briefing was exactly what he was looking for."*

In order to execute the security measures we recommended to the President, the decision was made by Secretary Ridge to activate the IIMG and recall all of the members via our new emergency notification recall systems with instructions to arrive at the NAC by noon. In the interim, during the next several hours, Secretary Ridge held conference calls with Governor George Pataki and the Homeland Security Advisor in New York, David Sheppard, Mayor Michael Bloomberg, and the Chief of Police in New York City, Ray Kelly. This was followed by additional conference calls to the Governors, mayors, police officials, and Homeland Security Advisors in New Jersey, Pennsylvania, Delaware, Maryland, Virginia, and Washington, DC. Lastly, Secretary Ridge held conference calls with the governors and senior homeland security officials in the remaining states to bring them up to speed on the threat followed by conference calls with officials from the private sector. In addition to discussing the threat, the purpose of the conference calls was to provide suggested random anti-terrorism security measures along the lines of what Secretary Ridge had prepared back on 11 September 2002 involving "little or no cost actions" and "actions that might bear some cost". Thanks to our Recorder, a person that writes down and logs in every action in order to make it a matter of record, the following day we were able to reconstruct the timeline when these calls took place when questioned by the White House.

* * *

One of the first actions that Secretary Ridge undertook shortly after standing up the IIMG was to designate the threat an Incident of National Significance so that he could appoint a Principal Federal Official (PFO), a PFO cell, and establish a Joint Field Office (JFO) as outlined in the National Response Plan (NRP).

After discussing it, the decision was made to appoint A.T. Smith, the USSS Special Agent in Charge of the New York Field Office, as the PFO for this period of increased threat since A.T. had already been selected to serve as the PFO during the Republican National Convention (RNC), which was scheduled to take place from 30 August to 4 September 2004. Informing A.T. that he would be serving as the PFO during this period of increased threat as well as at the RNC, we advised that we would be sending him a PFO cell, consisting of counterparts to many of the components in the IIMG, to assist him in coordinating the Federal resources, which would be deployed to combat this threat. For example, when several hundred-radiation detectors arrived in New York City that evening, one of the first things that A.T. had to coordinate with the FBI Joint Terrorism Task Force (JTTF) was the distribution of these detectors. As background, per HSPD-5, a PFO is designated by the Secretary of DHS to act as the Secretary's senior Federal official on-scene to oversee and execute the incident management responsibilities under HSPD-5 for Incidents of National Significance.

In his role as the PFO, A.T. was responsible for ensuring the overall coordination of Federal domestic incident management activities and resource allocation on scene as well as the seamless integration of Federal incident management activities in support of State and Local requirements. In this capacity, he was also responsible for providing strategic guidance to Federal entities and facilitating interagency conflict resolution to enable timely Federal assistance. Lastly, A.T. was responsible for coordinating the overall Federal public communications strategy at the State and Local levels, and clearing Federal interagency communications to the public regarding the incident.

Part of the security measures that the IIMG recommended included the implementation of "Project Constellation", designed by DHS' Critical Infrastructure and Protection Directorate under Assistant Secretary Bob Liscouski, to develop robust protective programs through the collaboration of Federal, State, Local and private sector resources to meet the security challenges due to this threat. The critical infrastructure target spectrum included major financial, chemical, emergency, communications, utility, and transportation networks, food, water, and natural resource development and supply chains. "Project Constellation" linked target-specific vulnerability and incident date from critical infrastructure to DHS via local "first preventers". It provided lateral collaboration tools for the private sector and local law enforcement; provided a comprehensive mechanism for analysis of observable target-specific data against existing vulnerability assessments to evaluate inside information across geographic areas; and facilitated the identification of sector-specific incident based targeting trends across sectors and geographic areas. Once implemented, "Project Constellation" enabled all participating Federal agencies, as well as local first responders, to have increased near term understanding of vulnerabilities of critical infrastructures in multiple regions and areas and group methods of operation.

On 12 August 2004, I broke away from the IIMG for a few hours to participate in a Senior Official Exercise known as "Crimson Dawn" hosted by the FBI at their Headquarters on 935 Pennsylvania Avenue. The purpose of this exercise centered on the "trade off considerations" regarding elevation of the HSAS level to Red (Severe Risk of Terrorist Attacks). In the midst of the threat to the financial institutions in New Jersey, New York City and Washington, DC and preparing for the upcoming Republican National Convention at the end of August 2004 the IIMG also had to monitor two fast-moving wildfires in Northern California north of Sacramento. These blazed across 1,000 acres leaving more than 40 structures damaged or destroyed, forcing the evacuation of more than 100 residences, and involving more than 700 firefighters.

* * *

Hurricane season was upon us and the IIMG, although stretched thin covering the threats and events, had to contend with several major hurricanes. Although the Atlantic hurricane season officially began on 1 June 2004 and lasted through 30 November 2004, the season was well above average in activity, with fifteen named storms and one of the highest accumulated cyclone energy totals ever observed.

The season was notable as one of the deadliest and most costly Atlantic hurricane seasons on record with at least 3,132 deaths and roughly $42 billion in damage. The most notable storms for the season were the four hurricanes that made landfall in Florida, three of which had at least 115 mph sustained winds–Hurricanes Charley, Frances, Ivan and Jeanne. Frances and Jeanne hit Florida in nearly the exact same location within three weeks of each other and, afterwards, floodwaters in the southeastern United States were brought to near-record levels.

Hurricane Charley was the third named storm, the second hurricane, and the second major hurricane of the 2004 Atlantic hurricane season. Charley lasted from nine to 15 August 2004, and at its peak intensity, it attained 150 mph winds, making it a strong Category 4 hurricane on the Saffir-Simpson Hurricane Scale. The storm made landfall in southwestern Florida at maximum strength, at the time, making it the strongest hurricane to hit the United States since Hurricane Andrew struck Florida in 1992. After moving briskly through the Caribbean Sea, Charley crossed Cuba on 13 August 2004 as a Category 3 hurricane, causing heavy damage and four deaths. That same day, Charley crossed over the Dry Tortugas, just 22 hours after Tropical Storm Bonnie struck northwestern Florida. This was the first time in history that two tropical cyclones struck the same state in a 24-hour time period. At its peak intensity of 150 mph, Hurricane Charley struck the northern tip of Captiva Island and the southern tip of North Captiva Island, causing severe damage in both areas. Charley, the strongest hurricane to hit southwest Florida since Hurricane Donna in 1960, then continued to produce severe damage as it made landfall on the peninsula near Port Charlotte. The hurricane continued to the Northeast and passed through East Orlando still carrying winds gusting up to 106 mph. Although Charley initially was expected to hit further north in Tampa, it caught many Floridians off-guard due to a sudden change in the storm's track as it approached the state. Damage in the State of Florida alone totaled over $13 billion while throughout the United States, Charley caused 10 deaths and $15.4 billion, making it the fourth costliest hurricane in United States history at the time.

Hurricane Frances was the sixth named storm, the fourth hurricane, and the third major hurricane of the 2004 Atlantic hurricane season forming on 25 August 2004 and dissipating on 10 September 2004 causing damages estimated at $9.6 billion dollars. The storm's maximum sustained wind speeds were 145 mph, a Category 4 on the Saffir-Simpson Hurricane Scale. The eye passed over San Salvador Island and very close to Cat Island in the Bahamas, and its outer bands affected Puerto Rico and the British Virgin Islands. Frances then passed over the central sections of Florida, moved briefly over the Gulf of Mexico on the other side of Florida, and made a second U.S. landfall at the Florida Panhandle. Frances affected the central regions of Florida, just three weeks after Hurricane Charley, before it moved northward into Georgia as a tropical depression, and then northeast along the spine of the Appalachians.

Hurricane Ivan was the strongest hurricane of the 2004 Atlantic hurricane season. The storm formed as a Cape Verde-type hurricane on 24 September 2004 and became the ninth named storm, the sixth hurricane, and the fourth major hurricane of the year in 2004 dissipating on 24 September 2004. Ivan reached Category 5 strength, the highest possible category and the only one of the season. At the time, it was the sixth most intense Atlantic hurricane on record and at its peak, in the Gulf of Mexico Hurricane

Ivan was the size of the State of Texas. It also spawned off more than 120 tornadoes, which we monitored in the IIMG. Ivan caused catastrophic damage to Grenada, which it struck directly at Category 3 intensity, and heavy damage to Jamaica, Grand Cayman, and the western tip of Cuba. After peaking in strength, it moved north-northwest across the Gulf of Mexico and made landfall as a strong Category 3 storm in the United States, in Gulf Shores, Alabama causing very heavy damage there. Ivan dropped heavy rains on the southeastern United States as it looped across Florida and back into the Gulf of Mexico. The remnant low from the storm regenerated into a new tropical system, which moved into Louisiana and Texas, causing minimal damage. Ivan caused an estimated $13 billion worth of damage in the United States, making it the fifth costliest hurricane to ever strike the U.S.

Hurricane Jeanne was the tenth named storm, the seventh hurricane, and the fifth major hurricane of the 2004 Atlantic hurricane season becoming a Category 3 storm on 13 September 2004 and dissipating on 28 September 2004. It was also the third hurricane and fourth named storm of the season to hit landfall in Florida. Jeanne affected the U.S. Virgin Islands, Puerto Rico, the Dominican Republic and Haiti, the northeastern Bahamas, and Florida. The worst damage occurred in Haiti, where over 3,000 people died as a result of flooding and mudslides caused by the storm. Total estimated damages for Hurricane Jeanne were $7 billion dollars.

* * *

The 2004 Republican National Convention, the Presidential nominating convention of the Republican Party of the United States, took place from 30 August to 2 September 2004 at Madison Square Garden in New York City, New York.

The convention was one of a series of historic quadrennial meetings at which the Republican candidate for President of the United States and party platform were formally adopted. Attendance included 2,509 delegates and 2,344 alternate delegates from the states, territories and overseas dependencies. The convention marked the formal end of the active primary election season, although the primaries were essentially uncontested since there was no major candidate to challenge the incumbent, George W. Bush.

Like the 2004 Democratic National Convention in Boston, Massachusetts, DHS declared the 2004 Republican National

Convention a NSSE and, as such, the USSS was charged with employing and coordinating all Federal and Local agencies including the various bureaus of DHS, the FBI, and the NYPD to secure the venue from terrorist attacks. A.T. Smith, who was already serving as the Principal Federal Official for the period of increased threat to the financial institutions in New York City, also served as the PFO for the RNC. Security expenditures reached $70 million–$50 million of which was funded by the Federal Government. The City of New York employed an active beat of 10,000 police officers deployed as Hercules Teams–police officers in full riot gear and body armor, and equipped with submachine guns and rifles. Commuter and Amtrak trains entering and exiting Penn Station were scoured by bomb-sniffing dogs as uniformed police officers were attached to buses carrying delegates. All employees of buildings surrounding Madison Square Garden were subjected to thorough screening and background checks. Later, following the RNC, I attended a National Capitol Region Command Post Exercise on 27 September 2004 hosted by Tom Lockwood, the new DHS National Capitol Region Coordinator. The purpose of the exercise was to facilitate the improvement of communications and coordination among the homeland security organizations at the Federal, State and Local levels within the National Capitol Region.

Several days later, on 9 October 2004, much to my delight, I was glad to see that interim President Hamid Karzai, who had been heading the Afghan Interim Government since early 2001, win the presidency in what appeared to be a fair and honest election over 17 other candidates. Two days later, on 11 October 2004, I received a phone call that my father had passed away. He was found in his chair, in front of his television set in his bedroom, early in the morning after completing his daily ritual of making breakfast, working on a crossword puzzle, handicapping the local horse races, donating small amounts of money to every charitable organization that asked, and then working on his roses prior to returning to his room to watch the news. Losing one parent is not easy; losing both parents within two years was extremely difficult. I soon realized that the only thing that gets you through this type of difficult period is your family and close friends.

Later on in early November of 2004, DHS finally rolled out the long anticipated National Response Plan (NRP), which delineated the Federal organizing principles, coordinating structures, resource allocation and mobilization processes used for domestic incident management. The NRP was all-hazards, was applicable to all types of events, and provided an integrated system for Federal response activities in the context of an incident across domains. The NRP expanded the concept of an 'incident' to begin with actionable information, covering the full 'life cycle of an incident', not just the consequences, and preserved existing elements as much as possible from established plans, structures, and organizations. Today, the NRP is known as the National Response Framework (NRF).

* * *

On 10 November 2004, the HSAS was lowered from "Orange" to "Yellow" for the financial services sectors in New York City, Northern New Jersey and Washington, DC. In a follow-up statement released by DHS, it was reported that, "Since the threat level was raised on 1 August 2004, State and Local leaders, as well as the private sector, have worked hard to strengthen security in and around specific buildings and locations throughout the financial services sector. Today there are permanent protective measures in place that did not exist before 1 August 2004."

The IIMG was up and running 24/7 for almost 3 ½ months since 2 August 2004 and I cannot emphasize the sacrifices that all of the IIMG members made during this period, me included. After standing down the IIMG, during the morning of 10 November, later in the day I had to attend a Senior Officials exercise known as "Storm Cloud" at the U.S. Secret Service Headquarters at 950 H Street in Washington, DC. This was designed to examine the policy and operational aspects of contending with a campaign of "suicide bombings" within the borders of the United States. This exercise was followed by a 7 December 2004 NSSE 2005 Presidential Inauguration Senior Official Tabletop exercise hosted by the North American Aerospace Defense Command (NORAD) and U.S. Northern Command that was held in Crystal City to prepare for the upcoming Presidential Inauguration.

The following day, on 8 December 2004, I attended yet another 2005 Presidential Inauguration Senior Official Tabletop exercises hosted by the USSS prior to departing for England with the Under-Secretary for Intelligence and Infrastructure and Protection (IAIP) at DHS, Lieutenant General Frank Libutti (USMC, Retired); the Assistant Secretary for Information Analysis, Lieutenant General Pat Hughes (USA, Retired); the Assistant Secretary for Infrastructure and Protection (IAIP), Bob Liscouski; the Director of the Homeland Security Operations Center (HSOC), Brigadier

General Matthew Broderick (USMC, Retired); and the Director of Response and Recovery for FEMA, Eric Tolbert, to name a few.

The purpose of our trip was to meet with our British homeland security counterparts and to conduct a tabletop exercise in preparation for DHS' Top Officials Three Exercise known as TOPOFF 3 scheduled from 4 to 8 April 2005. This exercise involved biological and chemical weapons in Connecticut and New Jersey with participation from the United Kingdom and Canada. All I can say was that we "smoked the British" during our visit. Meeting in their emergency operations center (known as "COBRA"), I am proud to say that the team assembled under Lieutenant General Libutti was at its best rolling out courses of action and security measure after security measure of what we, in the United States, would do during an incident which, ironically, involved terrorists conducting "suicide bombings" on buses and underground subways in England. How prophetic because on 7 July 2005, a series of bomb blasts hit London's public transportation system during rush hour killing 52 commuters.

Upon returning from London, on 17 December 2004, Secretary Ridge hosted a small Christmas party for members of his staff at one of his favorite restaurants in Georgetown, "Café Milano", from 6:00 to 8:00 p.m. As the function was breaking up that night, the Secretary's lead USSS agent informed him that Former President Bill Clinton, his wife Hilary, and their daughter Chelsea were on their way into the restaurant. After greeting the Secretary, I think both President Clinton and Hilary were shocked to see a steady stream of people coming up to Secretary Ridge that night to introduce themselves, while thanking him for his service as the Secretary of DHS. Comically, almost everyone asked to have their photograph taken with Secretary Ridge as they talked to him much to the chagrin of the former President and First Lady whose table just happened to be directly behind where the Secretary was standing as flash after flash from the cameras went off.

Three days later, on 20 December 2004, Secretary Ridge hosted a retirement ceremony for me in the chapel on the DHS Headquarters, Nebraska Avenue Complex (NAC). In addition to the Secretary, my good friends Bob Stephan and Ken Hill spoke to the packed audience that had braved the freezing cold that day to honor my family and me.

With President George Bush in the Oval Office December 2004

Epilogue

"In Closing"

Looking back at my time at the Office of Homeland Security (OHS), the Homeland Security Council (HSC), and the Department of Homeland Security (DHS), little did I know how much time I would be spending together with my co-workers–during Christmas' and New Year's, 4th of July's, hurricanes, wildfires, blackouts, exercises and even a space shuttle crash. With all that, I can honestly say that I was extremely fortunate to have worked with Secretary Tom Ridge, Admiral Jim Loy, General John Gordon, Vice Admiral Steve Abbot (USN), and Dr. Richard Falkenrath who, during various crises, always displayed incredible leadership, remained calm, and always provided clear-cut instructions.

Earlier in the year, on 24 September 2004, I had put my retirement paperwork in at the Agency, the same day that Porter Goss was sworn in by President Bush to be the new DCI. As I sat in the auditorium that day with Executive Director Buzzy Krongard, and heard Porter Goss speak to the packed auditorium, my mind drifted to the first day I arrived to work in the Agency and sat in the same auditorium hearing Charlton Heston on a video providing a "welcome aboard" speech. My, times had certainly changed in that actor Jennifer Gardner is now the celebrity providing the same speech. My mind also raced to many sad memories that the auditorium evoked including the ceremonies honoring the former chief of our office in Beirut, William Buckley, Larry F. killed in East Africa, and Mike Spann who was killed in Afghanistan.

On 31 December 2004, I officially retired from the CIA and entered the Agency's transition program. During the 28 years that I spent with the CIA, the Agency had been very good to me and I had a great career. Thanks to the Agency and Uncle Sam, I have stood on the Equator in both South America and in Africa; visited the Cape of Good Hope and the Cape of Good Horn; have visited the Mayan, Aztec, and Inca ruins; and even the Pyramids. Everybody kids me about the fact that Karen and I lived in two European countries for six years during the 1990s, while few remember the fact that we also lived in Honduras for three years while Kelly and Matthew were infants when Honduras was the second most impoverished country in the Western Hemisphere and Americans were being targeted and killed. Few people also remember that I spent an enormous amount of time in Central and South America during the 1980's.

The only sad memory that I have when reflecting on my Agency career, which spanned almost half of the CIA's existence, is that I know almost half of the individuals who died in the line of duty which are represented by the 87 stars on the CIA's Wall of Honor today.

Bill Rooney and General John Gordon at my CIA Retirement Ceremony April 2005

* * *

As noted in the CIA's *"Factbook on Intelligence,"* situated on the hillside between the Original Headquarters Building and the Auditorium, is a Memorial Garden.

Designed in 1995 by Sheila Brady of the landscape architects of Oehme, Van Sweden and Associates, and dedicated in 1996, an inscribed brass plaque reads, *"In remembrance of those whose unheralded efforts served a grateful Nation"*, is set in fieldstone surrounded by a large pond filled with goldfish. The blend of natural and landscaped plants amid the stone outcroppings, from which a cascade of water continuously falls, has created a tranquil and reflective retreat for Agency employees–*me included.*

Glossary

A

ARSO	Assistant Regional Security Officer
ASAC	Assistant Special Agent in Charge
ATF	Bureau of Alcohol, Tobacco, and Firearms

B

BFO	Boston Field Office

C

CAP	Combat Air Patrol
CATF	Central American Task Force
CBIRF	Chemical Biological Incident Response Force
CD	Clearance Division
CDC	Center for Disease Control and Prevention
CIA	Central Intelligence Agency
CNC	Counternarcotics Center
CODEL	Congressional Delegation
COG	Continuity of Government
COI	Community of Interests
COOP	Continuity of Operations
CSG	Counterterrorism and Security Group
CST	Clandestine Service Trainee
CT	Counterterrorist
CTC	Counterterrorist Center

D

DA	Directorate of Administration
DCI	Director of Central Intelligence
DDCI	Deputy Director of Central Intelligence
DDO	Deputy Director of Operations
DEA	Drug Enforcement Agency
DHS	Department of Homeland Security
DI	Directorate of Intelligence
DIA	Defense Intelligence Agency
DNC	Democratic National Convention
DO	Directorate of Operations
DOC	Department of Commerce
DOD	Department of Defense

Glossary

DOE	Department of Energy
DOI	Department of Interior
DOJ	Department of Justice
DOS	Department of State
DOT	Department of Transportation
DST	(French) Direction del la Surveillance
DS&T	Directorate of Science and Technology
DTRIM	Domestic Threat Response and Incident

E

EAC	Emergency Action Committee
ECG	Enduring Constitutional Government
EEOB	Eisenhower Executive Office Building
EPA	Environmental Protection Agency
ERT	Emergency Reaction Team

F

FBI	Federal Bureau of Investigation
FCO	Federal Coordinating Office
FDN	Fuerza Democratica Nicaraguense
FEMA	Federal Emergency Management Agency
FEST	Foreign Emergency Support Team
FFCD	Full, Final, and Complete Disclosure
FLIR	Forward Looking Infrared
FMLN	Frente Farabundo Marti para la Liberacion
FRP	Federal Response Plan
FSB	(Russian) Federal Security Service

GETS	Government Emergency

H

HHS	Health and Human Services
HLZ	Helicopter Landing Zones
HMRU	Hazardous Materials Response Unit
HSAS	Homeland Security Advisory System
HSC	Homeland Security Council
HSOC	Homeland Security Operations Center

HSC/PC	Homeland Security Council Principals
HSC/DC	Homeland Security Council Deputies
HSC/PCC	Homeland Security Council Policy
HSPD	Homeland Security Presidential Directive

I

IAEA	International Atomic Energy Agency
IAD	International Activities Division
IAIP	Intelligence and Analysis, Infrastructure and
ICSIS	Intelligence Community System
IIMG	Inter-Agency Incident Management Group
IMPT	Inter-Agency Management Planning Team
INS	Immigration and Naturalization Services
IRT	Incident Response Team
ISG	Incident Support Group

J

JCS	Joint Chief of Staff
JFO	Joint Field Office
JSOC	Joint Special Operations Command
JTTF	Joint Terrorism Task Force
JWICS	Joint Intelligence Worldwide

M

MRE	Meals Ready to Eat
MST	Mobile Search Teams

N

NAC	Nebraska Avenue Complex
NALT	Northern Alliance Liaison Team
NASA	National Aeronautics and Space
NAVSECSTA	U.S. Naval Security Station
NCTC	National Counterterrorism Center
NDS	National Directorate of Security
NEF	National Essential Functions
NERC	North American Electrical Reliability
NIC	National Intelligence Council
NIMS	National Incident Management System

Glossary

NOC	National Operations Center
NOC	Non-Official Cover Officers
NRP	National Response Plan
NSA	National Security Agency
NRC	Nuclear Regulatory Commission
NSC	National Security Council
NSSE	National Special Security Events

O

OAS	Organization of American States
OHB	Old Headquarters Building
OHS	Office of Homeland Security
OIC	Officers in Charge
OMS	Office of Medical Services
ONDCP	Office of National Drug Control Policy
OPSEC	Operational Security
OPEC	Organization of Petroleum Exporting
OSSB	Overseas Security Support Branch
OSD	Office of Secretary of Defense
OSI	Office of Strategic Information
OVP	Office of the Vice President

P

PCC	Post Communications Center
PCC	Policy Coordination Committee
PDB	President's Daily Brief
PDD	Presidential Decision Directive
PDF	Panamanian Defense Forces
PEO	Program Evaluation Office
PEOC	President's Emergency Operations Center
PFO	Principal Federal Official
PHS	Personal History Statement
PMEF	Primary Mission –Essential Functions
PRTC	Partido Revolucionario de Trabajadores
PT	Professional Trainee

R

RICC	Regional Intelligence Coordination Centers
RNC	Republican National Convention

RPG	Rocket Propelled Grenade
RPV	Remote Piloted Vehicle
RSO	Regional Security Officer

S

SAC	Special Agent in Charge
SAD	Special Activities Division
SCI	Special Compartmented Information
SCIF	Secure Compartment Information Facility
SDR	Surveillance Detection Route
SFOD-D	Special Forces Operational Detachment –
SIOC	Special Intelligence Operations Center
SIS	Senior Intelligence Service
SVTS	Secure Voice Telecommunications System
SWAT	Special Weapons Assault Team

T

TDY	Temporary Duty Assignment
TMC	Threat Monitoring Center
TSA	Transportation Security Administration
TTIC	Terrorist Threat Integration Center

U

UNSCOM	United Nations Special Commission
UNSCR	United Nations Security Council Resolutions
USCG	U.S. Coast Guard
USDA	U.S. Department of Agriculture
USPS	U.S. Postal Service
USSOCOM	U.S. Special Operations Command

V

VA	Veterans Administration

W

WMD	Weapons of Mass Destruction

CPSIA information can be obtained
at www.ICGtesting.com
Printed in the USA
BVOW06*0901080817
490795BV00003BA/3/P